THE ANCIENT ECONOMY

EDINBURGH READINGS ON THE ANCIENT WORLD

GENERAL EDITORS
Michele George, *McMaster University*
Thomas Harrison, *University of St Andrews*

ADVISORY EDITORS
Paul Cartledge, *University of Cambridge*
Richard Saller, *University of Chicago*

This series introduces English-speaking students to central themes
in the history of the ancient world and to the range of scholarly
approaches to those themes, within and across disciplines. Each
volume, edited and introduced by a leading specialist, contains a
selection of the most important work, including a significant
proportion of translated material. The editor also provides a guide
to the history of modern scholarship on the subject. Passages in
ancient languages are translated; technical terms, ancient and
modern, are explained.

PUBLISHED
Sparta
Edited by Michael Whitby

Greeks and Barbarians
Edited by Thomas Harrison

The Ancient Economy
Edited by Walter Scheidel and Sitta von Reden

IN PREPARATION
Ancient Slavery
Edited by Keith Bradley

Sexuality in Ancient Greece and Rome
Edited by Mark Golden and Peter Toohey

Ancient Myth
Edited by Richard Gordon

Alexander the Great
Edited by Simon Hornblower

The 'Dark Ages' of Greece
Edited by Ian Morris

Roman Religion
Edited by Clifford Ando

Augustus
Edited by Jonathan Edmondson

THE ANCIENT ECONOMY

Edited by

Walter Scheidel and Sitta von Reden

EDINBURGH UNIVERSITY PRESS

© Editorial matter and selection Walter Scheidel and
Sitta von Reden, 2002

Edinburgh University Press Ltd
22 George Square, Edinburgh

Typeset in Sabon
by Norman Tilley Graphics, Northampton
and printed and bound in Great Britain
by MPG Books Ltd, Bodmin, Cornwall

A CIP Record for this book is available from the British Library

ISBN 0 7486 1322 6 (hardback)
ISBN 0 7486 1321 8 (paperback)

Contents

Acknowledgements

The sources of the readings in each chapter are given in the footnotes. The editors and publishers thank the copyright holders for permission to include the material in this book. The editors and publishers also thank Cambridge University Press for permission to reprint maps 1–3, which are taken from P. Jones and K. Sidwell, *The World of Rome*, Cambridge, Cambridge University Press 1997, maps 1, 2 and 3.

We are grateful to Leslie Kurke and Richard Saller for providing us with previously unpublished work for this volume, to an anonymous reader for perceptive comments that encouraged us to broaden the scope of our selection, to Antonia Nevill for speedy and competent translations from the French, and to John Davey of Edinburgh University Press for his patient support and advice.

Note to the Reader

The articles included in this volume were, with two exceptions, originally published in a range of different journals and books. A degree of uniformity has been imposed (for example, in the abbreviations used), but many of the conventions of the original pieces have been preserved. This applies to spelling and punctuation (UK or US) and to different modes of referencing: chapters using the Harvard system (giving name and date) are followed by individual bibliographies, whereas those using 'short titles' usually have footnotes and no bibliography. (In Chapter 10, the author uses Harvard-style references as 'short titles'.)

The two exceptions published here for the first time are Chapters 5 and 12. The latter, by Richard Saller, will appear shortly after the publication of this volume in J. Manning and I. Morris (eds), *The Ancient Economy: Evidence and Models*, Stanford University Press.

Editorial notes and translations of ancient texts are introduced either within square brackets [ ] or in daggered footnotes †. Some Greek terms, especially those in use in English, have been transliterated.

All abbreviations of ancient texts, modern collections, books and journals used in this volume are listed and explained on the pages following. Full references to the works of ancient authors given in the original articles have not been changed. We hope that the absence of abbreviations from the 'Guide to Further Reading' will make it easier to use.

Abbreviations

1 ABBREVIATIONS OF REFERENCES TO ANCIENT SOURCES

Aelian *VH*	Aelian, *Varia Historia* (Miscellany)
Arist. *Pol.*	Aristotle, *Politics*
Aristoph.	Aristophanes
Ath. Pol.	Aristotle, *Athenaion Politeia* (Athenian Constitution)
Athen.	Athenaeus
B Afr.	[Caesar], *Bellum Africanum* (African War)
Cato, *De Agr.*	Cato, *De Agri Cultura* (On Farming)
Cod. Theod.	*Codex Theodosianus* (Theodosian Code)
Columella, *Rust.*	Columella, *De Re Rustica* (On Farming)
Dig.	*Digesta* (Digest)
D.S.	Diodorus Siculus
Gal.	Galen
Hdt.	Herodotus
Hes.	Hesiod
Theog.	*Theogony*
W&D	*Works and Days*
Mart.	Martial
NE	Aristotle, *Nicomachean Ethics*
Nep.	Cornelius Nepos
Them.	*Themistocles*
Or.	Aelius Aristides, *Orationes* (Speeches)
Paus.	Pausanias
Pindar	Pindar
O.	*Olympian Ode*
P.	*Pythian Ode*
Plin. *Ep.*	Pliny (the Younger), *Epistulae* (Letters)
Plin. *HN*	Pliny (the Elder), *Historia Naturalis* (Natural History)

Plut.	Plutarch
Arist.	*Life of Aristides*
Them.	*Life of Themistocles*
Ps.-Xenoph. *Ath. Pol.*	Pseudo-Xenophon, *Athenaion Politeia* (Athenian Constitution)
Sen., *Ep.*	Seneca, *Epistulae* (Letters)
SHA	*Scriptores Historiae Augustae*
Theoph[r].	Theophrastus
Char.	*Characters*
Hist. pl.	*Historia Plantarum* (Research into Plants)
Thuc.	Thucydides

2 ABBREVIATIONS OF REFERENCES TO JOURNALS AND MODERN EDITIONS

ABSA	*Annual of the British School at Athens*
Acta Antiqua Hung.	*Acta Antiqua Academiae Hungaricae*
AHR	*American Historical Review*
AION *(archeol.)*	*Annali Istituto Orientale di Napoli: Archeologia e Storia Antica*
AJA	*American Journal of Archaeology*
AJAH	*American Journal of Ancient History*
AJP	*American Journal of Philology*
Annales ESC	*Annales: Économies, Sociétés, Civilisations*
Annales HSS	*Annales: Histoire, Sciences Sociales*
ANRW	*Aufstieg und Niedergang der Römischen Welt*
AntAfr	*Antiquités Africaines*
ARHE	*Amphores Romaines et Histoire Économique. Dix Ans de Recherches. CEFR, 114, Rome, 1989*
BA	*Bollettino di Archeologia*
BAR	*British Archaeological Reports*
BASP	*Bulletin of the American Society of Papyrologists*
BCH	*Bulletin de Correspondance Hellénique*
BEFAR	*Bibliothèque des Écoles Françaises d'Athènes et de Rome*
BIFAO	*Bulletin de l'Institut Français d'Archéologie Orientale* (Cairo)
CA	*Classical Antiquity*

CAH	Cambridge Ancient History
CAS	Cahiers d'Archéologie Subaquatique
CEFR	Collection de l'École Française de Rome
CIL	Corpus Inscriptionum Latinarum
CJ	Classical Journal
ClAnt	Classical Antiquity
CP/CPh	Classical Philology
CR	Classical Review
G&R	Greece and Rome
ID	Inscriptions de Délos
IG	Inscriptiones Graecae
JAOS	Journal of the American Oriental Society
JEA	Journal of Egyptian Archaeology
JHS	Journal of Hellenic Studies
JNES	Journal of Near Eastern Studies
JRA	Journal of Roman Archaeology
JRS	Journal of Roman Studies
JS	Journal des Savants
LGPN	Lexicon of Greek Personal Names
MBAH	Münstersche Beiträge zur antiken Handelsgeschichte
MEFRM	Mélanges de l'École Française de Rome: Moyen Âge
MélRome	Mélanges de l'École Française de Rome: Italie et Méditerrannée
OGIS	Orientis Graecae Inscriptiones Selectae
Pap. Colon.	Papyrologica Coloniensia
Pap. Lugd.-Bat.	Papyrologica Lugduno-Battavia
P. Cair. Isid.	A. E. R. Boak and H. C. Youtie, The Archive of Aurelius Isidorus in the Egyptian Museum, and the University of Michigan. Ann Arbor 1960
P. Dion.	E. Boswinkel and P. W. Pestman, Les archives privées de Dionysios, fils de Kephalas. Leiden 1982
Perry	B. E. Perry, Aesop: Aesopica: A Series of Texts Relating to Aesop or Ascribed to him Closely Connected with the Literary Tradition which Bears his Name. Urbana, Ill.
P. Kron.	D. Foraboschi, L'archivio di Kronion. Milan 1971

PMG	D. L. Page, *Poetae Melici Graeci*. Oxford 1962
P. Oxy.	*The Oxyrhynchus Papyri*
Proc. Int. Cong. Pap.	*Proceedings of the International Congress of Papyrologists*
P. Soterichos	S. Omar, *Das Archiv von Soterichos*. Opladen 1979
P. Tebt.	*Tebtunis Papyri*
QS	*Quaderni di Storia*
RA	*Revue Archéologique*
Radt	S. Radt, *Tragicorum Graecorum Fragmenta*, vol. iv. Berlin 1977
RAN	*Revue Archéologique de Narbonnaise*
RE	A. Pauly, G. Wissowa and W. Kroll (eds), *Realencyclopädie der klassischen Altertumswissenschaft* (Stuttgart 1893–1978)
REA	*Revue des Études Anciennes*
REG	*Revue des Études Grecques*
SIG	W. Dittenberger, *Sylloge Inscriptionum Graecarum*. 3rd edn.
Snell-Maehler	B. Snell, 8th rev. edn H. Maehler, *Pindar*. Bibliotheca Scriptorum Graecorum et Romanorum Teubneriana. Leipzig and Stuttgart 1987–8
YCS	*Yale Classical Studies*
ZPE	*Zeitschrift für Papyrologie und Epigraphik*

Glossary

aggregate	see *per capita*
amphora	two-handled jar used for storage and transport
Annales School	school of thought associated with the French historians Marc Bloch, Fernand Braudel and Lucien Febvre and their journal *Annales* who argued that environmental and demographic factors have a major bearing on social, economic and political history, and strongly favoured quantitative methods (*histoire sérielle*)
annona	public grain supply in Rome
artaba	corn measure in Graeco-Roman Egypt of *c.*40 l*
aroura	square measure in Graeco-Roman Egypt of *c.*2760 square metres
aureus	Roman gold coin (equivalent to 25 denarii)
choregia	Athenian liturgy involving the production of a chorus at the musical or dramatic festivals
classical economics	generally refers to the body of economic ideas stemming from the works of Adam Smith and David Ricardo in the late eighteenth and early nineteenth centuries
deduction	argumentative method where particulars are inferred from general principles or a model (*contr.* induction)
deme	local district or village in Greece
demography	the study of human populations with respect to their size, structure and development
denarius	Roman silver coin (equivalent to 4 sestertii)

xiii

Digest	compilation of Roman civil law in fifty volumes (published in AD 533)
drachma (dr)	Greek silver coin (equivalent to 6 obols)
Dressel (Dr)	typological classification system for Roman amphorae devised by and named after the German scholar Heinrich Dressel
embedded/ disembedded economy	refers to the distinction made by Karl Polanyi between economies which are embedded in social and political relationships, and those which are based on anonymous market relationships
eisphora	tax on capital levied especially when the city was at war
epigraphy	inscriptions, the study of inscriptions
eranos	friendly loan
ethnoarchaeology	the archaeological study of recent or contemporary peasant societies; used for comparison with the ancient world
garum	fermented fish sauce
HS	sestertius
horos	boundary stone marking debt on land
induction	mode of reasoning from particular cases, or evidence, to general conclusions
iugerum	Roman square measure of c.2500 square metres*
kotyle (pl. kotylia)	Greek liquid measure of c.0.25 l*
liturgy	in Athens an institution which required wealthy men to undertake certain work for the state at their own expense
medimnos	Attic corn measure of c.54.5 l*
metretes	Greek liquid measure of c.30.4 l*
micro/macro economics	micro-economics is concerned with the economy of individual economic units (households, companies, etc.) while macro-economics focusses on the interplay of these units and the economy of a state or region as a whole
mna (mina)	Greek monetary unit equivalent to 100 drachmae; also a unit of weight*
modius	Roman corn measure of c.8.62 l*
neo-classical economics	refers to the enhanced version of classical economics that was developed in the late

	nineteenth century primarily by Alfred Marshall and Leon Walras; introduced the idea of the supply-and-demand mechanism as a regulation of prices
New Archaeology	school of thought, especially among pre-historic archaeologists, promoting a deductive and comparative approach to archaeology
nome	administrative subdivision or local district in Graeco-Roman Egypt
numismatics	the study of coins
nummular tesserae	see *tesserae nummulariae*
obol (ob)	Greek fractional coin equivalent to one-sixth of a drachma
oikos	ancient household, comprising family, slaves, house and land
opus africanum	architectural structure consisting of upright pillars separated by sections of smaller stones or rubble
ostraka	small potsherds used in antiquity for everyday notes, in particular receipts (Egypt) and voting (democratic Athens)
palaeobotany	the biological study of fossil plants and animals
palaeoethnobotany	the biological study of fossil plants and animals in low-technology societies
per capita	'by heads'; average production, consumption, etc. of each individual, in contrast to 'gross', 'aggregate' or total
polis	Greek city-state consisting of an urban centre and its hinterland
positivism	belief in absolute truths or knowledge in contrast to relativism where knowledge is taken to be dependent on the observer and his/her way of understanding
sestertius	Roman base metal coin (copper–zinc alloy)
solidus	Roman monetary gold unit introduced by Diocletian
stadion	a fixed standard of length of *c*.177 m*
subsistence economy	an economic system in which most of the population produce enough for their own sustenance, but little or no surplus for sale
symmory	in Athens a group of men liable to pay

	eisphora or liturgies
talent (tal)	Greek monetary unit equivalent to 6000 drachmae; also a unit of weight*
tesserae nummulariae	short inscribed rods affixed to sealed coin containers as proof of authenticity
trierarchy	Athenian liturgy involving responsibility for a warship (trireme) for a year

---

* Weights and measures could vary widely from place to place.

Map 1: Greece and the Near East

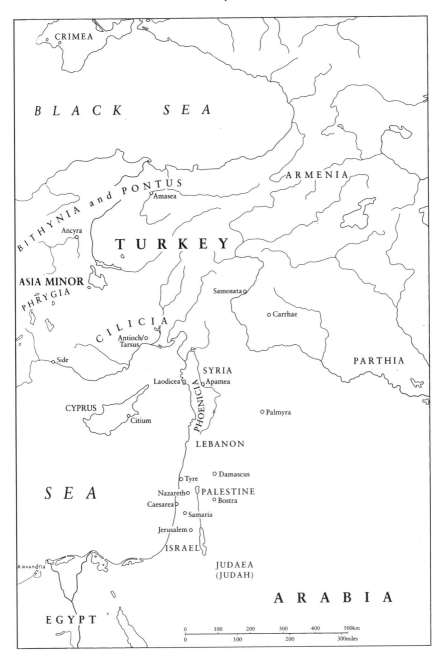

Map 2: Italy and the West

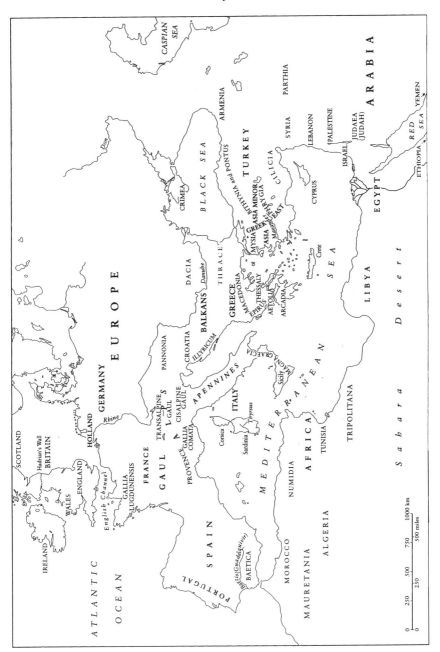

Map 3: The Roman Empire

Introduction

APPROACHING THE ANCIENT ECONOMY

In his celebrated study of *Structure and Change in Economic History*, the Nobel-prize-winning economist Douglass North takes it 'as the task of economic history to explain the structure and performance of economies through time'. While 'performance' is expressed in aggregate and per capita output and income distribution, 'structure' arises from 'those characteristics of a society which we believe to be the basic determinants of performance', such as political and economic institutions, technology, demography and ideology. Change over time of economic structure and performance calls for explanation.[1] In pursuing this goal, economic historians analyse the interaction of significant factors within a given economic system. Economic systems are institutional frameworks which co-ordinate human competition for scarce resources. They are created by the combination of various economic institutions and organisations. Organisations, such as markets and states or communities and households, develop in consequence of institutional frameworks, which have been defined as 'the humanly devised constraints that shape human interaction', such as formal rules and informal codes of conduct. Mediating the processes of production and exchange that are governed by the laws of supply and demand, these institutions and organisations inhibit as well as stimulate economic growth and development.[2]

Students of the ancient Greek or Roman economy, however, have rarely if ever discussed their subject matter in these terms. In fact, the only scholar to design a coherent and comprehensive general model

[1] D. C. North, *Structure and Change in Economic History*, New York: W. W. Norton, 1981, p. 3.
[2] For these concepts, see, e.g., D. C. North, *Institutions, Institutional Change and Economic Performance*, Cambridge: Cambridge University Press, 1990, pp. 3–4; Y. Hayami, *Development Economics*, Oxford: Oxford University Press, 1997, pp. 198, 241.

I

of the ancient economy deliberately avoided the terminology and conceptualisation of modern economics. For Moses Finley, ancient economic activity followed different rules. In his seminal book of 1973, *The Ancient Economy*, Finley argued that considerations of status and civic ideology, rather than the laws of supply and demand, governed economic decision-making.[3] In this, Finley adopted Karl Polanyi's 'substantivist' perspective, which rejects the 'formalist' assumption of the existence of an economic sphere separate from social relations.[4] As a consequence, he saw economic development in antiquity as constrained by (elite) values which determined status. Moreover, despite regional and temporal variation, a single model of an 'ancient economy' could be applied to the Graeco-Roman Mediterranean as a whole during the first millennium BC and the first half of the first millennium of the Christian era. The opening lines of his preface reminded the reader that 'the title of this volume is precise'. Thus, 'although change and variation are constant preoccupations ... it is not a book one would call an "economic history"'. Rather, in focusing on what he perceived to be 'the dominant types, the characteristic modes of behaviour', he outlined the structure of a distinctively Graeco-Roman type of economic systems, one in which economic activities were embedded in a network of social relationships that determined values, attitudes and actual behaviour.

In his recent foreword to a new edition of Finley's book, Ian Morris identifies various ways in which this model makes Greek and Roman preoccupations with status affect economic performance: thus, concerns about image and appropriate behaviour inhibited the growth of markets in land, labour and capital, and therefore of technology and trade; encouraged the social marginalisation of commercial activities (such as trading and banking); reinforced the primacy of the political over the economic; favoured coercive exploitation and redistribution over market exchange; and were instrumental in the expansion of chattel slavery and predatory imperialism.[5] As a result, economic growth could never 'take off': subsistence farmers and elite rentiers alike aimed for self-sufficiency; most market exchange was local and small-scale; agricultural rents and taxation rather than trade generated upper-class wealth. Urbanisation was parasitical upon the rural economy, providing little incentive for intensive growth and technological progress.

---

[3] M. I. Finley, *The Ancient Economy*, Berkeley and Los Angeles: University of California Press, 1973, 2nd edn 1985, updated edition 1999 (quotations from pp. 9 and 29).

[4] For the substantivist/formalist contrast see Cartledge, below pp. 14–15.

[5] I. Morris, 'Foreword', in Finley, *Ancient Economy*, pp. xxii–xxiii.

With Finley, the choice came to be between social embeddedness and independent, rational economic development rather than between different developmental stages. In this, Finley's work echoed and continued the older debate between proponents of a 'modernist' position, taking ancient to differ from modern economies in scale but not in substance, and the 'primitivist' camp, considering the backwardness of ancient economic systems as symptomatic of an earlier and hence structurally different stage of human attainment.[6] Although his perspective encouraged a pessimistic assessment of the scale of ancient economic activity, he was more concerned with its socio-political dimension and dynamics. However, whilst successful in redefining the terms of the debate, Finley's model predictably failed to establish a consensus on the nature of the ancient economy or, indeed, on the validity of the mere notion of a single 'ancient economy'. Ten years after the publication of *The Ancient Economy*, it was fair to call the study of the ancient economy 'an academic battleground'.[7] Critics question the real-life impact of elite mentality and identify apparent tensions between the historical record and the model that was meant to make sense of it. They tend to emphasise the considerable scale of economic activities (above all trade), and make a case for significant economic growth in the Roman imperial period when political and fiscal unification boosted market exchange. As our knowledge of numismatic, epigraphic and papyrological material from the margins of the Graeco-Roman world continues to improve, claims that Finley seriously underestimated the scale and significance of monetisation and market exchange are mounting.

The turn of the millennium, however clichéd, offers a fitting opportunity to take stock of this debate. The first two chapters of this collection cover the most salient arguments of recent years. A generation after *The Ancient Economy*, there is a growing feeling that Finley's questions, stimulating though they have proven to be, can take us only so far. Calls to move the debate 'beyond' the agenda of his work are becoming more insistent. Novel approaches differ widely in terms of method and purpose. Ecological studies seek to analyse the ways in which economic development was conditioned by the physical environment. The concerns of the new cultural

---

[6] The 'Guide to Further Reading' provides references for these and the other issues raised in this introduction.

[7] K. Hopkins, 'Introduction', in P. Garnsey, K. Hopkins and C. R. Whittaker (eds), *Trade in the Ancient Economy*, Berkeley and Los Angeles: University of California Press, 1983, p. ix.

history have spurred enquiries into the economic as a sphere of representation that relates to and conflicts with other, equally value-laden, models of behaviour. Finally, the first attempts are under way to reconcile the study of ancient economies with the models of and approaches to the economic history of more recent periods: a shift in understanding towards the contingency of economic performance upon the underlying institutions and organisations of economic systems may enable ancient historians to benefit from the conceptual and analytical repertoire of modern economics.

THE FORMAT OF THIS VOLUME

This volume straddles the divide between the 'Finley era' of the 1970s and 1980s, in which most pertinent scholarship engaged – expressly or implicitly – in a debate with *The Ancient Economy*, and the more diverse and forward-looking research that has now begun to appear at an accelerating pace. It goes without saying that it is impossible for a collection of this kind to cover all the bases. A weighty cased set of volumes would be required to do justice to the variety and intensity of the discussion. For this reason, we have had to strike a number of uneasy compromises. In keeping with the overall objective of this series, our collection is primarily retrospective in nature. However, while we have given pride of place to contributions of the late 1980s and 1990s, we have also felt the need to offer some glimpses of the most recent reorientations. Further difficulties arise from the tension between our brief to select the most crucial pieces – the 'classics' – and our wish to make important but less accessible work available to a wider audience. Scholarship in languages other than English has inevitably suffered most, and no more than token examples from a wide range of international research can be accommodated within our collection. Furthermore, we have made no attempt to cover the largest possible number of different aspects or segments of economic activity in the ancient world. Instead, we have placed particular emphasis on what are commonly perceived to be the most important and controversial issues of ancient economic history, and sought to showcase different types of source material and interpretative strategies.

Our collection opens with two recent survey articles which together take the place of what would otherwise have been a more comprehensive editorial introduction. A number of reasons have prompted us to decide on this somewhat unusual format: we would perforce have drawn heavily on these pieces in any survey of our own; they are complementary in that the former deals exclusively with Greek and the latter predominantly with Roman matters, and in that they shed light on the debate from two different academic backgrounds; and their inclusion adds to the number of reprints we were able to fit into this volume and so broadens our selection. Because of its place of publication, Paul Cartledge's article may not be as widely known as it deserves, while Jean Andreau's piece, originally published in a leading French periodical, is here made available in English for the first time.[8]

There is no obvious or 'proper' way of arranging the following ten chapters that form the core of this volume. In grouping these contributions in thematic sections, we have aimed to identify the pivotal areas of recent scholarly debate and to enable the reader to appreciate the true scale of variation in ancient economic structure as well as in modern interpretative approaches. Thus, the section on primary production juxtaposes Paul Halstead's reappraisal of Mediterranean subsistence farming with Robert Bruce Hitchner's work on large-scale, capital-intensive production of cash crops for an imperial market. The segment on money and markets brings together Leslie Kurke and Robin Osborne's substantively different readings of literary evidence alongside Gary Reger and Dominic Rathbone's regional studies that primarily draw on epigraphic and papyrological sources. Our understanding of ancient trade and other forms of the transfer of goods rests as much on the scrupulous accumulation and inductive interpretation of empirical data – represented by Clementina Panella and André Tchernia's survey of Roman amphorae – as on the imaginative modelling of significant structural mechanisms and variables advocated by Keith Hopkins. In the final section, Scott Meikle and Richard Saller probe the difference between 'ancient' and modern economies from very different angles.

At the same time, our decision to mix 'Greek' with 'Roman' – or the deliberately evocative title of our volume – should not be construed as an uncritical endorsement of Finley's belief in the structural unity of a single 'ancient' economy. The fact that specialised scholarship has taken rather different directions renders it difficult to test the validity of this concept.[9] Unlike their colleagues in Roman

---

[8] By contrast, two comparable survey articles – by Ian Morris and William Harris – are more readily accessible to a wider student audience: see 'Guide to Further Reading' below.

[9] See, however, Cartledge in this volume (Ch. 1) and J. K. Davies, 'Ancient Economies: Models and Muddles', in H. Parkins and C. Smith (eds), *Trade, Traders and the Ancient City*, London and New York: Routledge, 1998, pp. 255–7, who emphasise the diversity of ancient economies.

studies, Greek historians of the post-Finleyan era tend to be reluctant
to develop synthetic models of the ancient economy. They have concentrated on individual micro-economic issues such as domestic
production, unfree as opposed to free peasant labour, or credit and
exchange, in order to describe economic behaviour as rational and in
many cases market-oriented.

A key factor in the discussion is the role of money and markets.
Thus, Scott Meikle argues in purely theoretical terms that, however
much the ancient economy was influenced by monetary exchange,
there was no market for capital, that is, a market for credit used for
productive investment. It was for this reason, and not because the
ancients avoided markets and monetary exchange, that the ancient
economy was dissimilar to the modern. Paul Halstead – while not
exclusively concerned with the Greek world – warns us not to take
comparative data from contemporary peasant and pastoral communities as proxy evidence for the ancient world. On the one hand,
even traditional communities today have not remained unaffected by
the modern market economy. Conversely, the apparently low potential for accumulating (monetary) wealth in small-scale agriculture
concealed the fact that rich landowners in the ancient world could
exploit large fluctuations in annual yields to make a fortune by selling out their storage.

From a different theoretical perspective, Leslie Kurke offers
another, non-'primitivist', explanation for the absence of monetary
analysis from archaic and classical Greek texts. In her view, scholars
were quite mistaken in their attempts to discover any reflection of
historical reality in literary representation. Instead, she demonstrates
how representations of economic behaviour were bound up with
images of political abuse. If 'primitivists' deplore the lack of distinction made between economic and political matters in the minds of
the Greeks, they ignore the degree to which the economy enters
ancient texts largely as a tool for misrepresenting politics. Robin
Osborne, by contrast, does use Athenian oratory for looking at the
strategies of monetary accumulation among estate owners in classical Athens. On the basis of what he regards as a representative case
from the fourth century BC, he suggests that the high demands
on wealthy citizens for cash to meet their political obligations
drew them into the market. Production on large estates was clearly
market-oriented and based on a careful balance of risk avoidance
and maximisation of returns.

Once market exchange becomes re-established as a functionally
indispensable institution in the regional economies of ancient Greece,

the question of whether markets were linked by an inter-regional mechanism of supply and demand cannot be left aside. Gary Reger argues on the basis of the temple accounts of Hellenistic Delos that although the temple routinely supplied itself via the market, its major source for produce was the island itself and its direct neighbourhood. While prices on Delos were a function of supply and demand (*contra* the 'primitivist' position), the island was unlikely to have been integrated into an inter-regional market of necessities (*contra* 'modernist' claims). Dominic Rathbone bridges the divide between the Greek and Roman worlds. Again, he offers a distinctly optimistic outlook on the importance of the market in Egyptian rural production. Yet, equally importantly, he raises the question to what extent this first 'Hellenised' and subsequently 'Romanised' region can be treated as part of the ancient economy. As Egypt provides us with by far the most extensive amount of material which can be used for the purpose of economic investigation, answers to this question will crucially influence the direction of future discussions on the ancient economy.

Significant contributions to the study of the Roman economy have commonly addressed the pivotal issue of economic growth. In which ways and to what extent did the political unification of the Mediterranean under Roman rule and the attendant – albeit invariably partial and limited – homogenisation of taxation, currencies and legal institutions trigger market exchange, increased division of labour, urbanisation, technological progress and information transfer, and ultimately intensive, per capita growth in output and consumption? Each of the papers selected here approaches this question from a different angle.

In general, recent research has increasingly pushed away from the 'minimalist' end of the spectrum of modern interpretation. Thus, in a case study of olive cultivation in Roman imperial North Africa, Robert Bruce Hitchner argues for substantial intensive growth in provincial agriculture, a development facilitated by rising urban demand and documented by extensive archaeological evidence. A recent synthetic overview by Clementina Panella and André Tchernia represents the important field of amphora studies, which seeks to reconstruct Roman trade routes and trace changes in the objects and directions of inter-regional exchange by studying the distribution patterns of surviving ceramic containers of wine and olive oil. Drawing on ancient and comparative evidence as well as probabilistic estimates, Keith Hopkins advocates a dynamic model of public and private surplus extraction and market exchange: responding to criticism of an earlier version of his interpretation of the workings of the Roman imperial economy, he explores the interaction of different economic variables from taxation and productivity to urbanisation, long-distance trade and coin circulation. Finally, Richard Saller questions the terms of the debate between 'modernism' and 'primitivism'. He applies the perspective of modern economics to the question of Roman economic growth, highlighting the methodological pitfalls involved in the interpretation of ancient source material.

We have aimed to cover a variety of different topics, approaches and types of evidence without losing sight of the main issues of the recent debate. In the following papers, ancient archaeological, literary, epigraphic, papyrological and numismatic sources as well as comparative data are marshalled to explore agricultural production, trade, price formation, economic growth and integration, urbanisation, fiscality, economic thought and cultural poetics, ranging from archaic Greece to late antiquity. Nevertheless, much more would have been worthy of attention. Work on slavery, one of the most central aspects of ancient economic development, will be covered by Keith Bradley's reader in this series and has therefore been omitted on purpose. Constraints of space forestall the proper representation of further archaeological work – from field surveys to studies of shipwrecks – or important issues such as banking and finance, pastoralism, mining, manufacturing, non-slave labour, markets and fairs, technology, consumption, demography, gender, and explains the relative underrepresentation of early Greece, the Roman Republican period and the Later Roman Empire.[10] We have focused instead on controversial issues, and sought to avoid unsuitably technical or thematically narrow papers. In the end, this collection can do no more than give a flavour of recent debates, and – we hope – whet the appetite for more.

---

[10] Once more, readers are referred to the 'Guide to Further Reading' for pertinent literature.

PART I

After Finley

1 *The Economy (Economies) of Ancient Greece*

PAUL CARTLEDGE[†]

This bibliographical survey provides a thematic overview of post-Finleyan research on economies of the ancient Greek world. One strand of scholarship is concerned with the material conditions of rural production and exchange as well as with their social and geographical environment. Intensive field survey, ethnoarchaeology and palaeobotany open up new methodological approaches to the material culture of the ancient world, especially in their attempt to interpret ancient remains in the light of comparative data. Others are less preoccupied with new types of evidence than with new questions, concentrating above all on ideological aspects of the ancient economy. These scholars emphasise that a very different discourse surrounded the economy in the ancient world and explore the difference between ancient and modern understandings of economic problems. Both strands of research have moved the debate considerably away from the controversies that spun around Finley's *Ancient Economy*, but they have also triggered a new controversy over what might be regarded as the proper task of economic history. Unfortunately, these two scholarly perspectives share little common ground. While culturally oriented historians tend to question the status of archaeologists' 'data', 'new archaeologists' point out that cultural arguments ignore the harsh facts of life.[‡]

Cartledge's survey reminds us that research on the ancient economy has not taken place in an intellectual vacuum. Over the past few decades, the discipline of history has undergone a general transition from the belief that the past can be, however incompletely, reconstructed to the idea that historical research can only tentatively bridge the distance between past and present. Thus, as the reality of past economies may be irretrievably lost, historians might at best be able to engage in a dialogue between past representations and modern perceptions. It is for this reason that Cartledge takes modern economic theory to be of little help to the economic historians in their task to translate an alien culture into the modern world of thought.[§]

[†] Originally published as 'The Economy (Economies) of Ancient Greece', *Dialogos* 5 (1998), 4–24 (© Frank Cass).

[‡] See for this esp. Ian Morris, 'The Athenian Economy Twenty Years After *The Ancient Economy*', CP LXXXIX (1994), 351–66.

[§] For a different view, compare Ch. 12 (Saller) below.

OLD AND NEW HISTORY[1]

[...] Theodore K. Rabb observed in 1982, with a note of palpable surprise, or shock, 'it is almost as if there were a shrinking from the physical world'.[2] Historians, that is, or at any rate 'new' historians, seemed to Rabb to be in headlong 'flight from materialism', driven by an 'uneasiness with the material conditions of life that until recently seemed so compelling', an uneasiness itself inspired by 'doubts ... about the explanatory power of economic developments, and ... the defensiveness of the economic historians themselves'. Since 1982, that tendency has if anything accelerated, with the widespread, if premature, discrediting of materialist historiography of any kind and an avoidance of pure (or mere) economic history.

We ancient historians of course tend to be congenitally suspicious, or positively contemptuous, of novelty, on the quasi-Aristotelian principle that what is new is not true, and what is true is not new. But by a coincidental paradox, during the past couple of decades we have found ourselves walking or running in parallel with our more progressive colleagues in other historical fields regarding the economic in history. It is not that the flight from economics in ancient Greek history has been by any means total. But here too there has long been discernible a distinct turn from 'how it might actually have been' empiricist historiography to 'how it seems to have been thought or represented' intellectual-cultural studies.

ECONOMY (ECONOMIES): WHAT'S IN A NAME?

All the main words of my title require prior definition, delimitation and specification. Spatio-temporally, 'ancient Greece' will be taken to mean pretty much Plato's metaphorical 'pond',[3] that is the Mediterranean and Black Sea Hellenic world, between about 500 and 300 BCE. 'Economy' or 'economies', let alone 'the ancient Greek econ-

---

[1] In memoriam M.I.F. This essay appears exactly a quarter of a century after the first editon of the groundbreaking *The Ancient Economy* (Berkeley 1973; 2nd edn., 1985) by Moses Finley, to whose memory in affectionate gratitude it is dedicated. Compare also Finley, *Economy and Society in Ancient Greece*, ed. B. D. Shaw and R. P. Saller (London 1981); H. Schneider, 'Der moderne Markt und die antike Gesellschaft. Über Moses Finley', *Freibeuter* (1986) 143–6; I. Morris, 'The Athenian economy twenty years after *The Ancient Economy*', *Classical Philology* 89 (1994) 351–66 [; Ch. 2 (Andreau) below].

[2] T. K. Rabb in Rabb and R. I. Rotberg (eds.), *The New History: the 1980s and beyond. I. Studies in Interdisciplinary History* (Princeton 1982) 321.

[3] Plato, *Phaedo* 109b.

omy', are more complex issues. Perhaps one might approach them first by asking *whose* 'economy' or 'economies'?

Objectively, students of ancient Greek economic life are faced with the problem of generalizing usefully about a world of more than a thousand separate political units, which were on the whole radically self-differentiated. Perhaps there is a useful sense in which we might say that by 500 BCE the Greek world was unified by intersecting lines of economic exchange via the long-distance trade in staple goods (human as well as vegetable and mineral). But there is surely no useful sense in which we might speak of the Greek world of 500 as one economic system. When Herodotus attempted to define Hellenism (*to Hellênikon*), in terms of what all Greeks uniquely and distinctively had in common, economic life was conspicuously not among his chosen ingredients, let alone economic 'system'.[4] Indeed, what strikes us perhaps most forcefully about ancient Greece is rather its heterogeneous pluralism, in economic life as in other fundamental aspects of both individual and communal activity.[5] The economy of Sparta, for instance, however precisely it is to be classified and analysed, is surely a different animal from the economy of Athens – not to mention such further complications as whether Athens and Sparta themselves can be said to have had a single economy or, rather, to have comprehended a plurality of micro-economies.[6]

Subjectively, the issue turns in part on what one wishes to understand by economy or economics: is it need-satisfying production, distribution and exchange of the goods required for the purpose of securing life? or is it want-satisfying behaviour of those kinds with a view to achieving the good life? or something of each, or something in between? Failure to make the *explananda* [what is to be explained] clear from the outset is one reason for the long-running and now rather exhausted debate between the so-called 'primitivists' and

[4] Hdt. 8.144.2. It is at least more plausible to speak of the Greco-Roman world of (say) CE 1 as constituting such a system, and therefore of 'the ancient economy' in the singular. However, R. Duncan-Jones, 'Trade, taxes and money', in his *Structure and Scale in the Ancient Economy* (Cambridge 1990) 30–47, has taken cogently strong issue with the unitarian view of M. K. Hopkins, 'Taxes and trade in the Roman empire, 200 BC–AD 400', *Journal of Roman Studies* 70 (1980) 101–25; and id. in P. Garnsey, K. Hopkins and C. R. Whittaker (eds.), *Trade in the Ancient Economy* (London 1983) esp. x–xiv.

[5] E. Ruschenbusch, 'Zur Wirtschafts- und Sozialstruktur der *Normalpolis*', *Annuario della Scuola Normale Superiore di Pisa*, 13 (1983) 171–94, has sought to define a sort of model or ideal-typical Greek city; this construct's chief value is to demonstrate unequivocally the abnormality of classical Athens, from which most of our fine-grained evidence comes, and on which most of the debate concerning the nature of the ancient Greek economy is explicitly or implicitly focused.

[6] On the objective question of the nature of classical Greek economy in comparative perspective see further Finley (ed.), *The Bücher-Meyer Controversy* (New York 1979).

'modernizers': those who argue that the Greeks' economy (or economies) differed wholesale from any modern (Western, capitalist) economy, and those who discern in ancient Greece smaller-scale or inchoate versions of modern economic life and thought. Another reason for its persistence is that the primitivists tend to be trying to explain how the 98% of Greeks 'economized', that is, secured a bare livelihood within the framework of the ideally (yet rarely) self-sufficient *oikos* or household; whereas the modernizers focus instead on the 2% of exceptions for whom macro-economic activity at a regional or international level was the sole or prime source of their wealth. (My percentages are of course purely notional and rhetorical.)[7]

The other pivotal subjective factor in understanding 'economy' or 'economies' is the modern interpreter's choice of models or theory. One of the targets of Moses Finley's attack on the importation of anachronistic theory and assumptions into ancient Greek economic history was John Hicks's 'model for the "First Phase of the Mercantile Economy", in the city-state, which presupposes that "the trade (oil for corn) is *unlikely to get started* unless, to begin with, it is a handsome profit"'.[8] Hicks at least was using an explicit model, but it was Finley's persuasive view that he (like many other, if usually less distinguished, scholars) had got hold of the wrong one. For Finley's reading of Weber and his follower Johannes Hasebroek had honed his appreciation of cross-cultural comparison by way of economic and cultural anthropology (especially that of Karl Polanyi out of Richard Thurnwald) and had led him to embrace what came to be known as the 'substantivist' position as opposed to that of the 'formalists' on the location, mental as well as material, of the economic in ancient Greece.[9]

[7] The debate is neatly summarized by E. Will, 'Trois quarts de siècle de recherches sur l'économie grecque antique', *Annales (ESC)* 9 (1954) 7–22; cf. M. M. Austin and P. Vidal-Naquet, *Economic and Social History of Ancient Greece: an Introduction* (London 1977); E. M. Burke, 'The economy of Athens in the classical era: some adjustments to the primitivist model', *Transactions and Proceedings of the American Philological Association* 122 (1992) 199–226.

[8] Finley, *Ancient Economy*, 26 (Finley's italics), citing J. Hicks, *A Theory of Economic History* (Oxford 1969) 42–3. Note also Hicks, *A Market Theory of Money* (Oxford 1989); but for some of the problems with contemporary market theory, see F. Hahn, 'Incomplete market economics', *Proceedings of the British Academy* 80 (1993) 201–19, esp. 211. See further my review of E. E. Cohen, *Athenian Economy and Society: a Banking Perspective* (Princeton 1992), *Times Higher Education Supplement*, 17 April 1993, where I draw attention to the dangers of interpretative polarization (*either* primitive, non-market, embedded economy *or* full-blown, disembedded market economy). A more favourable response to Cohen's important book may be found in the review by T. Figueira, *Bryn Mawr Classical Review* 5 (1994) 109–13.

[9] On Hasebroek see briefly Cartledge, '"Trade and Politics" revisited: archaic Greece', in

For the formalists, the ancient economy was a functionally segregated and independently instituted sphere of activity with its own profit-maximizing, want-satisfying logic and rationality, less 'developed' no doubt than any modern economy but nevertheless recognizably similar in kind. Substantivists, on the other hand, hold that the ancient economy was not merely less developed but socially embedded and politically overdetermined and so – by the standards of neoclassical economics – conspicuously conventional, irrational and status-ridden. It is crucially important that this much more interesting and important substantivist–formalist debate should not be confused, as it often is, with the primitivist–modernizer debate. Not even the most ardent primitivist would deny that quite a bit of extra-household economy was practised in ancient Greece. Not even the most fervent modernizer would deny that some quite basic aspects of ancient Greek economy were really rather primitive. The most serious misunderstandings can arise when the debate about the level and quantity of Greek economic life becomes confused with the argument over its politico-social location.[10]

Finley, however, made things too easy for himself. From his almost tautological demonstration that the categories of neoclassical economic analysis had no useful application to 'the ancient economy' he proceeded to the illegitimate inference that the ancients did not employ economic analysis because there was no economy for them to analyse.[11] Granted that there is no question of 'economics' having been conceptualized by ancient Greeks in the terms of an Adam Smith or an Alfred Marshall, yet one might still prefer to use the non-applicability of neoclassical theory as merely a preliminary heuristic.

Garnsey, Hopkins, Whittaker (eds.), *Trade in the Ancient Economy*, 1–15. Polanyi's views are best read in K. Polanyi, *Primitive, Archaic and Modern Economies*, ed. G. Dalton (New York 1968), with the useful critiques of: S. C. Humphreys, 'History, economics and anthropology: the work of Karl Polanyi', in *Anthropology and the Greeks* (London 1978) 31–75; F. Block and M. Somers, 'Beyond the economistic fallacy: the holistic social science of Karl Polanyi', in T. Skocpol (ed.), *Vision and Method in Historical Sociology* (Cambridge 1984) 47–84; W. Nippel, 'Ökonomische Anthropologie und griechische Wirtschaftsgeschichte', in *Griechen, Barbaren und "Wilde". Alte Geschichte und Sozialanthropologie* (Frankfurt 1990) 124–51; D. W. Tandy and W. C. Neale, 'Karl Polanyi's distinctive approach to social analysis and the case of ancient Greece: ideas, criticisms, consequence', in C. M. Duncan and D. W. Tandy (eds.), *From Political Economy to Anthropology: Situating Economic Life in Past Societies* (Montreal 1994) 9–33.
[10] See further Morris, 'Athenian economy', 354: 'reducing substantivism to primitivism misses its political program, and with it everything that made Polanyi's and Finley's work – and ancient Greece – interesting to a wider audience.'
[11] See S. Meikle, 'Aristotle and exchange value', in D. Keyt and F. D. Miller (eds.), *A Companion to Aristotle's Politics* (Cambridge, Mass. 1991) 156–81; 'Modernism, economics and the ancient economy', *Proceedings of the Cambridge Philological Society* 41 (1995) 174–91 [= Ch. 11 below].

It might then be allowed that the ancient Greeks both had an economy and practised economic analysis, perhaps of an incommensur-
ably different nature from anything familiar to or recognizable by us
as such.[12] It is in these broader terms that both Plato and Aristotle
have been claimed on independent grounds as 'discoverers' of 'the
economy'.[13] However, it should go without saying that neither would
have dreamed of – nor could reasonably be imagined as – writing
either *An Inquiry into the Nature and Causes of the Wealth of
Nations* or *The Principles of Economics*.

SOURCES: EVIDENCE AND/OR MODELS?

How then should we set about formulating usable and useful
models? According to Geoffrey de Ste. Croix, we should 'formulate
the necessary categories, from the ground up' on the basis of 'a very
large body of evidence about the economic life of the Greek city ...
the great bulk [of which] comes from the late fifth and (more
especially) the fourth century'.[14] This is right in principle, but right
for the wrong reasons. Actually, there did not exist a single, homo-
geneous, normative 'Greek city', nor can we, as Ste. Croix claims,
'steadfastly clear our minds of all preconceptions derived from other
periods of history'; and, finally, his phrase 'a very large body of data'
may be seriously misleading.

Notoriously, there are few good, let alone statistically significant,
quantitative data available, and so no possibilities of *histoire sérielle*
on the *Annales* model. We cannot even test anachronism-free qualitative hypotheses numerically. Documents generally are in very short
supply.[15] In theory, inscriptions and coins might be thought our best

[12] H. Kloft, *Die Wirtschaft der griechisch-römischen Welt: eine Einführung* (Darmstadt
1992), seems to be saying something like that, even if his work is otherwise theoretically
flawed; see S. von Reden, *Classical Review* 43 (1993) 321–3. It is not irrelevant that, although
our words are Greek in etymology, the semantic fields of 'economy' and 'economics' overlap
only marginally with those of ancient Greek *oikonomia* and *oikonomika*: C. Ampolo,
'*Oikonomia*: tre osservazioni sui rapporto tra la finanza e l'economia greca', *Archeologia e
storia antica* 1 (1979) 119–30; cf. F. Roscalla (ed.), *Senofonte. Economico* (Milan 1991) (with
an important introduction by D. Lanza); G. Audring (ed.), *Xenophon. Ökonomische Schriften*
(Berlin 1992).
[13] M. S. Schofield, 'Plato on the economy', in M. H. Hansen (ed.), *The Ancient Greek City-
State* (Copenhagen 1993) 183–96; Polanyi, 'Aristotle discovers the economy', in Polanyi,
C. M. Arensberg and H. W. Pearson (eds.), *Trade and Market in the Early Empires* (Chicago
1957) 64–9. Xenophon too has been hailed as the 'earliest Greek economist' in S. B. Pomeroy,
Xenophon's 'Oeconomicus'. A Social and Historical Commentary (Oxford 1994) 42; but for
a critique of her modernizing and economistic reading of Xenophon see V. J. Hunter, *Classical
Philology* 91 (1996) 184–9.
[14] Ste. Croix, *Journal of Hellenic Studies* 87 (1967) 180, reviewing M. I. Finley (ed.), *Trade
and Politics in the Ancient World* (Aix-en-Provence 1965).
[15] Finley, 'Le document et l'histoire économique de l'antiquité', *Annales (ESC)* 37 (1982)
697–713.

prospects, but they are both flawed in practice. Inscriptions disappoint chiefly by their incompleteness or limited scope.[16] Coins do so, rather, because it is often unclear what exactly it is that they represent.[17] Archaeology more broadly, including wrecks and amphora-stamps as well as intensive field-survey and limited site-excavation, can, again, take us only so far.[18] Modern so-called 'proxy-data', drawn from *ex hypothesi* [stated in the hypothesis] relevantly similar contemporary societies are quantitative, to be sure, even serial, and have a solidly empirical base in accurate records. But they also have their own, rather different, problems in retrospective application, above all the difficulty of ensuring that like is being compared with, or substituted for, like.[19]

It is sooner rather than later, therefore, that we find ourselves driven back on 'literary' sources of one sort or another. Empirically, their limitations are obvious. Suppose, then, that we take them not as a *pis aller* [expedient] but rather as primary in the significatory sense, that is, as evidence of ancient Greek mentality, the whole nexus of ideas in Greek culture;[20] and suppose we assume, further, that mentality does not merely reflect but also up to a point determines economic (as other) reality. Yet this move too involves further, interconnected problems, namely how to evaluate both the representativeness and the ideology of the extant writings. Arguably, Aristophanes, Plato, Xenophon, Demosthenes and Aristotle shared an identical or closely similar economic mentality, but were their views representative of a wider 'Greek' mentality, and, even supposing they were, how justified would we be in assuming a snug fit between them and the economic realities on the ground (in the agora

[16] H. W. Pleket (ed.), *Epigraphica* I. *Texts on the Economic History of the Greek World* (Leiden 1964).

[17] Kloft, *Wirtschaft,* 55ff.; cf. M. H. Crawford, 'Numismatics', in Crawford (ed.), *Sources for Ancient History* (Cambridge 1983) 185–233, esp. 205–7, who remarks, with reference to P. Grierson, 'Commerce in the Dark Ages: a critique of the evidence', *Transactions of the Royal Historical Society,* 9 (1959) 123–40, that 'as far as the distribution of goods, including coins, is concerned, plunder and gift and such things as indemnities may be much more important than trade as a vehicle' (207). See also now C. Howgego, *Ancient History from Coins* (London 1995).

[18] A. M. Snodgrass, 'Archaeology', in Crawford (ed.), *Sources,* 168–72; cf. Morris, 'Athenian economy', 361 ('excavated materials are no more of a transparent window on the past than are written sources'). Note also esp. the determined attack on the 'positivist fallacy' (the correlation of the economic significance of an artefact or class of artefacts with its propensity to survive in archaeologically recoverable form) in D. Gill, 'Positivism, pots and long-distance trade', in I. M. Morris (ed.), *Classical Greece. Ancient Histories and Modern Archaeologies* (Cambridge 1994) 99–107. Field-survey: below, nn. 31, 35.

[19] See below n. 34.

[20] C. Gill, *Personality in Greek Epic, Tragedy, and Philosophy. The Self in Dialogue* (Oxford 1996) 4 n. 11, 30, 468.

and port, as well as within the private *oikos*)? Secondly, since a crucial part of the evidence these writings provide is ideological – both explicitly formulated theoretical reflections and pragmatic expressions of inexplicit ideological assumptions – should that disqualify such evidence entirely as a basis for our notionally non-ideological analyses?

In a sense, ideology is where Finley started – and ended. His 'ancient economy' was a unitary construct because in his view the ruling élites of Greco-Roman antiquity shared, morally and operationally, a single economic outlook. Finley, however, failed to allow sufficiently for ideology in the guise of false consciousness, the deliberate resistance to and distortion of reality in defence of a precarious or challenged *status quo*. On the other hand, he was surely right about the nature and function of dominant ideology: ruling ideas do tend to be the ideas of a society's rulers, and the writers mentioned above, like almost all our literary sources, belonged in some sense to the ruling class. Certainly, there were those outside the ruling classes or élites of ancient Greece who adhered to alternative ideologies, but as long as politics dominated economics and traditional landed property-owners dominated politics, 'commercial' or 'market' mentalities or ideologies were not actually going to prevail. However reactionary one takes Aristotle to be, in his economic as in his political and social theory more broadly, nevertheless his outlook ought still to have reflected with some fidelity the norms governing the vast bulk of economic activity throughout the classical Greek world – excepting perhaps only that which went on at Athens and, more particularly, in the Piraeus.[21]

POLITICS

Aristotle wrote on practically everything under the sun, but what he conspicuously did not write was economics.[22] Nor can it be shown that in works devoted in significant part to what might plausibly be labelled 'political economy' Aristotle engaged in economic analysis properly so called.[23] *A fortiori* [all the more], on the imaginary spectrum that runs from practical politicians, at one pole, through

[21] On class in antiquity see G. E. M. de Ste. Croix, *The Class Struggle in the Ancient Greek World. From the Archaic age to the Arab conquests* (London 1981, corr. impr. 1983). On the Piraeus economy, see further pp. 26–7 below, with n. 62.

[22] The Aristotelian work known under the Latin title *Oeconomica* was not written by Aristotle himself, nor does it comprise much that could be dignified with the label 'political economy', let alone economic analysis.

[23] Finley, 'Aristotle and economic analysis' (1970), repr. in Finley (ed.), *Studies in Ancient Society* (London 1974) 26–52; S. Meikle, *Aristotle's Economic Thought* (Oxford 1996).

economic political theorists, political economists, and economic actors to economists, at the other pole, the ancient Greeks in general can barely be said to have transcended the stage or status of 'economic political theorists'.

On the other hand, almost everything that Aristotle wrote on interpersonal social transactions can comfortably be placed under the general rubric of 'politics'. It is simply not possible to overstate the degree to which ancient Greek life – communal and private, individual and collective – was politicized.[24] It is this politicization which explains, for instance, the necessity (rather than the mere desirability) of alienating market-exchange as far as possible beyond the tight bonds of the civic community, displacing it for preference onto sub-citizen classes excluded from full civic participation by reason of their legal status as women, aliens or unfree.[25]

Politics, however, is one thing, 'the state' quite another. That Latin-derived term is harmless enough if it is used to denote the *polis*, a citizen-state or civic community in a strong sense, united by constitutional and other laws defining who was and who was not a 'shareholder', and especially (but not always, most notably not in the case of democratic Athens) on the basis of the ownership of landed property.[26] Its use can, however, be quite gravely harmful if it conjures up an entity in any significant way resembling the modern State: that is, a strongly institutionalized and differentiated, centralized and bureaucratized public sphere of professional government, in contradistinction from and opposition to the non-political, private sphere of 'civil society'. That modern State (capital 'S') is an invention of the early modern and modern periods, and is simply not to be found in ancient Greece, in which, as Aristotle succinctly put it, 'the same ideals [literally 'things'] are best in both public and private life, and it is the lawgiver's task to implant them in the souls of mankind'.[27]

---

[24] On politics and 'the political' in ancient Greece, see e.g. C. Meier, *The Greek Discovery of Politics* (Cambridge, Mass. 1990); further references and discussion in Cartledge, 'La Politica', in S. Settis (ed.), *I Greci*, I. *Noi e I Greci* (Turin 1996) 39–72 [, and in C. Rowe and M. Schofield (eds), *The Cambridge History of Greek and Roman Political Thought* (Cambridge 2000)].

[25] Morris, 'The community against the market in Classical Athens', in Duncan and Tandy (eds.), *From Political Economy*, 52–79, at 68; a point not sufficiently appreciated by Cohen, *Athenian Economy.*

[26] 'Share-holder': P. B. Manville, *The Origins of Citizenship in Ancient Athens* (Princeton 1990). 'Citizen-state': W. G. Runciman, 'Doomed to extinction: the *polis* as an evolutionary dead-end', in O. Murray and S. Price (eds.), *The Greek City from Homer to Aristotle* (Oxford 1990) 347–67.

[27] Arist. *Pol.* 1333b36–8. I am esp. indebted here to the unpublished Cambridge PhD thesis of M. Berent, 'The Stateless Polis. Towards a Re-evaluation of the Classical Greek Political Community' (1994).

AGRICULTURE, ECOLOGY AND
ETHNOARCHAEOLOGY

This absence will have a particular bearing on our discussion of trade and commerce. But I begin my substantive discussion of ancient Greek economics with the normal and the normative rather than the exceptional and possibly antinomian [abnormal].[28] The ancient Greek world was massively and unalterably rural. The overwhelming majority of its inhabitants lived in and off the country, as farmers. That much is not in dispute, though precise percentages and the nature of farming activity undoubtedly are. Within the modern historiography of ancient Greece, agriculture has been comparatively neglected, for two main reasons. First, the ancients themselves whose writings have come down to us tended to despise or affected to ignore its sordid realities.[29] The ancient literary sources, therefore, are not only relatively poor in reference to matters agricultural, but are also skewed by the perceptions and perspectives of the rich and leisured élite. Secondly, many modern students of the ancient world have shared their contempt for the base material factors of history, the economic infrastructure of civilized living.[30]

Yet although, or rather because, the available literary sources are inadequate, especially for purposes of quantification, the study of ancient Greek agriculture has in the last dozen years or so been re-fertilized and fructified by both the development of new, and the more productive application of old, theories and methodologies. These include: techniques of intensive field-survey inspired by the 'New Archaeology' that pay minute attention to how it actually was – and is – on the ground, as opposed to how it is represented in either the élite texts of ancient armchair agronomists or the digbooks of modern excavators;[31] ethnoarchaeology, that is the participant observation and recording of contemporary Greek or other Mediterranean peasant agrarian communities that farm in *ex hypothesi* relevantly

---

[28] In this section I resume Cartledge, 'Classical Greek agriculture: recent work and alternative views', *Journal of Peasant Studies* 21 (1993) 127–36, a review-article of A. Burford, *Land and Labor in the Greek World* (Baltimore 1993) and S. Isager and J. E. Skydsgaard, *Ancient Greek Agriculture: An Introduction* (London 1992), in which I pay due tribute to the inspirational pioneering work of the prehistorian Paul Halstead [see Ch. 3 below].

[29] R. Osborne, *Classical Landscape with Figures: the Ancient Greek City and its Countryside* (London 1987) makes what he can of what sources there are.

[30] Even a scholar like Alison Burford, who has written with sympathy on ancient craftsmen (typically humble people, often slaves), in her *Craftsmen in Greek and Roman Society* (London 1972), can claim that 'the Greeks rose to greater heights above the furrowed field in more spheres of intellectual and artistic activity than other people': *Land and Labor*, 2.

[31] S. E. Alcock, J. Cherry and J. L. Davis, 'Intensive survey, agricultural practice and the classical landscape of Greece', in Morris (ed.), *Classical Greece*, 137–70. Se also n. 35 below.

similar environments;[32] experimental history and archaeology, that is the modelling by computer-simulation of the domestic household life-cycle, or the attempted replication of ancient farming procedures; palaeoethnobotany; and then the renewed scrutiny, in the light of some or all of these novelties, of the available literary and epigraphical documents.[33] Many problems remain, however, and many fundamental issues are still open. Particularly furious debate rages over the legitimacy of using modem 'proxy data' to substitute for the original evidence we shall never have.[34] But some incontrovertible gains can surely be registered.

Few intensive field-surveys in Greek lands are as yet either completed or fully published; this is still new and largely uncharted territory.[35] But even the most inchoate have already transformed our picture of the settled countryside. We now have such a huge increase of raw information about human rural settlement in Greek lands from the Neolithic age to the modern era that debates have inevitably become more sophisticated or have shifted to different levels of analysis. For example, what is it that the visible artefactual remains represent? If a 'farm', was it the farmer's sole or principal residence, all year round or seasonally? Was it part of a nucleated or dispersed pattern of agrarian settlement? Did farmers deliberately disperse their holdings to spread and thereby minimize risks and/or to maximize efficient exploitation of different micro-environments?

Behind such questions, which are often unanswerable finally or globally, lurks the will-o'-the-wisp of economic rationality. Were ancient Greek farmers as rational in their choice, and as efficient in their pursuit, of economic goals as (some) Greek philosophers and mathematicians famously were in their respective fields of activity? Rationality? – *whose* rationality, it might well be asked, especially

[32] H. A. Forbes, 'The ethnoarchaeological approach to ancient Greek agriculture', in B. Wells (ed.), *Agriculture in Ancient Greece* (Stockholm 1992) 87–101.

[33] Household cycle: T. W. Gallant, *Risk and Survival in Ancient Greece. Reconstructing the Domestic Rural Economy* (Oxford 1991). Palaeoethnobotany: R. Sallares, *The Ecology of the Ancient Greek World* (London 1991).

[34] P. Garnsey, *Famine and Food Supply in the Graeco-Roman World: Responses to Risk and Crisis* (Cambridge 1988) and Gallant, *Risk and Survival,* are broadly – and to me persuasively – positive on this issue; Isager and Skydsgaard, *Ancient Greek Agriculture,* rather vehemently negative.

[35] This was a considerable handicap to S. Alcock, *Graecia Capta. The Landscapes of Roman Greece* (Cambridge 1993). But see now M. H. Jameson, C. N. Runnels and T. Van Andel, *A Greek Countryside* (Stanford 1994), with Cartledge, 'Classical Greek agriculture II', *Journal of Peasant Studies* 23 (1995) 131–9, a review-article of Jameson et al., and of V. D. Hanson, *The Other Greeks. The Family Farm and the Agrarian Roots of Western Civilization* (New York 1995); and L. Foxhall, H. A. Forbes and C. Mee, 'Six hundred years of settlement history on the peninsula of Methana: an interdisciplinary approach', *Dialogos* 3 (1996) 72–94.

since the collocation of 'the Greeks' and 'the irrational' is not quite as paradoxical and outrageous now as it appeared in 1951.[36] However, the general consensus would seem to be that ancient Greek farming practices were on the whole well adapted to terrain, climate, labour-supply and other environmental and social variables, given of course the universally and distinctly 'low' technological base and absence of what is understood today by infrastructure.

Some scholars indeed would go further. Sallares, for instance, has innovatively, if speculatively, drawn attention to the palaeoethnobotanical possibilities of seed-evolution by both natural and human selection. Gallant has reconstructed theoretically, with the aid of 'proxy data', a 'working-model of the average Greek peasant household life-cycle' comprising a nicely calibrated scale of responses to risk and crisis; this is certainly not intrinsically implausible (if as yet insufficiently fine-grained). Exponents of the so-called 'Alternative' or 'New Model' of Greek agriculture have even argued for not just the possibility, but the necessity, of regular deviations from a regime of strict biennial fallowing and the evolution of genuinely mixed farming, which would have involved systematic crop rotation and much manuring (human as well as animal), and thus what has been dubbed 'agro-pastoralism'.[37] Probably the principal common factor behind these radically positive constructions is the concern to account for seeming population explosion(s) in many parts of the Greek world between about 500 and 250 BCE, which have even prompted talk of a 'great transformation', a sort of ancient Greek agricultural revolution.[38] That is doubtless premature, but defenders of the traditional model of biennial-fallow dry-farming without benefit of animal manure are finding themselves having to fight a rearguard action.[39]

INDUSTRY, TECHNOLOGY AND LABOUR

To label the classical Greek world 'pre-industrial' is too vague; to call it 'third-world' too precise.[40] But if 'primitive' in its culturally loaded sense does have any application to ancient Greece, surely it is in the domain of industrialization, technology and labour. Whether or not

---

[36] E. R. Dodds, *The Greeks and the Irrational* (Berkeley 1951).

[37] S. Hodkinson, 'Animal husbandry in the Greek polis', in C. R. Whittaker (ed.), *Pastoral Economies in Classical Antiquity* (Cambridge 1988) 35–74.

[38] Morris, 'Athenian economy', 364.

[39] See esp. Isager and Skydsgaard. *Ancient Greek Agriculture.*

[40] As Ste. Croix remarks, *loc. cit.* (n. 14), '"underdeveloped countries" [are] powerfully affected by the advanced industrial societies towards whose condition they aspire'.

the Greeks knew the wheelbarrow (a perennial and partly humorous debate), this was unarguably a world still very largely of human energy and man-power, and deficient in artificially generated energy or power.⁴¹ The major exception in ancient pre-Roman Greece was wind-power, used, however, not to turn mill-sails, but to fill the sails of the specialist merchantmen that had been developed already by 600 BCE.⁴² The contrast between the ingenuity, time and material resources expended by the Greeks on sacred constructions, on the one hand, and on industrial or agricultural ergonomics, on the other, remains very striking indeed.⁴³

Three quarters of a century ago, a valuable account was published of the major written sources on ancient agriculture, Roman as well as Greek, 'from the point of view of labour'.⁴⁴ Since then, there have been studies of the Greek ideology of labour in general: the pagan Greeks were mostly agreed that working for one's living was not an intrinsic good, and their term for hard physical toil, *ponos*, is generally pejorative; to be without *ponos* was, according to Hesiod, to live like the blessed immortal gods.⁴⁵ Labour, moreover, as an abstract theoretical category (as in 'labour power', or a 'labour theory of value') was unknown to the ancient Greeks, by whom it was understood in the most concrete, physical sense.⁴⁶

Three major problems might be worth further consideration. First, was ancient Greece in broad terms a 'peasant' economy (or society)? First find – or define – your peasant. For some modern interpreters, the word is inherently negative, because peasant status necessarily

---

⁴¹ J.-P. Vernant, 'Some remarks on the forms and limitations of technological thought among the Greeks' [1957], in *Myth and Thought in Ancient Greece* (London 1983) 279–301; Finley, 'Technical innovation and economic progress in the ancient world' [1965], repr., with bibliographical addendum, in *Economy and Society*, 176–95, 273–5; H. W. Pleket, 'Technology and society in the Graeco-roman world', *Acta Historiae Neerlandica* 2 (1967) 1–25; id., 'Technology in the Greco-Roman world: a general report', *Talanta* 5 (1973) 6–47. For a specific instance see L. Foxhall, 'Oil extraction and processing equipment in Classical Greece', in M-C. Amouretti and J-P. Brun (eds.), *La production du vin et de l'huile en Méditerranée* (Paris 1993) 183–200.
⁴² L. Casson, *The Ancient Mariners. Seafarers and Sea Fighters of the Mediterranean in Ancient Times* (2nd edn., Princeton 1991).
⁴³ See Osborne, *Classical Landscape*, esp. 81–92.
⁴⁴ W. E. Heitland, *Agricola: a Study of Agricultural Life in the Graeco-Roman World from the Point of View of Labour* (Cambridge 1921).
⁴⁵ Vernant, 'Work and nature in ancient Greece' (1955), and 'Some psychological aspects of work in ancient Greece' (1956), in *Myth and Thought*, 248–70, 271–8; N. Loraux, '*Ponos*: some difficulties regarding the term for "labor"' [1982], in *The Experiences of Tiresias. The Feminine and the Greek Man* (Princeton 1995) 44–58.
⁴⁶ Esp. S. von Reden, 'Arbeit und Zivilisation: Kriterien der Selbstdefinition im antiken Athen', *Münstersche Beiträge zur antiken Handelsgeschichte* 11 (1992) 1–31, at 31 (English summary): 'in antiquity labour was conceptualized in terms of toil and achievement, rather than in terms of production'.

involves multi-directional subjection to powerful outsiders and so is inappropriate at least for free Greek citizen farmers.[47] For others, there is no shame in peasant status – on the contrary: the Athenian democracy was a 'peasant' republic.[48] Still others find the term unhelpful for various reasons: because there was no ancient Greek equivalent term, because ancient Greek farmers differed crucially from medieval and modern peasantries, and because use of the term has given rise to contradictory interpretations.[49] There is, I suggest, a *via media* [middle path]. Provided 'peasant' is allowed to retain its etymological sense of country(wo)man and does not necessarily connote political subordination or subjection, it may be helpful in picking out a category of farmer below that of the rich landed estate-owner and also in pointing unambiguously to the rural and agrarian economic base of all ancient Greek culture and societies.

In the eyes of Burford, however, true peasants were to be found only 'in all the various tied populations ... of the Greek world, men genuinely under obligation and rendering labor services in return'.[50] That includes populations such as the Helots of Lakonia and Messenia, whose status, functions and social organization constitute the second of my three major problems. It was on their backs that there rested the peculiar economy and society of Sparta, one of the two great powers of classical Greece before the rise of Macedon. Of that there is no question. On the other hand, to use 'peasants' or 'sharecropping tenants' to categorize their status seems seriously misleading and inappropriate.[51] Although the Helots were ethnically Greek, chiefly agriculturalists, and certainly a dependent population, in official Spartan parlance they were also *douloi* ('slaves' or 'unfree'), and they were not merely 'tied' to the land and its citizen owners, but also laboured constantly under pain of summary death. In the nature of the evidence we shall never attain anything like certainty or even consensus over the precise nature and efficiency of

---

[47] Esp. Burford, *Land and Labor*, 85–6 and n. 92.

[48] Esp. E. M. Wood, *Peasant-Citizen and Slave: the Foundations of the Athenian Democracy* (London 1988), and 'Labour and democracy, ancient and modern', in *Democracy Against Capitalism. Renewing Historical Materialism* (Cambridge 1995) 181–204.

[49] E.g. M. H. Jameson, 'Agricultural labor in ancient Greece', in Wells (ed.), *Agriculture*, 135–46.

[50] Burford, *Land and Labor*, 201.

[51] I have in mind here Hodkinson, 'Sharecropping and Sparta's economic exploitation of the Helots', in J. M. Sanders (ed.), ΦΙΛΟΛΑΚΩΝ. *Fest. H. W. Catling* (Athens 1992) 123–34, though I must add that Hodkinson seems to me to be currently the leading exponent of Spartan social and economic history [a view confirmed by his *Property and Wealth in Classical Sparta* (London 2000)].

Helot agricultural production, but perhaps we may at least avoid terminological inexactitude in classifying their status.[52]

Fortunately – or sadly – no such doubt surrounds the proper classification of all *douloi* in Athens: in our parlance, they were chattel slaves, wholly owned, natally alienated, socially, culturally and of course politically deracinated, and legally construed as quasi- or un-persons. Scholarly doubt concerns rather the nature, extent and effect of slaves' enforced participation in agriculture. In 1992 Michael Jameson restated the case he had made some fifteen years earlier that 'in classical Attica the prevailing pattern was that of independent farmers who worked their own land intensively and were commonly assisted by slaves belonging to their household'.[53] Behind that deceptively bland statement lies a massive controversy about the political economy of Athens. Against Jameson are ranged both those who wish to minimize the role of slavery in agriculture[54] and those who wish to maximize the role of slaves (and others) in the non-agricultural sector of 'the Athenian economy'.[55]

That controversy may never be finally resolved; the role of slavery in manufacture presents a further seeming paradox. Wherever anything like industrial craft-production existed in ancient Greece (shield-making, silver-mining, temple-building, pottery-manufacture, textiles for non-domestic consumption, wine for export), slaves constituted an important or major part of the workforce.[56] Yet for Aristotle, keen to defend the necessity of slavery for 'politics' as he understood them, slavery was an essential component, not of *poiêsis* ('production'), but of *praxis* ('behaviour', 'action', in the sense of living the good life of the citizen). The explanation is political, in the sense of that word discussed above: shields (etc.) could have been and sometimes were produced by free labour, but without slaves no free Greek could in Aristotle's view live the only truly good, civic life of moral-political activity in the *polis*. That depended upon the leisure

---

[52] J. Ducat, *Les hilotes* (Paris 1990), is comprehensive and acute, but by no means entirely satisfactory: see my review in *Classical Philology* 87 (1992) 260–3.

[53] Jameson, 'Agricultural labor', 135. But note his explicit qualification in 'Class in the ancient Greek countryside', in P. N. Doukellis and L. G. Mendoni (eds.), *Structures rurales et sociétés antiques* (Paris 1994) 55–63, at 60 n. 29: 'I would not claim that [agricultural slave-owning] characterized the Athenian lower classes or deny that most slave-owners were of middling or higher status'.

[54] Esp. Wood, *Peasant-Citizen and Slave*.

[55] Esp. Cohen, *Athenian Economy*; id., 'The Athenian economy', in R. Rosen and J. Farrell (eds.), *NOMODEIKTES. Fest. M. Ostwald* (Ann Arbor 1993) 197–206.

[56] Y. Garlan, *Slavery in Ancient Greece* (Ithaca 1988), confirms the conclusion of Finley, 'Was Greek civilisation based on slave labour?' (1959), repr. in *Economy and Society*, 97–116.

that slaves provided, and were themselves by definition denied, that is, precisely, freedom from the *ponos* of *poiêsis*.[57]

Aristotle's privileging of *praxis* above *poiêsis* is therefore in large part ideological, and yet it did also have a basis in material actuality. The observation passed by David Hume on the non-association of the growth of any ancient city with the establishment of a manufacture is still generally valid.[58] To the extent that manufacture of goods for exchange on the domestic or external market always played second fiddle to primary domestic production for autarkic home consumption, the ideal-typical Greek city was always a 'consumer' not a 'producer' city.[59] Defence of the territory and the securing of an external supply of basic foodstuffs in case of domestic shortfall (a constant preoccupation at Athens from, at the latest, 450 BCE) were regularly on the civic agenda figuratively speaking, and literally so in democratic Athens.[60] Yet there was no overall city 'budget' nor any global concern with a 'balance of payments', nor indeed with 'the' (or an) economy as such, partly because of the nature of the political in Greece, and partly for reasons that the next section should make clear.[61]

TRADE, COMMERCE AND PLUNDER

It is probably in the context of trade and commerce that the question of the nature of 'the' ancient economy has been most hotly disputed. There is, to be sure, still plenty of room for legitimate disagreement over just how rational, profit-maximizing and disembedded ancient Greek economy or economics could become, at any rate in fourth-century Athens, and even more specifically in the fourth-century world of the Piraeus *emporion* [commercial harbour], with its

---

[57] Cartledge, '"Like a worm i' the bud"? A heterology of Greek slavery', *Greece & Rome* 40 (1993) 163–80; id., *The Greeks: a Portrait of Self and Others* (rev. edn., Oxford 1997) ch. 6.

[58] Hume is quoted by Finley, *Ancient Economy*, 137; but see now also L. Neesen, 'Zur Rolle und Bedeutung der produzierenden Gewerbe in antiken Städte', *Ancient Society* 22 (1991) 25–40, at 27–33.

[59] Finley, 'The ancient city: from Fustel de Coulanges to Max Weber and beyond' [1977], repr. in *Economy and Society*, 3–23, has been besieged but not stormed by D. Engels, *Roman Corinth. An Alternative Mode for the Classical City* (Chicago 1990): see the review by R. Saller, *Classical Philology* 86 (1991) 351–7.

[60] Garnsey, *Famine and Food Supply*, Part III.

[61] L. Migeotte, *Les souscriptions publiques dans les cités grecques* (Quebec City 1992), shows that the phenomenon of the public subscription was an index of neither political nor financial crisis, and that it had little to do with the budget gaps, deficit reductions, and belt-tightenings familiar to us.

sumbola [contracts], *dikai emporikai* [maritime law-courts], bankers, maritime loans, and *nauklêroi* [shipowners].[62]

As a vehicle for the distribution of goods, trade may have to take its place in the queue behind plunder and gift.[63] Trade may also have to be distinguished from commerce (i.e. 'big business'): the transfer and exchange of goods over long distances can be accomplished without developed market mechanisms, let alone state regulation, and do not necessarily have major economic implications.[64] Finley, it is true, was over-impressed by Marcel Mauss's *Essai sur le don* (1925)[65] and so exaggerated the narrowly economic, as opposed to the social-political and ideological, importance of gift-exchange in his 'world of Odysseus'.[66] Homer was after all epic poetry, composed mainly about and for the élite, which largely screened out lower-class trade in a manner that a conservative eighteenth-century English aristocrat might have found congenial.[67]

But Finley was not wrong to draw attention to the large amount of non-market transfer of goods and to the non-commodification of exchange in the world of the early Greek states.[68] Serious changes, both structural and functional, are not in fact clearly visible before about 600 BCE in round figures; and for some considerable time after that the Greeks remained backward by comparison with Phoenicians and Etruscans, filling the role of pupils rather than teachers. Indeed, it was not until the creation of the fifth-century Athenian empire and, in consequence, the development of the Piraeus as both a commercial and a naval harbour that anything resembling the State regulation of trade long familiar from, say, Egyptian Naukratis came into being in the world of the Greek city.[69]

Even then, it is striking that there was no preferential treatment legally prescribed for Athenian citizen traders; and, partly for that reason, most regular, long-distance traders frequenting the Piraeus

---

[62] E. E. Cohen, *Ancient Athenian Maritime Courts* (Princeton 1973); R. Garland, *The Piraeus from the Fifth to the First Century* BC (London 1987); P. Millett, 'Maritime loans and the structure of credit in fourth-century Athens', in Garnsey, Hopkins and Whittaker (eds.), *Trade in the Ancient Economy*, 36–52; J. Vélissaropoulou, *Les nauklères grecs* (Geneva 1980); Cohen, *Athenian Economy*.

[63] See quotation in n. 17 above.

[64] Cartledge, '"Trade and politics" revisited'.

[65] This is available in two, revealingly different English translations (1954, 1990): Morris, 'Athenian economy', 357 n. 32. Mauss himself actually said virtually nothing about ancient Greece.

[66] Finley, *The World of Odysseus*[2] (London 1978).

[67] Morris, 'The use and abuse of Homer', *Classical Antiquity* 5 (1986) 81–138.

[68] S. von Reden, *Exchange in Ancient Greece* (London 1995).

[69] U. Wartenberg, *After Marathon: War, Society and Money in Fifth-Century Athens* (London 1995).

were aliens, not resident aliens (*metoikoi*) but transient foreigners (*xenoi*), both Greek and non-Greek. The Athenian community, moreover, pursued always and only an import interest rather than an export interest. The city as such was not interested in economic growth, in 'developing the economy'. The wall between citizens and profit-motivated investment was not perhaps as thick and impermeable as Finley imagined.[70] But it was there all the same, most obviously in regard to the ownership of real property. In so far as the Piraeus economy (or economic activity focused on the Piraeus) developed its own values, both material and moral, this was perhaps something like the ancient equivalent of our black economy. It was at any rate no accident that Hermes, 'the god of good luck and whatever is shadowy and chancy', was patron god of thieves as well as of merchants.[71] However – contrast present-day Colombia or Russia – the ancient Greeks' black economy had no State, however weak, to contest, collude with – or evade.

Moreover, it was the loss rather than the acquisition of empire which prompted the most innovative and far-reaching civic measures of intervention and control. It cannot be emphasized too firmly that the extensive development by Athens of a legal apparatus of would-be regulation was but a second-best option. Force, military force, remained the ideal economic specific, in the fourth as it had been in the fifth century.[72] Hence in Aristotle's *Politics* war was automatically conceptualized as a 'natural' means of production – not only for arms-manufacturers and shipbuilders, but for the community as a whole, in the shape of the acquisition of new resources, especially new cultivable land. Note also Xenophon's choice of *episitismos* – a process of restocking, especially in grain or food more generally (*sitos* could mean either) – to describe a massive Spartan-led invasion of the rich territory of Elis in the immediate aftermath of the economically exhausting Peloponnesian War. On the high seas, too, piracy was not merely a relic of some pre-political mode of acqui-

---

[70] Finley, 'Land, debt and the man of property in classical Athens' [1953], repr. in *Economy and Society*, 62–76; id., *Studies in Land and Credit in Ancient Athens 500–200 BC* (New Brunswick 1952, repr. with intro. by P. Millett, 1984); *contra*: Cohen, *Athenian Economy*.

[71] The quotation is from the late Canadian novelist Robertson Davies *ap.* D. Buitron Oliver (ed.), *The Greek Miracle. Classical Sculpture from the Dawn of Democracy* (Washington, DC 1992) 75.

[72] Finley, 'War and Empire', in *Ancient History: Evidence and Models* (London 1985) ch. 5; Osborne, *Classical Landscape*, ch. 7; Millett, 'Warfare, economy and democracy in Classical Athens', in J. Rich and G. Shipley (eds.), *War and Society in the Greek World* (London 1993) ch. 9. Tabulation of booty reported in Greek historians: W. K. Pritchett, *The Greek State at War*, V (Berkeley 1991) 505–41, with Cartledge, 'Ancient warfare', *International History Review* 15 (1993) 323–8, at 326–7.

sition, but even more prevalent in the fourth century than earlier.[73] War-damage to agriculture or rather arboriculture (especially olives) can be exaggerated,[74] but it is difficult to overstate the Greeks' en-grained booty-raiding mentality.

Most foreign wars pitted Greek against Greek over some disputed frontier territory.[75] Civil war (*stasis*) also had profound economic effects, by no means all negative. Redistribution of land and cancel-lation of debts were the slogans of oppressed peasantries, and *staseis* could result in shifts in the balance of power and wealth of which modern political parties of Right or Left can only dream.[76]

SYMBOLIC CAPITAL

When Augustine spoke of the Passion in terms of a commercial trans-action – 'he bought us when he was crucified. There he poured out his blood, the price for us'[77] – he was using metaphorical language that we can instantly recognize; for us too, 'redemption' has a secu-lar economic as well as a transcendental spiritual meaning. The classical Greeks likewise would have found nothing odd in the assim-ilation or melding of the material and the spiritual, the political and the economic. What better example than *timê*? This good Homeric word for non-material value, such as the honour due to the gods, in classical Greece came to mean also 'census group', 'political office', and yet more concretely 'price' (material cost, reward, recompense, valuation), without sacrificing one whit of its original moral sense.[78]

Such interference between culture and economy, or manipulation of 'symbolic capital', is well attested both visually and verbally in the archaic period.[79] But it can be explored most tangibly in classi-

---

[73] Arist. *Pol.* 1255b37, 1256b23–7, 1333b35ff.; Xen. *Hell.* 3.2.26. Piracy: Garlan, *Guerre et économic en Grèce ancienne* (Paris 1989), ch. 8; C. R. Whittaker, 'I popoli del mare', in V. Castronovo (ed.), *Storia dell' economia mondiale* I. *Permanenze e mutamenti dall'antichità al medioevo* (Turin 1996) 153–76, esp. 159–75 [; P. de Souza, *Piracy in the Graeco-Roman World* (Cambridge 1999)].

[74] V. D. Hanson, *Warfare and Agriculture in Ancient Greece* (Pisa 1983) [2nd edition California 2000] is an admirable corrective.

[75] M. Sartre, 'Aspects économiques et aspects religieux de la frontière dans les cités grecques', *Ktema* 4 (1979) 213–24.

[76] D. Asheri, *Distribuzioni di terre nell' antica Grecia* (Turin 1966); id., *Leggi greche sul problema dei debiti* (Pisa 1969).

[77] *Sermon* *54 Mainz, ch. 17. I am grateful to Peter Garnsey for drawing this new text to my attention.

[78] Compare Latin *honores*, as in the Roman *cursus honorum* (ladder of political offices).

[79] 'Symbolic capital': P. Bourdieu, *Outline of a Theory of Practice* (Cambridge 1977) 179. L. Gernet, '"Value" in Greek myth' [1948], in R. Gordon (ed.), *Myth, Religion and Society. Structuralist Essays* (Cambridge 1981) 111–46, was early to explicate this interpenetration of the moral and the material in Greece; cf. R. Di Donato, *Per una antropologia storica del mondo*

cal texts, from Aeschylus to Aristotle.[80] One might perhaps note especially the telling chapter-titles of Leslie Kurke's exploration of 'the poetics of social economy' in Pindar: 'The economics of *nostos*', 'The ideology of aristocratic exchange', 'Guest-friends and guest-gifts', and the title of Part III, 'Pindar's political economy'.[81] Her more recent interpretation of 'the economy of *kudos*' as 'a circulation of powers and honors whose goal is to achieve a harmonious sharing of this special commodity within the city' neatly captures the undoubtedly increasing commodification of goods in classical Greece.[82]

This approach consciously reflects the turn of the so-called 'new cultural history' towards what have been described as 'agent-centered issues of meaning, treating "the economic" as a category of representation, a field of negotiations for knowledgeable actors in pursuit of their own goals'.[83] A further illustration, recalling the '*whose* economy or economies?' debate with which I began, is von Reden's skilful development, and application to classical Greece, of the distinction between a positive, 'long-term' social model and a more morally questionable, 'short-term' economic model of material exchange.[84]

Such an approach seems to me far more easily conformable to a model of balanced reciprocity among Athenian citizen peers and negative reciprocity between social and political unequals than to any modernizing market-centred, profit-maximizing model of disembedded economy, and far more fruitfully so.[85] This preference may be due simply to a blinkered 'Cambridge School' vision, but I submit that it is objectively based on the sorts of evidence discussed above, and plausibly informed by the 'substantivist' mode of interpretation.

---

antico (Pisa 1990). Also, L. Kurke, 'The politics of *habrosunê* in Archaic Greece', *Classical Antiquity* 11 (1992) 91–120, and 'The economy of *kudos*', in C. Dougherty and L. Kurke (eds.), *Cultural Poetics in Archaic Greece* (Cambridge 1993) 131–63.

[80] G. Crane, 'Politics of consumption and generosity in the carpet scene of the *Agamemnon*', *Classical Philology* 88 (1993) 185–233; and esp. von Reden, *Exchange in Ancient Greece*.

[81] Kurke, *The Traffic in Praise. Pindar and the Poetics of Social Economy* (Ithaca 1991).

[82] Kurke, 'Economy', 141. Likewise, Carol Dougherty, with reference to Thucydides 1.22.4 (*ktêma es aiei*), has percipiently noted the historian's 'success in packaging the past as a metaphorical commodity': leaflet accompanying a 1994 exhibition at Wellesley College entitled 'The Object of History and the History of Objects'. Cf. L. Kallet-Marx, *Money, Expense, and Naval Power in Thucydides' History 1–5.24* (Berkeley 1993) 1–20.

[83] Morris, 'Athenian economy', 351.

[84] von Reden, *Exchange*, following the anthropologists M. Bloch and J. Parry (eds.), *Money and the Morality of Exchange* (Cambridge 1989); cf. A. Appadurai (ed.), *The Social Life of Things* (Cambridge 1986).

[85] P. Millett, *Lending and Borrowing in Ancient Athens* (Cambridge 1991), e.g. 110–11. *Contra*: Cohen, *Bryn Mawr Classical Review* 3 (1992) 282–9.

PRESENTISM

No doubt, as Max Weber once put it, 'the interest in a story is always keener when the audience has the feeling, *de te fabula narratur* [the story is about you], and when the story-teller can conclude his yarn with a *discite moniti* [what can we learn from this]!' But what Weber went on to say, with regard to the world of late antiquity, applies no less to our present topic: 'Unfortunately, the discussion which follows does not fall into this enviable category. We can learn little or nothing for our contemporary problems … [which] are of a completely different character.'[86] To which, however, I would want to add that in other than directly practical ways difference, even polar otherness, of socio-economic and cultural formation can be as instructive as close similarity.[87] I close therefore with a concrete historical example that wears its revelatory difference on its sleeve. It is taken from Thucydides' famous account of the Kerkyra *stasis* of 427 BCE:

> The civil war at Kerkyra began when the [250 or so] prisoners taken in the battles for Epidamnos were released by the Corinthians and returned home. In theory they had been released on a payment of 80 talents as security by the Kerkyraians' diplomatic representatives among the citizens of Corinth, but in fact they had undertaken to bring over Kerkyra to Corinth. They set to work, approaching each of the citizens in the attempt to detach the city from Athens …
>
> A man called Peithias, who had volunteered to serve as diplomatic representative of the Athenians and was the leader of the common people, was brought to trial by these men on a charge of enslaving Kerkyra to Athens. He was acquitted, and in turn prosecuted the five richest men on a charge of repeatedly cutting vine-props from the sanctuary of Zeus and Alkinöos: a fine of one *statêr* was prescribed for each prop. These men were found guilty, and because of the size of the fine they went as suppliants to the shrines, hoping to come to an arrangement over the payment. But Peithias, who was also a member of the Council, persuaded it to enforce the law … They [the condemned] therefore banded together and, armed with daggers, suddenly burst into the Council chamber, killing Peithias and about sixty other Councillors and ordinary citizens.[88]

The monetization and size of the ransom-payments and fines are of course independently interesting and informative, and the evidence Thucydides provides is all the more valuable for coming from outside

[86] M. Weber, 'Die sozialen Gründe des Untergangs der antiken Kultur' [1896], repr. [1950], trans. in *Max Weber*, ed. J. T. Eldridge (London 1971) 254–75 (quotation at 256).
[87] This is the governing idea of Cartledge, *The Greeks*; cf. id., 'The Greeks and anthropology', *Anthropology Today* 10 (1994) 3–5.
[88] Thuc. 3.70, trans. P. J. Rhodes (modified); note that '80' is read instead of the '800' of the MSS.

the directly Athenian sphere. Yet what strikes one most strongly here is the quintessentially classical Greek mixture. Combined in this one episode are what *we* might want to call 'economics', together with war, civil war, politics (including both a highly politicized attempt to exercise legal justice and a flagrant illegality), and – centrally, not accidentally – religion. That peculiar cocktail surely exudes a strong aroma of the substantive alterity of classical Greek *oikonomia* [economy] and *oikonomika* [economic matters, esp. household management].

2 *Twenty Years After Moses I. Finley's* The Ancient Economy†

JEAN ANDREAU

Jean Andreau, a historian at the École des Hautes Études en Sciences Sociales in Paris, prepared this article as an introduction to a series of papers published to mark the twentieth anniversary of the French translation of Finley's *The Ancient Economy*. Andreau is known as the world's leading authority on Roman banking and finance.‡ In keeping with his main research interests, his discussion largely focuses on recent scholarship on the Roman economy, thereby complementing the article by Paul Cartledge reprinted above (Ch. 1). Thanks to the author's French background and British connections, Andreau's piece, while fully engaged in the ongoing debate, offers a critical perspective from outside the predominantly Anglo-American circle of Finley's followers and critics. Identifying what he perceives as the five major themes of recent scholarship in the field, Andreau tackles pivotal issues of the debate over the nature of the 'ancient economy' by assessing recent contributions and setting an agenda for future research.

Moses I. Finley's book *The Ancient Economy* was published in 1973, and subsequently translated into several languages.[1] It marked without doubt a decisive turning-point in the field of Greek and Roman economic history. The 'Finley Method' triumphed.

While the public at large, when they take an interest in antiquity, persist in seeking there the cultural origins of the modern world (which leads them to give greater importance to continuities and

---

† Originally published as 'Twenty Years After Moses Finley's *The Ancient Economy*' [translated by Antonia Nevill from the French: 'Vingt ans d'après *L'économie antique* de Moses I. Finley'], *Annales: Histoire, Sciences Sociales* 50 (1995), 947–60 (© Annales: Histoire, Sciences Sociales).

‡ *Les affairs de Monsieur Jucundus*, Paris: École Française de Rome, 1974; *La vie financière dans le monde romaine: les métiers de manieurs d'argent*, Paris: École Française de Rome, 1987; *Banking and Business in the Roman World*, Cambridge: Cambridge University Press, 1999.

[1] Moses I. Finley, *L'économie antique*, Paris, Éd. de Minuit, 1975 [= French translation of *The Ancient Economy*, 1973].

similarities), the majority of specialists, for their part, have moved perceptibly over the past thirty years towards an attention to differences. In social and economic questions, Finley and his students have played a role similar to that of historical psychology and anthropology in the religious and cultural domain. In ancient history, the influence of economic anthropology has, strictly speaking, been slender; its place has been occupied, as it were, by Finley's method.

Finley dealt with the ancient economy as a totality.[2] In spite of the chronological and geographical differences, in his estimation it continuously presented the same major characteristics, from the archaic Greek era to late antiquity; and its principal aim was self-sufficiency. The fundamental resource was agriculture, and trade made only a small contribution to the gross product. There were three reasons for this: production was more or less the same everywhere; transport costs were high; only luxury goods were in circulation, and the market for such products was insufficient. In the same way as the volume of trade was limited, the status of traders was fairly low. Local elites, even in the large ports such as Carthage, Aquileia or Alexandria, preferred land to trade. The town was a centre of consumption rather than of manufacture or trade, and the process of urbanisation was more the result of a cultural model than of economic growth. Lastly, the notion of 'status' was preferable to that of class, because it was less precise and allowed 'the incorporation of cultural values into an economic analysis'.

The field of research was completely reorganised as a result of Finley's work and of the themes he had emphasised. Those whom he had not convinced opposed him, and tried to refute him. Those who aimed at innovation spoke of 'overtaking' him. The more the years passed, the more clearly his influence was perceived; and he increasingly occupied a central position in the intellectual landscape. It was already noticeable ten years ago,[3] and it is even truer today.

But I would not say that Finley's model has triumphed, for, after years in which his conclusions continued to be advanced, chiefly in the English-speaking world but also everywhere else (except perhaps in Italy and Spain), this is no longer the case. The questions are Finleyan, the methods and ways of thinking bear the stamp of his influence, but the answers are moving farther and farther away from

---

[2] This very brief résumé of Finley's ideas on the economy was inspired by that of his disciple and friend K. Hopkins (see Peter Garnsey, Keith Hopkins and Charles Richard Whittaker (eds), *Trade in the Ancient Economy*, London, Chatto & Windus, 1983, pp. xi–xii).

[3] See Jean Andreau and Roland Étienne, 'Vingt ans de recherches sur l'archaïsme et la modernité des sociétés antiques', *REA* 86 (1984), 55–83.

his own. The very concept of an 'ancient economy' is becoming increasingly relativised by comparative studies, for example those of H. W. Pleket and L. De Ligt, which demonstrate that the originality and coherence of classical Graeco-Roman antiquity are far less obvious when ancient circumstances are compared with those of the Middle Ages.[4]

It is true that some of his closest former students have remained loyal to their master's thinking; but others had already distanced themselves some years ago. As for the young researchers, students of Finley's students, they are now following their own path, independently; it would be easy to show how their work breaks new ground by comparison with the orthodoxy of fifteen or twenty years ago.

It is now time to get away from the struggle between Finley's partisans ('the primitivists') and his adversaries ('the modernists'), not only because it is Manichean, but because it would end by considerably impoverishing historical analysis. To contrast, term by term, everything pre-industrial with everything modern, and endlessly to scour antiquity for all possible and imaginable signs of archaism, results in a very reductionist view of history. Besides, whether deliberate or not, such an approach has the effect of providing present-day institutions and situations with an intellectual justification which they do not always merit, and of strengthening our reassuring (but illusory) impression that they are eternal, or at least immortal, since we have now entered modernity.

In order to make progress, we must try to define the great original features of the Greek and Roman worlds, whose economies were without doubt historical, pre-industrial and non-capitalist, but could in no way be confused with those of China, medieval Islam or the western Middle Ages. [...] On the path to follow in this respect, much can certainly be learnt from the work of P. Veyne.[5]

From this perspective, various recent works appear very fruitful, as they increasingly offer a less schematic picture of the ancient economy. [...]

Finley's work drew attention to four or five major topics, obviously interconnected, but the subject of separate research or debates.

[4] Henry Willy Pleket, 'Wirtschaft', in Friedrich Vittinghoff (ed.), *Europäische Wirtschafts- und Sozialgeschichte in der römischen Kaiserzeit*, Stuttgart, Klett-Cotta, 1990, pp. 25–260; L. De Ligt, 'Demand, Supply, Distribution: The Roman Peasantry between Town and Countryside', *MBAH* 9, 2 (1990), 24–56, and 10, 1 (1991), 33–77.
[5] Paul Veyne, *Le pain et le cirque. Sociologie historique d'un pluralisme politique*, Paris, Seuil, 1976 [abridged Engl. trans. 1990]; id., 'Foucault révolutionne l'histoire', 'Postscript' to *Comment on écrit l'histoire*, Paris, Seuil, 'Points Histoire', 2nd edn, 1979, pp. 203–42; id., *La société romaine*, Paris, Seuil, 1991.

These five themes are: the problem of the unity of the ancient economy; the existence or absence of a market economy (in the sense of 'market principle'); the place of the economy in the ancient state; rationality; and the status of agents of the economy. [...]

UNITY OF THE ANCIENT ECONOMY
AND EXISTENCE OF THE MARKET
('MARKET PRINCIPLE')

The first theme is that of the unity of the ancient economy. Must we conclude that, between the classical era of the Greek city-states, the beginning of the Roman Empire and late antiquity, the economy hardly changed, and thus favour arguments of continuity instead of breakdowns and crises?

The second concerns the market, in the abstract sense of the word (what Steve Kaplan has called the 'market principle'):[6] was the ancient economy a market economy? Finley was convinced that it was not, without envisaging any middle road in between. Either one could talk of a market economy, as for the twentieth century, or there was no market at all. He therefore denied that ancient commerce and its evolution could be studied according to ideas such as competition or the law of supply and demand.

In both instances, recent research seems to point us in directions going beyond Finley's position, without, however, returning to the 'modernist' visions of Rostovtzeff.[†] D. Hollard's article, of course, places much emphasis on the discontinuity represented, in money matters, by the 'third-century [AD] crisis' (and may therefore be felt to be opposed to Finley).[†1] But, for certain regions, or in regard to other aspects of the economy, the impression of continuity will probably win the day. Depending on the circumstances, the conclusions vary and tend to become more complex.

The absence of a large modern market (in the abstract sense) does not preclude the existence of partial markets whose operation we must try to understand. R. Descat emphasises several changes that took place in Greece in the fifth and fourth centuries BC: the modification of the relationship between agriculture and market, between

---

[6] Steve Kaplan, *Provisioning Paris*, Ithaca, Cornell University Press, 1984, pp. 23–40. S. Kaplan contrasts the *'market principle'* (called 'marché comme principe' in the French translation of his book) with the *'market place'* ('marché comme site' in French).

[†] For Rostovtzeff's position see p. 135.

[†1] D. Hollard, 'La crise de la monnaie dans l'empire romain au 3e siècle après J.-C.: synthèse des recherches et résultats nouveaux', *Annales HSS* 50 (1995), 1045–78.

agriculture and non-agricultural activities; the appearance of the *oikonomia attike* ('economic behaviour characterised by the dual act of selling and buying'); the existence of artisanal or commercial wealth that had nothing at all to do with landed property; an advance in the sale of land; etc.† These were important transformations which did not, however, mean that Athens had turned capitalist or that the Industrial Revolution was at hand. Nevertheless, R. Descat does not believe that the archaic Greek economy can be described in the same way as that of the Periclean period. He thus diverges from Finley on the first aspects (unity of the ancient economy, existence of a market).

'QUANTITATIVE' STUDIES

These two topics lead to questions of quantities: from what point in time did variations in the levels of production and, above all, marketed produce become sufficient to bring about structural transformations? And for which commercial activity can one begin to speak of a market? Those who have insisted on the economic discontinuities of the ancient world have relied on quantitative variations, some probable or even certain, and others more arguable. Archaeologists such as D. Manacorda, G. Pucci or J.-P. Morel have rightly stressed that the quantities of artefacts attested in the excavations and field-surveys of the early second century BC were incomparably higher than those of the preceding eras.[7] For his part, K. Hopkins has shown that between the middle of the second century BC and the middle of the first, the Roman state had increased one hundredfold its issues of denarii, and that henceforth the quantity of coins minted no longer bore any relation to that which had been issued by a city such as Athens in the fifth or fourth century.[8]

Under the Empire, between the first and second century AD, it was no longer so much the overall quantity of marketed goods (for instance, pottery) that was involved as that of goods produced and sold within Italy. These indeed seemed to dwindle to the advantage

---

† R. Descat, '*L'économie antique* et la cité grecque; un modèle en question', *Annales HSS* 50 (1995), 961–89.

[7] See Jean-Paul Morel, 'La céramique campanienne: acquis et problèmes', in *Céramiques hellénistiques et romaines*' (collective work), Paris, Belles Lettres, 1980, pp. 85–122; id., 'Marchandises, marchés, échanges dans le monde romain', *AION* (*archeol.*) 4 (1982), 193–214; and Andrea Giardina and Aldo Schiavone (eds), *Società romana e produzione schiavistica*, 3 vols, Rome-Bari, Laterza, 1981 (volumes to which notably the above-named archaeologists contributed).

[8] Keith Hopkins, 'Taxes and Trade in the Roman Empire, 200 BC–AD 400', *JRS* 70 (1980), 101–25.

of products from the provinces.[9] Archaeological research also seems to indicate a (fairly slow) decline in Italy, revealing the abandonment of certain sites and growth in the size of properties and enterprises. But none of these signs provides compelling evidence. Some scholars, therefore, stress the serious nature of discontinuities and crises, whereas others are more receptive to the signs of permanence.[10]

Quantitative data are not limited to revealing an advance or a decline in marketing; they also help us to grasp the cultural or social differences. For instance, in the protohistoric sites of the south of Gaul, during the last centuries BC, the relatively large amounts of black-glazed pottery, the presence of which is attested at nearly all the sites, enable us to distinguish Greek settlements from those of the indigenous peoples. In the first two centuries AD, in the same regions, rural sites are characterised, in comparison with urban ones, by lesser quantities of sigillata and slipped pottery. By means of typologies and quantifications, archaeology meets the concerns of both economic history and cultural anthropology.[11] This important development is very alien to the sensibilities of Finley, who nurtured a lively mistrust of archaeology.

Over the last ten to fifteen years, therefore, many efforts have been made to attain a more detailed quantitative picture. Figures for prices, production and output, supplied by ancient texts (figures that are very rare and sometimes hardly credible), have been collected.[12] Just lately, two other methods, described as 'inductive' and 'deductive', have been much used to establish other quantitative data.[13] They can serve either as indications of trends, or as a quantitative frame, or even as absolute figures.

The 'inductive' method consists of reciting the available evidence, in particular archaeological material (although coins, inscriptions, etc. may also be listed). It implies consideration of the methods of counting, and comparison of the results obtained and of their histori-

---

[9] On this see Jean Andreau, 'Mercato e mercati', in Aldo Schiavone (ed.), *Storia di Roma*, 2, vol. 2, Turin, Einaudi, 1991, pp. 367–85.

[10] On these questions, see the recent synthesis by Philippe Leveau, Pierre Sillières and Jean-Pierre Vallat, *Campagnes de la Méditerranée romaine, Occident*, Paris, Hachette, 1993.

[11] In a brilliant book, N. Bats has shown what the study of ceramics can teach on the development of dietary habits (see M. Bats, *Vaisselle et alimentation à Olbia de Provence (c. 350– c. 50 BC)*, *Modèles culturels et catégories céramiques*, Paris, CNRS, 1988).

[12] For example, by Tenney Frank in the five volumes of the *Economic Survey of Ancient Rome*, Baltimore, Johns Hopkins Press, 1932–40. See also Richard Duncan-Jones, *The Economy of the Roman Empire, Quantitative Studies*, Cambridge, Cambridge University Press, 1st edn 1974, 2nd edn 1982.

[13] Some people, for example W. Jongman (*The Economy and Society of Pompeii*, Amsterdam, Gieben, 1988, 2nd edn 1991), describe the inductive method as the '*artefact approach*' and the deductive method as the '*simulation approach*'.

cal significance. The outstanding specialists in this method, which has made an effective contribution to the history of production and trade,[14] are obviously archaeologists, as well as a few numismatists. [...]

The 'deductive method' seeks to construct hypothetical figures not supplied by the ancient evidence, by reasoning from other data, depending on likelihood, analogy or comparison. It was introduced by Finley, but was spread mainly by his students, especially K. Hopkins, and is practised hardly anywhere but Britain. Let us take an example: W. Jongman explored whether in the first century AD the city of Pompeii's external sales of wine were as great as in the previous century (he was convinced that they were not).[15] He asked how much of their land the Pompeians needed to cultivate in order to keep themselves supplied with cereals. He started from an average of individual consumption of cereals (which is not known, but we have a few clues; before W. Jongman's book, some speculative assessments were made varying by as much as a factor of two),[16] the population figure for Pompeii, and the average grain production per agricultural unit, these figures also being unknown and needing to be worked out by means of other indications. One may speculate, too, on the quantity of cereals and dry vegetables which the Pompeians were able to buy from the provinces via Puteoli, Rome's great port [70 miles north of Pompeii]. W. Jongman concluded that the Pompeians did not sell large amounts of wine outside the city.

It may be seen how this method, multiplying enormous margins of error, can make conclusions risky; it is a dangerous method, circulating apparently reliable figures which in fact are questionable. It can be profitable only if used with great caution and in very clearly defined situations, for example in ancient demography where sound comparative models are available, especially those of the United Nations.[17]

[14] See for example D. P. S. Peacock and D. F. Williams, *Amphorae and the Roman Economy, An Introductory Guide*, London, Longman 1986; A. Giardina and A. Schiavone (eds), *Società romana e produzione schiavistica*, pt 2, *Merci, mercati e scambi nel mediterraneo*, Rome–Bari, Laterza, 1981; and Andrea Giardina (ed.), *Società romana e Impero tardoantico*, pt 3, Rome–Bari, Laterza, 1986.

[15] Jongman, *The Economy and Society of Pompeii*.

[16] On cereal consumption in the town of Rome (very important to determine in order to evaluate the degree of private trade in grain, since broadly speaking the size of the free distributions regularly carried out by the Emperor is known), see Lionel Casson, 'The Role of the State in Rome's Grain Trade', in John H. D'Arms and E. C. Kopff (eds), *The Seaborne Commerce of Ancient Rome: Studies in Archaeology and History*, Rome, American Academy in Rome, 1980, pp. 21–33; Geoffrey Rickman, 'The Grain Trade under the Roman Empire', ibid., 1980, pp. 261–75; Peter Garnsey, 'Grain for Rome', in Garnsey, Hopkins and Whittaker (eds), *Trade in the Ancient Economy*, pp. 118–30.

[17] In this area, one must hail the work of B. W. Frier, who during the past ten years, has

Quantitative methods arose partly from Finley's concern to develop a problem-oriented form of history. But subsequently scholars have pursued quite different objectives; introducing the inductive method they have helped to show that the ancient economy changed considerably from one period to another, for example as the result of increasing, or conversely, dwindling marketing of produce. In many instances it challenged Finley's conclusions.

THE MODELS

Like the 'inductive' and 'deductive' methods, the use of 'models', *a priori* schemas which have to be subjected to the test of evidence, had its origins in Finley's work. Warmly recommended by his students P. Garnsey and R. Saller,[18] it is frequently revealed as stimulating and fruitful. Paradoxically, it brought together aspects of economic theory which Finley, however, did not consider useful for the understanding of ancient phenomena. Where, indeed, could more varied and stimulating models be found than in economic theory?

Let me say a few words about the 'taxes and trade model' of K. Hopkins,[19] recently modified and completed by H. U. von Freyberg.[20] Hopkins set it out in a few pages, without really trying to back it up with sound documentary evidence. He caused much gnashing of teeth, including from those of Finley's most faithful students (they reckoned that this model gave too much importance to trade and its developments, as well as to the role of money and its transfer). But it is the best known of the models worked out for ancient history, and continues to wield a far from negligible influence. As I have already said, in the early Empire, during the first century AD, scholars observe a considerable shift in the trade balance between Italy and the provinces, to the advantage of the latter and to Italy's cost. The reality of this phenomenon has been debated – one

transformed the demography of antiquity and caused it to make great advances (see Roger S. Bagnall and Bruce Woodward Frier, *The Demography of Roman Egypt*, Cambridge, Cambridge University Press, 1994).

[18] M. I. Finley, *Ancient History: Evidence and Models*, London, Chatto & Windus, 1985 (most of which has been translated into French in *Sur l'histoire ancienne, la matière, la forme et la méthode*, Paris, La Découverte, 1987); and P. Garnsey and R. Saller, *The Roman Empire, Economy, Society and Culture*, London, Duckworth, 1987, pp. 43–51 (corresponding to pp. 91–102 of the French translation).

[19] Hopkins, 'Taxes and Trade in the Roman Empire', and below, Chapter 10.

[20] H. U. von Freyberg, *Kapitalverkehr und Handel im römischen Kaiserreich* (27 BC–235 AD), Freiburg im Breisgau, Rudolf Haufe, 1989. On these models, and chiefly on von Freyberg's book, see Jean Andreau, 'L'Italie impériale et les provinces, Déséquilibre des échanges et flux monetaires', in *L'Italie d'Auguste à Dioclétien* (collective work), Rome, École française de Rome, 1994, pp. 175–203.

may wonder, for instance, how representative the products for which we have evidence are: we know a great deal about pottery and very little about textiles – but the most recent archaeological research seems, on the whole, to confirm the trend.[21] How is it to be explained? M. I. Rostovtzeff thought that the cause of the development lay in the relative qualities of the employers and workers in the various regions, and that the provincials, through their management abilities and the level and profitability of their products, had been able to take over the markets. This explanation, which is a matter of supply, is no longer convincing, and has been superseded by economic explanations concerning demand: production centres moved because consumption centres moved (a notion supported by indisputable evidence), and the characteristics of products changed in accordance with consumers' preferences (something which, conversely, cannot be verified).

K. Hopkins, arguing on the macro-economic level, connected the development of marketing with the tax system. It was the regions paying direct taxes without receiving much in return from the imperial treasury (in other words, provinces without soldiers) which were the sellers, to compensate for the flow of assets, monetary or not, that they were losing to Italy's gain. This is assumed to be the reason, or at least one of the reasons, why, beginning in the first century AD, Gallo-Roman and Proconsular African pottery replaced Arretine on the sites of the entire western Mediterranean. Such hypotheses remain much disputed, but the link between the tax system and marketing should be kept in mind. Earlier, M. H. Crawford had placed some emphasis on the links between the development of the currency and the tax system, but without including trade in the monetary circuit – on the contrary, he minimized the importance of commerce.[22]

THE ECONOMY IN THE CITY-STATE: ECONOMIC RATIONALITY

Another two of the five topics I listed are closely connected to each other, and both are concerned with the following problem: was the economy in antiquity inserted in something else that was not

[21] On this see Andreau, 'Mercato e mercati'.
[22] Michael H. Crawford, *La moneta in Grecia e a Roma*, Rome–Bari, Laterza, 1982; id., *Coinage and Money under the Roman Republic, Italy and the Mediterranean Economy*, London, Methuen, 1985. On relations between tax system and economy, see also Claude Nicolet, *Rendre à César*, Paris, Gallimard, 1988.

economic (i.e. was, what Finley called an 'embedded' economy)? One topic, however, has to do with the city, the state, and the other with relations between economy and society.

Did the city in antiquity have the same relationship with the economy as the medieval city or the modern and contemporary state? Finley borrowed his answer from Max Weber: the ancient city was a 'consumer city', and not a 'producer city'; but the interpretation of this model of the consumer city is not self-evident. Finley and, in his wake, C. Goudineau, laid much emphasis on the relations between town and country: in the consumer state, the town produces hardly anything for the rural areas, it lives at their expense. We must therefore speak of a consumer town, or even a parasite town.[23] H. Bruhns thinks that this was not Max Weber's understanding of the consumer state, but was the matter of a state considering its inhabitants as consumers and not producers, so that keeping them supplied was its prime concern.[24] W. Jongman, in the book already quoted, gives yet another definition.

Those who reacted against Finley's line of thought worked out other models. Beginning with a monograph on Corinth, D. Engels spoke of a service state.[25] But it was chiefly P. Leveau who, with his 'organising state', forming and running its territory, provided another way of analysing the ancient city, which was as far away from modernism as Finley's was, but much less schematic and taking better account of diversity.[26]

The fourth topic for debate also has a bearing on relations between the economic and non-economic, but in private and social life. Did specifically economic forms of behaviour exist in antiquity? To what extent did social traditions stifle any attempt at economic inno-

---

[23] Christian Goudineau, 'Les villes de la paix romaine', in Georges Duby (ed.), *Histoire de la France urbaine*, Paris, Seuil, vol. 1, *La ville antique*, pp. 233–391 (chiefly pp. 365–81).

[24] Hinnerk Bruhns, 'De Werner Sombart à Max Weber et Moses I. Finley: la typologie de la ville antique et la question de la ville de consommation', in Philippe Leveau (ed.), *L'origine des richesses dépensées dans la ville antique*, Aix-en-Provence, Université de Provence, 1985, pp. 255–73.

[25] Donald Engels, *Roman Corinth, An Alternative Model for the Classical City*, Chicago–London, University of Chicago Press, 1990; reviewed by Richard Saller, *CP* 86 (1991), 351–7.

[26] Philippe Leveau, 'La ville antique, "ville de consommation"? Parasitisme social et économie antique', *Études rurales* 89–91 (January–September 1983), 275–83 (followed by C. Goudineau's reply, 283–7); id., 'La ville antique et l'organisation de l'espace rural: villa, ville, village', *Annales ESC* 38 (1983), 920–42. On these 'models' of the city, see Chs 8, 'The Consumer City Revisited: The Vicus', and 9, 'Do Theories of the Ancient City Matter?', in C. R. Whittaker, *Land, City, and Trade in the Roman Empire*, Aldershot, Ashgate, 1993. At first very persuaded by the idea of the consumer city, Whittaker now doubts the scientific interest of such models.

vation? Many questions arise from this problem, and they must not all receive the same response; but all are connected with the more general problem (and one which is absolutely central to our debates) of economic rationality, posed earlier by M. Godelier.[27]

The problem of economic rationality can be approached from various angles, one of which is the study of accounting. Ancient accounting practices have given rise to an extensive literature, despite very meagre evidence, apart from the papyri of Egypt.[28]

By emphasising the idea of autarky [self-sufficiency] (applicable to people as well as cities), which he took up from P. Veyne,[29] and by giving it a precise definition, R. Descat appears to advance in Finley's direction. But here again, differences are noticeable, which he expresses in finely shaded terms, closely analysing Finley's text. For this search for autarky became a sort of marketing policy; not, of course, of the same kind as that of modern states, and in no way implying that the economy was conceived of as an independent sphere. But it presupposes, on the part of government, a certain consciousness of the specific nature of commerce, independent of the political and social motives there might have been for intervening in the transactions which, for example, concerned the grain supply. If, as C. Meillassoux affirmed, pre-industrial societies had a form of economy (and not only of material economic life), but one that obeyed specific laws (those of the non-capitalist market society),[30] the principal difficulty is to define those particular laws. On this line of argument, the analysis of R. Descat regarding the economic strategies of the classical Greeks and their cities is very instructive.

THE SOCIAL STATUS OF AGENTS OF THE ECONOMY

The last of these five major themes is the social status of the economy's agents in the non-agricultural sectors. What role did the members of the elites play in commerce, production (arts and crafts as well as manufacture), money-lending and banking? To what extent did they use their freedmen and slaves as intermediaries to

[27] Maurice Godelier, *Rationalité et irrationalité en économie*, Paris, Maspero, 1966.

[28] In this regard I must mention the fine recent book by Dominic Rathbone, *Economic Rationalism and Rural Society in Third-Century AD Egypt, The Heroninos Archive and the Appianus Estate*, Cambridge, Cambridge University Press, 1991.

[29] Paul Veyne, 'Mythe et réalité de l'autarcie à Rome', in *La société romaine*, pp. 131–62.

[30] Claude Meillassoux, 'Essai d'interprétation du phénomène économique dans les sociétés traditionnelles d'auto-subsistance', *Cahiers d'études africaines* 1, 4 (1960), 38–67.

acquire a greater or lesser share of the profits of non-agricultural activities?

Here, the argument of A. Łoś is far more social than economic: the place of freedmen in the Roman social hierarchy; the characteristic features of that hierarchy; remarks on the possibilities of social mobility. But the social questions he raises are constantly approached, directly or indirectly, in the setting of the theme of economic history that I have just sketched out.†

This last topic could seem more social than economic anyway. Does the social status of the subjects matter to economic history or not? Following Max Weber and J. Hasebroek, Finley always gave a positive reply to this question, and tried to show that these social components helped to make the ancient economy distinct from the modern. This way of posing the problem undoubtedly rendered his answer compelling. Even those who challenged his conclusions paid the greatest attention, as he did, to the social status of entrepreneurs. Like Finley, they were convinced that the status of agents of the economy could not have failed to have consequences for economic life itself. Other things being equal, a business run by a landlord possessing an aristocratic heritage was not operated in the same way as that of a freedman who had started from nothing.

There is, however, an exception to this consensus; H. Pleket considered that the role of the elites was a purely social, and not economic, matter.[31] For, he argued, economic activity is the same regardless of the status of those engaged in it and benefiting from it. Whether the business was the affair of a bourgeois or a noble made it neither more archaic nor more modern. The individual is certainly of interest to H. Pleket, but from the point of view of social history, so as better to define the hierarchies and balances of Roman society. Few scholars, however, share this perspective.

Are the prosperity and modernity of an economic sector broadly in proportion to the social rank and wealth of the entrepreneurs who dominate it? Hasebroek and Finley, speaking for antiquity, have always answered this question in the affirmative. They considered that, if the entrepreneurs were of modest status, their influence on the authorities would be much smaller and would only increase the gap existing between the city and the economy. Furthermore, the sums of money invested by petty artisans were limited, as well as the volume

---

† A. Łoś, 'La condition sociale des affranchis privés au 1er siècle après J.-C.'. *Annales HSS* 50 (1995) 1011–43.
   [31] Pleket, 'Wirtschaft'.

of their business. The richer and closer to the seat of power were the economy's agents in the non-agricultural sectors, the more they were identified with the ruling aristocratic elite, and the more the economy had opportunities to be developed. That was one of the conditions, or one of the elements, of its 'modernisation'. Nearly all present-day students of antiquity, Finleyans or not, share this viewpoint. Are they right? I am not sure.

Finley believed that the bulk of traders and craftsmen, in Greece as in Rome, had an inferior social status. Moreover, attributing a great deal of weight to differences in status, he tended to emphasise the dependence of freedmen and the obstacles which they encountered, even when rich, in their efforts to climb the social ladder. And he did not, finally, believe in the existence of a middle class in antiquity. On all these points, as far as Rome is concerned, J. H. D'Arms argued against him.[32] Convinced that, contrary to their public image, the loftiest personages in the Roman city and other cities in the Empire were among the most active entrepreneurs in the economy, especially in trade, he tried to minimise the importance of differences in status. He stressed the relative social prestige of rich freedmen, who, in his view, had little difficulty in penetrating the higher ranks, or at least arranging for their sons to do so.

Literary and legal texts provide contradictory evidence, which is often difficult to interpret. Did members of the elite conceal their actions in the economic field that were deemed to be scarcely in keeping with the demands of their status, and what exactly did their possible operations comprise? For the last ten or fifteen years, the debate has broadly shifted towards the archaeological and epigraphical evidence, and chiefly the 'epigraphy of the *instrumentum*' – in other words, inscriptions bearing on objects of daily life: the marks stamped at the time of manufacture on tableware, amphorae and their lids, bricks and tiles, glass and metal articles, ingots, anchors, pipes; painted inscriptions on amphorae; painted or well-incised graffiti, for example on terracotta after baking; and texts carved on labels, tokens or counters in metal or bone. Some material provides much more information than others; for instance, bricks and tiles from the region of Rome or 'Dressel 20' oil amphorae from Baetica. For each object, there is argument between those who insist on the

---

[32] John H. D'Arms, 'M. I. Rostovtzeff and M. I. Finley: The Status of Traders in the Roman World', in John H. D'Arms and John W. Eadie (eds), *Ancient and Modern: Essays in Honor of Gerald F. Else*, Ann Arbor, University of Michigan Press, 1977, pp. 157–79; and id., *Commerce and Social Standing in Ancient Rome*, Cambridge, Mass., Harvard University Press, 1981.

role of members of the elite (generally speaking, the 'anti-Finleyans', who are far more numerous in Italian scholarship) and those who are inclined to play it down or, at least, as I would be inclined to do, stress the indirect nature of that role. This archaeological and epigraphical research has greatly enriched ancient economic history. Simultaneously demonstrating the limits of Finleyan orthodoxy and of the opposing arguments, it has led to more carefully worked out and less radical conclusions.[33] Even though A. Łoś, a specialist in social history who has mainly worked on freedmen and Pompeian society, does not deal with the epigraphy of the *instrumentum*, it is in the framework of such debate that his article is to be understood. Very well informed about Polish and German scholarship (sometimes little known in France), he offers at the same time a whole series of lucid research based on epigraphic material.

The evidence that has reached us enables us to measure social prestige far better than wealth. Membership of orders, and the exercise of official duties such as magistracies for the freeborn of the elite or the quasi-magistracies of the imperial cult for freedmen, provide good information about the prestige of an important personage in Rome or its empire. A freedman's wealth is almost always unknown to us, except in the very rare instances when a text gives the amount of an inheritance. By its precise and exhaustive nature, the article by A. Łoś helps to reveal the limits of what Pompeii itself, on a par with Rome as the best-known city in the Empire, has to teach us on the subject. The result is often (though not by A. Łoś who pays constant attention to the diversity of situations and the subtlest evolutions of Roman society) an all too rigid vision of Roman society – the idea that, because of legal, social and political status, everyone is confined in a compartment from which he cannot escape, and that his wealth is proportionate to the compartment in which he finds himself. Of course, this view links up with one of the fundamental characteristics of the Roman state, and then Empire: the fact that the political elite was at the same time the social elite, and that its members were certainly among the richest inhabitants of the Empire. But frequently the picture one forms of Roman society pushes this characteristic to the extreme, and radicalises it excessively.[34]

[33] On these problems, see the following two collaborative works: W. V. Harris (ed.), *The Inscribed Economy*, Ann Arbor, *Journal of Roman Archaeology*, Supplementary Series 6 (1993); and *Epigrafia della produzione e della distribuzione*, Rome, École française de Rome, 1994.

[34] Ten or fifteen years ago, in the debate between Finley and D'Arms, I rather sided with Finley on these questions, but with reservations and slight differences (see Jean Andreau, 'Modernité économique et statut des maniers d'argent', *Mélanges de l'École française de*

In matters pertaining to the ancient economy the last twenty years have therefore been fruitful (infinitely more so than the previous twenty). [...] By way of conclusion, I should like to suggest some lines of research that are likely to make the debate advance still further.

We still lack detailed case studies although many more exist than ten years ago. The syntheses by C. Domergue on mines and primary metallurgy,[35] those by B. Liou and A. Tchernia on the epigraphy of the oil amphorae of Baetica,[36] and recent studies on the epigraphy of wine amphorae[37] have much to tell on the subject of the organisation of production and trade. For instance, they have shown that the role of the landowner, often a member of the elite, was more indirect and circumscribed than we could be led to believe by the pure and simple catalogue of the names appearing on amphorae (the list is of great value, of course, but in itself does not help us to grasp how trade was organised). On many questions, there is a painful lack of detailed analyses. As a result, either we do not know what conclusions to draw from the available evidence (this is the case with the nummu-lar tesserae and the metal seals bearing their owner's name, the '*signacula*'), or we incorrectly reconstruct a whole story on the basis of one small part of material, or from an isolated case.

The principal objectives are to continue to define the original features of ancient economies and to understand their significance. If, for example, in company with J. H. D'Arms and J.-P. Morel, we agree that the VIPs of the Roman state, senators and knights, had large commercial and industrial interests, how is that to be explained? Was it a constant of pre-industrial societies (European or other)? Or, conversely, are we dealing with an exception? Was it a feature shared between Rome and classical as well as Hellenistic Greece, or was Finley right in considering classical Greece as typical?

Rome, *Antiquité* 97 (1985), 373–410). But D'Arms opportunely recalled a certain fluidity in Roman society, which the existence of differences in status and the place accorded to them by documentation were apt to make us forget.

[35] Claude Domergue, *Les mines de la péninsule Ibérique dans l'Antiquité romaine*, Rome, École française de Rome, 1990; also the contributions of Claude Domergue to the collective works cited in n. 36, as well as Jean Andreau, Jean-Pierre Vernant and Raymond Descat (eds), *Les échanges dans l'Antiquité: le rôle de l'État*, Entretiens d'Archéologie et d'Histoire, Saint-Bertrand-de-Comminges, Musée archéologique départemental, 1994.

[36] Bernard Liou and Jean-Marie Gassend, 'L'épave Saint Gervais III à Fos-sur-Mer (milieu du IIe siècle apr. J.-C.), Inscriptions peintes sur amphores de Bétique, Vestiges de la coque', *Archaeonautica* 10 (1990), 157–259; Bernard Liou and André Tchernia, 'L'interprétation des inscriptions sur les amphores Dressel 20', in *Epigrafia della produzione e della distribuzione* (collective work), Rome, École française de Rome, 1994, pp. 133–56.

[37] Besides André Tchernia (*Le vin de l'Italie romaine*, Rome, École française de Rome, 1986), I must mention Piero Gianfrotta, Antoinette Hesnard, Daniele Manacorda and Clementina Panella.

Was it a sign of modernity or archaism? But what went on in the medieval and early modern eras?

In the wake of the scholarly work (whether on literary texts, inscriptions on stone, coins or sherds), comparative methods are necessary. In recent years it has been practised chiefly in the English-speaking countries which are currently much more open to such approaches, at least in the fields dealt with here. In my view, it must be used much more. Inevitably the method takes several directions.

It is first a comparison between the various periods of Roman antiquity (for instance, the comparison between classical Rome and late antiquity, which is too rarely made except from the angle of the study of archaeological material), and a comparison between Rome and Greece. Some years ago, F. Hartog and I attempted a trial comparison of this kind, which we centred on the idea of the city-state, in homage to Finley and in dialogue with his work.[38] Such attempts must be increased, because they open up broad perspectives, as varied as they are problematical: cultural, political and social differences between the Greek cities and their Italic counterparts; the importance of the conquests which, as early as the late fourth century BC, transformed Rome into a state with a vast territory; the continuity and evolution of the Greek world, at first under the rule of Macedon, and then of Rome; and the continuity and evolution of the Italic world. The Hellenistic and Roman Greek world, which, unfortunately, is on the whole less studied than classical Greece (and above all Athens), must occupy a central position in those comparisons, since it can enable a better understanding of the relative importance of continuities and transformations. An inventory must be drawn up of what is valid for the Greek world (but is there only one Greek world?) and what for Rome.

Take, for example, the city's attitudes to trade and the economy in general: R. Descat's propositions do not seem to me to carry over to Rome's situation (this in no way implies that he is wrong as regards Greece). Autarky, as he defines it in regard to the city–state, does not appear to occupy the same place in the behaviour of the Roman authorities.

Comparisons may be made outside antiquity, with the medieval and modern periods in western Europe, and with other societies in history. Who can fail to see the need for such approaches – all the more delicate because in many instances they require the collabor-

---

[38] Jean Andreau and François Hartog (eds), *La Cité antique? A partir de l'oeuvre de Moses I. Finley*, vols 6–8 of the journal *Opus*, 1987–9.

ation of specialists in several disciplines? Fernand Braudel once said: 'If you do not emerge from Antiquity seeing what happened afterwards, you cannot form a history of Antiquity!'[39] This remark is more appropriate than ever, and one cannot say that it makes the task any easier.

---

[39] Fernand Braudel, 'L'Antiquité et l'histoire ancienne', interview conducted by Jean Andreau and Roland Étienne, *QS* 24 (July–December 1986), 5–21 (see 21).

PART II

Production

3 Traditional and Ancient Rural Economy in Mediterranean Europe: plus ça change?[†]

PAUL HALSTEAD

Paul Halstead is well known for his comparative and ethnoarchaeological assessments of early rural economies.[‡] His paper challenges attempts – widely embraced among ancient historians – to reconstruct ancient agricultural systems and practice on the basis of comparative data derived from modern peasant economies. In the wake of the famous French 'Annales' historians, who emphasised long-term continuities in the environmental and social conditions of rural production in the Mediterranean, many ancient historians have turned to contemporary peasant and pastoral communities for insights into the workings of ancient farming. Halstead, however, argues that inferences from comparative material can be misleading and simplistic. Looking more closely at the historical background of so-called 'traditional' peasant economies, he shows that bare fallowing and transhumance, which are generally regarded as common strategies of ancient rural production, are related not so much to natural features of the Mediterranean as to developments of the more recent past. While transhumance in Greece depended among other things on large-scale (man-made) deforestation of the lowlands and the access to lowland markets enjoyed by highland pastoralists, bare fallowing was not the only viable option in Mediterranean agriculture but could be replaced by intensive farming enhanced by (natural) fertilisation, or a system of crop/pulse rotation. In his view, what historians do stand to learn from traditional agriculturalists is that they tend to be highly flexible in their responses to local conditions, annual climatic changes, and fluctuations in the supply of labour and demand for produce. Whereas comparative data are instrumental in illustrating the range of options that may have been available to ancient communities, they cannot serve as proxy evidence for 'normal' behaviour in prehistoric and classical times.

† Originally published as 'Traditional and Ancient Rural Economy in Mediterranean Europe: plus ça change?', *Journal of Hellenic Studies* 107 (1987), 77–87 (© The Society for the Promotion of Roman Studies).

‡ See, e.g., his co-edited volume (with J. O'Shea), *Bad Year Economics: Cultural Responses to Risk and Uncertainty*, Cambridge: Cambridge University Press, 1989, as well as numerous articles on the ancient rural economy.

The study of recent 'traditional' Mediterranean rural economy has long been a predilection of ancient historians and archaeologists working in that area. Traditional practices and production norms have been used by ancient historians in the interpretation of the often enigmatic testimony of the ancient agronomic writers, while archaeologists have used the same information to fill in the many gaps in the material record supplied by the spade. Many of the relevant data on traditional rural economy are gleaned from the accounts of early travellers or of modern geographers, ethnographers and agronomists. But *comparanda* [comparative data] acquired at first-hand enhance the credibility of archaeologists and ancient historians as fieldworkers, and chance summer encounters with Cretan shepherds or Cycladic fishermen are valuable currency in competitive displays at academic conferences.

More crucial than the *source* of traditional analogies, however, is the issue of their relevance to the prehistoric and historic past. In some quarters an implicit assumption of relevance perhaps arises from a rather romantic notion of the Mediterranean rustic, both ancient and modern, as a being in communion with nature.[1] Others have argued more explicitly for an essential continuity in rural economy as a reflection of the strong constraints imposed by the natural environment of the Mediterranean.[2] Yet it is clear that many aspects of traditional rural life are integrally bound up with elements of the contemporary natural and social environment which have not remained unchanged since time immemorial. The purpose of this paper is to caution against the uncritical use of traditional practices and norms as analogies for antiquity and to suggest that the greatest value of studying traditional farming may be as a guide to the questions we should be asking about the past.

I TRADITIONAL MEDITERRANEAN FARMING

Most descriptions of traditional Mediterranean farming recognize the influence of two distinctive features of the Mediterranean natural environment – climate and relief.[3] The climate of the coastal

[1] For a critique of such uniformitarian assumptions about rural life in Greece, see L. M. Danforth, *Journal of Modern Greek Studies* ii (1985) 53–85.
[2] E.g. M. R. Jarman, G. N. Bailey and H. N. Jarman (eds.) *Early European agriculture* (Cambridge 1982).
[3] E.g. E. C. Semple, *The geography of the Mediterranean region and its relation to ancient history* (London 1932); D. B. Grigg, *The agricultural systems of the world: an evolutionary approach* (Cambridge 1974); G. Barker, *Prehistoric farming in Europe* (Cambridge 1985).

lowlands, where most human settlement is concentrated, is characterized by an alternation between mild winters and hot summers and by a winter rainfall regime. Annual crops like wheat take advantage of the mild winters to complete their growth cycle by early summer, while perennial crops such as the olive are adapted to surviving the summer drought. The relief is heavily broken, such that the plains and hills of the lowlands usually lie within days, if not hours, of high mountains which are snow-bound in winter but cool and well-watered in summer. The flocks of sheep and goats which overwinter in the lowlands can thus escape the summer drought by moving to the high pastures of the mountains and there are 'transhumant' pastoral communities which undertake such a pattern of twice-yearly movement between lowland and mountain throughout the Mediterranean.

Clearly one consequence of broken relief is considerable *local* diversity of topography and climate, but certain generalizations about land-use can still be made. Traditionally the Mediterranean landscape has been dominated by the seasonal pastures of sheep and goats and by wheat or barley fields sown on a two-year fallowing cycle. The fallow fields have been cultivated to prevent weed growth (hence 'bare fallow') and so to preserve two years' moisture for the succeeding cereal crop. A much smaller area is devoted to vegetable gardens and to orchards or vineyards, though the value of their produce is disproportionately large. Locally, olives and vines may take up a large part of the total cultivated area, partly because of their ability to thrive on soils to which shallow rooting cereals are ill-adapted.

Scholars have extrapolated a number of traditional features back into the past. In Greece, some sort of seasonal use of mountain pasture by early historical times is clearly implied in the story relating how the infant Oidipous was handed over by a Theban shepherd to a Corinthian shepherd on Mt. Kithairon,[4] but full-scale transhumant pastoralism has been suggested for later prehistory on archaeological grounds in Greece, Italy and Spain.[5] Indeed a broadly similar pattern of movement has even been suggested for a population dependent on animals such as red deer in northwest Greece during the last Ice Age.[6]

---

[4] Semple (n. 3) 323.
[5] G. Barker, 'Prehistoric territories and economy in central Italy', in E. S. Higgs (ed.) *Palaeoeconomy* (Cambridge 1975) 111–75; Jarman *et al.* (n. 2).
[6] E. S. Higgs, C. Vita-Finzi, D. R. Harris and A. E. Fagg, *Proceedings of the Prehistoric Society* xxxiii (1967) 1–29.

The alternation of cereals and bare fallow has also widely been assumed to be the norm in historical times[7] and perhaps in pre-history.[8] This assumption is integral to many estimates of past labour requirements or productivity and has contributed to the widespread belief that ancient agriculture was woefully unproductive, with rare insights by the early agronomists being effectively neutralized by technological shortcomings. Local specialization in olives or vines has also aroused interest, and is a basic prerequisite of Renfrew's argument that the palaces of Bronze Age southern Greece developed as centres for the redistribution of the fruits of locally specialized agricultural production.[9]

Unfortunately the direct historical or archaeological evidence for extrapolating these traditional forms back as widespread elements of past rural life is rarely unambiguous. For this reason circumstantial arguments as to what is likely to have taken place assume great importance. Clearly such circumstantial arguments are dependent on understanding the social and natural environmental context of traditional transhumance, bare fallowing or tree-crop specialization. For example, the geographical pattern of local specialization in crops such as olives and vines has changed radically during the last three centuries for a variety of locally and historically specific reasons – in response to the development of new urban markets, to the construction of new transport links such as canals and railways or to the growth and decline of competing producers because of government intervention or because of natural disasters such as the phylloxera which wiped out the vineyards of France and Spain, then Italy and Dalmatia.[10] In Greece itself local specialization in olives in areas ill-suited to cereal growing is clearly related to the opportunities of an international market economy: thus olive growers in the infertile Mani peninsula of southern Greece cut down their trees and reverted to cereal production when World War II disrupted international trade and forced them to rely on local subsistence agriculture. This

---

[7] Semple (n. 3) 386; M. I. Finley, *The ancient economy* (London 1973) 108; R. Duncan-Jones, *The economy of the Roman empire; quantitative studies*[2] (Cambridge 1982) 49; but *cf.* K. D. White, *Roman farming* (London 1970) 119–21.

[8] H. J. van Wersch, 'The agricultural economy', in W. A. McDonald and G. R. Rapp (eds.) *The Minnesota Messenia expedition* (Minneapolis 1972) 183–4; A. G. Sherratt, *World Archaeology* xi (1980) 313–20; M. Wagstaff, S. Augustson and C. Gamble, 'Alternative subsistence strategies', in C. Renfrew and M. Wagstaff (eds.) *An island polity: the archaeology of exploitation in Melos* (Cambridge 1982) 177; J. L. Bintliff and A. M. Snodgrass, *Journal of Field Archaeology* xii (1985) 142.

[9] C. Renfrew, *The emergence of civilisation: the Cyclades and the Aegean in the third millennium BC* (London 1972).

[10] Grigg (n. 3) 141–4.

does not, of course, mean that local specialization did not take place in the distant past, but it does cast doubt on Renfrew's model in which local specialization is a prerequisite for the initial development of the very institutions which would have made specialized communities viable.[11]

Two other traditional features noted above are rather harder to dismiss. Transhumance and bare fallowing (and hence the absence of manuring or crop rotation) together account for what many see as the single most fundamental distinction between traditional Mediterranean and temperate European farming – the divorce between stock husbandry and arable farming [crop fearming].[12] In essence, transhumance removes livestock from the lowlands for half of the year, thus depriving the arable sector of half of the available manure.[13] Bare fallow, in turn, produces less fodder than a weedy (i.e. uncultivated) fallow and far less than a rotation including fodder crops: thus the grazing potential of the lowlands is kept low and livestock are forced into seasonal transhumance.[14] Together the most distinctive characteristics of traditional stock and crop husbandry have locked the pastoral and arable sectors of the rural economy into a vicious circle of increasing separation.

But was this pastoral: arable divorce equally characteristic of rural economy in antiquity? To answer this question, we must first look critically at the natural and social context of transhumance and bare fallowing in traditional rural economy.

II TRANSHUMANCE

Most studies of traditional Mediterranean transhumance have rightly stressed the complementary nature of the lowland winter grazing areas and the highland summer pastures. A few of these studies have argued that the lowlands are in fact too hot and dry in summer for stock to survive, while winter conditions in the mountains are equally severe. Under this extreme formulation, transhumance is literally an inevitable consequence of environmental constraints and can be extrapolated back into the distant past with absolute confidence. All the common farmyard animals, however,

[11] See also S. Aschenbrenner, 'A contemporary community', in McDonald and Rapp (n. 8) 49; J. G. Lewthwaite, 'Acorns for the ancestors: the prehistoric exploitation of woodlands in the west Mediterranean', in S. Limbrey and M. Bell (eds.) *Archaeological aspects of woodland ecology* (British Archaeological Reports International Series cxlvi [Oxford 1982]) 218.

[12] Semple (n. 3) 297; Grigg (n. 3) 125.

[13] Semple (n. 3) 300.

[14] Grigg (n. 3) 125.

can and do survive the heat and aridity of the lowland summers and a few even overwinter in the mountains, albeit at a considerable cost in stall-feeding.[15] A more usual, and less contentious, 'environmental' interpretation of transhumance sees such twice-yearly movements as evading the season of scarce grazing in both the lowlands and the mountains and so permitting the maintenance of larger populations of livestock (and people).[16] In other words, transhumance is a necessary response to the Mediterranean environment *if livestock are kept on a sufficiently large scale.* Stock husbandry on the necessary scale in the past cannot be assumed and has rarely, if ever, been demonstrated.

In later prehistory, at least, the ecological niche occupied by traditional transhumant pastoralists simply did not exist. Firstly, the present summer pastures in the mountains are, to a large extent, not a 'natural' feature of the Mediterranean landscape.[17] Although tree growth may be prevented locally in the mountains by steepness of slope, absence of soil, waterlogging and so on, no Mediterranean mountain is high enough (for its southerly latitude) for extensive alpine meadows to be the inevitable product of harsh winter conditions. On the contrary, tree growth tends to be associated in the mountains of the Mediterranean region with wet, rather than warm, topographical situations. In northern Greece, for example, the tree-line is higher on west- than on east-facing slopes, higher on high mountains than on low ones, and higher on impermeable than on permeable rocks, all of which suggests summer aridity, rather than winter cold, as the major *climatic* factor favouring grassland.[18] Even if insufficient to prevent tree growth, aridity could seriously retard regeneration of high mountain forests in the face of clearance by shepherds and woodcutters, which is very well documented in the recent past.[19] Most mountain pasture seems to be the product of human interference – either directly through the fire and axe or indirectly through grazing livestock – and, as the decline of the traditional pastoral economies leads to relaxation of grazing pressure, trees are widely recolonizing these areas. Throughout much of later

[15] E.g. J. K. Campbell, *Honour, family, and patronage* (Oxford 1964) 10–11.

[16] Higgs *et al.* (n. 6); Barker (n. 5); Jarman *et al.* (n. 2); J. M. Frayn, *Sheep-rearing and the wool trade in Italy during the Roman period* (Liverpool 1984).

[17] Higgs *et al.* (n. 6); G. Mavrommatis pers. comm.

[18] Admiralty, Naval Intelligence Division, *Greece, i: physical geography, history, administration and peoples* (Geographical Handbook Series [Andover 1944]); P. Quezel, *Vegetatio* xiv (1967) 127–228.

[19] W. B. Turrill, *The plant-life of the Balkan peninsula* (Oxford 1929).

prehistory, therefore, and perhaps well into early historical times, mountain pasture may have been very limited in extent.

Secondly, the fertile lowlands occupied by the earliest Mediterranean farmers in the sixth millennium BC were also well wooded.[20] This does not mean that a dense arboreal canopy prevented the growth at ground level of accessible graze and browse, but herding large numbers of animals would have been very difficult and a variety of large predators and competitors will have made close herding necessary. Moreover the trees will have offered browse for domestic livestock during the months when the more shallow-rooting grasses died back[21] and in some areas seasonal wetland will have provided an alternative source of graze for small numbers of animals, so summer will not have been such a season of scarcity for lowland livestock as has been the case in recent times. Thus seasonal use of distant mountain pastures may only have become advantageous, let alone necessary, once extensive clearance had created a surfeit of winter grazing in the lowlands and this surfeit had been taken up by greatly increased numbers of livestock.

Thirdly, the social environment in which the transhumant pastoralism of recent centuries flourished is quite unlike any which existed in the distant past. The unusual political and economic conditions under which the long distance systems of Spain (the 'Mesta') and Italy (the 'Dogana') developed to supply the mediaeval wool trade are well known. More recently Lewthwaite has discussed the international political and economic factors which underpinned smaller scale pastoral economies in Corsica and Sardinia.[22] In northern Greece the traditional economy of the Vlachs and Sarakatsani, who inspired much of the recent archaeological fascination with transhumant pastoralism, also warrants further investigation. Though many Vlach and Sarakatsani shepherds did make the prescribed annual moves with their flocks to and from the high mountain pastures of the Pindhos range, others stayed in the mountains as

---

[20] E.g. W. van Zeist and S. Bottema, 'Vegetational history of the eastern Mediterranean and the Near East during the last 20,000 years', in J. L. Bintliff and W. van Zeist (eds.) *Palaeoclimates, palaeoenvironments and human communities in the eastern Mediterranean region in later prehistory* (British Archaeological Reports International Series cxxxiii [Oxford 1982]) 277–321.

[21] G. Williamson and W. J. A. Payne, *An introduction to animal husbandry in the tropics*[2] (London 1965) 79.

[22] J. G. Lewthwaite, 'Plain tails from the hills: transhumance in Mediterranean archaeology', in A. Sheridan and G. Bailey (eds.) *Economic archaeology: towards an integration of ecological and social approaches* (British Archaeological Reports International Series xcvi [Oxford 1981]) 57–66.

sedentary mixed farmers, while others travelled widely in Greece, the Balkans and eastern Europe making a living as merchants, tinkers or builders.[23] In recent times, at least, the shepherds have sold the produce of their flocks (wool, cheese, lambs) in the markets of the lowland towns and have bought in relatively cheap agricultural staples, such as flour and oil,[24] and up to the nineteenth century some of the highland population was employed in guiding, guarding and robbing traders passing through the mountains. Thus in a number of ways the recent highland economy has been heavily subsidized by and parasitic upon the market economy of the lowlands.[25] Without this 'subsidy', pastoral communities would need to maintain far larger flocks to support a given human population.

Quite when the niche occupied by traditional transhumant pastoralists was first created and exploited is a difficult question, the answer to which doubtless varies from area to area within the Mediterranean. Firm palynological [pollen research] evidence for the impact of early farmers on lowland vegetation is notoriously hard to find,[26] suggesting that clearance was in most cases a very gradual process, and extensive deforestation in the mountains seems, in some areas at least, only to have taken place in the last few centuries. There is also a tendency among ancient historians to play down the importance in classical antiquity of the urban market upon which recent pastoralists have been dependent.[27] The appearance in northern Greece towards the end of the first millennium AD of the Vlachs, the linguistically and culturally distinct group which has traditionally occupied much of the high Pindhos, may then reflect the colonization of a new economic niche.[28] Locally, specialized pastoralism may well have existed much earlier, particularly in agriculturally marginal areas,

---

[23] A. J. B. Wace and M. S. Thompson, *Nomads of the Balkans* (London 1914); Campbell (n. 15); N. Gage, *Eleni* (London 1983).

[24] Campbell (n. 15) 363–4.

[25] See also S. H. Lees and D. G. Bates, *American Antiquity* xxxix (1974) 187–93; P. Briant, *État et pasteurs au moyen-orient ancien* (Cambridge 1982) 235.

[26] See e.g. the extensive pollen record from central and northern Greece: H. E. Wright, 'Vegetation history', in McDonald and Rapp (n. 8); S. Bottema, *Late quaternary vegetation history of northwestern Greece* (Groningen 1974); *Palaeohistoria* xxi (1979) 19–40; *Acta Botanica Neerlandica* xxix (1980) 343–9; *Palaeo-historia* xxiv (1982) 257–89; J. R. A. Greig and J. Turner, *Journal of Archaeological Science* i (1974) 177–94; J. Turner and J. Greig, *Review of Palaeobotany and Palynology* xx (1975) 171–204; N. Athanasiadhis, *Flora* clxiv (1975) 99–132.

[27] Finley (n. 7).

[28] The antiquity of transhumant pastoralism cannot be resolved by archaeological survey alone: the often ephemeral habitations of mobile pastoralists can be archaeologically invisible, especially in the difficult terrain of the mountains; conversely, to interpret all high mountain occupation sites as the remains of transhumant pastoralists is begging the question.

but the wholesale seasonal removal of livestock from the arable lowlands was probably not commonplace in antiquity.[29]

III BARE FALLOWING

The popular explanation for the traditional prevalence of bare fallowing (and near-absence of soil-improving practices such as manuring and cereal/pulse rotation) is that the limiting factor on crop production in the Mediterranean is the availability of water, rather than nutrients, and that bare fallowing allows two years' rainfall to be stored for one crop.[30] At best, therefore, manuring offers an irrelevant improvement in soil fertility and at worst it accelerates water loss by opening up the soil, and so is actually deleterious.[31] Similarly a pulse rotation crop, which adds nitrogen to the soil, is at best irrelevant and at worst competes with the ensuing cereal crop for moisture and so is positively disadvantageous. The fact that cereal/pulse rotation has only begun to oust bare fallowing very recently, and at the behest of modern agronomists, even though its theoretical advantages were appreciated by the ancient agricultural writers, apparently confirms the unsuitability of this practice to the Mediterranean.

That soil moisture can be a limiting factor on crop production in the Mediterranean is made amply clear by the frequent coincidence of severe drought and crop failure.[32] Moisture is evidently not the only limiting factor, however, because the widespread abandonment of bare fallowing since World War II has been accompanied by the adoption of weed killers and artificial fertilizers, but only rarely of irrigation. In fact experiments conducted during the 1930s, 1940s and 1950s in Cyprus showed that fertilizers improved cereal yields dramatically.[33] Fertilized plots produced more *every year* than did bare fallowed plots in alternate years. Moreover, sheep manure produced the same effect as artificial fertilizers. In fact manure is applied to tree crops, gardens and cereals throughout the Mediterranean and is evidently beneficial – at least if the timing and quantity

[29] P. Garnsey, 'Mountain economies in southern Europe or: thoughts on the early history, continuity and individuality of Mediterranean upland pastoralism' in M. Mattmüller (ed.), 'Wirtschaft und Gesellschaft von Berggebieten', *Itinera* v/vi (Basel 1986), 7–29.

[30] Semple (n. 3) 386; White (n. 7) 113, 118.

[31] Semple (n. 3) 411; White (n. 7) 129.

[32] E.g. D. Christodoulou, *The evolution of the rural land use pattern in Cyprus* (World Land Use Survey Regional Monograph ii [Bude 1959]) 28–33.

[33] H. M. James and A. Frangopoulos, *Cyprus Agricultural Journal* xxxiv (1939) 5–19; L. Littlejohn, *Empire Journal of Experimental Agriculture* xiv (1946) 123–33; P. A. Loizides, *Empire Journal of Experimental Agriculture* xxvi (1958) 25–33.

are appropriate. So manured annual cropping is far more productive than a bare fallow/cereal rotation, if sufficient manure is available.

Alternatively, cereals may be grown in rotation with pulse crops, and again modern experimental data are instructive. The Cypriot experiments showed that wheat yields following a pulse crop were slightly lower than those after bare fallow, while experiments in northern Greece indicate a slight improvement in wheat yields after a pulse crop.[34] Data from the semi-arid south of Australia, however, suggest that in the long term the benefits of pulse rotation to alternate year wheat yields are quite unequivocal[35] – and of course a pulse crop is also produced in the intervening years

If, as seems inevitable, bare fallowing is so much less productive per unit area than either manured annual cropping or cereal/pulse rotation, why was it so pervasive in the recent past? As was noted above, manuring is not in fact unknown in traditional farming and has probably tended to be concentrated in small-scale gardens, orchards and so on because of the scarcity of manure[36] – which in turn partly results from the traditional prevalence of transhumance.[37] The key to the rarity of cereal/pulse rotation in traditional farming seems to be the higher labour costs of (harvested) pulse crops compared with cereals:[38] though more productive per unit area than bare fallowing, cereal/pulse rotation may be less productive per unit of human labour.

In both cases the *scale* of traditional farming is crucial. Traditionally, most of the rural population of the Mediterranean has lived in nucleated villages or towns, far from the majority of their fields. Even small settlements, which are often located with an eye to security rather than for proximity to their fields, may face the same problem and the need to farm at a distance from home is widely exacerbated by broken terrain and by a highly fragmented and dispersed pattern of land tenure.[39] In consequence subsistence agriculture has been

[34] Β. Θ. Κοκόλιος, Γεωπονικά 110–111 (1963) 1–15; Σ. Ε. Σωτηριάδης, Γεωργική Ἔρευνα i (1977) 125–36.

[35] M. Williams, *The making of the south Australian landscape* (New York 1974); B. A. Chatterton and L. Chatterton, *Libyan Studies* xv (1984) 157–60.

[36] E.g. P. A. Loizides, 'The cereal–fallow rotation in Cyprus', *Proceedings of the first Commonwealth conference on tropical and subtropical soils* (Commonwealth Bureau of Soil Science, Technical Communication xlvi [Harpenden 1948]) 210.

[37] Also, in the recent, heavily deforested landscape, farmers have sometimes needed to use available dung as fuel – e.g. A. C. de Vooys, *Tijdschrift van het Koninklijk Nederlandsch Aardrijkskundig Genootschap* lxxvi (1959) 31–54.

[38] F. Dovring, *Land and labor in Europe 1900–1950* (The Hague 1960) 404; M. Wagstaff and C. Gamble, 'Island resources and their limitations', in Renfrew and Wagstaff (n. 8) 103.

[39] Dovring (n. 38) 15, 26–7; Christodoulou (n. 32); M. Chisholm, *Rural settlement and land use*[2] (London 1968); S. F. Silverman, *American Anthropologist* lxx (1968) 1–20; H. A. Forbes,

dominated by extensive cultivation of distant fields in which cereals alternate with bare fallow, while the more labour intensive pulses have tended to be relegated to a minor role, often restricted to intensively worked in-field gardens.[40] This labour-saving tactic rules out the possibility of widespread cereal/pulse rotation.

Why was bare fallowing characteristic of the cereal fields? Significantly, in the Cypriot experiments referred to earlier, the main obstacle to manured annual cropping of cereals was found to be the proliferation of weeds. The extensively cultivated cereal fields of traditional farming received only low levels of manuring, tilling and weeding and so produced poor crops which did not compete well with weeds. Bare fallowing, by ploughing up fallow weeds before they seed, is an effective means of checking weed growth and, because ploughing can take place in late spring in the agricultural slack season between sowing and harvest, it makes economical use of scarce manpower and plough animals.[41] This scarcity is in turn a consequence of the extensive and unproductive nature of traditional land-use.

Like transhumance, therefore, traditional bare fallowing is integrally related to a specific historical context and should not be extrapolated back into the distant past uncritically. If traditional extensive farming is integrally related to the traditional nucleated pattern of settlement, dispersed settlement in farmsteads and villages located nearer to the arable land might well be associated with more intensive farming. In fact a relatively dispersed pattern of settlement does seem to have been the norm for most of prehistory[42] and has recently been documented for classical antiquity in a host of intensive archaeological surveys.[43] Even if some of the smallest rural 'sites' located in these surveys are not permanent farmsteads, the presence of substantial (i.e. archaeologically visible) field-houses may have rather similar implications for the intensity of land-use.[44] Thus if the deconstruction of traditional agricultural practice offered here is basically valid, intensive cultivation involving regular manuring

---

Annals of the New York Academy of Sciences cclxviii (1976) 236–50; M. Wagstaff and S. Augustson, 'Traditional land use', in Renfrew and Wagstaff (n. 8) 108.

[40] E.g. Wagstaff and Augustson (n. 39) 119.

[41] E.g. H. A. Forbes, *Expedition* xix. i (1976) 5–11.

[42] P. Halstead, 'Counting sheep in Neolithic and Bronze Age Greece', in I. Hodder, G. Isaac and N. Hammond (eds.), *Pattern of the past: studies in honour of David Clarke* (Cambridge 1981) 307–39.

[43] P. D. A. Garnsey, *Proceedings of the Cambridge Philological Society* ccv (1979) 1–25; D. R. Keller and D. W. Rupp (eds.), *Archaeological survey in the Mediterranean area* (British Archaeological Reports International Series clv [Oxford 1983]).

[44] R. Osborne, *ABSA* lxxx (1985) 110–28.

and cereal/pulse rotation may have been commonplace in antiquity. Indeed the widespread 'background' scatter of ancient pottery, documented in parts of the lowland Mediterranean landscape as a spin-off of recent surveys,[45] surely reflects intensive agricultural activity and was perhaps largely created by manuring or middening.[46]

IV LAND-USE IN ANTIQUITY – AN ALTERNATIVE MODEL

Transhumance and bare fallowing, the twin interrelated pillars of the traditional divorce between livestock and crop husbandry, have both been shown to be integrally bound up with the nucleated nature of human settlement and the consequently extensive nature of land-use in the recent past. During later prehistory and early historical times, much of the rural population of the Mediterranean lived relatively close to the fields they worked and small-scale intensive farming was a practicable alternative. Under such a regime, cereal/pulse rotation may well have been the norm rather than the exception and changes in animal husbandry are also likely. The traditional system of farming a scatter of distant and dispersed plots makes it difficult for individual households to graze their small herd of livestock on their own arable land. Instead most livestock were run in large consolidated herds, either on a communal basis or under the ownership of specialized pastoralists, and fields under cereals and those in fallow tended to be grouped into large blocks to facilitate herding These large herds both permitted and encouraged transhumance. With dispersed settlement and closer plots, herding at the household level would be more practicable and more complex rotation schemes might be a substantial obstacle to large consolidated herds. Transhumance would then be less likely and the consequent integration of crop and livestock husbandry would in turn make manure more freely available and so reinforce the viability of intensive arabic farming.

Viewed in this light, discussion by the ancient agricultural writers of the benefits of intensive practices like manuring and cereal/pulse rotation should perhaps be interpreted not as exploring the boundaries of contemporary agronomic theory, but rather as advocating the application to extensively farmed estates of techniques used on small farms since time immemorial.

[45] T. W. Gallant, 'The Ionian Islands paleo-economy research project', in Keller and Rupp (n. 43); Bintliff and Snodgrass (n. 8).

[46] A. M. Snodgrass, *Annales (É.S.C.)* v–vi (1982) 800–12; see also T. J. Wilkinson, *Journal of Field Archaeology* ix (1982) 323–33; D. Crowther, *Scottish Archaeological Review* ii (1983) 31–44; T. M. Williamson, *Britannia* xv (1984) 225–30.

This contrast between traditional extensive farming and the alternative intensive model has a number of quite radical implications for attempts by ancient historians to quantify the likely labour requirements and productivity of classical agriculture. For example, traditional agriculture is heavily dependent on work animals – both pack animals, for carrying labour to and produce from the distant and scattered fields, and plough animals for tilling the extensive areas under cereals or cultivated fallow. The feeding costs of such work animals are prodigious[47] and Roman colonial land allotments may often have been too small to justify the capital cost of keeping work animals: as little as 7–8 jugera *(c.* 2 ha) worked by hand could feed a family, but 20 jugera *(c.* 5 ha) would be needed if work animals were kept.[48]

Spade and hoe cultivation is still the norm for in-field gardens today and has on occasion replaced ploughing both in recent centuries and in classical antiquity.[49] For the Roman period spades and hoes are richly attested by archaeological finds[50] – though many of these were doubtless used to complement rather than to replace the plough.[51] The wider implications for farming societies of plough versus hoe cultivation have been discussed by Goody,[52] but two particular points deserve mention here. Firstly, with plough agriculture, the capital-expensive plough team sets the limit on productivity, whereas hoe cultivation can make far fuller use of a household's human labour force. Secondly, the alternative cultivation technologies affect the costs of crop production at a number of levels.

Under the traditional extensive system, much agricultural labour is directly geared to the maintenance of work animals which, because they are working during the day, need to be stall fed for much of the year. Crops are therefore harvested together with much of the straw, which could otherwise have been left in the field and grazed *in situ*. Reaping thus becomes even more back-breaking and a far greater

[47] E.g. Christodoulou (n. 32) 182–3.

[48] White (n. 7) 336; *cf.* G. Delille, *Agricoltura e demografia nel regno di Napoli nei secoli xviii e xix* (Naples 1977), who cites *maximum* cultivable areas of 3.5 ha and 10 ha respectively for smallholdings without and with a pair of oxen (pp. 127–9) and a requirement of up to 10–12 ha of grazing to maintain a single ox (p. 135).

[49] H. A. Forbes, *Strategies and soils: technology, production and environment in the peninsula of Methana, Greece* (Ph.D. dissertation, University of Pennsylvania 1982) 217; Delille (n. 48); White (n. 7) 484 n. 5.

[50] K. D. White, *Agricultural implements of the Roman world* (Cambridge 1967).

[51] E.g. Delille (n. 48) 118 fig. 39.

[52] J. Goody, *Production and reproduction*, Cambridge Studies in Social Anthropology xvii (1976); see also A. Gilman, *Current Anthropology* xxii (1981) 1–23; A. G. Sherratt, 'Plough and pastoralism: aspects of the secondary products revolution', in Hodder *et al.* (n. 42).

volume of crop must be transported from the fields and then threshed and winnowed. Trampling the crop under the hooves of work animals, rather than flailing by hand, offsets the greater volume of crop to be threshed, but the need to save straw and chaff for fodder means that the crop must be winnowed laboriously in only a light breeze.[53]

The different cultivation technologies may also entail very different seed:yield ratios. Extensive plough agriculture is traditionally associated, and again clearly for reasons of scale, with broadcast sowing, which is very wasteful of seed. Intensive gardening, on the other hand, is compatible with dibbling – a sparser but more even method of sowing which permits much higher seed:yield ratios.[54] Thus extensive and intensive farming are characterized by different cultivation technologies, by different harvesting and crop processing techniques and so by different labour inputs and production outputs at almost every stage in the agricultural cycle.

These differences might account for some of the 'discrepancies' in ancient literary estimates of labour requirements or productivity noted so despairingly by Duncan-Jones.[55] Of course, additional variation is introduced by other factors. Speed of ploughing, for example, depends on the heaviness of the soil and number of plough animals. Threshing is faster on a hot day, but slower if the crop is a glume wheat rather than a free-threshing cereal or pulse. Consideration of decision making by modern farmers, however, suggests other, perhaps more fundamental, reasons for caution in the search for labour and production norms for ancient agriculture.

V THE ECONOMICS OF AGRICULTURE – NORMS AND VARIABILITY

When modern peasant farmers are questioned about *average* yields or labour requirements, they are often unwilling, even unable to give a straight answer. Though frustrating for the amateur ethnographer, this experience can also be instructive.

Through the life-cycle of an individual household, the number of mouths to be fed changes, additional production requirements occur for dowries and the like, and the number of available workers

---

[53] G. Jones and P. Halstead, 'Traditional crop processing in Amorgos, Greece' (in preparation).

[54] P. McConnell, *The agricultural notebook* (London 1883).

[55] Duncan-Jones (n. 7), 330.

changes.[56] In effect the farmer is aiming at a moving target with a weapon of gradually shifting calibre. Upon this foundation of a gradually (and largely predictably) changing ratio of producers to consumers is superimposed a morass of unpredictable variation in both input and output.[57]

Key members of the labour force, human or animal, may be lost through death, injury or illness. Crop returns from a given plot of land fluctuate in response to external factors such as variation in the amount and timing of rainfall. Stored crops are subject to unpredictable losses through fire, spoiling or pest damage. To complicate the issue, one of the many ways in which farmers absorb temporary surplus or deficit may be to buy or sell land or labour.[58] So each year the farmer may be aiming for a different production target, from a different area of land, with a different labour force and with the cushion of a greater or lesser amount of produce in store.

He may adjust a number of aspects of agricultural practice as a tactical solution to these problems. If stores are running out and a dry winter has ruined the main cereal crop, he may try a late spring-sown crop such as millet. If stores are plentiful, he may try a high risk crop with a high market value. His choice of fallowing and rotation regime will reflect the relative availability of land, human labour, work animals, manure, stored produce and so on – as will the frequency of ploughing, hoeing and weeding. Most sinister of all from the perspective of the quantitative ancient historian, he may vary his sowing rate, and thus his seed:yield ratio.

For a given soil type, the more sparsely a farmer sows, the more shoots or tillers each seed will put out. If a farmer has access to enough good soil for normal subsistence, he may sow fields with marginal soil very sparsely on the grounds that he loses little when the crop is a failure and secures a windfall bumper harvest when weather conditions are ideal.[59] If a farmer needs a good return from all his land to be confident of an adequate harvest, and yet is short of labour for tilling and weeding, he may sow thickly so that a dense crop outcompetes the weeds which would otherwise choke it.[60] Evidently the miserably low seed:yield ratios from mediaeval estates

[56] M. Sahlins, *Stone age economics* (London 1974).

[57] Forbes (n. 39); (n. 49); J. O'Shea, 'Coping with scarcity: exchange and social storage', in Sheridan and Bailey (n. 22).

[58] P. Hill, *Rural Hausa: a village and a setting* (Cambridge 1972).

[59] *Cf.* P. A. Rowley-Conwy, 'Slash and burn in the temperate European Neolithic', in R. J. Mercer (ed.), *Farming practice in British prehistory* (Edinburgh 1981) 85–96.

[60] E.g. E. A. Skorda, 'Constrains to cereal production and possible solutions in Greece', *Fifth regional cereals workshop, Algiers, i* (Algiers 1979) 30.

in northwest Europe,[61] often used in modelling prehistoric and classical agriculture, likewise reflect particular local factors (such as the availability of land and labour or the price of grain),[62] as well as the relatively high rates of sowing required in a region of cold and wet climate.[63] At any rate, the dangers of an uncritical search for 'normal' seed:yield ratios for classical antiquity are apparent.

VI AGRICULTURAL NORMS AND THE ANCIENT ECONOMY

These issues of rotation and fallowing regime, sowing rates and so on are clearly important *per se* from the point of view of the agricultural historian. They are also relevant to certain broader questions in social and economic history, such as the relationship in Roman Italy between free peasantry and landowners and the relative importance to the latter of slave and seasonally hired free labour.[64]

The preceding discussion also suggests the need for reevaluation of Finley's conviction that the goal of self-sufficiency extolled by the Roman writers was a moral precept with no basis in economic rationality.[65] In fact, as Finley himself points out, because transport costs were high in the ancient world, local surpluses and deficits could not easily be evened out by trade.[66] The outcome was violent fluctuation in the prices of agricultural produce, and in such an environment to aim for self-sufficiency and so avoid being at the mercy of extortionately high prices would have been very hard-headed economic rationality indeed.[67]

This leads on to what is arguably the most important problem in the ancient economy – how did rich Greeks and Romans in classical antiquity acquire their wealth? The current consensus among ancient historians seems to be that farming was, with very few exceptions, the only really important area of economic activity, at least until well into the Roman period.[68] Yet agriculture seems to offer only modest

[61] B. H. Slicher van Bath, *The agrarian history of western Europe AD 500–1850* (London 1963); G. Duby, *Rural economy and country life in the medieval west* (London 1968).
[62] E.g. E. van Cauwenberghe and H. van der Wee (eds.) *Productivity of land and agricultural innovation in the Low Countries (1250–1800)* (Leuven 1978) 125–39.
[63] J. Percival, *The wheat plant* (London 1921) 421–2; I. Arnon, *Crop production in dry regions, 2: systematic treatment of the principal crops* (London 1972) 48.
[64] E.g. K. Hopkins, *Conquerors and slaves* (Cambridge 1978); D. W. Rathbone, *JRS* lxxi (1981) 10–23.
[65] Finley (n. 7) 109.
[66] Finley (n. 7) 127.
[67] Cf. J. du Boulay, *Portrait of a Greek mountain village* (Oxford 1974) 33–7; Forbes (n. 49).
[68] Finley (n. 7).

potential for accumulating wealth: the average returns on cereals were low and, because of their bulk, they could not easily be traded, while cash crops such as vines yielded higher returns, but only high quality produce was really profitable and that was traded on a small scale.[69] The problem of how the rich first got rich – before they had accumulated extensive estates[70] – is even more difficult to resolve from this perspective.

Here the variability and uncertainty inherent in agriculture, instead of being an obstacle to the discovery of norms, become a useful heuristic device in their own right. Though the returns from cereal agriculture were normally low, a killing could evidently be made from exceptionally high prices in times of famine – a range of cultural and legal prescriptions against excessive profiteering are documented for the Greek world[71] and, for the Romans, Varro clearly advocates the storing up of produce for this very purpose.[72] Cereal farming does not emerge in the ancient writers as the primary economic goal of landowners, because the rewards of such famine-broking must have been as unpredictable as the risks.[73] But occasional windfall profits could well, over the timespan of a generation or two, have made a major contribution to the income of elite households – and may well hold the key to the original emergence of a rich minority, given that current ancient historical orthodoxy seems, on a mixture of theoretical and empirical grounds, to have ruled out all the obvious alternatives.

VII CONCLUSION

This paper has perhaps taken a rather tortuous path through the Mediterranean rural landscape, but its message is simple. Before archaeologists and ancient historians seek to transfer the behaviour of those they meet on their Mediterranean travels back into the past, they should look closely at what their informants are doing and why. And though the complexity of traditional agricultural ecology may obstruct the search for simple production norms, the unravelling of this complexity may also help to identify new and important questions which should be asked about the past. It is certainly not

---

[69] Duncan-Jones (n. 7).
[70] E.g. Finley (n. 7) 102–3; Hopkins (n. 64).
[71] E.g. Finley (n. 7) 169–70; M. M. Austin and P. Vidal-Naquet, *Economic and social history of ancient Greece: an introduction* (London 1977) 291–4.
[72] Duncan-Jones (n. 7) 38.
[73] Duncan-Jones (n. 7) 146.

intended to discourage ancient historians and prehistorians from
using their knowledge of traditional rural economy in the investigation of the past. On the contrary, such knowledge is essential both
to evaluate and to supplement the ancient literary sources. Moreover,
the intensive model of land-use proposed here as an alternative (or
complement) to the extensive traditional pattern is consistent with,
but cannot really be tested against, the ancient literary sources, given
their systematic lack of interest in small-scale, subsistence farming.[74]
Further progress is heavily dependent on developing improved
archaeological methods for the study of ancient agriculture – and to
this end ethnoarchaeological study of the last vestiges of traditional
rural economy in the Mediterranean is a matter of the greatest
urgency.

---

[74] *Cf.* Duby (n. 61) 23, suggesting that Pliny is describing *extensive*, but Columella *intensive* agriculture; *cf.* also M. H. Jameson, *CJ* 73 (1977–8) 122–45.

4 Olive Production and the Roman Economy: The Case for Intensive Growth in the Roman Empire[†]

ROBERT BRUCE HITCHNER

This is the first of four chapters (followed by Chapters 9, 10 and 12) that address the central problem of Roman economic history: the structure and scale of economic development engendered by the success of Roman imperial expansion and provincial administration. Robert Bruce Hitchner is an archaeologist at the University of Dayton (Ohio) who has conducted fieldwork in the former Roman provinces of North Africa. In this paper, he seeks to utilise archaeological evidence for an interpretation of economic processes. Expressly positioning himself against minimalist assessments of Roman economic growth, he draws attention to the apparently large scale of investment in market-oriented olive oil production in North Africa, and explores several factors that were conducive to this expansion. Hitchner's paper not only illustrates the contribution of archaeology to the study of the Roman economy but may also be considered representative of a school of thought that tends to interpret source material indicative of large-scale production and transactions as proxy evidence of intensive growth. 'Intensive' or 'real' growth, however, is a technical economic term referring to an increase in per capita output and income. Like other critics of minimalist models of ancient economic development, Hitchner makes no sustained attempt to distinguish between aggregate and per capita growth. This issue will be taken up in Saller (Ch. 12 below).

INTRODUCTION

Current orthodoxy holds that the Roman economy was under-developed and thus capable, at best, of only modest growth.[1] The

---

† Originally published as 'Olive Production and the Roman Economy: The Case for Intensive Growth in the Roman Empire', in M.-C. Amouretti and J.-P. Brun (eds), *La production du vin et de l'huile en Méditerranée* (*Bulletin de Correspondance Héllenique* Supplément XXVI), École Française d'Athènes: Athens, 1993, pp. 499–503 (© École Française d'Athènes).
[1] Finley (1985), Hopkins (1980), Garnsey and Saller (1987).

reason for this, it is argued, is that Roman (and more generally Ancient) cultural, political, and social values discouraged 'rational' economic behavior and thus created conditions inimical to economic growth. Yet an analysis of the evidence pertaining to olive production in the Roman Empire suggests that significant growth may have occurred in this important sector of the economy. If so, this raises fundamental questions, not only about our present understanding of the performance of the Roman economy, but also about the supposedly limited rationality of Roman economic impulses, attitudes, and behavior. This paper will, accordingly, investigate the evidence for the growth in olive production and export, and consider the implications of this development for the Roman economy in general.

DISCUSSION

1 Factors favorable to growth in olive production and export

A dominant tendency in recent scholarship on the Roman economy has been to spotlight those elements of Ancient society that prevented the empire from experiencing an industrial revolution or economic growth on a scale comparable with, say, early modern Europe. However, this comparative approach overlooks or undervalues institutions and structures present in the Ancient World which were conducive to real growth.[2] In the case of olive product production and export, for example, it is possible to isolate a number of infrastructural catalysts to its growth in the Roman period.

1.1 THE CENTRAL IMPORTANCE OF OLIVE PRODUCTS TO THE ANCIENT ECONOMY

The olive and its by-products were universally employed as foodstuffs, unguents, medicaments, lubricants, and sources of energy. It is estimated that per capita consumption of olive oil, alone, in Antiquity was probably in the vicinity of 20–25 liters per year and may have accounted for up to one-third of an individual's annual caloric intake.[3] The olive's ability to fulfil numerous and diverse needs may have made it the single most important agricultural commodity in the ancient economy.

---

[2] Reynolds (1985), 7–10 and Jones (1988) and see below note 31.
[3] Amouretti (1986), 177–96; Forbes and Foxhall (1978); Foxhall and Forbes (1982); Mattingly (1988a), 34.

1.2 INCREASED DEMAND FOR OLIVE PRODUCTS IN THE ROMAN PERIOD

Although the archaeological evidence from the late republican and early imperial period in Italy does not show olive oil production rising at nearly the rate of viticulture,[4] an emerging market of some scale for olive products is implied in the attention accorded to all aspects of oleoculture in the agricultural treatises of Cato, Varro, Pliny, and Columella. (The treatises themselves are signs of growth potential in that they indicate an interest in the dissemination of the stock of knowledge.) There are clear indications, moreover, that oil was being imported in considerable volume to meet the demands of Rome, a market comprising the largest non-elite urban population of the Ancient World. Caesar's fine of 3 million pounds of olive oil on *Lepcis Magna* (*B. Afr.* 97.3), for example, looks very much like a calculated attempt to curry favor among the Roman populace by providing either an annual or one time windfall of this valuable commodity. The thousands of Spanish and Tripolitanian oil amphorae sherds dating to the 2nd century from Monte Testaccio in Rome and the 1st–4th century African amphorae recovered at Ostia also stand as a clear testament to the considerable demand for olive products in the city prior to the addition of oil to the *annona* in the early 3rd century.[5] Some of the imported olive oil no doubt came as part of the 'internal supply' system of the Roman aristocracy,[6] though the bulk of it is likely to have been purchased in the vectigal market. Although no precise figures exist, annual Roman requirements for olive oil may have exceeded 25,000,000 liters.

Another source of increased demand in the Roman period was the army. From an economic standpoint, the legions may be viewed as a new, large, and non-elite market. Indeed the supply of the military with oil products ought not to be under-interpreted as a part of a simple redistributive process designed to balance shortages in an important commodity, but as a new source of demand for olive products which, like Rome, contributed to the stimulation of olive production under the Roman period.

1.3 INFRASTRUCTURAL CONDITIONS WITHIN THE EMPIRE FAVORABLE FOR GROWTH IN OLIVE PRODUCTION

The favorable location of the Roman empire around the long

---

[4] Tohernia (1986); Carandini (1989).
[5] Rodriguez-Almeida (1974–5), (1984); Panella (1983).
[6] Whittaker (1985); Fulford (1987).

indented coastline of the Mediterranean and the general political and military security provided by the empire made the movement of commodities over great distances cheaper and safer than ever before. Roman maintenance and expansion of the land transport network of the Mediterranean will also have facilitated the movement of goods and commodities and promoted the growth of agriculture in non-core production areas away from the Mediterranean coast.

The 'boom' in olive production in the western Mediterranean provinces, in particular, may be attributed to the prior existence in these areas of olive cultivation and of long-distance trade in other agricultural and non-agricultural commodities. The olive was a well-established crop along the coast of southern Gaul, Africa, and Tripolitania well before the Roman conquest. Moreover, with the rise of grain shipments to Rome and the army from Africa as early as the 2nd century BC, regular shipping routes and supply and distribution mechanisms were initiated which olive producers in the imperial period could exploit to their own advantage.[7]

Spain's emergence as a major olive producer in the imperial period is, likewise, probably explained by its well-established trade in metals, which provided the capital base both for investment in olive cultivation and the necessary subsidization of transport costs of bulk-load oil and other agricultural goods to Rome and the Rhine.[8] In Spain, as well as Africa, furthermore, esparto grass, used in the making of bedding, fuel, footwear, cloth, mechanical appliances, and ship rigging (Plin. *HN* 19.7–8, 26–9; 37.77, 201), may also have played a role in stimulating olive production, for it is precisely in areas where esparto grass was grown that Roman period olive cultivation later emerged. Lastly, the presence in Spain and Africa of a substantial, unexploited labor force (free or servile status notwithstanding) in the indigenous tribal populations may have served as a strong incentive to the development of large tenant-dominated agricultural estates.[9]

1.4 ROMAN GOVERNMENT ACTIONS AND POLICIES DID NOT ACT AS A DETERRENT TO GROWTH IN OLIVE PRODUCTION IN THE EARLY EMPIRE

It is frequently argued that the role of the Roman government in the economy was [deleterious] to growth. In the case of the olive industry this argument is difficult to sustain. We have already seen that oil

[7] Carandini (1983); Mattingly (1988a), 53–4.
[8] Mattingly (1988a), 52–4.
[9] Hitchner et al. (1990).

production to meet urban and military needs did not constitute a deterrent to olive growth. Indeed, even when olive oil became part of the *annona*, a government monopoly over its production and distribution was not an end result. Where there is evidence of administrative intervention in oil production as in the case of the Spanish (and perhaps Tripolitanian) amphorae stamps, it is at first, evidently, a local responsibility and, in any case, likely to have been a regulatory mechanism designed to minimize fraud and other corrupt activities detrimental to trade.[10] In Africa, Roman government interest in agricultural development, including olive cultivation, is intimated in two surviving pieces of agrarian legislation, the *Lex Manciana* and *Lex Hadriana de rudibus agris*, and indirectly in the growth of agricultural settlement in treaty-determined territories of formerly pastoral tribes.[11]

2 Evidence for real growth in olive production and export

2.1 THE LARGE NUMBER OF RURAL SITES WITH PRESSES DATING TO THE ROMAN PERIOD

The best summary, analysis, and interpretation of the evidence for the expansion of olive production in the West is provided by Mattingly.[12] Working primarily from the archaeological record, he has amassed data showing that between the late 1st and 4th centuries there was substantial growth in the number of rural agricultural settlements devoted to olive production, and that this growth was not restricted to areas under olive cultivation but extended to areas previously underdeveloped agriculturally. In an area of 1 500 km² in the djebel [mountain or hill] to the west of *Lepcis Magna*, for example, Mattingly estimates that there were more than 750 presses established in the Roman period, approximately 1 press for every 2 km.[13] Over 350 presses are known in an area of 1,500 km², in

---

[10] Mattingly (1988a), (1988b).

[11] Leveau (1988); Hitchner (1989). This is not a new argument, but in recent years it has been challenged on the grounds that it imputed to the Roman government a degree of *dirigisme* in its policies toward the African provinces which was not possible either in theory or practice in view of the limited nature of Roman administration, and the supposedly immutable character of traditional African society (Whittaker [1978]). It is important, however, to avoid terms or concepts which arbitrarily restrict debate, for even if it is true that the nature of Roman government was underdeveloped by comparison with the modern bureaucratic state and thus more *ad hoc* in its provincial policy, and that African society was perhaps less altered by Rome than once believed, neither of these revisions preclude *perforce* programmatic Roman state intervention in African affairs for the purpose of achieving specific policy ends.

[12] Mattingly (1988a).

[13] Mattingly (1988a, 1988).

the Sbeitla–Kasserine–Thelepte region of central Tunisia.[14] In the Guadalquivir valley in Spain as many as 161 of the 1,500 recorded Roman period rural sites show evidence of pressing facilities, and the actual number of presses in the valley 'could have been well in excess of 1000'.[15]

In Africa and Tripolitania, where environment and post-Antique historical developments have contributed to a high level of site preservation, a significant number of sites show evidence of having had multiple presses (17 in one example, more often 3–5). The presses were frequently grouped in banks and located within a large, well-constructed (either *opus africanum* or ashlar masonry) buildings. Although ancillary settlement is common around the buildings, the unpretentious character of most of the associated structures is an unequivocal indication of the intensely industrial character of oil production at these sites, suggestive of an intent to produce large volumes of surplus olive oil on a regular basis. Indeed, from the standpoint of economic attitudes and responses, the construction of these oilery sites reflects considerable capital investment in the future potential of the mass oil market noted above. By any standard, this must be considered a marked exception to the supposed heavy rent-seeking mentality of Roman elites.

Almost certainly related to this phenomenon is the proliferation of small farms with one or two presses often in close promixity to oileries, and frequently on agricultural marginal lands (piedmont and mountain zones). That is, the decision to construct a large stone, lever press (see 2.2 below), particularly when much more modest means for extracting oil for subsistence needs were available, implies that surplus oil production was the ultimate objective of the small farm occupants. Although the capital for these presses is likely, in many instances, to have come from the owners of the nearly oileries interested in the oleocultural development of marginal lands in or around their estates, we may also see in these arrangements an effort by the farms' occupants, whether independent small-holders, free tenants or even slaves, to better their lot.[16]

---

[14] Mattingly (1988a); Hitchner (1989).
[15] Mattingly (1988a).
[16] It is precisely these types of economic alliances which were probably being encouraged in the *Lex Manciana* and *Lex Hadriana*; see Kehoe (1984), (1988); Mattingly (1988b); Hitchner (1988), (1989); Hitchner et al. (1990); Leveau (1988); Foxhall (1990); Leveau (1984); Hitchner and Mattingly (1991).

2.2 TECHNOLOGICAL MODIFICATION AND
SERIALIZATION OF PRESSES TO INCREASE PRODUCTION

Recent analysis of well-preserved Roman lever presses in Africa and Tripolitania suggests some serializations in their materials and design for the purpose of increasing oil yields per pressing unit.[17] Specifically, the use of stone: 1) for the posts (*arbores*) that anchored and adjusted the press beam; 2) as masonry to pin down the posts; and 3) as counterweights to bear down on the free end of the beams[18] seems to have been a calculated attempt, within the limits of the technology, to generate the greatest possible force in the pressing operation in order to maximize the amount of oil expressed. A general bid at high volume olive pressing in a single operation at sites in the Kasserine region and Libya in particular is implied by the construction of what seem to be very large presses and the discovery of monolithic press beds capable of holding baskets of olive paste of up to 1 m in diameter.[19] Whether the modifications cited above were a consequence of recent tinkering designed to increase oil productivity per pressing unit (2,500–10,000 kg oil per year on Mattingly's estimate)[20] cannot yet be determined. However, the timing of these modifications is less important for our purposes than their serialization at both large and small pressing operations, for this development stands as an important indicator of technological responsiveness to perceived economic opportunities, a necessary ingredient for economic growth. Indeed, when the estimate of individual lever press production is combined with the large number of presses in Tripolitania and the Kasserine region, the resulting total oil production calculations (18,000 metric tons and 5,000–10,000 tons of oil, respectively, in bumper years) point to Roman period production on a scale well beyond universal subsistence requirements.[21]

Another indicator of the expansion of oleoculture which may fall under the category of technological serialization is the expansion of irrigated agriculture into the arid upland regions of the North African hinterland. Recent survey in the Kasserine region, for example, indicates irrigated cultivation in association with Roman period olive farms extending far up the nearby ridges (600 m+ above

---

[17] See Mattingly (1988c) and Mattingly and Hitchner (1993), pp. 439–82.
[18] Mattingly (1988a).
[19] Hitchner et al. (1990); Hitchner and Mattingly (1991); Mattingly and Hitchner (1993), pp. 439–82; Mattingly (1993), pp. 483–96.
[20] Mattingly (1988c), (1993), pp. 483–96.
[21] Mattingly (1988a), (1988b); Hitchner and Mattingly (1991).

sea level).[22] While this form of agricultural technology was not new to North Africa, its extension in the Roman period to more marginal landscapes constitutes a huge long-term investment in land and labor designed to increase olive product production.

2.3 THE EMERGENCE OF INDUSTRIES WITH OPERATIONAL 'LINKAGES' TO OLIVE PRODUCTION

Another possible signifier of real growth in oil production and export is the emergence of amphora and pottery manufactories in the olive producing area of Spain and North Africa.[23] In the Guadalquivir Valley, there appear to have been 150–200 kilns with an estimated output of 200,000–300,000 amphorae in the mid-2nd century AD. At the Roman urban site, Ksar el Guellal, in the Kasserine region, where no fewer than 23 presses have been identified, a dense concentration of Red-Slip pottery and amphorae sherds indicative of a major kiln has been found.[24] These ceramic manufactories look very much like embryonic factory operations with complementary, and vertical, 'linkages' to local olive production operations. Both developments are normally indicators of economic growth.[25]

2.4 PROXY MANIFESTATION OF THE EXPANSION OF OLIVE PRODUCTION

The ostensible correspondence between the spread of olive cultivation, pottery manufacture, and monumental urban development in the North African hinterland has long attracted the attention of scholars. However, the precise nature of the linkage between these developments has not been easy to draw out empirically. A possible solution to this dilemma may be found in a recent study of the relationship between ARS [African Red-Slip] production and urban building activity by Fentress and Perkins.[26] The results of their inves-

[22] Hitchner (1988), (1989).
[23] Mattingly (1988a), (1988b); Peacock et al. (1990).
[24] Hitchner (1988); Hitchner and Mattingly (1991); Peacock et al. (1990).
[25] The emergence of a local Red-Slip production in the Kasserine region is worthy of further attention as a potential indicator of the region's economic expansion as a result of the introduction of the olive in the Roman period. Specifically, Kasserine region RS [Red-Slip] appears to have developed in response to rising local demand for Adrican Red-Slip wares from Carthage in the late 1st and 2nd centuries, and the Tunisian Sahel in the late 2nd and 3rd centuries. This demand was probably a direct consequence of the lucrative export of local oil and thus a form of revenue return to the region's economy. By the 4th century, Kasserine region RS, although continuing to imitate wares imported mostly from the Sahel, appears to have virtually monopolized the local market (see Neuru, Appendix 1, in Hitchner et al. [1990]). In development literature, this phenomenon, known as 'import substitution', is especially common in inland areas where imports can be fended off more easily because of high import costs; it is generally regarded as a sign of genuine economic growth (Reynolds [1985]).
[26] Fentress and Perkins (1988).

tigation reveal a close correlation in African towns between building activity and pottery production from the 2nd to 5th centuries and by inference 'an increase in capital availability and expenditure'. Although they do not attempt to locate precisely the source of this 'capital availability', they acknowledge (following Carandini)[27] that the rise of [C-type pottery] produced in Tunisia is probably to be associated with the growth of oil production in the area. In view of the connections already noted between oil and ceramic production, and the correlation in terms of capital expenditure between pottery production and public building noted by Fentress and Perkins, it would seem to follow that surplus revenues accrued from the massive export of olive products by large local producers (who no doubt formed the core of municipal elites) were directly invested in the construction of public buildings in African cities.

Another potential indicator of growth stemming from olive production is the emergence of a provincial elite in those non-core agricultural regions where olive cultivation was extended. This is especially evident in Tripolitania, where the rise of certain aristocratic families of *Lepcis Magna* to senatorial and even possibly imperial status (Septimius Severus) may be plausibly attributed to the wealth and status achieved through their large-scale production of olive oil.[28] A similar pattern can be detected at *Sufetula* (modern Sbeitla), an important olive town just to the north of the Kasserine region, where a number of local senatorial and equestrian families have been identified.[29] It is not, however, the mere emergence of new elites in these regions that stands out for our purposes. These individuals also constituted, for the most part, an educated and literate element of the population capable of disseminating knowledge, an important catalyst for economic development.

CONCLUSION

I have argued in this paper that significant growth was achieved in the olive production sector of the Roman economy. If my thesis is correct, its implications for our understanding of the Roman economy's overall performance and the economic mentalities, institutions, and activities that sustained it are profound. In terms of performance, for example, it is worth noting that many of the indicators of growth in olive production (e.g. a mass market, regional

[27] Carandini (1969).
[28] Mattingly (1988b).
[29] Duval (1989); Hitchner (1982).

security, a developed transportation infrastructure, agricultural expansion, technological serialization, spawning of complementary industries (ceramics), and urban development) appear to be present in the local economies of various regions of the Empire between the 1st and 5th centuries AD.[30] This raises the possibility that growth, even if glacial and tentative by modern standards, was achieved in the Roman economy.[31]

These same indicators, drawn, for the most part, from the more neutral archaeological record, as opposed to the more doctrinaire rhetoric of Roman litterateurs, seem to suggest that economic calculation, risk-taking, innovation, and other 'rational' economic activities were widespread in the Empire, and that Roman institutions and government did not offer serious impediments to efficient economic performance. Indeed, there is sufficient evidence that the Roman state, from time to time, encouraged activities and policies that would contribute to long-term growth in the Empire.[32]

These are, to be sure, rather radical assertions about the nature and performance of the Roman economy built on a very limited investigation of olive production in the Empire.[33] I have risked advancing them in the hope that they will serve as the stimulus for renewed debate on the Roman economy. For more than a decade, discussion on this subject has been dominated by the paradigm originally advanced by Finley.[34] The rapidly expanding archaeological record and the economic approach to reading a portion of that

[30] This is evident in Italy, Spain, Gaul, and Africa in the early Empire, and in Britain and the Danubian and Asian provinces in the late Empire; see Randsborg (1991). André Tchernia and Fanette Laubenheimer have also suggested to me that wine production in Italy and southern Gaul seems to have experienced growth similar to that found in the olive sector.

[31] Comparison of the Roman economy's performance with that of modern economies is, in my view, a flawed and misleading exercise, for it works under the implicit assumption that growth did not occur in pre-modern economies. It also contributes to a tendency to evaluate the Roman economy from a capitalist or marxist economic perspective, neither of which is appropriate to understanding economic behavior or performance in the Ancient World.

[32] The existence of universal values and governmental policies favorable to growth does not necessarily contribute to parity in the level of economic growth from one region to another. Reynolds (1985) points out, for example, that even countries which are considered economically underdeveloped show evidence of growth relative to their past performance and social and cultural values favorable to growth. What this means for the Roman economy is that, while attitudes, activities, and policies conducive to economic growth may have been generally present in the Empire, they will not necessarily have contributed to equal levels of growth everywhere; some areas of the Empire are likely to have remained relatively underdeveloped by comparison with others throughout their history. This is not the same as saying that these underdeveloped areas did not experience growth, however.

[33] I hope to test these assertions in the near future by extending my investigation to other aspects of the Roman economy.

[34] Finley (1985). Note in this regard the recent observation of E. L. Jones (1988): 'most ancient historians ... insist that there was a total lack of promise in the classical world. The occasional scholar who raises the possibility of early growth runs the risk of derision'.

record that I have advanced here indicates there is room for new theories which account, more positively than Finley's and those of his proponents, for the empirical evidence of growth and expansion in the economy of the Roman Empire.

BIBLIOGRAPHY

Amouretti, M.-C. (1986) *Le pain et l'huile dans la Grèce antique*, Annales Littéraires de l'Université de Besançon 328, Paris.

Brun, J.-P. (1986) *L'oléiculture antique en Provence, Les huileries du département du Var. RAN Suppl.* XV.

Brun, J.-P. (1989) 'La villa gallo-romaine de Saint-Michel à La Garde (Var), un domaine oléicole au Haut-Empire', *Gallia*, 103–62.

Camps-Fabrer, H. (1953) *L'olivier et l'huile dans l'Afrique romaine*. Algiers.

Camps-Fabrer, H. (1985) 'L'olivier et son importance économique dans l'Afrique du nord antique', in *L'huile d'olive en Méditerranée*. Aix-en-Provence, 53–78.

Carandini, A. (1969) 'Produzione agricola e produzione ceramica nell'Africa de età imperiale', *Studi Miscellanei* 15, 97–119.

Carandini, A. (1983) 'Pottery and the African Economy', in P. D. A. Garnsey, K. Hopkins and C. R. Whittaker (eds), *Trade in the Ancient Economy*. London, 45–62.

Carandini, A. (1985) *Settefinestre, una villa schiavistica nell'Etruria romana*. Modena.

Carandini, A. (1989) 'Italian Wine and African Oil: Commerce in a World Empire', in K. Randsborg (ed.), *The Birth of Europe. Archaeology and Social Development in the First Millennium* AD. Rome.

Duval, N. (1989) 'Inventaire des inscriptions latines païennes de Sbeitla', *MélRome* 101, 403–88.

Fentress, E. and Perkins, P. (1988) 'Counting African Red Slip Ware', *L'Africa Romana* 5, 205–21.

Finley, M. I. (1985) *The Ancient Economy*. Rev. edn, Berkeley and Los Angeles, University of California Press, and London, Hogarth Press.

Forbes, H. A. and Foxhall, L. (1978) 'The Queen of All Trees, Preliminary Notes on the Archaeology of the Olive', *Expedition* 21,1, 37–47.

Foxhall, L. 'The Dependent Tenant: Land Leasing and Labour in Italy and Greece', *JRS* 80, 97–114.

Foxhall, L. and Forbes, H. A. (1982) 'Sitometria: The Role of Grain as a Staple Food in Classical Antiquity', *Chiron* 12, 41–90.

Fulford, M. (1987) 'Economic Interdependence among Urban Communities of the Roman Mediterranean', *World Archaeology* 19, 58–74.

Garnsey, P. and Saller, R. (1987) *The Roman Empire. Economy, Society and Culture*. London.

Hitchner, R. B. (1982) *Studies in the History and Archaeology of* Sufetula *down to the Vandal Conquest*. Ann Arbor, University Microfilms.

Hitchner, R. B. (1988) 'The Kasserine Archaeological Survey (1982–1986)', *AntAfr* 24, 7–41.

Hitchner, R. B. (1989) 'The Organization of Rural Settlement in the Cillium-Thelepte Region (Kasserine, Central Tunisia)', *L'Africa Romana* 6, 387–402.

Hitchner, R. B. and Mattingly, D. J. (1991) 'Ancient Agriculture. Fruits of Empire – the Production of Olive Oil in Roman Africa', *National Geographic Research and Exploration* 7,1, 36–55.

Hitchner, R. B. et al. (1990) 'The Kasserine Archaeological Survey (1987)', *AntAfr* 26, 231–60.

Hopkins, K. (1980) 'Taxes and Trade in the Roman Empire', *JRS* 70, 101–25.

Jones, E. L. (1988) *Growth Recurring. Economic Change in World History.* Oxford.

Kehoe, D. P. (1984) 'Private and Imperial Management of Roman Estates in North Africa', *Law and History Review* 2, 241–63.

Kehoe, D. P. (1988) *The Economics of Agriculture on Roman Imperial States in North Africa.* Göttingen.

Leveau, P. (1984) *Caesarea de Maurétanie, une ville romaine et ses campagnes.* Rome.

Leveau, P. (1988) 'Le pastoralisme dans l'Afrique antique', in C. R. Whittaker (ed.), *Pastoral Economies in Classical Antiquity*, Cambridge Philological Society, Suppl. XIV, 177–95.

Mattingly, D. J. (1988a) 'Megalithic Madness and Measurement, or How Many Olives Could an Olive Press Press?', *Oxford Journal of Archaeology* 7, 2, 177–95.

Mattingly, D. J. (1988b) 'The Olive Boom. Oil Surpluses, Wealth and Power in Roman Tripolitania', *Libyan Studies* 19, 21–41.

Mattingly, D. J. (1988c) 'Oil for Export? A Comparison of Libyan, Spanish and Tunisian Olive Oil Production in the Roman Empire', *JRA* 1, 33–56.

Mattingly, D. J. (1993) 'Maximum Figures and Maximizing Strategies of Oil Production? Further Thoughts on the Processing Capacity of Roman Olive Presses', in M.-C. Amouretti and J.-P. Brun (eds), *La production du vin et de l'huile en Méditerranée.* Athens, 483–98.

Mattingly, D. J. and Hitchner, R. B. (1993) 'Technical Specifications for Some North African Olive Presses of Roman Date', in M.-C. Amouretti and J.-P. Brun (eds), *La production du vin et de l'huile en Méditerranée.* Athens, 439–62.

Panella, C. (1983) 'I contenitori presenti ad Ostia in età antonina: analisi tipologica, epigrafica, quantitativa', in *Production y comercio del aceite en la Antigüedad, Segundo congresso internacional, Sevilla (1982).* Madrid, 225–61.

Peacock, D. P. S., Bejaoui, F. and Ben Lazreg, N. (1990) 'Roman Pottery Production in Central Tunisia', *JRA* 3, 59–84.

Randsborg, K. (1991) *The First Millennium* AD *in Europe and the Mediterranean.* Cambridge.

Reynolds, L. G. (1985) *Economic Growth in the Third World (1850–1980).* New Haven.

Rodriguez-Almeida, E. (1974–5) 'Bolli anforari di Monte Testaccio', *Bulletino archeologico communale di Roma* 84, 109–35, 199–248.

Rodriguez-Almeida, E. (1984) *Il Monte Testaccio. Ambiente, storia, materiali.* Rome.

Rossiter, J. J. (1978) *Roman Farm Building in Italy.* BAR 52.

Tchernia, A. (1986) *Le vin de l'Italie romaine. Essai d'histoire économique d'après les amphores.* BEFAR 261, Rome.

Whittaker, C. R. (1978) 'Land and Labour in Africa', *Klio* 60, 2, 331–62. [repr. in Whittaker, *Land, City and Trade in the Roman Empire.* Aldershot and Brookfield 1993, ch. 1]

Whittaker, C. R. (1985) 'Trade and the Aristocracy in the Roman Empire', *Opus* 4, 49–75. [repr. in Whittaker, *Land, City and Trade in the Roman Empire.* Aldershot and Brookfield 1993, ch. 12]

PART III

Money and Markets

5 Money and Mythic History: The Contestation of Transactional Orders in the Fifth Century BC[†]

LESLIE KURKE

Ancient economic historians have long struggled with ancient texts that tell us much about what is wrong with money but little about price formation. 'Primitivists' tend to take this as an indication that ancient authors were unable to analyse money in economic terms and that they lacked a conception of the 'economic' within which the function of money could be analysed. Yet, more recently, this negative assessment has become the starting point of more positive arguments. Scholars with various theoretical interests have looked at culturally specific meanings of monetary exchange which go beyond the usual complaint that money encourages greed and selfishness. They have demonstrated, among other things, how money operated as a signifier by which relationships, identity and power could be negotiated.

Leslie Kurke has been at the vanguard of these novel theoretical approaches. She has argued that coinage in particular interfered with regimes of value that were associated with precious metal. Money in the form of silver coinage represented a considerable threat to the mythical hierarchy of metals, as espoused in the Hesiodic myth of the races (Hes. W&D 105ff), and to the class that identified themselves with it. In her view, Greek texts from the sixth century down to Aristotle reveal a political tradition associating the 'real' value of gold with power, sovereignty, religious authority and justice. From this perspective, the 'conventional' value of silver coinage figured only in hostile representations of new political elites, trickery, deceit and debased character. Texts of this kind did not simply express moral concerns about money, or look down on a class of traders, but were culturally specific expressions of political conflicts over values.[‡]

† (© Leslie Kurke).
‡ 'Herodotus and the Language of Metals', *Helios* XXII (1995), 36–64; *Coins, Bodies, Games, and Gold. The Politics of Meaning in Archaic Greece*, Princeton: Princeton University Press, 1999. Her earlier work on the economy of values includes *The Traffic in Praise: Pindar and the Poetics of the Social Economy*, Ithaca and London: Cornell University Press, 1991.

These observations provide the starting point for the present contribution. Looking at a variety of texts recalling the exploits of Themistocles (the democratic Athenian naval commander who persuaded the citizenry to use their silver to build a larger fleet), Kurke shows that his political enemies represented him within a whole range of related images: as a bad leader who was corrupt and involved in dubious monetary strategies for private gain. Sometimes he is even depicted as an inn-keeper and petty trader. Such texts did not present a true, or even a biased, picture of Themistocles, but constructed a political enemy within the abusive imagery of monetary exchange. As the political order could be envisioned as an exchange, or in Parry and Bloch's terms, as a 'transactional order', so power could always effectively be misrepresented as commerce: the direct exchange of goods for money in a non-political, self-interested, yet public sphere. Thus, Kurke's paper, written self-consciously by a 'literary scholar', highlights the necessity for economic historians to take proper account of the fictionality of much of the textual information that underpins their work.

I

Since I've been working for several years on the representation of money in archaic and classical Greece, it was perhaps inevitable that I would eventually come to Themistocles. For Themistocles seems constantly to be associated with money in its most corrupt and sordid forms – with graft, bribery, extortion and uncontrollable greed. It has been argued that Themistocles simply 'was like that', but this response fails to take account of the nature of our sources.[1] The figure of Themistocles, like many other phenomena in ancient economic history, is never available to us unmediated, but only filtered through ancient representations, visual and verbal. As the products of human construction and symbol-making, these representations require analysis and interpretation as cultural systems. Part of what I want to suggest here is that figures like Themistocles (and Aristeides, for that matter) enter the literary tradition always already mythologised – always already bearers of a cultural signification that exceeds their historical reality. Hence, I want to offer an 'imaginary history' of Themistocles – to consider the conceptual work the figure of Themistocles does in the texts and traditions in which he appears. As such, this is an object lesson in the styles of reading required by ancient representations and the kinds of history it is possible to do based on texts.

---

[1] See, e.g., Frost 1980.10–11: 'If [Herodotus] tells us that Themistocles took bribes from Euboeans and extorted money from the islanders, it may actually be because it was the truth.'

Let me begin with two very famous anecdotes about Themistocles and money. First, a story from Herodotus about the Greek fleet at Artemisium. Confronted with the overwhelming numbers of Persian ships arrayed against them, the Greek commanders plan to flee 'from Artemisium to the interior of Greece'. At this point, Herodotus tells us:

> The Euboians, having realised that they were planning these things, were asking Eurybiades to remain for a little while, until they could evacuate their children and households. And, when they were not persuading him, they went over to the Athenian commander Themistocles and they persuaded him for a wage of thirty talents, that [the Greeks] will remain and make the naval battle before Euboia. And Themistocles makes the Greeks hold on in the following way: from this money, he gives to Eurybiades five talents as if (of course) giving it from himself. And when this one had been persuaded (for Adeimantos the son of Okytos, the Corinthian commander, alone of the rest was resisting, saying that he would sail away from Artemisium and not remain), to this one Themistocles declared on oath, 'You will not abandon us, since I will give you more gifts than the King of the Medes could send you for abandoning the allies.' These things he said publicly and at the same time, he sends three talents of silver money to the ship of Adeimantos. And these men, struck [out of their wits] by the gifts, were persuaded and gratified the Euboians, and Themistocles himself made a profit, since he escaped notice keeping the rest, but those who got a share of this money assumed that it had come from Athens for this very purpose. (Hdt. 8.4.2–8.5.3)[2]

An even more famous story of Themistocles' greed and corruption rounds out Herodotus' narrative of Salamis and its aftermath (immediately after the Greek commanders have decided not to destroy Xerxes' pontoon bridge and Themistocles has secretly sent a messenger to Xerxes falsely claiming credit for that decision):

> And the Greeks ... were besieging Andros, wishing to take it. For the Andrians first of the islanders, when Themistocles demanded money from them, were not giving it. But when Themistocles put it to them this way,

---

[2] Plutarch repeats much the same story, though he offers us an interesting alternative in one detail. In place of Themistocles' bribery of Adeimantos, Plutarch substitutes the following account, which he tells us he derives from the fourth-century historian Phanias of Lesbos. (Phanias was 'a contemporary and friend of Theophrastus', according to Podlecki 1975.103–4):

> And Architeles was opposing him most of all the citizens, Architeles who was the trierarch of the sacred vessel and was eager to sail away because he didn't have the money to pay his sailors. At that point, Themistocles egged his crew on even more against him, so that running together, they snatched away his dinner. And when Architeles was dispirited because of this and took it badly, Themistocles sent to him in a box a dinner of bread and meat, having put a talent of silver underneath and urged him, for the moment, to eat his dinner and then, the next day, to take care of his crew. But if he didn't, [he threatened] to denounce him to his fellow citizens as having taken money from the enemy. And Phanias of Lesbos said these things. (*Life of Themstocles* 7.6–7)

that the Athenians had come attended by two great gods, Persuasion and
Necessity – so that they really must give them the money – the Andrians
responded to this by saying that it made perfect sense, then, that Athens
was great and blessed, since she came well [supplied] with the best gods.
But, [they said], since the Andrians, at any rate, had come to the greatest
extremity of poverty, and there were two useless gods who wouldn't leave
their island but really loved the place – namely Poverty and Resourcelessness
– since the Andrians were in possession of these gods, they weren't going
to give money. For never would the power of Athens be greater than their
own powerlessness. These then, having made this answer and refusing to
give money were being besieged. But Themistocles, since he [never] stopped
wanting more (*pleonekteôn*), was sending threatening messages to the other
islanders and demanding money ..., saying that if they will not give the thing
asked, he will lead against them the army of the Greeks and destroy them by
siege. And, saying these things, he collected a great deal of money from the
Karystians and the Parians, who had learned about Andros, that it was being
besieged for medising, and that Themistocles stood in the greatest repute
among the commanders, fearing all this, they were sending money. And
if indeed also others of the islanders contributed, I cannot say; though I
think that also some others gave and not just these alone. And yet, for the
Karystians at least there was no delay of evils on account of this [payment],
but the Parians, having propitiated Themistocles with money, escaped the
expedition. And so Themistocles, setting out from Andros, was amassing
money from the islanders in secret from the other commanders. (Hdt.
8.111–12)

Historians have long been sceptical about the truth-value of these
two anecdotes, pointing out the implausibilities and incoherences
Herodotus' stories contain. In the first anecdote, about the Greeks at
Artemisium, the most obvious objection is strategic: as Herodotus
himself tells us, the fleet at Artemisium was there to support and
protect Leonidas' force at Thermopylae from a rearguard action.
While that force held on, it is nearly inconceivable that the Spartan
admiral Eurybiades would abandon his position. Then there are the
inconsistencies within the account itself: why would the Euboians
bribe an underling when they could bribe the supreme commander
for much less? And why don't the Euboians then take advantage of
the respite thus dearly purchased, since their flocks are still not evacu-
ated several days and naval encounters later (at Hdt. 8.19)?[3] As for
the account of Themistocles' extortion of money from the islanders,
it wears its incoherences right on its face. We are told first that
the entire Greek force was besieging Andros because Themistocles,
threatening them with the *Athenians*, had failed to extort money

---

[3] For these objections (and others), see Macan 1908.(1.2) 363–64; How and Wells
1928.II.236–7, 373–4; Cawkwell 1970.41; Wallace 1974.22–5.

from them. And yet, a little later, it emerges that Andros was under siege 'for medising'; here the narrative, almost in spite of itself, reveals that this was the normal exaction of penalties or indemnities that often followed a successful campaign. Finally, given the presence of the entire Greek force investing Andros, how exactly did Themistocles manage to collect money 'in secret from the other commanders'?[4]

In both these cases, historians have argued, Herodotus' narrative reveals matters of public policy and finance, even as it misrepresents them as moments of private greed and corruption. Thus M. B. Wallace has suggested that the 30 talents from Euboia was in fact the normal *trophê* or support offered to one's naval allies for their assistance, properly divided among the commanders according to their proportional contributions to the entire fleet.[5] Likewise for the exaction of money from the islanders: this seems to have been a common venture by the successful Greek fleet to defray its costs after the Battle of Salamis.

Framed in these terms, Herodotus' strange and incoherent narratives make more sense, but, as often, ancient historians' procedures of reading treat the text simply as a screen or barrier, through which we must penetrate to get at 'the facts' concealed behind. Happily, according to this style of reading, seeing through the screen is ultimately unproblematic, so that we will eventually all agree on what 'the facts' at issue are. From my perspective as a literary scholar, the problem of this approach is that it completely ignores the *textuality* of texts – what's on the screen, what Herodotus actually says. For I take it as axiomatic that texts are systems of representations, not simple unmediated reflections – or distortions – of 'what really happened', but internally coherent signifying systems that stand in some complicated relation to cultural practice and ideology. Thus, as a literary scholar and cultural historian, I want to focus on the screen itself and ask why these particular details? Why are these particular stories told about *Themistocles*? Why (especially if these were public

---

[4] For critiques of this Herodotean narrative, see Macan 1908.(1.2) 534–7; How and Wells 1928.II.272; Barth 1965; Cawkwell 1970.42–3; Wallace 1974.27 with n.15; Cresci Marrone 1986. Cresci Marrone goes further, suggesting that the story of the dialogue between Themistocles and the Andrians was retrojected from the campaign of Perikles against the islands in 450 (Cresci Marrone 1986.115–21, following the lead of vague hints in Macan 1908.534). This theory, if correct, poses all the more urgently the question, why was this story felt to be appropriate to Themistocles? Cf. also Barth 1965, who understands Themistocles' *pleonexia* here as greed for empire, citing as parallels for this political use of the term Hdt. 7.149.3, 158.1; Thuc. 1.77.3, 4.61.5.

[5] Wallace 1974.22–9, following and elaborating Cawkewell 1970.41; cf. Pritchett 1971.46–8.

ventures and exchanges) are they represented as private profit,
secrecy and corruption? What does Phanias of Lesbos' elaboration
add to the tale as a signifying system? And finally, in the case of
Themistocles' little dialogue with the Andrians, what are the generic
affiliations of Herodotus' story – and what is the significance of these
generic and stylistic choices?[6]

II

But here I need to pause for a moment and put this in the context of
what I've found about the interrelation of money and representation
in earlier periods. It is my contention that coinage was adopted from
the East – from Lydia – by the Greek cities in the period 550–525 BC
at least partly as a political token, a means of asserting the city's
authority to constitute and control regimes of value. And this is an
assertion of the city's authority not just in relation to outside – other
cities with their own coinages – but also in relation to an internal elite
that had traditionally controlled the highest material and symbolic
values through the para-political order of gift exchange. This assertion of civic authority did not go unchallenged and unopposed: what
is striking is the almost complete occlusion of any mention of coinage
in contemporary literary texts.[7] This, I think, becomes explicable
when we recall Ian Morris's model of two opposing traditions in
archaic poetry – what he calls 'middling' and 'elitist' strands. According to Morris, the middling tradition supported the newly emergent
polis or city-state as its source of authority, while the elitist tradition,
in opposition, founded its authority, its right to rule, on privileged
links to the gods, the heroes and the East.[8] The great strength of
Morris's analysis (from my perspective as a literary scholar) is that
it attends to and makes sense of systematic correlations between
archaic Greek genre, performance context and ideological position.

---

[6] Furthermore, historians' explanations of why Herodotus' narrative should be distorted
in just this way rarely account for the particularity of the Themistocles narratives. Thus, historians suggest that Herodotus' anti-Themistoclean bias arises from (1) hostility to
Themistocles after his exile and defection to Persia; or (2) vilification of Themistocles by
political opponents in Athens – (a) Alkmeonids assumed to be Herodotus' sources (How and
Wells 1928.I.42–3; but against this, see Thomas 1989.264–82); or (b) pro-Spartan politicians
(Cawkwell 1970). And yet, none of these 'explanations' explains why the kinds of stories told
about Themistocles are different from those told, e.g., about the failure and fall of Miltiades
after Marathon (Herodotus 6.132–6). Conversely, Fornara 1971.66–74 strenuously denies
that Herodotus' portrait of Themistocles is hostile or biased at all, but he completely ignores
the Themistocles-money stories at 8.4–5, 111–12. For a more balanced account of
Themistocles in Herodotus, see Podlecki 1975.67–72.
[7] Cf. Laroche 1949.232–3; von Reden 1995.200, 205–6.
[8] Morris 1996, 2000.155–91.

Thus the middling position tends to be that espoused in the publicly performed genres of iambic and (some) elegy, while the elitist position represents the oppositional voice of monodic lyric, performed within the confines of the aristocratic symposium. Publicly performed choral lyric, finally, is often the space where the two positions are combined and mediated.[9]

Most of the literary production contemporary with the earliest use of coinage represents the oppositional voice of the symposium – Morris's elitist position. In so far as it implicitly rejects the city as the ultimate authority, this position is also suspicious of – even hostile towards – coinage as a symbol of the city's power to constitute and regulate value. We see this opposition most clearly in the way in which archaic sympotic poetry constitutes a set of highly value-laden binaries, opposing the pristine space of the elite symposium to the debased and corrupted exchanges of the agora; opposing the symbolic 'refined gold' of aristocratic *hetairoi* [friends] to the 'counterfeit coin' of the excluded *kakoi* [the 'bad' anti-elite], opposing the stable and secure circuit of elite gift exchange to the indiscriminate and promiscuous circulation of money in the public sphere. These oppositions construct a material symbology, if you will, through which divergent positions within the city contest the culture's most fundamental values. Long before the explicit articulation of abstract political theory, ideological battles are being fought through the deployment of material practices and material discourses.[10]

One such ideological battle I think we can detect in the literary remains is a fierce conflict raging (through the sixth century and even into the fifth) over what constitutes the long- and short-term transactional orders. I take these terms from the anthropologists Jonathan Parry and Maurice Bloch; according to Parry and Bloch, many societies constitute the activities of exchange and economics as two separate but organically articulated transactional orders (each with its own moral inflection). The long-term transactional order is always positively valued, for it reproduces the larger social and cosmic order through proper relations to the gods, to the dead, and between social agents. This sphere precludes the pursuit of individualistic profit. Yet, individuals must work and eat, so every culture must allow a space for 'individual acquisition'. This is the short-term transactional order, which 'tends to be morally undetermined since it concerns individual purposes which are largely irrelevant to the long-term

---

[9] This final claim is, in a sense, the weight of the argument of Kurke 1991.
[10] For detailed discussion of these oppositions, see Kurke 1999.

order'. Between the short- and long-term transactional orders, every culture must have a conversion system, whereby the profits of the short-term cycle can be transformed into the altruistic, community-building elements of long-term reproduction. Conversely, the short-term order only retains its moral neutrality as long as it remains separate from and subordinate to the needs and activities of the long-term cycle.[11]

I would suggest that the definition and balance of these two transactional orders are precisely what is being contested in sixth- and fifth-century Greece, between Morris's 'elitist' and 'middling' positions. Each position claims for itself and its practices privileged access to the long-term order, while relegating the other position to the short-term transactional order. The city constitutes itself as the final instance, the summit of the long-term transactional order, to which citizens owe their loyalty and their lives. Thus, for example, gift-giving, so positively valued in elitist terms, becomes negatively inflected as 'bribery' (*dôrodokia*) when it is felt to interfere with a citizen's obligations to his civic community.[12] In opposition to this civic ideology there exists a competing anti-civic ideology (most at home in the aristocratic symposium) which is, among other things, hostile to coinage. This hostility to coinage in the elitist tradition takes a particular form – it is part of the consistent misrepresentation of the public sphere as the domain of disembedded economics. In other terms, the elitist tradition misrepresents the agora as *only* an economic space, repressing its political dimension because it wants to deny the authority of the public sphere. Hence the association in elitist discourse of coinage with *kapêleia* [petty huckstering], deceit, and profit unconstrained by social value, as well as the linkage of coinage to other elitist representations of the public sphere as associated with counterfeiting, prostitution and general lowlife criminality. (An example of all these themes bundled together is Anakreon's poem abusing Artemon – fr. 358 *PMG*.)[13] Thus I would contend that the motivation for this kind of representation and misrepresentation is ultimately political, although it expresses itself as morally evaluative discourse about money and the economy.

[11] For 'long- and short-term transactional orders', see Parry and Bloch 1989.23–30; quotation taken from p. 26. For applications of Parry and Bloch's model of long- and short-term transactional orders to the ancient Greek economy, see Morris 1993, 2000.133–4, and von Reden 1995.3–4, 96–7.

[12] On bribery in ancient Greece, see Harvey 1985; von Reden 1995.94–5, 117–20, 132–4.

[13] For extended discussion of this cluster of associations in Anakreon's fragment, see Kurke 1999.187–191.

III

It is precisely in the context of these kinds of representational battles that I would like to locate the stories that cluster around Themistocles. For the figure of Themistocles in our texts presides over a period when the spending of money in the public sphere was being conceptualised in new ways and on a whole new scale. In contrast both to the para-political circuits of elite gift exchange and to liturgies performed by the richest citizens to earn the city's *charis* [gratitude], the city itself in this period invested its public funds on an enormous scale to build and maintain a fleet. The public fleet was the basis for Athenian naval hegemony and represented a whole new kind of military expenditure. Along with ships, there were public building programmes – first the city walls and the Long Walls, then the conversion of Peiraeus into a usable port, which required quite massive public works including dockyards and shipsheds (all three projects, according to tradition, were Themistoclean initiatives).[14] At the same time, within the city, we get the institution of pay for office, for jury duty and, at the end of the century, even for assembly attendance.

We can see all these developments as aspects of the city's assertion of its control of the long-term transactional order – indeed, we can see them as the invention of the concept of independent public-sphere spending. This argument conforms well to that of Lisa Kallet-Marx, who has recently pointed out how novel within a fifth-century context is the idea that money = power (which she traces in Thucydides and other texts of the second half of the fifth century).[15] Though it is a natural enough equation for us, Kallet-Marx insists that this formulation appears at a particular moment in Greek history, closely linked to the building and maintenance of an Athenian state fleet. For, as several historians have noted, the shift from land to sea power requires the expenditure of state money on an unprecedented scale.[16] Kallet-Marx also tentatively suggests that this way of thinking about money and power may first have been propounded for an Athenian civic audience by Themistocles himself, in the debate recorded by Herodotus at 7.144.[17] At this point, according to Herodotus, shortly

[14] On the public expense of a navy, see Cawkwell 1970.41; Lewis 1990.246, 254; Kallet-Marx 1993, 1994; Rosenbloom 1995.95–8, 107–10. On the substantial building projects required to convert Peiraeus into a usable port, see Frost 1980.175–7. The ancient sources which credit these building projects to Themistocles' initiative are Thuc. 1.90–3; Aristoph. *Knights* 815; Paus. 1.1.2; Plut. *Them.* 19; D.S. 11.39–40; Nep. *Them.* 6–7; Polyaenus 1.30.5.

[15] Kallet-Marx 1993, 1994.

[16] Lewis 1990.246, 254; Kallet-Marx 1993, 1994; Rosenbloom 1995.95–8.

[17] Kallet-Marx 1994.244–5.

before the Persian invasion of 480, Themistocles persuaded the Athenians to use the windfall of silver from Laureion to build a fleet, rather than distributing it among the citizens.

Kallet-Marx thus posits that the real Themistocles was himself the 'inventor' of the conception of this use of money in the public sphere. Though I find her argument about a shift in the ideology of money compelling, I am reluctant to follow her in this last step, because I think that the multifarious literary traditions we have suggest that the process was much more complicated. The Aristotelian *Ath. Pol.* preserves a very different tradition, according to which Themistocles and Aristeides worked in common (*koinêi, Ath. Pol.* 23.4) to rebuild the walls of Athens, and in which *Aristeides* was the prime mover of the shift from land to sea power and of *misthophoria* [payment for political office] in the democracy:

> Athens' confidence increased and she built up a significant financial reserve; Aristides recommended them to seize the hegemony and to live in the city rather than the countryside; there would be a livelihood for all, some on expeditions, others on duty, and others in government; in this way they would hold the hegemony. The people agreed, took control, and treated their allies more tyrannically except for the peoples of Chios, Lesbos and Samos; they used them as guards of empire, and so allowed them to retain their own constitutions and such possessions as they had.
>
> The result was also affluence for the masses, as Aristides had suggested. More than twenty thousand men earned their living as a result of the tribute, the taxation and the money the empire brought in. (*Ath. Pol.* 24.1–3; trans. J. M. Moore)

It is not my intention to claim that it was *really* Aristeides and not Themistocles who masterminded the major conceptual shifts that enabled Athenian empire:[18] instead, I would suggest that a whole set of canny politicians and leaders (including Themistocles and Aristeides as well as others) helped lay the ideological foundations for empire. What I want to emphasise instead is how consistently and compellingly the representations of Themistocles credit him with this radical reconceptualisation of transactional orders. Whether or not Themistocles achieved this all by himself, we'll never know; instead, I suggest we need to think of prominent figures like Themistocles and Aristeides as symbolic operators – magnets or focalisers through which Greek texts think through these issues. This is to turn 'great man' history on its head: to read these mythologised figures as allegories of complex ideological processes, rather than simply reinscribing ancient Greek allegories as literal historical 'fact'.

---

[18] Such is the argument of Piccirilli 1984 and part of the argument of Schmitt-Pantel 1992.179–208.

Much of the mythology around Themistocles (which we find already in our earliest textual references to him) turns around the proper relation of public and private, and the proper uses of money in relation to the navy and naval power. This is true of both positive and negative representations of Themistocles, but I would contend further that there's a whole set of topoi that belong to a coherent, anti-democratic, anti-imperial response to these civic developments, coded through Themistocles as a symbolic operator. To offer a template or blueprint for this hostile tradition, I'd like to do a reading of Timocreon fr. 1 (727 *PMG*), probably our earliest preserved literary reference to Themistocles. This will allow me first to demonstrate the ideological and discursive struggles we can find played out in literary texts, and then to establish a vocabulary of tropes and topoi that we will find repeated in portraits of Themistocles through the fifth century and later.

Timocreon, an exiled Rhodian aristocrat, wrote a poem abusing Themistocles, which is preserved in Plutarch's *Life*:

> But if you praise Pausanias, and you Xanthippos, and you Leotychides, *I* praise Aristeides as the single best man to come from holy Athens, since Leto conceived a hatred for Themistocles – liar, unjust traitor, who, persuaded by scampish money, failed to restore Timocreon to his homeland Ialysos, though he was his *xeinos* [guest-friend]. But taking three talents of silver, he went sailing off to the devil, unjustly restoring some, driving out others, and killing still others. But underhandedly crammed with silver, he entertained (*pandokeue*) laughably at the Isthmos, furnishing cold meats; but they were eating and praying that there be no attention paid to Themistocles (*or* 'that there be no sacrificial portion/joint for Themistocles').[19]

Although historians argue about the exact date, this poem (which seems to be complete) was probably composed in the early 470s. Traditionally, historians have read this poem to establish 'facts': did the Athenian fleet sail as far as Rhodes in 480? Or was it 478? When did Aristeides rise to prominence in the Delian League (for which Leto in line 4 has been read as an allegory)?[20] More recently, an ancient historian has used this text as proof that Themistocles tried to establish radical democracies throughout the islands in the 470s.[21] Again, as I noted with Herodotus, this is to treat the poem itself as

---

[19] This translation of *ôran* as 'sacrificial portion/joint' was suggested by W. J. Slater *apud* Robertson 1980.62n.9. For the usage, cf. SIG 1037 (a Milesian inscription of the fourth/third century BC).

[20] Kirchhoff 1876; von Wilamowitz-Moellendorff 1893.1.138; Beloch 1916.2.2.144; Bowra 1961.352–5; Fornara 1966; Meiggs 1972.414–5.

[21] Robertson 1980.

a screen through which we have to penetrate to get at the 'real facts' concealed behind.

Literary scholars in the meantime have had a different set of problems with this poem – problems of literary decorum. First, though the poem's brevity and content suggest that it was meant for sympotic performance, its metrical structure is that of choral lyric.[22] Second, whatever kind of lyric it is, the poem exhibits an unsettling mix of very high style and the coarse language of iambic abuse.[23] In 1983, Ruth Scodel proposed an elegant and compelling solution to the literary problems the poem presents – a solution which, I want to argue, has important implications for historians as well. Scodel suggested that Timocreon's poem is monodic sympotic lyric [solo song performed at private symposia] parodying or masquerading as choral victory ode [choral song performed in public in praise of an athletic victor], that is, blame pretending to be praise. This would account for both the metrical and stylistic anomalies of Timocreon's little poem.[24] Thus the triad begins in good epinikian fashion with praise, only to pivot on the mention of Leto's hatred into explicit abuse of Themistocles. The epode then ends with a scene at the Isthmos, a parody of the traditional banquet thrown by an athletic victor to celebrate his victory. As part of this interpretation, Scodel suggests that the mention of Leto is a play on the epinikian convention that the victor has won through the special favour of a particular divinity; that Themistocles is hated by Leto, the gentlest of all the gods,[25] is an argument *a fortiori* that his betrayal of *xenia* [guest-friendship] has made him an abomination to all divinities. Scodel adds (quite rightly) that Leto enters the poem as part of the private domain of *xenia* and Themistocles' betrayal of Timocreon, and is therefore highly unlikely to allegorise the Delian League. Thus in this case, formal, generic considerations preclude the kind of interpretation that historians have tried to impose on the poem. Ignoring

[22] On the metrical problem, see Bowra 1961.351–2; Smyth 1963.333, 335–6; Campbell 1967.406; Kirkwood 1974.182. Stehle (1994.510n.13) contends that the metre is not a problem at all, citing Pindar fr. 123 Snell-Maehler for an example of sympotic poetry composed in choral metre. Still, I think earlier scholars are correct, since Pindar's poem is the only other exception in extant lyric.

[23] This mix of high and low style has incurred the censure of literary critics; thus Bowra 1961.355; Kirkwood 1974.183. I would add to the category of those elements that violate proper lyric decorum the explicit mention of money (three times!). An investigation of all the occurrences of *to argurion* meaning 'money' down through the fifth century reveals that it is a term almost completely restricted to comedy and prose (history, oratory and philosophy); it occurs nowhere else in extant lyric.

[24] Scodel 1983.

[25] Scodel (1983.104–5) citing Hes. *Theog.* 404–6, Pindar *Paian* 12.12 S-M, and Plato, *Kratylos* 406a.

issues of form and genre is fatal for historical reconstructions based on literary texts.

That is a negative conclusion, but I believe that Scodel's analysis allows us to say a great deal that's positive about the surface of the text. Precisely this generic mixture – monody masquerading as choral, blame masquerading as praise – opens a space for challenging one model of 'regimes of value' and replacing it with another. Performing for a small group of like-minded reactionary symposiasts, Timocreon systematically inverts the public values endorsed by epinikion. Thus the introductory priamel and the shift from strophe to antistrophe implicitly reject the civic accomplishment of the heroes of the Persian Wars as the highest value.[26] Instead, the antistrophe asserts the absolute value of the para-political dimension of *xenia* and aristocratic relations, so that the worst crime of all is their betrayal for money (hence the shock value of the mention of money, emphatically repeated three times in five lines).[27] Finally, the epode rhetorically transforms Themistocles' pursuit of *timê* [honour] or symbolic capital into the most debased economic activity. Scholars are divided on whether we are to imagine the scene in the epode as Themistocles' competing for honour at the Isthmian Games (in 478 or later) or jockeying for the *aristeia* [prize for the bravest] of Salamis at the Isthmos in 480. There is no way to be sure, but, like Scodel, I am partial to the latter interpretation.[28] Herodotus tells us (8.123–4) that, after trying to extort money from Andros, the victors of Salamis dedicated *acrothina* [tithes of booty], divided the remainder of the booty, and sailed to the Isthmos in order to award the prize for valour to the Greek commander who was most worthy. Voting at the altar

[26] This is true whether the heroes of the priamel are meant to be read 'straight' or ironically; for different views on this problem (which is, I believe, insoluble), see Fornara 1966.257–61; Robertson 1980.65–6 Scodel 1983.103; Stehle 1994.510–16.

[27] Cf. Stehle 1994.516: 'the denunciation of Themistokles is organized around the contrast between money and friendship. Themistokles took a bribe to betray a guest-friend. For the members of the symposium, a group that relied on the power of friendship and was always vulnerable to betrayal, the theme was of immediate interest. The singer, by denouncing Themistokles, signals his own hierarchy of values, with friendship at the top.'

[28] For Themistocles at the Isthmian Games, see Maas 1935.1271; Fornara 1966.259n.9; Meiggs 1972.415; Robertson 1980.68; for a reference to the vote on the *aristeia* of Salamis, see Kirchhoff 1876.43–5; Meritt, Wade-Gery and McGregor 1950.185n.10; Podlecki 1975.53; Scodel 1983.106–7. This latter interpretation has been challenged by Stehle 1994, who argues that this event, as narrated by Herodotus, is too particular and not really so bad for Themistocles. Instead, Stehle sees in the reference to the 'Isthmos' simply an obscene sexual insult of Themistocles. While it seems quite plausible that many of Timocreon's terms (especially in the poem's epode) operate as sexual *doubles entendres* insulting Themistocles, I think Stehle is wrong to insist that this sexual reading must preclude other (e.g., political) readings of the poem. Thus, I would accept Stehle's reading, but combine it with Scodel's important insights about the poem's play with genre.

of Poseidon, each Greek commander voted for himself first, while the majority voted for Themistocles second. The result – just what you'd expect: only single votes for first place, but Themistocles wins second by a wide margin. At that point, Herodotus tells us, the other commanders were unwilling to give the prize to Themistocles out of envy, so instead they all sailed home with the issue undecided.

If we compare this narrative with the last lines of Timocreon's poem, we find distinct similarities of outcome, even if the emphasis is very different.[29] On this reading, the 'they' of the last line are the other commanders, who accept Themistocles' hospitality but pray that there be no 'regard' or 'attention paid' to him. And indeed, in the end, his position as everybody's second choice neatly reciprocates his stingy serving of 'cold meats' – that is, leftovers. The preceding lines of the epode, then, describe Themistocles' attempt to win votes by displays of hospitality, but in language that simultaneously transforms that activity from aristocratic liberality to the most debased, venal activity imaginable. The key term – the shifter – here is *pandokeue*, for in high style (as, for example, in the public praise of epinikion) it signifies the generous hospitality of gods and aristocratic victors.[30] But in low-class contexts, where money changes hands, this is the technical term for 'innkeeping'.[31]

This single word is perhaps Timocreon's most brilliant effect in projecting blame on the screen of praise, because, at least for the moment of its utterance, we see double: Themistocles the generous host overlaid with Themistocles the money-grubbing innkeeper. To be sure, the surrounding context nudges *pandokeue* almost immediately in the degraded direction of innkeeping – the collocation with *argurion* [silver], *geloiôs* [laughably] and finally 'cold meats' signals unequivocally its proper generic and socio-economic register. But I want to linger for a moment on the double effect of *pandokeue* to make a point. Sitta von Reden has emphasised that money in archaic and classical Greece is not bad in itself; everything depends on context.[32] This is an important and valuable point, but I would add that, on many occasions, context is unstable and contested, and it is precisely what is being forged and reforged *by* and *in* representation.

---

[29] As Kirchhoff (1876.43–5) already saw clearly.

[30] This is particularly true of the adjective *pandokos* (Pindar O.3.17, O.4.15, P.8.61; Aeschylus *Choephoroi* 662; Sophokles fr. 274 Radt), but also the verb *pandokeuô*: cf. Hdt. 4.95.3.

[31] For the technical terms *pandokeion, pandokeus, pandokeutria* and *pandokeuô*, see Aristoph. *Frogs* 114, 550, *Wealth* 426; Demosthenes 19.158; Aeschines 2.97; Plato *Laws* 918b–e; Theophr. *Char.* 6.5; Polybius 2.15.5–6; Arrian *Epiktetos* 1.24.14.

[32] von Reden 1995.171–216 and especially 1997.

Whether we think Themistocles is a war-hero and noble host or an innkeeper depends on whether we agree or disagree with the world of values Timocreon's poem conjures.

Thus the poem itself participates in a significant contest of paradigms, attempting to reinscribe an older aristocratic order. And I would contend it does this not just in its content, but also in its form. As a send-up of public, choral poetry in the context of sympotic monody, as blame overlaid on praise, Timocreon's poem enacts a generic displacement of the values of the city in favour of those of the elite symposium. Furthermore, as Eva Stehle points out, this poem owes its survival to an extended sympotic afterlife – to its continuous reperformance (probably in Athens and throughout Greece) as part of the repertoire of the symposium.[33] This performance context in turn opens up a vista for us, exposing the proper setting for a tradition that is equally hostile to Themistocles, the public sphere, and the monetary practices of naval hegemony. This is, then, a tradition of oligarchically inclined elites, both outside of Athens (like Timocreon, a medising aristocrat from Rhodes) and within Athens (those who reperformed and thereby preserved Timocreon's little *tour de force*).[34]

IV

At this point, I want to recap the anti-Themistoclean tropes and topoi that emerge most clearly from Timocreon's poem, and then consider briefly how elements of this tradition show up later in Herodotos, Aristophanes and Plato. First, I would suggest that Timocreon's poem begins by engaging in a popular sympotic game, asserting the speaker's opinion of who or what is 'the best' in a particular category.[35] Timocreon's opening priamel suggests an ironic turn on the question, 'Who was the best commander in the Persian Wars?'. Many other texts suggest that this was a game much indulged in after the Persian Wars: thus, for example, Herodotus cannot mention Aristeides without affirming that he was 'the best' (Hdt. 8.79.1,

---

[33] Stehle 1994; cf. Stehle 1997.14.

[34] See Meiggs 1972.406–12 on opposition to empire by an oligarchic Athenian elite. For Herodotos' sources on Themistocles as mainly aristocratic/oligarchic and mainly hostile to Athens, see Barth 1965.37; Fornara 1971.74. It is worth noting that many of the ancient sources we know of on Themistocles – Critias (ap. Aelian *VH* 10.17), Ion of Chios, Stesimbrotos of Thasos, Phanias of Lesbos – were oligarchic, while the last three came from cities oppressed by the Athenian empire. On Ion, Critias and Stesimbrotos, see Frost 1980.16–18.

[35] Fränkel 1955.90–2; Burnett 1982.280–90.

8.95.1), while he represents Themistocles himself laying claim to that status in a secret message to the Persian king (Hdt. 8.110.3). We might call this 'priamel history', but it is more than just a debate about who's the best; it is also a way of formulating issues by thinking in opposed pairs. In this context, it's worth noticing that Themistocles is almost always paired in anecdotes with a figure representing an opposing style of warfare, aristocratic display, or the constitution and running of empire: in Herodotus, implicitly with Aristeides; in Thucydides, the story of the fall of Pausanias seems inexorably to call forth the paired account of Themistocles (1.128–38); in Plutarch, Themistocles and Aristeides form perfect complements to each other, while, on occasion, Themistocles is also paired and contrasted to the proper aristocratic magnificence of Kimon (e.g., Aristotle *Eudemian Ethics* 1233b10; Plut. *Life of Themistocles* 5.4).[36]

And this brings me to my second point about Timocreon's abuse of Themistocles. Money in Timocreon's poem is associated with private profit and corruption, and opposed to the proper order of aristocratic *xenia*: in this way, the poem leaves no space for the honourable use of money in the public sphere. This technique of occlusion is perhaps clearest in the epode, which represents Themistocles' honourable public activity (providing feasts at the Isthmos) as debased private activity – as 'innkeeping' and 'furnishing cold meats'. This last characterization especially suggests the commodification of food in opposition to a sacral order of sacrifice – 'cold meat' is the product of sacrifice that has been sold in the market rather than shared out in a common sacrificial meal.[37] Innkeeping also for the Greeks represents the worst kind of venal, corrupt activity. Thus Plato's Athenian lawgiver in the *Laws* aligns it with *kibdêleia* [counterfeiting] and *kapêleia*, and wonders how to make it an honourable activity free from the basest reproaches. He suggests the following thought experiment:

[36] For acknowledgement that Themistocles and Aristeides already formed a schematic pair in the fifth century, see Meiggs 1972.42, 48; Podlecki 1975.71; Rhodes 1981.346; Stehle 1994.522 with n.63. For the opposition of Themistocles and Kimon, see Podlecki 1975.80.

[37] Berthiaume 1982.62–9. For the opposition of sacral and commodified economies of meat in the epode of Timocreon's poem, Slater's suggested pun on *ôra* (as 'joint of sacrificial meat'; specifically 'portion of honour' awarded to the officiating priest) becomes particularly appropriate (Slater *apud* Robertson 1980.62n.9). When Themistocles, acting as 'innkeeper', served 'cold meats', the others 'were eating and praying that there would be no sacrificial portion of honour' for him – i.e., that he would not be readmitted into a shared sacrificial community. It is perhaps significant that one of the very few texts in all antiquity that refers specifically to a butcher selling parts of sacrificial animals is the late, popular *Life of Aesop* (ch. 51–4 Perry) – a low text about a low (ugly, foreign, slave) character. On the significance of this scene of sacrificial and post-sacrificial practices, see Isenberg 1975.

Yet if someone … were to compel (now it's laughable to utter this, but nevertheless it's going to be uttered) the best men everywhere (*aristous andras*) to become innkeepers for a certain period of time, or to carry on retail trade, or do one of such things …, we would know how friendly and desirable each of these things is; and, if it were to be practised according to an uncorrupted principle, all such activities would be honoured in the guise of a mother and nurse. But now, when someone has established houses for the sake of innkeeping (*kapêleias heneka*) in deserted spots having lengthy roads in every direction, and receives, with welcome resting places, those who have come to be at a loss, providing calm tranquillity to those driven by the violence of savage storms, and refreshment in stifling heat, he doesn't proceed after this to follow up his welcome as he would if he were receiving comrades (*hetairous*), and give friendly guest-gifts (*philika … xenia*), but instead, as if they were enemy prisoners who had fallen into his hands, he releases them on payment of very large, unjust and impure ransoms! It is these and similar faults that have in all such cases correctly discredited the provision of assistance to those at a loss. So the lawgiver must always contrive medicine for these things. (*Laws* 918d8–919b4, trans. T. L. Pangle, with slight modifications)

The paradoxical force of Plato's thought experiment depends on the absolute disjunction commonly assumed between the protocols of elite *xenia* and the unscrupulous exploitation of innkeeping (precisely the opposition Timocreon's poem constructs). Theophrastus also shows us the negative associations of innkeeping, when he characterises the 'insane man' as

terribly good at innkeeping (*pandokeusai*) and pimping and tax-farming and not refusing any shameful business, but [he'll] act as herald, he'll cook, and play dice; he won't support his mother, he'll be led away on a charge of theft, and he'll spend more time in jail than in his own home. (Theophr. *Char.* 6.5–6)

Theophrastus' 'insane man' is the paradigm of disembedded economic shamelessness, prepared to take on the most degrading activities for personal profit. Together, innkeeping and furnishing cold meats locate Themistocles' activities squarely in a corrupt, short-term transactional order, systematically opposing them to the long-term transactional order of aristocratic guest-friendship (here even endorsed by the goddess Leto).

I focus on these potent images because I think that they, along with the corrupted values they figure, recur throughout a tradition of anti-Themistoclean rhetoric and anecdote – a tradition whose generic affiliations remain coherent over many centuries.[38] Thus I return

---

[38] To some extent, the coherence and continuity of this tradition undermine the confidence of many ancient historians that we can trust the fifth-century sources on Themistocles (and Aristeides), but that the fourth-century and later sources are 'tainted' by rhetoric and philo-

to Herodotus' Themistocles narratives, which represent a tradition hostile to public-sphere spending in the domain of Athenian foreign policy and imperial activity. Herodotus' account of Themistocles' extortion of money from the islanders (8.111–12), as has been noted, barely conceals a co-ordinated naval effort to exact war indemnities from the Greek states that had medised. What is striking from the perspective of the discourses we have been considering is how much Herodotus' account resonates with Plato's remarks on the moral corruption of innkeeping (so, for example, Plato's characterisation of the innkeeper's 'victims' as 'those who have come to be at a loss', from whom he exacts 'large, unjust and impure ransoms'). It is also worth noting that the low genre of fable (here of the competing gods Persuasion and Necessity vs. Poverty and Resourcelessness) erupts in Herodotus' text together with Themistocles. Thus, not only is Themistocles himself represented as low-class, but he is consistently affiliated with low-class literary genres.[39] Finally, Herodotus' narrative wryly represents Themistocles' exactions as the cynical debasement of a sacral order of exchange, since he claims 'Persuasion' and 'Necessity' as Athens' patron divinities. That Herodotus himself felt the inappropriateness of invoking divinity to extort money is revealed by the language he uses to close the anecdote: 'The Parians, having propitiated (*hilasamenoi*) Themistocles with money, escaped the expedition' (Hdt. 8.112.3). *Hilasamenoi*, as commentators have noted, is properly used of propitiating a god:[40] the use of the verb here with Themistocles as its object registers his corrupt replacement of the long-term transactional order with the basest profit-seeking of the short-term.

The same tension between transactional orders informs Herodotus' narrative of Themistocles' bribery by the Euboians (Hdt. 8.4–5), as Phanias' imaginative elaboration of the story confirms. Indeed, we might even say that the oppositions in Phanias' version

sophical agendas (cf. Meiggs 1972.8–10; Podlecki 1975.77–102; Frost 1980.19–39). Part of my purpose here is to demonstrate a coherent logic of representation that extends back to Timocreon, Aristophanes and Herodotus, and forward, through Plato and the philosophical tradition, to Plutarch.

[39] Notice Macan's reference to 'the fable of Themistocles and the Andrians' (Macan 1908.534). Themistocles' own low-class origin is, I think, part of the point of Herodotus' *neôsti* [recently] when Themistocles is first introduced (7.143) – he is an *arriviste*. (For debate on what *neôsti* here means, see Cawkwell 1970.40; Podlecki 1975.68–9; Evans 1987.) By the time of Plutarch, this intimation of low-class origin has hardened into fact: cf. Plut. *Them.* 1–2. Throughout the tradition, Themistocles is frequently associated with blame, beast fable and comedy, while Aristeides tends to be associated with the high genres of epic and tragedy (cf. Timocreon frr. 3/729, 4/730 PMG; Plut. *Them.* 11.6, 18.4, 18.6, 29.4; Plut. *Arist.* 3.5–4.3, 24.3, 24.6).

[40] Cf. Macan 1908.537; How and Wells 1928.II.273.

between a proper sacral order and private profit-mongering are overdetermined. Thus Phanias replaces the obstreperous Corinthian commander Adeimantus with the 'trierach of the sacred vessel, Architeles', while he foregrounds the commodification of food and bare subsistence in the form of Themistocles' bribe. Here, Architeles wants to withdraw not out of cowardice (as in Herodotus), but because he lacks the funds properly to pay his crew (*chorêgein*). Into this miniature community with its hierarchy of sacral duty and responsible liturgical service, Themistocles intrudes, pitting crew against captain and replacing proper pay with lawless theft. He then plays 'innkeeper' to Architeles, furnishing him with bread and 'cold meats' and making the honourable captain completely dependent on private graft.[41] Perhaps the oddest detail of all is Architeles' command of a sacred ship. As Frank Frost observes:

> One thing is almost certain: the story, with all its details, is false. The insistence of the crew on being paid, and even the very existence of a 'sacred ship', may be anachronistic. We know that in later times, at least, the crew of the *Paralos* was paid four obols a day by the state.[42]

Thus Phanias' little anecdote repeats – only more stridently – the same occlusion of state spending that Herodotus' original narrative had enacted. What replaces the public pay of sailors in both narratives is the officious private graft of the 'innkeeper' Themistocles. who feeds the navy yet still reaps an exorbitant profit for himself.[43]

The reduction of state spending to 'innkeeping' that Herodotus' and Phanias' narratives detail in the domain of Athenian naval activity is repeated in other sources for Themistocles' treatment of the demos at home. For example, in Aristophanes' *Knights*, Themistocles hovers behind the action of the play, a kind of 'patron saint' presiding over the corrupted activities of the demagogues of the 420s. In the play's representation, post-Periklean politicians are a series of low-class 'mongers' (*pôlai*, 129–43), for whom the public sphere is merely a degraded agora in which to hawk their wares.[44] But simultaneously, Aristophanes portrays the demagogues of the

---

[41] Notice that Phanias' contemporary Theophrastus, in the passage quoted above, also links theft and innkeeping as characteristics of the 'insane man'.

[42] Frost 1980.107, citing Harpokration s.v. *Paralos* and Jordan 1975.157–9.

[43] It may also be relevant, as Boromir Jordan argues, that the crews of the sacred ships in Athens were 'cult associations or artificial *genê* [tribes]' unified by worship of common cults and rituals like the *kreanomia*, or 'distribution of sacrificial meat' (Jordan 1975.167–76, quotation from p. 176). Thus Themistocles' intervention undermines a sacrificial community with self-interested thievery and deceit.

[44] Cf., e.g., *Knights* 168–76, 218, 394, 979. I take the translation 'monger' (which, like Greek *pôlês*, does not normally occur uncompounded) from Sommerstein 1981.150.

420s as unscrupulous slaves competing for the favour of their fickle master Demos by offering him ever-new culinary treats and by cynically manipulating his gullible faith in riddling oracles. In all these domains, Themistocles is an honoured precursor, so it is no accident that his shade is conjured early in the play by Nikias, suggesting a manly form of suicide by drinking bull's blood ('for the death of Themistocles is the best one to choose', 82–4).[45] Later, the association of Themistocles with current practices is made explicit; when Paphlagon dares to claim that he 'has done many more good things for the city than Themistocles' (811–12), the Sausage-Seller responds with an outburst of paratragic indignation:

> O city of Argos, do you hear what sorts of things he says! You vie (*antipherizeis*) with Themistocles?
> Themistocles, who made our city full to the brim when he found her half-full,
> And besides, when she was breakfasting, he kneaded Peiraeus-cake for her as a second helping,
> And taking away none of our ancient [privileges], he added new fish.
> But you have sought to make the Athenians nothing
> By walling through and singing oracles – you who vie (*antipherizôn*) with Themistocles!
> And that one is exiled from the land, while you wipe your fingers on Achillean cake! (*Knights* 813–19)

The repeated *antipherizeis–antipherizôn* locate us squarely in the domain of 'priamel history', in which current demagogues compete to outdo the achievements of Themistocles. And these achievements are precisely represented as 'innkeeping' – gratifying Demos' appetites with a full cup, the Peiraeus 'kneaded' for the city like bread, and 'new fish added to old [privileges]'.

Strikingly, when Demos appears rejuvenated at the end of the play, Themistocles emphatically disappears, along with all traces of naval empire and the commodification of food:

> Sau: Such as he was when he used to dine together with Aristeides and Miltiades.
>
> ...
>
> Sau: Here is that one to see, wearing [golden] cicadas, radiant in his ancient garb,

---

[45] In several passages, the characterisation of the Sausage-Seller echoes or conjures up Themistocles. Thus, for example, the Sausage-Seller's assertion that he 'doesn't even know *mousikê* [lit. 'music'; have proper education] except *grammata* [(basic) reading and writing] (*Knights* 188–9) echoes a story told by Ion of Chios about Themistocles (cf. Plut. *Them.* 2.4, *Kimon* 9.1). In addition, in the oracle contest late in the play, when Paphlagon's oracle mentions a 'wooden wall', the Sausage-Seller insists that he's the only one who can interpret that element correctly.

> Smelling not of mussel-shells, but of peace-libations, anointed with
> myrrh.
> Ch: Hail, O King of the Greeks! We too rejoice with you, for your current
> state is worthy of the city and of the trophy at Marathon! (*Knights*
> 1325, 1331–4)

Here, instead of the relationship of base innkeeping or bribery
between leader and populace, we get positive images of shared
commensality (*xunesitei*), conjoined with a proper sacral order
(*spondôn*). Demos appears transformed, in the garb of an archaic
aristocrat scented with myrrh, and Themistocles' hovering presence
is definitively exorcised by the shades of Aristeides and Miltiades and
the memory of Marathon.[46]

Precisely the same imagery, in the same contexts, informs Plato's
denunciation of fifth-century politicians in the *Gorgias*. Engaging
with Kallikles in a discussion of the 'Four Great Statesmen' of the
fifth century (Miltiades, Themistocles, Kimon and Perikles), Socrates
denies that they were good leaders or any better than current politicians (515d–519b).[47] Socrates' main argument is that a good statesman should, in principle, make the citizens better and more just, and
yet in the end, the demos turned against all four, ostracising, pros-
ecuting and exiling them. This is a negative argument against their
quality as leaders; when it comes to positive critique of their actual
policies, Socrates mentions only two. He initially criticises Perikles
for 'having made the Athenians idlers and cowards and talkers
and moneygrubbers, by first having established the *misthophoria*'
(515e5–7), and later refers generically to the skill of fifth-century
politicians in 'supplying ships and walls and shipyards and many
other such things' (517c2–3).[48] These two policies (as we have seen)
represent a new development of the use of state money in the public
sphere (in both domestic and foreign policy), which together enabled
the rise and dominance of Athenian naval empire. And, as Socrates
and Gorgias had themselves acknowledged earlier in the dialogue,
the building of 'ships and walls and shipyards' was largely the work

---

[46] The 'mussel-shells' negatively contrasted with 'peace-libations' here are a polyvalent
symbol, since they served as voting-tokens in the lawcourts (see Sommerstein 1981.216, citing
Wasps 333, 349), but they are also products of the sea. Thus they signify both democratic
political practice and naval empire.

[47] That this set of fifth-century leaders represented a conventional grouping (as heroes of
the democracy) is suggested by Aelius Aristides' reference to them simply as 'the Four Men'
(*Or.* 46); cf. Dodds 1959.325–6.

[48] Notice Kallikles' response to the charge against Perikles: 'You must have heard these
things from the cauliflower-ear crowd' (515e8–9); i.e., from Lakonising young oligarchs who
liked to hang out in the palaistra [wrestling ground] (cf. Dodds 1959.357).

of Themistocles and then, to a lesser extent, of Perikles (455de).[49] Significantly, it is the mention of 'ships and walls and shipyards' that immediately provokes Socrates' comparison of politicians to 'a retail trader or an importer or a craftsman of these same things, a baker or meat-chef or weaver or shoemaker or tanner' (517d6–e2). For, in comparison to the doctor or athletic trainer, these craftsmen have no knowledge of how to improve the body; they simply pander to its appetites. Socrates concludes his denunciation emphatically:

> You come back a little later saying that there are men who have proved themselves to be noble leaders in the city, and whenever I ask who they are, you seem to me to proffer men in the domain of politics who are most like this, just as if, when I ask you who are the good men concerning gymnastic training or who are good tenders of bodies, you would say to me in all seriousness, Thearion the baker and Mithaikos the one who wrote the handbook on Sicilian meat-cookery and Sarambos the tavern-keeper – that they are marvellous tenders of bodies, the first providing marvellous loaves, the second marvellous meat, and the third marvellous wine. (*Gorgias* 518b5–c1)

Here, the list of base trades has narrowed to the baker, the meat-chef and the tavern- or innkeeper (purveyors of bread, meat and wine), analogised (as Socrates says a little later) to 'those who, without moderation or justice, cram the city with harbours and shipsheds and walls and tribute and other such nonsense' (519a1–4); just as in Aristophanes' *Knights*, Themistocles plays tavern-keeper (filling Demos' cup to the brim) and baker (kneading a 'Peiraeus-cake' for the city). Plato's sweeping critique of the fifth-century architects of democracy and empire may be novel, but the imagery through which he condemns them is entirely traditional, reaching back through Old Comedy to Timocreon's sympotic lampoon.[50]

V

Rather than doing a full-scale survey of Plutarch's *Life of Themistocles* as it continues the tropes and topoi of the 'innkeeper' Themistocles, I'd like to conclude by focusing on a single moment of characterisation in Plutarch's text. Early in the *Life*, Plutarch sums up one main feature of Themistocles' character:

[49] For Themistocles and Perikles as the prime movers of these building projects, see Dodds 1959.209–10, 361–2.

[50] Dodds (1959.325–6) notes how shocking and unconventional Plato's attack on 'the Four Men' would have been to his contemporaries. It may also be significant that Aristeides makes a single appearance in the *Gorgias*, in the final myth – not as a good statesman, but as the *only* Athenian leader uncorrupted by power (526b1–2; priamel logic again!). As in *Knights*, he serves as a figure of closure, in implicit opposition to the other democratic leaders.

> And some writers say that he was intensely interested in making money on account of his generosity: for, being a lover of sacrifice and conspicuous in his expenditures on guests (*xenous*), he had need of abundant choregic funds; but others say just the opposite and accuse him of much greed and stinginess, on the grounds that he would even sell gifts of food that were sent to him. (*Life of Them.* 5.1)

This passage perfectly captures one opposition I have been tracing: Themistocles here hovers between the poles of a complete investment in the mystified economy of sacrifice ('being a lover of sacrifice') and the most shameless form of disembedding that sacral economy ('even selling gifts of food'). I would suggest that the competing sources Plutarch draws on, that offer such disparate characterisations of Themistocles, are engaged not just in biography (slanderous or otherwise), but in a kind of embedded or embodied political theorising. That is to say, the biographical Themistocles serves here as a symbolic operator, through which new developments in the use of money in the public sphere can be challenged and debated. I make this suggestion because precisely the same split representation on the desire for and use of money occurs in fifth-century sources, but significantly applied to the Athenian demos. Thus we find the positive version prominently featured in Perikles' Funeral Oration in Thucydides:

> Furthermore, we have furnished the most relaxations of the spirit, using contests and sacrifices that last through the year, and attractive private furnishings, whose day-to-day enjoyment drives out anxiety. And on account of the great size of our city, all things come to us from all the world and it befalls us to enjoy the things produced here with no more native enjoyment than those that come from the rest of mankind. (Thuc. 2.38)

Here Perikles lauds the city's institution of public sacrifices in terms that appropriate for the entire demos the aristocratic virtue of *megaloprepeia* [generosity], while the transition from the first sentence to the second implies that such cultivation of lavish expenditure is linked to naval hegemony and the goods it draws to Athens.[51]

We find a very different valuation of the same phenomena in the Old Oligarch, who complains that the Athenians cannot even get all their official business done, partly because of the sheer number of public festivals and sacrifices they enjoy (*Ath. Pol.* 3.2–4; cf. Thucy-

---

[51] See Loraux 1986.172–220 for the appropriation of aristocratic virtues for praise of the demos in the *epitaphios* [funeral oration] tradition. For another element relevant for Plutarch's representation of Themistocles' aristocratic *xenia* in 5.1, see Thuc 2.40.4: 'And in the things with regard to virtue (*aretê*), we are the opposite of the many, for it is not by being well treated, but by treating [others] well that we acquire friends.'

dides' 'contests and sacrifices that last through the year'). When it comes to the reason for these lavish public displays, the Old Oligarch accepts neither piety nor even Perikles' rationalising suggestion that they foster social cohesion and enjoyment. Returning twice to the subject of such public expenditure (which clearly rankles), the political pamphleteer ruthlessly demystifies the demos' interest:

> The demos has prevented those who cultivate physical exercise there and musical skill, considering this not to be noble because it knows that it cannot cultivate these things [itself]. And again, in *chorêgiai* and gymnasiarchies and trierarchies they know that the wealthy spend the money and the demos has the money spent on it, and the wealthy finance gymnasia and triremes, while the demos has money spent on triremes and gymnasia. Indeed, the demos sees fit to get money even for singing and running and dancing and sailing in the ships, in order that it itself have money and the wealthy become poorer. (*Ath. Pol.* 1.13)

> As for sacrifices and offerings and festivals and precincts, the demos, knowing that it is impossible for each one of the poor to sacrifice and feast and set up offerings and inhabit a large, beautiful city, has figured out how these things will come to be. So it is that the city sacrifices at public expense many victims, but, in fact, it is the demos that feasts lavishly and divides and allots the sacrificial victims. (*Ath. Pol.* 2.9)

In these two passages, both the (forced) liturgical spending of the wealthy and the expenditure of public funds on festivals and sacrifices are exposed as simply the private greed of individual poor citizens, conniving for money (*argurion*, 1.13) and meat (*ho dêmos ho euôchoumenos*, 2.9).[52]

Together, Thucydides and the Old Oligarch illustrate the very different representations of sacrifice available for public-sphere spending on an unprecedented scale. The demos could be figured on the model of an aristocratic *oikos*, spending lavishly in pursuit of honour among gods and men, or alternatively, dissolved from a collective into grasping private individuals engaged in a sordidly commodified economy of money and meat. It is worth noting that these are precisely the two poles between which Plutarch's Themistocles wavers in the conflicting representations of 'earlier writers' (*Them.* 5.1). In their debate, I suggest, we can just catch the reverberations of the ideological contests that raged over the redefinition of the long-term transactional order in the fifth century BC.

---

[52] Ironically, almost in spite of himself, the Old Oligarch's last phrase in 2.9 gives the game away: the demos' power to divide and apportion sacrificial meat figures in the sacral register the city's assertion of its ability to constitute and control value. I would contend that it is this constitution of the public sphere through the power to sacrifice that is the real issue. For the significance of the Old Oligarch's remarks here, cf. Schmitt-Pantel 1992.231–2; Morris 2000.126–7.

BIBLIOGRAPHY

Barth, H. 1965. 'Das Verhalten des Themistokles gegenüber dem Gelde.' *Klio* 43–5, 30–7.

Beloch, K. J. 1916. *Griechische Geschichte.* 2nd edn. Vol. 2.2: Truebner.

Berthiaume, G. 1982. *Les Rôles du Mágeiros: Étude sur la boucherie, la cuisine et le sacrifice dans la Grèce ancienne.* E. J. Brill.

Bowra, C. M. 1961. *Greek Lyric Poetry from Alcman to Simonides.* Oxford University Press.

Burnett, A. P. 1982. *Three Archaic Poets: Archilochus, Alcaeus, Sappho.* Harvard University Press.

Campbell, D. A. 1967. *Greek Lyric Poetry.* St Martin's Press. 2nd edn 1982.

Cawkwell, G. L. 1970. 'The Fall of Themistocles.' In *Auckland Classical Essays Presented to E. M. Blaiklock*, ed. B. F. Harris. Auckland University Press/Oxford University Press. 39–58.

Chantraine, P. 1962. 'A propos de ΞΥΝΩΡΚΕΥΕΤΑΙ.' *REG* 75, 384–95.

Cresci Marrone, G. 1986. 'Temistocle e la "Vigilia" dell' Impero.' In *Tre Studi su Temistocle*, ed. L. Braccesi. Editoriale Programma. 113–32.

Dodds, E. R., ed. 1959. *Plato Gorgias.* Oxford University Press.

Evans, J. A. S. 1987. 'The "Recent" Prominence of Themistocles.' *AJP* 108, 383–4.

Fornara, C. W. 1966. 'Some Aspects of the Career of Pausanias of Sparta.' *Historia* 15, 257–71.

Fornara, C. W. 1971. *Herodotus: An Interpretive Essay.* Oxford University Press.

Fränkel, H. 1955. *Wege und Formen frühgriechischen Denkens.* C. H. Beck.

Frost, F. J. 1980. *Plutarch's Themistocles: A Historical Commentary.* Princeton University Press.

Harvey, F. D. 1985. 'Dona Ferentes: Some Aspects of Bribery in Greek Politics.' In *Crux: Essays in Greek History Presented to G. E. M. de Ste. Croix on his 75th Birthday*, eds P. A. Cartledge and F. D. Harvey. Imprint Academic. 76–117.

How, W. W. and J. Wells. 1928. *A Commentary on Herodotos.* 2 vols. Oxford University Press.

Isenberg, M. 1975. 'The Sale of Sacrificial Meat.' *CP* 70, 271–3.

Jordan, B. 1975. *The Athenian Navy in the Classical Period.* University of California Press.

Kallet-Marx, L. 1993. *Money, Expense, and Naval Power in Thukydides' History 1–5.24.* University of California Press.

Kallet-Marx, L., 1994. 'Money Talks: Rhetor, Demos, and the Resources of the Athenian Empire.' In *Ritual, Finance, Politics: Democratic Accounts Presented to David Lewis*, eds R. Osborne and S. Hornblower. Oxford University Press. 227–51.

Kirchhoff, A. 1876. 'Der delische Bund im ersten Decennium seines Bestehens.' *Hermes* 11, 1–48.

Kirkwood, G. M. 1974. *Early Greek Monody:. The History of a Poetic Type.* Cornell University Press.

Kurke, L. 1991. *The Traffic in Praise: Pindar and the Poetics of Social Economy.* Cornell University Press.

Kurke, L. 1999. *Coins, Bodies, Games, and Gold: The Politics of Meaning in Archaic Greece.* Princeton University Press.

Laroche, E. 1949. *Histoire de la racine* **nem**- *en grec ancien.* Klincksieck.

Lewis, D. M. 1990. 'Public Property in the City.' In *The Greek City from Homer to Alexander*, ed. O. Murray and S. Price. Oxford University Press. 245–63.

Loraux, N. 1986. *The Invention of Athens: The Funeral Oration in the Classical City.* Harvard University Press.

Maas, P. 1935. 'Timokreon.' *RE* 6A.1. Munich: Alfred Druckenmüller. colls 1271–3.

Macan, R. W. 1908. *Herodotos: The Seventh, Eighth, and Ninth Books.* Macmillan.

Meiggs, R. 1972. *The Athenian Empire.* Oxford University Press.

Meritt, B. D., H. T. Wade-Gery and M. F. McGregor. 1950. *The Athenian Tribute Lists.* Vol. III. American School of Classical Studies at Athens.

Morris, I. 1993. Review of Millett, *Lending and Borrowing in Ancient Athens. CP* 88, 340–6.

Morris, I. 1996. 'The Strong Principle of Equality and the Archaic Origins of Greek Democracy.' In *Dêmokratia: A Conversation on Democracies, Ancient and Modern*, eds J. Ober and C. Hedrick. Princeton University Press. 18–49.

Morris, I. 2000. *Archaeology as Cultural History.* Blackwell.

Parry, J. and M. Bloch, eds. 1989. *Money and the Morality of Exchange.* Cambridge University Press.

Piccirilli, L. 1984. 'Aristide e *L'Athenaiôn Politeia*.' *L'Antiquité Classique* 53, 137–44.

Podlecki, A. 1975. *The Life of Themistocles: A Critical Survey of the Literary and Archaeological Evidence.* McGill–Queen's University Press.

Pritchett, W. K. 1971. *Ancient Greek Military Practices*, Part 1. University of California Publications in Classical Studies 7. University of California Press.

Rhodes, P. J. 1981. *A Commentary on the Aristotelian Athenaion Politeia.* Oxford University Press.

Robertson, N. 1980. 'Timocreon and Themistocles.' *AJP* 101, 61–78.

Rosenbloom, D. 1995. 'Myth, History, and Hegemony in Aeschylus.' In *History, Tragedy, Theory: Dialogues on Athenian Drama*, ed. B. Goff. University of Texas Press. 91–130.

Schmitt Pantel, P. 1992. *La cité au banquet: Histoire des repas publics dans les cités grecques.* École française de Rome.

Scodel, R. 1983. 'Timocreon's Encomium of Aristides.' *CA* 2, 102–7.

Smyth, H. W. 1963. *Greek Melic Poets.* Biblo and Tannen.

Sommerstein, A. H., ed. 1981. *Aristophanes: Knights*. Aris & Phillips.

Stehle, E. M. 1994. 'Cold Meats: Timokreon on Themistokles.' *AJP* 115, 507–24.

Stehle, E. M. 1997. *Performance and Gender in Ancient Greece*. Princeton University Press.

Thomas, R. 1989. *Oral Tradition and Written Record in Classical Athens*. Cambridge University Press.

von Reden, S. 1995. *Exchange in Ancient Greece*. Duckworth.

von Reden, S. 1997. 'Money, Law and Exchange: Coinage in the Greek Polis.' *JHS* 117, 154–76.

von Wilamowitz-Moellendorff, U. 1893. *Aristoteles und Athen*. Vol. 1. Weidmann.

Wallace, M. B. 1974. 'Herodotos and Euboia.' *Phoenix* 28, 22–44.

6 *Pride and Prejudice, Sense and Subsistence: Exchange and Society in the Greek City*†

ROBIN OSBORNE

The economic relationship between city and countryside is an important historical issue. It was only with the Industrial Revolution that the city replaced the countryside as the principal site of production and economic growth. It is generally agreed that in keeping with pre-modern patterns, ancient Greek cities played a subordinate role in the economy of the polis and beyond: manufacture was relatively unproductive and profits in urban food markets were limited. Finley further developed Max Weber's model of the 'consumer city' according to which ancient cities relied on their hinterland to sustain extensive levels of unproductive urban labour tied up in politics, administration and religion. Instead of generating wealth, cities absorbed food and manpower without reciprocating in products and services. A related concept is that of the peasant-citizen who, working primarily to ensure his family's subsistence, provisioned himself with his own products while discharging political duties in the urban centre.

Osborne qualifies these models by arguing that urban markets and monetary exchange were instrumental in generating the cash income wealthy citizens needed to finance their political obligations.‡ Rural production was as dependent on urban markets as the city was dependent on agricultural products. Osborne's model attributes significantly more importance to 'formal' economic rationality of estate management than the 'primitivist' model, although the incentives for profit-seeking behaviour are seen as political rather than economic in nature. He also demonstrates that despite his disagreement with Finley, the latter's emphasis on the meshing of the political with the economic remains essentially valid even if market activity occurred at a much larger scale than Finley suggested. As Osborne

---

† Originally published as 'Pride and Prejudice, Sense and Subsistence: Exchange and Society in the Greek City', in J. Rich and A. Wallace-Hadrill (eds), *City and Country in the Ancient World*, Routledge: London and New York, 1991, pp. 119–45 (© Routledge).

‡ Osborne's earlier work on the Greek rural economy includes *Demos: The Discovery of Classical Attika*, Cambridge: Cambridge University Press, 1985, and more specifically *Classical Landscape with Figures: The Ancient Greek City and its Countryside*, London: George Philip, 1987.

puts it, the relationship between city and countryside could not be calculated in terms of a balance sheet, and it is not possible to disentangle economic from ideological matters when it comes to the question of why Greek cities sought to feed their citizens from their own territories. The cash flow between urban markets and rural estates was not just an economic exchange but maintained relationships of power, and was stimulated by money brought into circulation by the political economy of the polis. As a consequence, agricultural historians and those concerned with the ideology of economic questions need to work more closely together than they currently do.§

The question of the economic relationship between city and countryside has been frequently addressed by ancient historians. There has, moreover, been virtually universal agreement about what is the key question to ask. Thus Moses Finley, in his chapter on 'Town and Country' in *The Ancient Economy*, repeatedly asks 'How did an ancient city pay for its necessities?', and Geoffrey de Ste Croix in his section on 'Polis and chora' in *The Class Struggle in the Ancient Greek World* picks out as the prime feature to be noted that:

> A Greek (or Roman) city normally expected to feed itself from corn grown in its own chora (*territorium*) or at any rate grown nearby.[1]

But asking *this* question, and this question alone, has two undesirable consequences: it leads to the treatment of the relationship between town and country in terms of a balance sheet;[2] and it effectively presupposes that town and country can be cleanly divided, despite the fact that in the Greek polis, at least, the actors themselves make no such clean division.[3] In this paper I want to approach the question of exchange between town and country from a very different angle, and I will argue that the economic relationship between town and country should be understood as much in terms of the need of wealthy landowners for cash as of the need of landless town residents for food.

The high priority put by Greek cities upon feeding their citizenry from the land is independent of the existence of the landless town resident and it has consequences which extend far beyond the question of the balance of trade, either within the city or between

§ See Cartledge (Ch. 1 Above), and I. Morris as referred to in the headnote to Ch. 1.
[1] Finley (1973/85) 131 (cf. 125, 139); de Ste Croix (1981) 11. A similar concern dominates Osborne (1987) 94ff.
[2] So Finley (1973/85) 139, the structure of whose analysis is not as far as all that from that of Gomme (1937), which he criticises.
[3] It is notable that de Ste Croix draws very heavily on the post-classical Greek world, with Jones (1940) providing his model city.

cities. The more securely a city could meet its own food needs from its own land the easier it was to maintain political independence. There seems therefore a direct correlation between the value put on growing at home the food needed for the city's subsistence, and the way that land was seen as the only proper investment, that land-ownership was, ideologically if not actually, tied to citizenship, and that all landowning was respectable, so that no 'class' divisions formed within the citizen body and no ideology of subordination developed.[4] Furthermore, the political implications of farming create a strong pressure for the landowner to dwell in the town, as the only place where citizen rights can be fully exercised, and to form the core of the citizen army by which both political independence and the fields are protected.

It is not simply that landowning was a socio-political act in the Greek city, but that the socio-political forces actually competed with the more purely economic forces. This is most graphically seen in the decision of active farmers to live in the town, away from the land that they own and work. But it is also the priority of the socio-political which makes for the complementarity of town and countryside which has been stressed as the peculiar feature of the Greek city (Humphreys 1978, 134). For where the town works as an enlarged village, which relates to the countryside as simply as a village to its fields, town and country are indivisible, and questions of feeding the town or of exchange between town and country simply do not arise.

This model of the city is consistent with two strongly contrasting means of land exploitation:

(i) systems of lordly surplus extraction by means of extra-economic compulsion (especially serfdom)
(ii) full peasant ownership of land.

The former is, broadly, the position at Sparta in the Classical period; the latter more or less the position in almost all other Greek cities. I have borrowed both categories from Professor Robert Brenner, who initiated a massive debate in *Past and Present* in the late 1970s and early 1980s with his claim that 'the original breakthrough in Europe to a system of more or less self-sustaining growth' was dependent upon the development of class relations through the breakdown of both the above situations – serfdom and peasant possession. Brenner's argument reinforces from a new direction the view that

---

[4] Thus, while English has various verbal ways of distinguishing small farmers from large landowners, Greek does not.

socio-political priorities in the Greek city competed with economic forces and impeded economic growth.

The model city is, however, something of a fictional construct. Cases of all landowners dwelling in the town were probably relatively rare, as perhaps were cities where landownership was really the necessary and sufficient condition for citizenship. However, departures from the strict letter of the model may be of only trivial importance, for the real issue is whether cities acted *as if* the model situation were true. One example which might be argued to support the model is provided by the history of Mantineia. In 385 Sparta compelled the Mantineians to split up their town and go back to living in villages. Xenophon, recounting this, explicitly notes that those with property came to be pleased with the change because they were now living closer to their fields. Yet in fact the new situation did not create any new type of community functioning along lines and according to norms divergent from those of the model city, for as soon as the external pressure was removed the Mantineians reverted to a single city centre.[5]

But if the model seems to hold good for some Greek cities, how far does it hold good for that exceptional city, Athens, about which we know most and on which most studies of the economic relationship between city and countryside in ancient Greece have been centred? Certainly not all Athenians dwelt in the political centre – scholars have probably consistently *over*-estimated the proportion doing so (Osborne 1985, 225 n.91) – but arguably the master-stroke of Kleisthenes was to divide the political centre, and by giving the villages of the countryside an integral and essential part in the political process to make it possible for all Athenians to live in *a* political centre. Athenians do seem to have continued to congregate together and not to have gone out and lived on their plots of land, and democracy probably could not have functioned had this not been so. Citizenship in Athens was not formally dependent on landownership: Lysias 34 makes it clear that some Athenians at least were aware of how enforcing such a link would alter the composition of the citizen body. But landownership was dependent on citizenship. Moreover, some Athenians were quite as ready as other Greeks to make a big thing of the moral value of landownership: Xenophon (particularly in the *Oikonomikos*) provides the prime, but not the only, example. At the heart of the ideology of Athenian democracy was the contention that the Athenians were autochthonous, born

---

[5] Xen. *Hell.* 5.2.7, 6.5.3, with S. and H. Hodkinson (1981) 286–8.

from the very land, and this autochthony provided the fundamental support for the equality of all Athenians (and also for citizen exclusiveness).

Furthermore it is at the heart of Finley's claims that on the economic plane Athens was not in fact different in kind from other cities. Finley stresses that although the non-agricultural workforce was relatively large it did not produce anything that was significant in the economy of the city (except the silver, mined in the countryside) and the town remained a centre of consumption and not of production.

Seen from the point of view of the question of how ancient cities paid for their 'food, metals, slaves and other necessities' it is clear that the model city is one which is economically stagnant, for it has a very low demand for necessities which are not produced by the citizen himself. For Finley the Athenian exploitation of silver meant that even without meeting her own demands for food from her own territory Athens could meet her impressive import bill, and hence the Athenian countryside could stagnate just as much as other cities could. Once this viewpoint is adopted it becomes plausible to take literally the view implied by Dikaiopolis in Aristophanes' *Akharnians* 33–6 that traders were unknown outside the town (even in so large and prosperous a community as Akharnai), and to believe that the failure of archaeology or written records to give evidence of market places outside Athens, the Peiraieus and the mining region is significant. The countryside, it might seem, could maintain itself without any significant need to buy and sell on the market.

But is this claim really true? One way of examining it is to look at specific cases. For Athens a small number of men are relatively well known because they became involved in law courts in cases in which matters of property were involved. One such man is Phainippos, a figure of whom we would know nothing were it not for a single court case from which the opponent's speech is preserved as the 42nd oration in the Demosthenic corpus. The claim made in court is that Phainippos is richer than the speaker and therefore ought to undertake liturgical commitments in his stead. As a result, the speech contains considerable detailed information about both the estate of Phainippos and the estate of the speaker, and even though we can be confident that this information is distorted, probably systematically distorted, it proves to be of exceptional interest when considered closely.

Kallippos' son Phainippos had inherited the properties of two families, his own paternal family and also his wife's, for he had been adopted as son by his father-in-law. His opponent alleges that both properties were so large that they had previously borne liturgic liabilities (21–3). As described in the speech the property consisted of a single landed estate, at Kytherros, a deme almost certainly in the Mesogaia area and which the most recent discussion (Traill 1986, 47–51) places in the Erasinos valley, south of Brauron. We do not know what Phainippos' paternal deme was, but his father-in-law was of Kolonai, not Kytherros.[6]

In an unprecedented, and notorious, measurement, Phainippos' opponent gives the circumference of the Kytherros estate as 'more than forty stades' (5), a measurement which, even if true, is consistent with the estate being of a wide range of areas (de Ste Croix 1966). More usefully the speaker described the nature of the agricultural exploitation and makes claims about the agricultural yield. Barley, vines and wood form the core of the estate's production: barley production is put at more than 1,000 *medimnoi* (which may imply that around 40 hectares were so cultivated), wine production at 800 *metretai*, and wood production is supposed to bring in 12 drachmas a day (7.20). The estate has two threshing floors (just possibly an indication that it combines two previously separate estates?), and a number of buildings used for storage of grain (7).

The only labour force mentioned by the speaker consists of six donkeys and two or more donkey-drivers who are referred to over the transport of wood, and the claim is made that these were employed year-round for this purpose. No other labour force, animal or human, is mentioned: given that the speaker wants to maximise, rather than minimise, the impression of the size and wealth of the estate there seem to be two possible reasons for this: either the six donkeys and their drivers were the only workforce and were employed on woodcutting only in the season in which the speaker visited the estate, or else the permanent workforce otherwise employed by Phainippos was so small that it would have undermined the case being made. In favour of the former it might be noted that the speaker did visit the estate in Metageitnion (August), a month when, for example, the Eleusis accounts show that beasts of burden were free to be released from agricultural tasks in order to be used for the transport of marble; and close to the time at which Hesiod recommends that the farmer should devote his energies to wood-cutting. Moreover it might be argued that the employment of such a force on woodcutting all the year round would imply a very large area devoted to woodland which it would be odd for the speaker not

---

[6] See generally Davies (1971) no. 14734 and D22.

to make more of than he does.[7] In favour of the second suggestion, it might be noted that there probably was quite large-scale use of hired labour in Attic agriculture to meet the peak period of labour demand.[8]

Phainippos' opponent is concerned to show the scale of Phainippos' resources, and he may omit from his description much that went on on the estate but was of trivial economic importance. It is simply impossible to tell whether Phainippos aimed to grow all the sorts of food his household needed on the estate or not: we certainly cannot assume that barley and wine were the only foodstuffs the estate produced. What is clear is that there is no way that his household (consisting, let us say, of twenty members), would consume more than 10% of the claimed barley yield. The opponent puts into Phainippos' own mouth the admission that he had already sold part of the grain crop, and he further claims that Phainippos subsequently sold off more of the grain than was in store (6.8).

The speaker certainly exaggerates; and the barley price quoted (18 drachmas) is atypically high as a result of a particularly bad harvest in much of Attica. Nevertheless, even if we halve the figures given, Phainippos' estate must have yielded something approaching 5,000 drachmas of *cash* per annum. The opponent claims an income of 3,500 drachmas for wood (12 drachmas a day for the working year; if the wood was worked only in slack seasons the figure would be more like 1,000 drachmas), 18,000 drachmas for barley (1,000 *medimnoi* at 18 drachmas per *medimnos*; a price of 3–5 drachmas would be more realistic), and 9,600 drachmas for wine (800 *metretai* at 12 drachmas a *metretes*). This gives a total of about 31,000 drachmas (or about 15,000 on a reduced working year for wood and reduced price for barley).

What did Phainippos spend this cash on? The running costs of the estate cannot have been inconsiderable: even if we allow that subsistence food needs were met by home production, there remain donkeys and slaves to replace, hired labour to be paid, non-food necessities to purchase (clothes, tools, buildings and building maintenance), and so on. But it takes a massive stretch of the imagination to make these items reach even the conservative estimate of cash income I have posited. Yet, unless we are to believe that Phainippos

---

[7] The type of wood is not specified, but Meiggs (1982) 205–6 supposed it to have been firewood, in which case if this is more than casual exploitation Phainippos must have gone in for coppicing. There is plenty of evidence for coppicing in the Roman agronomists (see Meiggs 1982, 263, 266-9) but no explicit allusions in Greek authors.

[8] Cf. Osborne (1985) 142–6, Wood (1983, 1986) and, more generally, Wood (1988).

is an utter liar, there is evidence in the speech that this cash income had been unable to cover his cash outlay. The speaker claims that, although there were no *horoi* marking debts visible on the estate when he visited it, Phainippos had since alleged that he had a whole series of debts: 6,000 drachmas owed to Pamphilos and Pheidoteles of Rhamnous; 4,000 drachmas to Aiantides of Phlya; and 1,400 drachmas to Aristomenes of Anagyrous (26–8). Only the last of these debts does the speaker claim to be able to show to have been repaid. For our purposes it is immaterial whether the debts were in fact outstanding at the time of the speech; what is important is the evidence they provide that in the recent past Phainippos' cash outlay had exceeded his cash income.

The speaker of [Demosthenes] 42 does not disclose the circumstances in which Phainippos contracted, or claimed to have contracted, these debts, for he wants the dikasts [jurors] to believe them invented or no longer relevant. The best guide which we can get to the sort of reason why Phainippos might have contracted these debts is provided by our information about the circumstances in which other fourth-century Athenians have borrowed money. The evidence, from the orators and from the *horoi* themselves, was collected and analysed by Finley some 35 years ago in *Studies in Land and Credit.*[9] In summary, two common reasons for raising loans of a substantial size on the security of real estate were the raising of a dowry and the leasing of an orphan estate; loans to purchase plant or land, to pay for liturgical obligations, to pay for a family funeral, and to meet another man's temporary crisis are also known. Had Phainippos borrowed money to lease an orphan estate, or purchase plant or land, his opponent could not have been silent about it, for anything which increased the productive capacity of Phainippos' estate was grist to his mill in persuading the dikasts of Phainippos' wealth. Similarly, Phainippos cannot have borrowed money to perform a liturgy, for the opponent's very complaint is that Phainippos should be, but is not, performing a liturgy (22–3). Although no borrowing seems to be involved, Phainippos did claim that 1 talent of his property was not his to dispose of because it represented the dowry for the remarriage of his widowed mother.

It seems true that at least one of Phainippos' fathers had died quite recently, but although funerals could be expensive (a sum of 1,000 drachmas is involved in Demosthenes 40.52), the entire body of Phainippos' debt can hardly be put down to this. Again, although

---

[9] Finley (1951/85); for a thoroughgoing examination of credit at Athens see Millett (1991).

Apollodoros can claim to have bailed out his neighbour to the tune of 16 mnas (Demosthenes 53.12–13), and although the speaker certainly would not mention any philanthropic gestures on Phainippos' part, it is unlikely in the extreme that altruism lies behind Phainippos' debts. That we are left with no clear idea of what was behind Phainippos' borrowing is itself important: it is a sign of how little we understand of the major demands for cash that a wealthy Athenian might face. Further to speculate on the origins of Phainippos' need for cash in large quantities would be futile; but there is much to be gained from the scrutiny of the way in which Phainippos ran the estate in the light of his manifest need to generate cash.

Phainippos' opponent describes his estate as an *eskhatia* [border land]. This almost certainly implies that it was brought into cultivation relatively late, and probably implies that the land was to some extent marginal (Lewis 1973, 210–12). The grain crop is sometimes referred to simply as *sitos*, but when specification is given it is always that the crop is barley. The Eleusis 'First-fruits' account, of very similar date to this speech, suggests that much more barley was grown in Attica than wheat (Garnsey 1985; 1988, 102). Barley was certainly eaten by men as well as by animals, but there is some sign of a preference for wheat (Gallo 1985; Garnsey 1988, 99 n.27). Phainippos' decision to grow barley rather than wheat may reflect the marginality of his estate: barley is more tolerant of drought than is wheat. But the decision must also be seen in the light of the presence of vines on the estate. That Phainippos had a productive vineyard implies that at least part of the estate had an adequate water supply, and yet Phainippos does not use that well-watered land for wheat. Growing barley may well have given a consistent yield of a not very profitable crop on the less good land of the estate; growing vines gave a cash crop that was regularly in high demand, and which could be stored for relatively long periods to be disposed of when need arose or when market conditions were particularly favourable. The estate was bound to produce more, perhaps much more, than the subsistence needs of the household, and it seems that Phainippos directed his farming activities to low risk enterprises on the one hand, and high cash yielding enterprises on the other.

That Phainippos had one eye on the market seems to be further confirmed by his exploitation of the woodland. If the suggestion that exploitation of woodland was seasonal rather than permanent is correct, then it illustrates nicely the need of the farmer who employs permanent rather than just casual labour to fill the slack periods of the agricultural year productively. Full employment is much more of a priority for the owner of draught animals and slaves than for the peasant who has neither. But the decision to exploit wood is also interesting. The wood seems to be of no intrinsic use for the estate, it is being carted away and sold (perhaps in Athens, as John Davies suggests (1971, 553), or perhaps in the mining region?). Phainippos' opponent expresses the yield in terms of drachmas a day, and although it is in his interest to allege a cash income it would be perverse not to accept that woodcutting on the scale alleged must have generated some cash return. Hamish Forbes has stressed that the exploitation of woodland resources has traditionally been one of the main sources of cash for small farmers in Greece:[10] Phainippos may have had a larger cash need than most of his neighbours, but this way of meeting the need may have been quite widely employed.

In sum, it seems reasonable to claim, on the basis of his opponent's allegations, that Phainippos had a very considerable need for cash and that he organised the exploitation of his estate in such a way as to bring in as steady a cash income as possible. He sells off his barley little by little from shortly after the harvest, apparently keener to get cash in hand than to gamble on the future movement of prices. His opponent alleges that he has broken the seals put on the grain stores and has continued to sell grain, and also that he has continued to sell wood (8–9): if this is true it looks as if Phainippos was not prepared to let a vexatious court case stand in the way of his established marketing practices.

It must be admitted that the information that we have about Phainippos is exceptional; but was he atypical in his needs and practices? A glance at the situation of his opponent, only partially revealed, suggests that many Athenian rich may have been in similar circumstances and faced similar demands. The speaker in Demosthenes 42 claims that he himself was left 4,500 drachmas by his father, as was his brother, and that it is difficult to live off so little. He admits that he increased his fortune by activities in the mining region, claiming that he made this money by working and labouring with his own body (whatever that may mean). But he then 'shared a common misfortune with others labouring in the mines', and lost some money 'privately' by incurring great fines, and then finally had to pay a fine of 3 talents to the city – 'a talent per share' – because he had an interest in a mine which was confiscated (3, 20, 22, 29).

Scholars who have discussed this speech have frequently followed

[10] Forbes (unpublished). I am very grateful to Dr Forbes for letting me read this stimulating paper. See also Jolas and Zonabend (1973/78). Phainippos seems to have no pastoral interests.

the lead of the speaker and suspected Phainippos of some sort of cover-up; but it was not in his opponent's interest, either, to reveal all about himself. The picture which he draws of turning a moderate estate into one of the largest in Athens (he was one of the 300 established by Demosthenes' Naval Law of 340) through his own labour in the mines is one designed to win sympathy, from dikasts and modern readers alike. That picture cannot have been obviously false, but since money invested in the mines was not easily visible we cannot be confident that the 4,500 drachmas which his father left to him was the totality of the legacy: it is not beyond the bounds of possibility that that was the value of the landed estate which he was left, and that there were already established mining interests on top of that. Certainly the speaker must have been able to pay off his mining fines in order to bring this case at all, and that means that he has been able to produce cash to settle a number of fines including one amounting to perhaps 3 talents.[11]

However sceptical we may be of the details, we are certainly faced here with a man who has met major demands for cash and has been left still in a position where he is not self-evidently incapable of bearing a trierarchy. The demands to which he admits are not at all of the same sort as those faced by Phainippos, but they are of a very similar scale. Both these rich men could represent themselves as having to meet very heavy demands for cash and expect that the dikasts, who might be unfamiliar with the situation of such very rich men, but who were likely to be suspicious, would believe them. Yet in the very nature of the case neither of them is counting public demand for cash in the form of liturgies or *eisphorai* into his obligations and expenditure.

What we know of *eisphorai* and liturgies suggests that the demands which these imposed upon the rich were at least as great as the private demands. *Eisphorai* were periodic levies on the rich, occasional in the fifth century, more systematic and regular in the fourth. Our information is not such that we can accurately assess the impact of these levies on individual households in either century, but the random selection of preserved figures gives some impression of the scale of the demand. The first *eisphora* of the Peloponnesian War is said to have been intended to raise 200 talents (Thucydides 3.19) – far more than the tribute paid by any ally. During the period from 411/10 to 403/2 one wealthy man (Lysias 21.3) paid out 3,000 and

---

[11] It may have been possible, depending on the precise arrangements for sharing the mine, for Phainippos' opponent to represent his share of the fine as larger than it was in fact.

4,000 dr. in two *eisphorai*. In the fourth century an assessment of the total capital value of property holdings in Attica was made and *eisphora* were then raised at 0.5%, 1% or 2% of capital in the belief that such levies would yield 30, 60 and 120 talents respectively.[12] It seems likely that at the same time that this assessment of property was made those liable to pay the levy were organised into symmories and that, then or shortly afterwards, the richest members of each symmory were responsible for advancing the whole sum due from the symmory and for recovering the sums due from the other members of the symmory. The number of those liable to pay the *eisphora* is much disputed and is closely bound up with the question of whether or not the same symmories were employed for raising *eisphora* and for the performance of liturgies.[13] No modern scholar, however, seems to want to maintain that *fewer* than 1,200 Athenian property holders were liable to pay the *eisphora*: i.e. just less than 5% of Athenians probably had to contribute to these levies. The impact that the *eisphora* made on the fortunes of these rich men obviously depended in part on the frequency with which the levies were made. The amounts demanded from an individual on each occasion were not large but they would still make a substantial hole in cash holdings: if we accept Phainippos' own account of his debts and assume that they will not have amounted to more than half the total value of the estate, then for him *eisphora* will have meant payment in the order of 150 to 600 drachmas a time (cf. Davies 1971, 554).

In the case of liturgies our information for cost comes almost exclusively from litigious contexts, and is therefore subject to forensic inflation. However, a conservative estimate of the amount paid out on festival liturgies in Athens suggests that in a normal year around 100,000 drachmas may have been expended by around 100 citizens, and that in every fourth year, when the major Panathenaic celebration fell, this expenditure rose to something over 120,000 drachmas with about 20 more men to share it (Davies 1967; 1971, xxi–11). But this expenditure on festivals is almost negligible compared to the cost of maintaining the Athenian fleet. Even on a fairly conservative reckoning of 3,000 drachmas for a trierarchy (and some individuals and groups certainly spent more), the cost of maintaining 120 ships at sea (as recorded for 356) would have been some

---

[12] Demosthenes 14.27, cf. 27.7. The ancient testimonia on the fourth-century reform of Athenian finances are usefully collected and translated in Harding (1985) no. 39.

[13] See most recently Rhodes (1982, 1985) and MacDowell (1986). The debate badly needs to be put in a wider context.

60 talents (360,000 drachmas), and the cost of 170 ships at sea (as recorded in 322) 85 talents (510,000 drachmas).[14]

For liturgies alone therefore, the richest individual Athenians, probably numbering no more than 1,000 (Demosthenes 14.16–19), will have had to find up to 100 talents a year of spare cash. No individual could be called upon more frequently than one year in two to bear a festal liturgy, and no more frequently than one year in three to bear a trierarchy, but the sums which they had to find were only more lumpy, not in the end smaller, for that. Some rich men certainly mortgaged their land to raise the cash for a trierarchy: two cases of this are known in the fourth century, and it may not have been uncommon.[15] Property was only mortgaged to other citizens, and thus even if the practice was widespread the amount of cash that had to be extorted from the wealthier section of the citizen body is unaffected. Moreover mortgaging was only in the end helpful for the individual if he either could pay off the sum mortgaged before next being called upon to bear a liturgy or was so reduced in means by the mortgage that he would not in future be liable, at least for the trierarchy.

In sum, large numbers of wealthy Athenians needed large amounts of cash, and needed them not just occasionally but regularly. *Horoi* illustrate some of the more publicly proclaimed reasons for raising cash in large sums; Phainippos' financial position suggests that there were also other private reasons which might be less publicly proclaimed; Phainippos' opponent's fines indicate the way in which the Athenian fondness for litigation could also take its financial toll; *eisphora* and liturgies illustrate, but probably do not exhaust, the massive public demand, for as well as these payments which were legally unavoidable it remained true in fourth-century Athens that wealth obliged the holder to contribute philanthropically to both local community and polis as a whole. All of this suggests that a picture of Athens which shows exchange in the society purely in terms of the city's need to obtain food and other necessities misses an important dimension: the country also needed cash from the market.

How, then, was cash generated to meet these demands? The

[14] On the cost of being trierarch see Davies (1971); 120 ships at sea in 356: Diodoros 16.21.1; 170 ships at sea in 322: Diodoros 18.15.8; for further figures see Davies (1981) 20–2. The number of ships possessed by the Athenians was far in excess of the number that appear ever to have been manned in a single year: 283 in 357–356 (*IG* ii² 1611 3–9), 412 in 325/324 (*IG* ii² 1629 783–812). The naval lists regularly give both the total number of ships (at sea and in the dockyards) and also separately the number of ships at sea.
[15] Demosthenes 28.17–18 with 21.78–80, and Demosthenes 50.13.61. See Finley (1951/85) 84 and no. 56.

parties to the Phainippos case illustrate two traditional ways of raising cash: Phainippos himself relies on relatively unsophisticated agricultural practices; his opponent reaps most of his money from mining silver. But the demand for cash may have led to the development of agricultural and business practices less traditional than these. Various lease documents from the fourth century point to an apparently booming demand for public land to lease, and rich men eagerly snap up even small plots of such land (Osborne 1985, 54–9). Such men clearly do not require such plots in order to meet their own food needs. Pride and the high social value of landowning certainly play some part in such leases, but a desire for an additional source of income, exempt in some cases from liability to the *eisphora* (see Osborne 1987, 42–3), may well have influenced such men and encouraged such leasing. Private leasing of land also went on on a scale rather greater than has been appreciated in the past (Osborne 1988). Here the advantages to the lessor must be very largely economic, and while the lessee may have non-economic motives this is increasingly unlikely when leases are for short terms. Potential economic advantages for the lessee might include the possibility of making more efficient use of a labour force through economies of scale, possibilities of diversification, or simply the gamble on making a quick profit without having to face the consequences of agricultural malpractice.

The administration of city taxes also offered some opportunities for passing on the demand for cash to others, some of them outside the citizen body. Alarmingly, a high proportion of our knowledge of such taxes comes from chance mentions in inscriptions, and it is impossible to quantify even the number of taxes, let alone to attempt to calculate what they raised or what was in it for the tax farmer. Typical of the sources of our knowledge is the document recording the selling off of the property of one Meixidemos of the deme of Myrrhinous after he had been unable to pay off a debt of more than half a talent to the public treasury. He had incurred this debt by giving surety for a number of individuals who had contracted to raise various taxes but had never produced the cash. Either Meixidemos' friends were criminally exploiting him, or they did not find the activity of raising taxes as easy or as profitable as they had expected, but their activities show something of the theoretical possibilities for profiting from undertaking public services of this kind. That some of the taxes involved very large sums and could yield very considerable profit to those who farmed them is strongly suggested by the story told by Andokides about the bidding and counterbidding for the privilege of exacting the 2% tax on imports and exports, in which sums of 30 and 36 talents are involved (Andokides 1.133f.).

Leases and taxes, like mortgages, do not create wealth, they simply redistribute it, leases among the citizen body, taxes among a slightly wider circle. For the Athenian rich to meet their private and public demands for cash in large quantities something other than cash had to be turned into cash somewhere along the line. War itself brought in large amounts of booty (cf. Austin 1986) which could be converted into Athenian 'owls', but it hardly brought it in regularly enough for the rich in general to rely upon it. In the end we must contemplate the possibility that one or both of the following propositions are true:

1) that manufacture did in fact play a significant part in the creation of wealth at Athens;
2) that agriculture itself was, for substantial landowners at least, highly profitable, and if highly profitable then, given that Athenians did not go in for protectionism, also highly productive.

Both of these propositions go against firmly held modern convictions. Yet only by exalting the silver mines to a massively predominant place in the Athenian economy can both propositions be rendered unnecessary. That this is unjustified is indicated by the survival of Athens during the first third of the fourth century, when very little seems to have been done in the mines, and by the evidence for who grew wealthy from mining activities. Phainippos himself, whose mining connections consist at most in the mines providing a market for his wood, witnesses to the possibilities of creating wealth and producing cash at Athens without dabbling in silver.

Finley's arguments against ascribing a major economic importance to manufacture in any Greek polis, even Athens, remain strong. But could agriculture have produced a cash income on the scale demanded? One crude way of assessing this is to convert the cash demand into barley production. Even if we assume a highish barley price of 5 drachmas a *medimnos*, 120,000 *medimnoi* have to be *sold* in order to raise the 100 talents needed, in some years at least, to meet *public* demand. 120,000 *medimnoi* (almost 5 million kg) would feed almost 25,000 people for a year. Given that, if Phainippos is at all typical, the rich will have been spending as much on private as on public outlay, we should be thinking of, say, 10 million kg of barley (or equivalent) needing to be *sold* by rich Athenian farmers every year to supply the cash they required. Using the assumptions employed by Peter Garnsey (1985) and supposing that one quarter of Attica was in cereal production, this would mean that something over a quarter of the grain produced in Attica would have to be marketed. Perikles, in the anecdote related by Plutarch (*Perikles* 16), may be unusual in selling *all* the produce of his land immediately after the harvests, but if the cash demands of the Athenian rich were met largely from agriculture then it seems inevitable that they were committed very heavily indeed to market transactions.

Even if it was possible for agriculture to generate a sufficient supply of agricultural produce to raise the cash, is it possible to generate sufficient demand for such produce? There will have been some demand for agricultural produce in the countryside itself, both from those whose land was insufficiently productive to meet their needs and from those who concentrated on producing only one or two crops from their land. That heavy specialisation was at all widespread seems unlikely, however: whenever the produce of an estate is described (as in the Attic stelai, or in Demosthenes 42) or prescribed (as in some lease documents) a variety of crops can be seen to be grown, and this is exactly what we would expect in a situation where most estates consisted of discrete plots of land enjoying different ecological conditions and suited to different use. The two primary markets for agricultural produce within Attica must have been the town and, at least for the middle half of the fourth century, the mining region, where perhaps 10,000 or more slaves could be employed (see Conophagos 1980, 341–54, or speculations about numbers). That the mines did create an extraordinary demand seems to be indicated by the exceptional settlement pattern of the Sounion region, and the density of purely classical, particularly fourth-century, agricultural activity in the Kharaka valley, west of Sounion, which has been revealed by the recent German survey.[16] Barley might be regarded as food particularly suitable for slaves, and if Phainippos were sending his wood to the mines then that might be in virtue of connections established through marketing his barley there also (and one might further speculate that his selling in the mining region may have been what brought him to the notice of his opponent, himself heavily involved with mining). For all that, however, the bulk of the demand must have come from the town.

How, then, did the town pay? In some considerable degree the town may have paid because, directly or indirectly, it was in receipt of much of the money that the rich were producing in *eisphorai* and liturgical contributions. The beneficiaries of liturgical activity must

---

[16] Osborne (1985) 29–36 plus Lohmann (1985) 71–96, whose findings have to be considered in the context of the history of the silver mines.

have been widely spread, for there was probably no area of public life that residents of the town monopolised, but it seems undeniable, even if very hard to demonstrate, that town residents took more than their fair share of and in public activities. Private services and craft activities will have played a further part in enabling the town to pay, and will have contributed to a small degree by bringing in cash from outside the city.

All these considerations point to a very considerable volume and complexity of exchange within the city of Athens. It is difficult to believe that this can have been achieved without a high degree of monetisation. The ability of the wealthy to meet public and private demand seems to have depended on a high degree of liquidity, not just in their personal economies but in the economy of the city as a whole, and a rapidity of exchange transactions which a partially monetised economy could hardly have achieved. But it also depended on a high level of general prosperity, for it was only a relatively prosperous citizenry that could maintain the buoyant markets upon which the rich depended. In a tight circle the expenditures by which the rich justified and maintained their social, and indeed political, dominance required the public payment of magistrates, dikasts and those who attended the assembly which maintained democracy; while in turn those not liable for liturgies or *eisphorai* depended upon the rich being able to bear such burdens in order to free the funds to pay themselves for their democratic activities by which they kept the edge on their prosperity. [...]

BIBLIOGRAPHY

Aston, T. H. and Philpin, C. H. E. (eds) (1985), *The Brenner Debate: Agrarian Class Structure and Economic Development in Pre-industrial Europe*. Cambridge.

Austin, M. M. (1986), 'Hellenistic kings, war and the economy', *Classical Quarterly* n.s. 36, 450–66.

Conophagos, C. (1980), *Le Laurium antique*. Athens.

Davies, J. K. (1967), 'Demosthenes on liturgies: a note', *JHS* 87, 33–40.

Davies, J. K. (1971), *Athenian Propertied Families 600–300 BC*. Oxford.

Davies, J. K. (1981), *Wealth and the Power of Wealth in Classical Athens*. New York.

Finley, M. I. (1973/85), *Studies in Land and Credit in Ancient Athens, 500–200 BC*, reprinted with introduction by P. C. Millett (1985). New York.

Finley, M. I. (1973/85), *The Ancient Economy* (revised edn 1985). London.

Forbes, H. (unpublished), 'The struggle for cash: the integrated exploitation of the cultivated and non-cultivated landscapes in the southern Argolis, Peloponnesus, Greece'.

Gallo, L. (1985), 'Alimentazione e classi sociali: una nota su orzo e frumento in Grecia', *Opus* 2, 449–72.

Garnsey, P. D. A. (1985), 'Grain for Athens', in P. A. Cartledge and F. D. Harvey (eds), *Crux. Essays in Greek History Presented to G.E.M. de Ste Croix*, 62–75. London.

Garnsey, P. D. A. (1988), *Famine and Food Supply in the Graeco-Roman World. Responses to Risk and Crisis*. Cambridge.

Gomme, A. W. (1937), *Essays in Greek History and Literature*, Oxford.

Gudeman, S. (1978), *The Demise of a Rural Economy*. London.

Harding, P. (1985), *Translated Documents of Greece and Rome 2. From the End of the Peloponnesian War to the Battle of Ipsus*. Cambridge.

Hodkinson, S. and Hodkinson, H. (1981), 'Mantineia and the Mantinike. Settlement and society in a Greek polis', *Annual of the British School at Athens* 76, 239–96.

Hopkins, M. K. (1983), 'Introduction' in P. Garnsey, K. Hopkins and C. R. Whittaker (eds), *Trade in the Ancient Economy*. London.

Humphreys, S. C. (1978), *Anthropology and the Greeks*. London.

Jolas, T. and Zonabend, F. (1973/78), 'Gens du finage: gens du bois', *Annales ESC* 28 (1973), 285–305, reprinted and translated in R. Forster and O. Ranum (eds), *Rural Society in France* (1978), 126–51.

Jones, A. H. M. (1940), *The Greek City from Alexander to Justinian*. Oxford.

Lewis, D. M. (1973), 'The Athenian *rationes centesimarum*', in M. I. Finley (ed.), *Problèmes de la terre en Grèce ancienne*, 181–212. Paris.

Lohmann, H. (1985), 'Landleben im klassischen Attika. Ergebnisse und Probleme einer archäologischen Landesaufnahme des Demos Athene', *Jahrbuch Ruhr-Universität Bochum* (1985), 71–96.

MacDowell, D. M. (1986), 'The law of Periandros about symmories', *Classical Quarterly* n.s. 36, 438–49.

Meiggs, R. (1982), *Trees and Timber in the Ancient Mediterranean World*. Oxford.

Mickwitz, G. (1937), 'Economic rationalism in Greco-Roman agriculture', *English Historical Review*, 577–89.

Millett, P. C. (1991), *Lending and Borrowing in Ancient Athens*. Cambridge.

Osborne, R. G. (1985), *Demos. The Discovery of Classical Attika*. Cambridge.

Osborne, R. G. (1987), *Classical Landscape with Figures. The Ancient Greek City and its Countryside*. London.

Osborne, R. G. (1988), 'Social and economic implications of the leasing of land and property in classical and hellenistic Greece', *Chiron* 18, 225–70.

Renfrew, A. C. (1982), 'Polity and power: interaction, intensification and exploitation', in A. C. Renfrew and J. M. Wagstaff (eds), *An Island*

Polity. The Archaeology of Exploitation in Melos, 264–90. Cambridge.

Rhodes, P. J. (1982, 1985), 'Problems in Athenian *eisphora* and liturgies', *American Journal of Ancient History* 7, 1–19.

Ste Croix, G. E. M. de (1966), 'The estate of Phainippus (Ps-Dem. xlii)', in E. Badian (ed.), *Ancient Society and Institutions: Studies Presented to Victor Ehrenberg*, 109–14. Oxford.

Ste Croix, G. E. M. de (1981), *The Class Struggle in the Ancient Greek World*. London.

Traill, J. S. (1986), *Demos and Trittys. Epigraphical and Topographical Studies in the Organisation of Attica*. Toronto.

Wood, E. M. (1983, 1986), 'Agricultural slavery in classical Athens', *American Journal of Ancient History* 8, 1–47.

Wood, E. M. (1988), *Peasant-citizen and Slave. The Foundations of Athenian Democracy*. London.

7 The Price Histories of Some Imported Goods on Independent Delos[†]

GARY REGER

Quantitative data which are suitable for economic analysis become more readily available from the Hellenistic period onwards. This paper is based on a particularly rich source of inscriptional evidence which has survived on the island of Delos. The author, Gary Reger, builds on his own ground-breaking analysis of the temple accounts of the Delian sanctuary of Apollo.[‡] In emphasising the essentially regional character of the economy of the island, he takes issue with Rostovtzeff's modernistic model of the Hellenistic economy and seeks to bring his data to bear on the more recent debate on the integration of the ancient economy. The latter is a complex controversy raised in various chapters of this volume. Much depends on our definition of the term 'economic integration': does it refer to the free movement of goods, labour or money and the compatibility of different currencies, or to the synchronised and parallel variation of prices, wages and interest rates in different markets across large regions? Reger adopts the latter view when he argues that prices for different commodities developed independently over time, and denies that general economic trends determined price formation on Delos. Even so, attempts to identify the underlying causes of significant local price changes remain problematic. For example, as Reger himself concedes, he cannot exclude the possibility that the prices of goods were affected, but in different ways, by broader inter-regional developments. Nor can his analysis control for a variety of other factors that might have been responsible for changing price levels in the records of the Delian priests. Reger's argument effectively undermines earlier assumptions about a single, fully integrated market economy of the Hellenistic world in the

---

† Originally published as 'The Price Histories of Some Imported Goods on Independent Delos', in J. Andreau, P. Briant and R. Descat (eds), *Économie antique: Prix et formation des prix dans les économies antiques* (Entretiens d'archéologie et d'histoire, Saint-Bertrand-de-Comminges, Musée archéologique départemental), Musée archéologique départemental: Saint-Bertrand-de-Comminges, 1997, pp. 53–72 (© Musée archéologique départemental, Saint-Bertrand-de-Comminges).

‡ *Regionalism and Change in the Economy of Independent Delos, 314–167 BC*, Berkeley: University of California Press, 1994.

third and second centuries BC. At the same time, his data cannot support
positive conclusions about the nature of price formation in the Hellenistic
world.

The great appeal of Delos for any scholar of the ancient economy can
be found between the covers of three volumes of inscriptions published between 1912 and 1929 by Felix Durrbach.[1] Under numbers
135 through 498 appear the accounts of the Delian ἱεροποιοί
[*hieropoioi*], a board of two to four officials who, every year,
recorded the income and outgoings of the temple of Apollo in the
most excruciating detail, and then oversaw the publication of their
accounts on great marble stelai erected in the temple and discovered,
broken but still eloquent, two thousand years later by the French
excavators, most prominently Théophile Homolle.[2]

Many of these documents were presented, whether completely or
in a preliminary fashion, by Homolle in the *BCH*[3] or in his monograph *Les archives de l'intendance sacrée à Délos (315–166 av. J.C.)*,[4]
but it was the appearance of the first fascicle of the never-completed
Delian volume of *Inscriptiones Graecae* that excited the first attempts
to place the rich Delian data in an interpretative context. In a review
published in 1913 and entitled 'Les prix des denrées à Délos,'[5]
Gustave Glotz stressed the capital importance of this material:

> Maintenant nous possédons une masse considérable, une série à peu près
> continue de renseignements exacts sur la vie matérielle; pour certains objets
> les chiffres se suivent presque d'année en année … Depuis que les historiens
> de l'Antiquité sont entrés dans la voie des études économiques et sociales,
> ils ont beaucoup souffert … de n'avoir rien de pareil à leur disposition …
> Au contraire, les hiéropes de Délos … nous ont laissé, sous une apparence
> de chiffres fastidieux, un tableu d'une précision unique et d'une ampleur
> inespérée.[6]

These great Delian data, so rich in prices, wages, rents, and other

---

[1] *Inscriptiones Graecae* XI 2 (Berlin, 1912); *Inscriptions de Délos. Comptes des hiéropes
(nos. 290–371)* (Paris, 1926); *Inscriptions de Délos. Comptes des hiéropes (nos. 372–498),
lois ou réglements, contrats d'entreprises et devis (nos. 499–509)* (Paris, 1929). Too many
corrections and additions have appeared in the subsequent decades to list here; for a full bibliography, see Reger 1994b, pp. 289–349.
[2] For a history of the excavations, see Plassart 1972, pp. 5–16.
[3] For example, Homolle 1890, pp. 398–511, publication of *IG* XI 2.161.
[4] Homolle 1887.
[5] Glotz 1913a; see also Glotz 1913b.
[6] ['Now we have a considerable body of material, an almost uninterrupted series of exact
information about economic life; for some goods the figures follow on almost year by year …
Since ancient historians committed themselves to the study of economic and social history, they
have suffered badly … from not having anything like this as a source … The *hieropoioi* of
Delos, by contrast, … have left us, beneath what are apparently tedious figures, a picture that
is uniquely precise and of an extent we could never have hoped for.'] Glotz 1913a, p. 17.

figures that they surpass any other source for the Hellenistic period outside of Egypt, came at an important moment in the history of the study of the Greek economy. In the struggles to conceptualize its workings, a new model was emerging in the early twentieth century. Most starkly stated, this 'modernist' model argued that modern economic concepts like 'capitalism' and 'the market' could be applied directly to classical antiquity. The Hellenistic world came particularly to be seen through the modernist lens. For scholars like Fritz Heichelheim, J. A. O. Larsen, and Michael Rostovtzeff,[7] who, despite their very real differences, nevertheless shared the modernist model, the entire Hellenistic world, from Upper Egypt to Olbia, from Epeiros to Afghanistan, was bound together in a universal price-setting market in which the 'demand for Greek goods of speciality types was large, the buying capacity of the markets was continually increasing,' and 'the successful efforts of the Hellenistic kings to intensify production ... [led to] a steady fall of prices in the Aegean Sea.'[8] The Delian data provided a crucial underpinning because they were believed to track the rise and fall of commodity prices *throughout the Greek world*: they were, that is to say, relicts of the universal price-setting market, and could substitute for prices for the same goods anywhere Greeks were settled (minus of course the costs of transportation).

The claim that Delian prices were universal prices was supposed to be proven most particularly by the movement of olive oil prices. A graph of Delian oil prices (Figure 7.1) starts high and declines to a roughly steady level by about 279 BC. Heichelheim argued that this trend could be explained by the ramifications of the great expansion of territory under Greek control thanks to Alexander. Greeks settled in the East continued to want their home products, like oil, but could not be satisfied from local production because there were no olive groves in the Middle East. Their demand pushed prices up until orchards could be planted locally and come into production. As that happened, demand slackened and prices fell. Hence the price curve. And if oil prices were set so in a universal market, then so must other goods have been.

Heichelheim put this case in the strongest terms. Some scholars, notably Glotz himself,[9] expressed certain reservations while never-

---

[7] Heichelheim 1930; Heichelheim 1954–5; Larsen 1938; Rostovtzeff 1941.

[8] Rostovtzeff 1935–6, pp. 235, 239–40.

[9] In a review of Heichelheim 1930, after praising Heichelheim for producing 'le meilleur travail et le plus compréhensif qui ait été écrit d'après la méthode que j'ai préconisée depuis 1913' (Glotz 1932, p. 241), Glotz adds, 'Si les variations de prix, considérées en gros, démontrent l'existence, d'un marché universel au temps des monarchies hellénitiques, il en est cependant, et en grand nombre, qui semblent contredire cette thèses (p. 248).

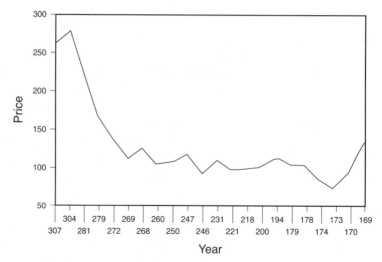

Figure 7.1 Oil prices

theless accepting the general scheme; others, like Rostovtzeff, embraced it wholeheartedly. And it was with Rostovtzeff's great book
on the social and economic history of the Hellenistic world, a book
that was thoroughly informed by the notion of a universal price-
setting market, that the study of the Delian material *as economic data*
virtually ceased.

In the meantime, of course, understanding of the ancient economy
continued to evolve, and surely no figure came to dominate its study
in the 1960s, 1970s, and 1980s like M. I. Finley. In an outpouring
of articles and books, he attacked the entire modernist edifice and
assembled in its place a 'primitivist' view of the ancient economy that
sometimes seemed even to deny that the Greeks had an 'economy'
at all.[10] In turn, Finley's dominating view has come under attack.
Notions of 'economic rationalism' have crept back into the literature,
and increasingly in the 1990s concepts from both sides of the debate
have cropped up in particular studies: as one recent commentator has
remarked, 'the old battle lines have blurred.'[11]

It was precisely in 1985, the year that Finley produced the second
edition of *The Ancient Economy*, that, quite by accident, I began my
studies of the Delian material. The more I read, the more I found
to trouble me. The great mass of Delian data had been analyzed

[10] Of his many works, perhaps the most influential was his Sather lectures, first delivered in
1972 and published as *The Ancient Economy* (Finley 1985).

[11] Van Wees 1995, p. 235. For some examples of 'economic rationalism,' Rathbone 1991;
Carandini 1983. For an anti-primitivist study of the economy of fourth-century Athens, see
Cohen 1992.

and incorporated into the literature under the modernizing paradigm described above; it had never been brought to bear on either the primitivist model that succeeded, or the various newer approaches already emerging in the later 1980s. Despite great changes since the 1930s in the way the Greek economy was conceptualized, the framework within which the Delian data had been fitted had never been subjected to criticism. These two issues alone seemed to me to justify reopening the Delian dossier. Moreover, the Delian inscriptions still provided one of the best and most coherent bodies of economic data delivered by the Hellenistic world: they ought, it seemed to me, to be applied as a test against the suppositions and theoretical constructions of scholars of every view.

I began by examining the data on which the notion of a universal price-setting market rested: olive oil prices. I discovered (to make a long story short) that the long-term history of oil prices on Delos did not conform to Heichelheim's model. In its place I offered a different scenario, based on the assumption that the Delians sought their oil (which did have to be imported) from sources as close by and reliable as possible. I suggested that before the Delians were liberated from Athens in 314, Athenians had been their prime suppliers; that in subsequent decades they relied on Rhodians, suffering greatly in 304 BC when Demetrios, son of Antigonos and soon to be Poliorketes, was besieging the island; and that in turn the Delians promoted, by their new demand for oil, the establishment of orchards in nearby islands, which, as they began to yield crops, ultimately provided a reliable local source, less likely to be disrupted except by local problems, which could explain the steady prices seen after about 279 BC.[12] The result is a regional model for the setting of prices which, on the one hand, does not abandon the concept of a price-setting market mediated through the open exchange of goods, but, on the other hand, tries to take into account the overwhelmingly local character of almost all economic activity in antiquity, including that which occurred outside the boundaries of the market, and to place longer-distance trade in that local perspective.

My own model for oil price formation on Delos over the long term rests on a preference for seeking first local explanations for economic phenomena. I tried to argue the 'localness' of the Delian economy from various sources, and have offered a model for the emergence

---

[12] Reger 1994b, pp. 155–71, with Reger 1994a, pp. 79–85, which offers an explanation for the emergence of the Kyklades as a region in the late fourth and early third centuries. (The citation of this article in the bibliography of Reger 1994b, pp. 372–3, should now be modified as in the references here.)

of the Kyklades as a region; but it is not an unreasonable criticism of my approach, implicit in the observation of Roland Étienne and Véronique Sablé in their very useful and stimulating review of my book that pitch prices seem to move in conjunction with oil prices,[13] that it may overlook or downplay the impact of factors outside Delos in setting prices. I would like to have a look here at the price histories of some goods apparently imported into Delos from outside the Kyklades.

It must be admitted that candidates are few. Ivory, expensive and obtainable from only a few sources, would have been a marvelous test case, but unfortunately we have only three prices, of 8, 5, and 3.5 dr/mna in 276, 269, and 250 BC.[14] Is this a trend? In this price decline W. W. Tarn thought he could detect rivalry between Ptolemaios Philadelphos and Antiokhos II for the favor of the Delians;[15] while Tarn's suggestion is pure speculation, it serves to remind us, as Glotz did too, that political considerations may sometimes overwhelm the market. In any case, three prices do not make a trend, and the absence of any prices for the crucial second half of the third century, where Étienne and Sablé have seen 'une tendance à uniformisation des cours, pour les denrées différentes, sur une période qui s'étend de 245 environ jusque vers 200,' with a stabilization of price between 220 and 200,[16] precludes testing their views.

Some other candidates fare no better. The inscriptions provide a long series of lead prices, 17 from the late fourth century to 246 (again missing the crucial years thereafter), but unfortunately in only three cases do we know the price per unit: 5 dr/talent probably in the 290s, 6 dr/tal in 274, and 7.5 and 7 dr/tal in 269.[17] If three prices made a trend then the direction here would be ominous: precisely the opposite of that for ivory! While we cannot legitimately conclude anything about long-term trends from this comparison, I do think we

[13] Étienne and Sablé 1995, pp. 557–8: [It is a shame that the comparative analysis of price levels does not consider the case of other goods which are dependent on import from a more or less long distance: pitch and luxury products, such as incense or papyrus. If one analyzes price developments, one can observe a tendency towards uniform price levels for different goods during the period between *c*. 245 and about 200. Prices stabilize in the period between 220–200; this is the case for oil, pitch and papyrus, all being imported goods.]

[14] *IG* XI 2.163Aa7 (279), 203A71 (269), 287A118 (250).

[15] Tarn 1928, p. 258 (approved by Rostovtzeff 1941, p. 389): early in the reign of Ptolemaios II, ivory came only through Seleukid territory and was expensive, but 'between 269 and 250 Ptolemy threw enough African ivory on the market to break the price.' Tarn gives this as an example of the king's 'personal keenness as a trader.'

[16] Étienne and Sablé 1995, p. 558: [a tendency towards uniform price levels for different goods during the period between *c*. 245 to about 200]; also quoted more extensively above, n. 13.

[17] *IC* XI 2.153.13 (for the date, see Reger 1994b, p. 226), 199A63–4 (274), 203A52 and 71–2 (269).

are entitled to one observation: the prices of different imported goods may well be set by completely different factors, that is to say also, in completely different markets (I use the term metaphorically, not literally, here). Of course the lead the Delians bought may not have been imported from farther away than neighboring Keos, whose lead and silver mines may have continued to produce, albeit at a low level, in the Hellenistic period.[18]

There are four more promising candidates.[19] Frankincense [...] is a good possibility. Produced only in Arabia (Theoph. *Hist. pl.* 9.4.2), it was clearly imported over a long distance. We have fifteen prices from 250 to 169 BC, thus covering the crucial later third century. But as with lead, we are frustrated by the *hieropoioi*'s cavalier attitude toward recording amounts as well as prices. In only four cases do they tell us *how much* frankincense they bought as well as how much they paid. But these cases are interesting. In 250 BC they bought one-quarter of a mna in Lenaion, the first month of the Delian year (roughly equivalent to our December–January), for 6.668 dr/mna. Nine months later, in Bouphonion (roughly August–September) they bought a half-mna for 5.333 dr/mna. The price had fallen by 20%. This decline is perhaps no surprise for an imported good, for the first purchase was made in winter, when merchant ships did not ply the Aegean, and the second occurred in high summer, well after the sailing season had opened and still a good month or two from its closing. The same phenomenon can be traced in other goods.[20]

So far so good. But further prices may give us pause. The two other prices attended by amounts both fall in Lenaion, in 246 and 231 BC, when the *hieropoioi* paid 5 dr/mna and again 6.668 dr/mna. These seem to confirm the pattern, with the additional information that frankincense prices could fluctuate over the years, itself no surprise. Taken as a trend, these prices might suggest a changing price between two stable extremes, as can be seen for olive oil. But there is another possibility. If the amount bought is plotted against price per talent, the result is a very good correlation: one quarter of a mna costs 6.668 dr/mna (in 250 and 231), one-half a mna costs 5.333 dr/mna (in 250), and one mna costs 5 dr/mna (in 246). In other words, it may

---

[18] For lead (and possible silver) extraction at Petroussa in the late nineteenth and early twentieth centuries, see Cherry, Davis, and Mantzourani 1991, p. 68 n. 2. Cf. also Mendoni 1985–6 and Mendoni and Belogiannes 1991–2. For Glotz 1913a, p. 27, the exhaustion of the mines at Laureion explains the price rise.

[19] For the references for these goods, see Appendix I [not reproduced here].

[20] Reger 1994b, pp. 54–5 (sailing season), 134–7, 141–4, 145–6 (fluctuations tied into the sailing season).

be that the *hieropoioi* were able to secure a quantity discount.[21] Some of the later prices for frankincense recorded without amount of purchase fit this pattern too. In particular, the outlay in 194 BC of 1.667 dr conforms perfectly to a purchase of one-quarter of a mna at 6.668 dr/mna, the outlays of 4 dr in 201, 200, and 179 come as close as you could hope to a price for three-quarters of a mna (predicted as 3.975 dr by the formula in n. 21), and the 6 dr spent twice in 174 would be exactly one and one-half mna at a price of 4 dr/mna (predicted = 4.08). The outlays of 3.5 dr in 224 and 3.167 (plus a bit?) in 169 could also be made to fit the pattern, with perhaps a bit of adjustment. What this suggests is the possibility of an absolutely uniform price for frankincense, governed by amount purchased, of 5 dr/mna for a mna over 71 years from 250 to 169 BC. This would be striking. Every other item known from Delos shows an adjustment in typical level of price between 250 and 169 BC. Olive oil prices, for example, show three distinct patterns in the years between 279 and 169.[22] It is very hard to understand why frankincense prices should show no such changes if they are somehow related to oil prices. It may be, of course, that the temple secured its frankincense through some mechanism other than the market which guaranteed a stable price. For example, some rental agreements from temple estates in Mylasa in Karia include the provision of fixed amounts of frankincense as part of the rent.[23] But the complexities and uncertainties render any arguments from frankincense about *general* price trends risky, and they may also serve as a warning: the same data can sometimes be interpreted in two (or more) completely different ways, and it may not always be possible to decide which interpretation is correct, or even the more likely.

Two other goods offer firmer ground. Perfume expenditures present the same difficulties as frankincense and lead in that amounts bought are rarely recorded.[24] Since, however, the two times the amount is stated it is exactly the same, one and a half kotylia (269 and 250 BC), I have permitted myself the assumption that the *hieropoioi* always bought one and a half kotylia. On this basis a

[21] As they could not, or would not, for oil: Reger 1994b, p. 10. The data fit a curve described by the formula $y = 6.8865 \times 10^{(-0.15089\,x)}$ where y is the price/mna and x is the amount bought, with an R^2 of 0.771.

[22] Reger 1994b, pp. 156, 169–71.

[23] IK Mylasa 216.9 (Mylasa itself), 818.7, 822.12, 828.7 (Olymos, then [forming one city] with Mylasa).

[24] For the sources of perfumes (especially Egypt and Persia), see Rostovtzeff 1941, pp. 84, 92 with 1245, 389 with 1391 n. 113 and 920, 699, 1258. I have assumed that there is no substantive distinction between μύρον ῥόδινον and μύρον plain and simple (see Appendix I [not reproduced here]).

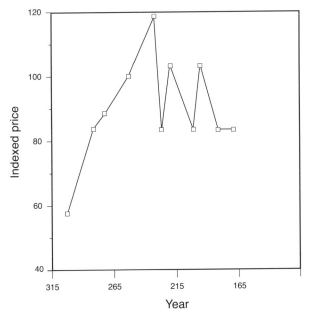

Figure 7.2 Perfume prices

trend for prices between 302 and 169 can be constructed (Figure 7.2). The pattern is striking. From 302 to 231 prices rise inexorably, doubling over 71 years. Then from 224 to 169 they fluctuate by 14% above and 6% below the mean price of just over 4 dr/kotylion. For the first period, the trend is exactly the opposite of that for oil, and the rise persists for at least 48 years beyond the point at which oil prices stabilize. In the second period, despite a superficial similarity, oil and perfume prices behave differently too, for oil price levels undergo two adjustments, while perfume price levels remain unchanged; nor do the directions of price movements match, neither linked or lagged (Figure 7.3). Clearly perfume and oil prices were set in different markets, even though both were imported.

Papyrus, which of course was essentially an Egyptian monopoly,[25] tells a different tale (Figure 7.4). Wild fluctuations in the price per roll characterize the years from 279 to 250 BC; prices vary from 1 dr 3 ob in 267 to 2 dr 1 ob in 269 and 258; I leave aside the extraordinary price of 10 dr in 267. From 250 on, however, papyrus prices stabilize. The variability is only about 10% and the level of price is low. But again, the pattern bears only a superficial resemblance to

---

[25] Préaux 1939, pp. 187–96. See Glotz 1929, where he argues that papyrus prices were low between 332 and 296, when Ptolemaios I reinstituted the Egyptian monopolies disrupted by the invasion of Alexander the Great.

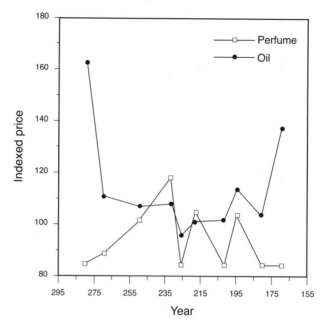

Figure 7.3 Perfume and oil prices

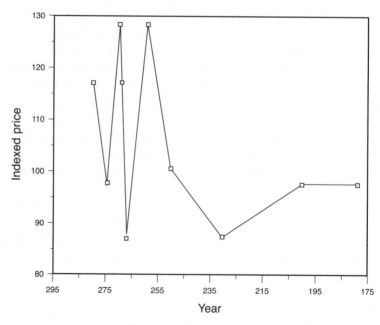

Figure 7.4 Papyrus prices

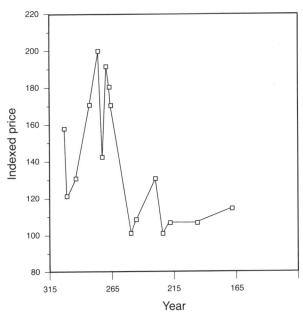

Figure 7.5 Pitch prices

that for oil, if indeed we can say anything at all on the basis of four prices; and in any case, as we shall see in a minute, there may be a very good explanation for the price history of papyrus.

Finally, pitch. Here again two periods can be distinguished (Figure 7.5). Between 303 and 269 BC prices are high, ranging from 17 to 40 dr/met; from 250 to 169 they are low, ranging from 9 to 18 dr/met. If in both periods the anomolous prices are deleted, an interesting pattern emerges. Pitch prices swing up and down, but tend generally to rise over time, and in both cases this trend accounts for about 45% of the variation in price from year to year.[26] The fluctuations of prices around the mean are also very similar.[27] The only difference between the two periods is the level of price: the mean in the first is about 22.2 dr/met, but in the second only about 15.2 dr/met (Figures 7.6 and 7.7).

In other words, pitch prices obey exactly the same rules throughout the entire span of Delian independence; the only difference is the level of price around which fluctuations occur. It will come as no surprise that pitch price behavior in the early period bears no resemblance to that of oil prices. After 250 BC, however, the two goods

[26] The R^2 is in each case 0.464.
[27] For the early period, 21.6% above and 20.3% below the mean; for the later, 18.5% above and 8.2% below (these figures rise to 38% and 31.5% if the price of 179 is included).

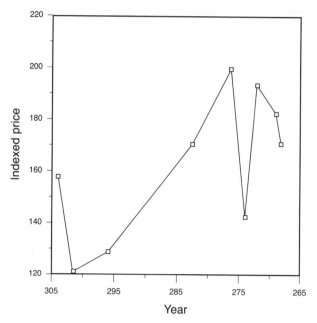

Figure 7.6 Pitch prices before 250

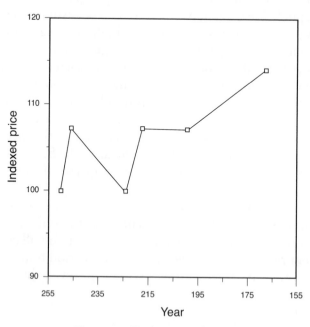

Figure 7.7 Pitch prices after 250

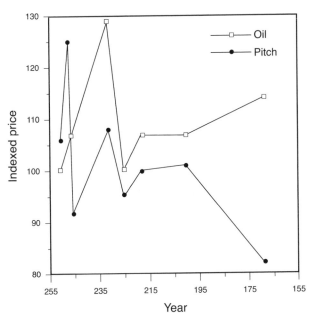

Figure 7.8 Oil and pitch prices after 250

track each other extraordinarily well, rising and falling virtually in tandem (Figure 7.8).

We have now examined the price histories of four imported (or presumably imported) goods. These histories seem to justify a few conclusions. First, no two prices histories behave in the same way in the first half of the third century. This strongly suggests that any explanation for a particular individual price history must be sought in the particularities of that good, and not in a general appeal to a common price-setting market for imported goods. This result supports the argument that the modernist reconstruction of the operation of a general Greek price-setting market in the early Hellenistic period is indeed mistaken. The fact that oil prices too follow their own trajectory in these years adds weight to the case. Second, the behavior of prices in this first period should caution against any totalizing view of price histories in the later third and second centuries. It is true that, for every good except frankincense, some structural change occurs after about 250 BC (though the precise timing of these changes varies widely from good to good). But the character of those changes is in each case different; for perfume, a change from a steady rise to fluctuation about a mean, for pitch a decline in level of price without any change in the character of the fluctuations over time. (I return to the question of papyrus and oil below.) This implies that in seeking explanations for price behavior in these goods too, we should first look to the particularities of each good. At the same time, however, even if the structural changes in price histories are dissimilar, we must not deny the reality of the synchronicity of those changes, which itself needs some explanation.

Pitch and papyrus prices are a good place to start. In a justly famous article, Gustave Glotz long ago offered an explanation for the price history of pitch. He argued that pitch, a strategic good because of its use in warships, was available essentially from only two sources: Makedon and the region around Mt. Ida. He then divided the history of pitch prices into three periods of low, high, and low prices, and attributed them to the interests of the Aegean hegemonic power: between 314 and 296 BC, Antigonos Monophthalmos and Demetrios promoted pitch export to Delos from Mt. Ida, and prices were low; between 282 and 268 BC both Antigonos Gonatas and the Seleukids blocked exports to the Ptolemaic dominated Kyklades; finally, a return to Antigonid hegemony after 250 brought renewed availability of Makedonian pitch. Special circumstances, he thought, explained the remarkably high pitch price of 279 BC and the low of 179: the former a result of the Celtic invasion of Greece, the latter Philip's attempt to curry favor in the Aegean.[28]

In its details, Glotz's theory no longer wholly coheres; in particular, his Antigonid domination of the Kyklades after 250 can no longer be accepted. Further, prices in Glotz's first period are notably higher than those in his third, and seem to go better with those of his second period than to form a separate group. But it is in fact the prices of papyrus that offer a crucial test of Glotz's theory. Papyrus was obtained virtually exclusively from Egypt, and, like pitch, it too was crucial for ship construction and maintenance, for from it were fashioned sails and ropes.[29] Thus papyrus too was a 'strategic good,' and the Ptolemies should have been interested in blocking its export to its enemies. But the highest attested papyrus price falls during the period of Ptolemaic control of Delos (in 267 BC), and prices are generally lower in the second half of the third century than in the first.

In fact, pitch and papyrus prices track each other in an extremely interesting fashion (Figure 7.9). Before 250 BC, pitch and papyrus prices rise and fall in tandem. After 250, however, they decouple: for

---

[28] Glotz 1916.

[29] Hermippos apud Athen. 1.27f, Theoph., *Hist. pl.* 4.8.4. See Gabrielsen 1994, pp. 139–40; Casson 1986, pp. 19–20.

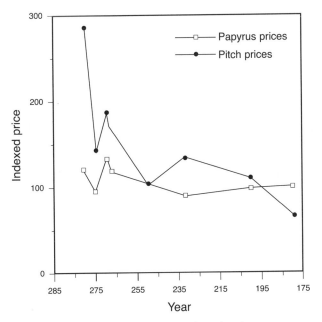

Figure 7.9 Papyrus and pitch prices

the years where we can match prices, papyrus generally rises, while pitch generally falls. (This does not contradict the claim above that the general trend for pitch is upward; the point here is just that the movements of pitch and papyrus are in opposite directions *for the years in which we have matched prices.*) We can test the reality of these phenomena in another way, by tracing the movement of papyrus and oil prices. Since oil and pitch prices do not match in the period before 250, when papyrus and pitch do, but do match after 250, when papyrus and pitch do not, we would expect that oil and papyrus prices never link. And indeed, that is precisely what happens: papyrus and oil prices never move in tandem except briefly during the phase change (if I may borrow a metaphor from physics) when pitch and papyrus prices are decoupling (Figure 7.10).

Glotz's theory cannot explain these phenomena, but another explanation is at hand. Between 314 and 246 BC the central Aegean saw a great deal of naval activity. Antigonos Monophthalmos and Demetrios moved fleets through the Kyklades almost annually; Ptolemaios I and II projected their power by sea; the Khremonidean War was fought in part at sea, and either ended with, or was followed by, the famous battle of Kos; the battle of Andros took place in 246

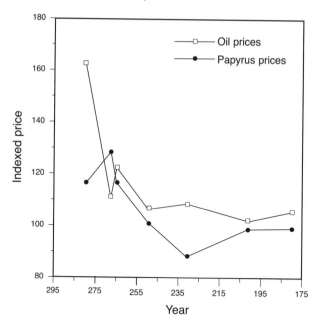

Figure 7.10 Oil and papyrus prices

or 245.[30] Throughout these years the Kyklades were organized into the Nesiotic League by these outside hegemons [leaders], who stationed troops and ships in the islands and made other demands. After the battle of Andros, however, the Kyklades were left relatively alone. Fleets still moved occasionally through the islands, of course (most notably during the Second Makedonian War and its preliminaries and during the Third Makedonian War), but the constant presence of ships that characterized the earlier years was no longer there.[31] We can therefore hypothesize that before 250 BC the military uses of both pitch and papyrus overwhelmed the market, becoming the primary agents for setting the price. Once this military demand waned, the other uses for both goods became predominant and prices decoupled. This result is very important for another reason: its implication that pitch and papyrus prices are set in different markets except under conditions of high military demand in turn suggests that all imported goods did not behave in the same way after 250 and that pitch and papyrus were produced, marketed, and priced in

[30] I discuss the evidence and cite secondary literature in Reger 1994c and 1985; see also Reger 1994b, pp. 181–8.

[31] See Reger 1994b, pp. 16–47. The slightly elevated pitch prices of 218, 200, and 169 might be associated with the Kykladic raid of Demetrios of Pharos, Philip V's expedition to Asia Minor, and the Kykladic naval operations of the Third Makedonian War.

different markets; the lack of correlation between oil and papyrus prices reinforces this view.

Where does all this leave Glotz's notions of blockage by great powers? Certainly, it is not inherently implausible that sea powers did try to monopolize straategic goods; in a famous passage about late fifth-century Athens, the Old Oligarch remarks that the 'power that controls the sea' can always prevent the shipment of vital goods to its enemies.[32] It would not be surprising if the Antigonids and the Seleukids did try to stop the shipment of pitch to their enemies, although given the way ancient trade worked there was bound to be lots of leakage. But Glotz is far too pessimistic about the sources of pitch. Theophrastos' account of its manufacture makes it perfectly clear that pitchmaking was no high technology industry; anyone with a few vats and other simple equipment could do it (*Hist. pl.* 9.3.1–4; cf. also 9.2.1, 9.2.3). The only other vital ingredient was the trees; as Russell Meiggs has remarked, 'Wherever there were pines there could be pitch.'[33] The Kyklades and nearby Asia Minor were certainly not bereft of pines in antiquity (nor indeed are they today),[34] and I would suggest that, as for so many other products, a certain amount of pitch was locally produced (I have no good explanation for the link between pitch and oil prices after 250 BC [Figure 7.8].) Further, the lack of correlation between pitch and papyrus prices after 250 can now also be cited as an indication that, as papyrus is indisputably an imported good (albeit from the medium, rather than long, distance) and pitch prices do not move together with papyrus prices after 250, the pitch marketed in the Kyklades consisted at least in large measure in pitch produced locally. Finally, local production might also help account for the long-term upward trend in pitch prices generally, at least in the later period, when there is other evidence for upward pressure on the prices of wood products.[35]

There is one more matter on which I would like to touch. I have not yet mentioned a subsidiary component of Glotz's argument about pitch price history, viz.: that the identity of the sellers supports his views of the origin of the good. Nannakos and Hestiaios, pitch suppliers in 302, were, Glotz argued, Phrygian and Ionian (or from a neighboring region), perfect for merchants bringing pitch from Mt. Ida; during the years of Ptolemaic hegemony, Delian citizens, not

[32] Ps.-Xenoph. *Ath. Pol.* 2.11–12; see also Gabrielsen 1994, p. 141.
[33] Meiggs 1982, p. 470.
[34] See, for example, Dalongeville and Renault-Miskovsky 1993, p. 42; Rackham 1982, p. 192 (Samos); for the lower Maiandros valley, Rowton 1967, p. 264.
[35] Reger 1994b, pp. 171–6.

foreigners (as a general rule), procured this 'denrée macédonienne.'[36]

The correspondence Glotz sets up is not perfect; he does not explain why a Euboian [...] is supplying pitch in 304[37] and a citizen of Klazomenai in 269. More important, however, is the assumption that lies behind the argument. For Glotz, as for all adherents of the modernist model, trade was conducted largely by specialists who moved back and forth between production centers and customers. These pitch suppliers, who are called explicitly 'marchands de poix' [pitch merchants] in the first volume of the *Index* of Delian inscriptions, are fit into this category. But examined more closely, they look rather different. Glotz's 'Phrygian' Nannakos recurs twice in the inscriptions as the man who paints the *agalma* (statue) of Dionysos in 304 and again in 272 or 271.[38] Whatever his origin, he is clearly long established on Delos, that is to say, he is no itinerant trader, and he does other things for the temple than supply pitch. (The *Index* calls him a 'painter.') Amphithales, whom *LGPN* and *Index* both take to be a Delian, not only supplies pitch in 282 BC but also applies it to the Keraton. Menon, again taken to be Delian, supplies pitch and Makedonian wood in 274 BC, and boards in 304; I am inclined to identify him also with the Menon who, with a companion, cleaned the channels in the theater in 268 BC.[39] Antigenes of Klazomenai, pitch seller in 269 BC, sold the *hieropoioi* something else in 272 or 271. But it is sellers of perfume who clinch the case. Two of the three known (one name is too mutilated to reckon on) are women: Kombaris (or Kombaphis) in 269 BC and Komodia, who not only supplies perfume in 279 but also a fillet, ταινία, in 269.[40] There can be no doubt that women were not sailing off to the East to buy perfume, and their situation may cast doubt on the construction usually put on the men who sell goods to the temple, too.

The entire matter of the status and roles of the many people who sold goods to Apollo needs careful study. From the data presented above, I am inclined to see many of them as jobbers: laborers, sellers, buyers, ready to do what is needed. The temple needs pitch; Amphithales goes off to buy it, and offers himself as the man to slap

---

[36] Glotz 1916, pp. 304, 312 (quotation). For the suppliers, see Appendix II [not reproduced here].

[37] Clearly an ethnic, not a name: [παρὰ] Καρυστίου (*IG* XI 2.144A112); but cf. Vial 1984, p. 311, on the name.

[38] Bruneau 1970, pp. 312–22.

[39] There are no more than three Menones attested on independent Delos, two if I am right: Fraser and Matthews 1987, s.v. (16)–(18).

[40] *IG* XI 2.203A39 with Tréheux 1992, p. 57; *IG* XI 2.161A93, 203A65. The mutilated name appears at *ID* 316.84.

it on the Keraton too; Menon deals in wood products generally, but also happily cleans out the gutters of the theater. Nothing in the texts compels us to see any of these people as merchants or traders; indeed, the indications are that they were not. Other people, anonymous in this context, were the ones who brought the goods to Delos, in many cases (I would argue) from quite nearby; perhaps Epigenes the Naxian, seller of pitch in 272 or 271, was one.

Here we need to return to the larger question of what happened in the second half of the third century that enabled the price structures of many items to undergo changes at about the same time. It must be stressed that the price histories of perfume and frankincense still stand out, and that they are also now the only items on our list that we can still say with assurance were imported via long-distance trade. Papyrus, too, came from outside the Kyklades, and as we have seen its price history diverges strikingly from that for pitch once the two decouple, for reasons I have explained. I cannot help but suspect that the explanation for many of these changes should be sought in the withdrawal of outside hegemons from the central Aegean in these years. The disappearance of elevated demand from troops and sailors, the end to withdrawal of wealth in the form of tribute and manpower, and the termination of disruptions caused by a continuous outside military presence would permit the local economy to 'find its levels' both for goods produced locally and for medium-distance imports like papyrus.

I have stressed here the question of demand, which seems reasonable with respect to pitch and papyrus. In *Regionalism and Change* I argued instead the role of supply in setting olive oil prices. In a sense these two approaches are two sides of the same coin. In the scale of a Kykladic regional economy, demand on Delos for any item will have been small; high demand from outsiders may easily have disrupted local markets. But the tale olive oil prices tell is tellingly different from that for papyrus and pitch, for two reasons. First, oil prices decline and stabilize by *c.*276 BC, long before the structural change for papyrus and pitch and while outside powers are still competing in the central Aegean; second, once pitch and papyrus prices decouple, the latter behave in a different pattern from oil. Consequently, the same reasons cannot be invoked to account for the structural changes in oil prices as for pitch and papyrus, and we must reject the view that some forces are acting on these prices in the same way simply because they are imported goods (a proposition to be doubted in any case, as we have seen, with respect to pitch).

It would be nice to be able to test some of these conclusions. Most obviously, they imply that the price histories of the same goods ought to look different in different regional economies. Even with exiguous data, it may be possible, from time to time, to link a price or a handful of prices from elsewhere that are well dated to the Delian data in order at least to ask whether it looks as if prices differ in different regions.[41] We also need to know a great deal more about the specifics of commodity production in the Hellenistic world and the ways in which goods passed from producers through transporters and middlemen to consumers.

In the end, we must remember the limitations of our data and our understandings. We do the best we can with what we have, but that is precious little; new insights, new inscriptions, new techniques may overthrow even the most apparently solidly founded interpretation. There remains a great deal to do in the study of the economy – or I should write, economies – of the Hellenistic world.

BIBLIOGRAPHY

Bruneau, P. (1970), *Recherches sur les cultes de Délos à l'époque hellénistique et à l'époque impériale*, Paris, BEFAR, 217.

Carandini, A. (1983), 'Columella's Vineyard and the Rationality of the Roman Economy', *Opus*, 2, pp. 177–204.

Casson, L. (1986), *Ships and Seamanship in the Ancient World*, 2nd edn, Princeton.

Cherry, J., Davis, J. L. and Mantzourani, E. (1991), *Landscape Archaeology as Long-term History. Northern Keos in the Cycladic Islands*, Los Angeles (Monumenta Archaeologica, 16).

Cohen, E. (1992), *Athenian Economy and Society: A Banking Perspective*, Princeton.

Dalongeville, R. and Renault-Miskovsky, J. (1993), 'Paysages d'île de Naxos', *Recherches dans les Cyclades*, Lyon, pp. 9–57.

Davis, P. (1937), 'The Accounts of the Theatre on Delos', *AJA*, 41, p. 109.

Étienne, R. and Sablé, V. (1995), 'Review of Reger 1994b', *Topoi*, 5, pp. 555–60.

Finley, M. I. (1985), *The Ancient Economy*, Berkeley, 1973, 2nd edn, 1985.

Fraser, P. M. and Matthews, E. (1987), *A Lexicon of Greek Personal Names*. Volume I. *The Aegean Islands, Cyprus, Cyrenaica*, Oxford.

Gabrielsen, V. (1994), *Financing the Athenian Fleet. Public Taxation and Social Relations*, Baltimore, London.

Glotz, G. (1913a), 'Les prix des denrées à Délos', *JS*, 11, pp. 16–29.

Glotz, G. (1913b), 'Les salaires à Délos', *JS*, 11, pp. 206–15, 251–60.

---

[41] I tried to do this, at least a little, in my study of the Delian grain trade (Reger 1993).

Glotz, G. (1916), 'L'histoire de Délos d'après les prix d'une denrée', *REG*, 29, pp. 281–325.

Glotz, G. (1929), 'Les prix du papyrus dans l'antiquité grecque', *Annales d'histoire économique et sociale*, 1, pp. 3–12.

Glotz, G. (1932), 'Un livre d'histoire économique', *REG*, 45, pp. 241–9.

Heichelheim, F. (1930), *Wirtschaftliche Schwankungen der Zeit von Alexander bis Augustus*, Jena (Beiträge zur Erforschung der wirtschaftlichen Wechsellagen. Aufschwung, Krise, Stockung, 3).

Heichelheim, F. (1954–5), 'On Ancient Price Trends from the Early First Millennium BC to Heraclius I', *Finanz Archiv*, 15, pp. 498–511.

Homolle, T. (1887), *Les archives de l'intendance sacrée à Délos (315–166 av. J.-C.)*, Paris, BEFAR, 49.

Homolle, T. (1890), 'Comptes et inventaires des temple déliens en l'année 279', *BCH*, 14, pp. 398–511.

Larsen, J. A. O. (1938), 'Roman Greece'. In Frank, T. (ed.), *An Economic Survey of Ancient Rome*, 4, Baltimore, pp. 334–414.

Meiggs, R. (1982), *Trees and Timber in the Ancient Mediterranean World*, Oxford.

Mendoni, L. (1985–6), Ἀρχαιολογικὲς ἔρευνες στὴν Κέα, *Archaiognosia*, 4, pp. 149–84.

Mendoni, L. and Belogiannes, N. (1991–2), Μεταλλευτικὲς και μεταλλουργικὲς δραστηριότητες στην αρχαία Κέα, *Archaiognosia*, 7, pp. 91–104.

Plassart, A. (1972), 'Un siècle de fouilles à Délos', *Études déliennes*, *BCH*, suppl. 1, pp. 5–16.

Préaux, C. (1939), *L'économie royale des Lagides*, Brussels.

Rackham, O. (1982). 'Land-Use and the Native Vegetation of Greece'. In [Bell, M. and Limbrey, S.], *Archaeological Aspects of Woodland Ecology*, London, pp. 177–97 (BAR, International Series, 146).

Rathbone, D. (1991), *Economic Rationalism and Rural Society in Third-century AD Egypt. The Heroninos Archive and the Appianus Estate*, Cambridge.

Reger, G. (1985), 'The Date of the Battle of Kos', *AJAH*, 10, [1993], pp. 155–77.

Reger, G. (1993), 'The Public Purchase of Grain on Independent Delos', *ClAnt*, 12, pp. 300–34.

Reger, G. (1994a), 'Some Boiotians in the Hellenistic Kyklades'. In [Fossey, J. (ed.)], *Boiotia Antiqua IV. Proceedings of the 7th International Congress on Boiotian Antiquities, Boiotian (and Other) Epigraphy*, Gieben, pp. 71–99.

Reger, G. (1994b), *Regionalism and Change in the Economy of Independent Delos*, Berkeley (Hellenistic Culture and Society, 14).

Reger, G. (1994c), 'The Political History of the Kyklades 260–200 BC', *Historia*, 43, pp. 39–46.

Rostovtzeff, M. (1935–6), 'The Hellenistic World and its Economic

Development', *AHR*, 41, pp. 231–52.

Rostovzteff, M. (1941), *The Social and Economic History of the Hellenistic World*, Oxford.

Rowton, M. B. (1967), 'The Woodlands of Ancient Western Asia', *JNES*, 26, pp. 261–77.

Tarn, W. W. (1928), 'Ptolemy II', *JEA*, 14, pp. 246–60.

Tréheux, J. (1948), 'Les dernières années de Délos sous le protectorat des amphictions', *RA*, 31–2, pp. 1008–32.

Tréheux, J. (1986), 'Un document nouveau sur le *Néôrion* et le *Thesmophorion* à Délos', *REG*, 99, pp. 293–317.

Tréheux, J. (1988), 'Une nouvelle lecture des inventaires d'Apollon à Délos.' In [Knoepfler, D. (ed.)], *Comptes et inventaires dans les cités grecques*, Neuchâtel, Genève, pp. 29–35.

Tréheux, J. (1992), *Inscriptions de Délos*. Index. Tome I. *Les étrangers à l'exclusion des Athéniens de la clérouchie et des Romains*, Paris.

Vallois, R. (1944), *L'architecture hellénique et hellénistique à Délos jusqu'à l'éviction des Déliens 1. Les monuments*, Paris.

van Wees, H. (1995), review of Reger 1994, *G&R*, 42, pp. 234–5.

Vial, C. (1984), *Délos indépendante (314–167 avant J.-C.). Étude d'une communauté civique et de ses institutions*, BCH, suppl. 10.

8 *The Ancient Economy and Graeco-Roman Egypt*†

DOMINIC RATHBONE

As we saw in the previous chapter, the study of the ancient economy has recently moved beyond the centres of the Graeco-Roman world and turned towards its geographical and temporal borders, the Hellenistic world and the Roman provinces. Although less well documented by ancient authors, and often ignored by modern scholars, these areas have produced an abundance of numismatic, epigraphic and papyrological material which is only beginning to be explored. Yet this material also poses new problems and questions, especially how it should be used and what it can tell us given that its ideological context is frequently unknown. Moreover, while material on costs, prices, wages, rents and so forth is rich by ancient standards, it may not be sufficient for reliable quantitative or statistical analysis. The nature of the relationship between these Hellenised and Romanised regions, on the one hand, and the centres of Greek and Roman society and culture, on the other, is also open to debate.

Dominic Rathbone, who is best known for his book on *Economic Rationalism and Rural Society in 3rd century BC Egypt*,‡ addresses several of these problems here. He suggests that Egypt, both as a Hellenistic kingdom and subsequently as a Roman province, was not as exceptional as is often assumed. Rather, it was part of the classical world. Its economic system therefore cannot be considered in isolation, all the more so as it offers valuable insights into the workings of the 'ancient economy' as a whole. Key economic factors, such as the social position of the rural population, the economic rationalism of agricultural producers, and systems of taxation, were essentially brought in line with practices elsewhere in the classical world. Rathbone also seeks to demonstrate the historical potential of papyrological material, especially for quantitative analyses and our understanding of estate management, accounting and public

† Originally published as 'The Ancient Economy and Graeco-Roman Egypt', in L. Criscuolo and G. Geraci (eds), *Egitto e storia antica dall'ellenismo all'età araba: bilancio di un confronto*, Cooperativa Libraria Universitaria Editrice Bologna: Bologna, 1989, pp. 159–76 © Cooperativa Libraria Universitaria Editrice Bologna).

‡ Cambridge: Cambridge University Press, 1991.

administration. His model of the Egyptian – and, by implication, the ancient – economy is distinctly anti-primitivist, allowing for considerable complexity of economic strategies, a high degree of rationalism in agrarian production, and a degree of monetisation that offered reliable market information.

The ancient economy, it has been said, is an academic battlefield; indeed it has been an academic Hundred Years' War. The crippling shortage of munitions – especially of reliable, factual, quantitative data, the essential material of economic analysis – makes for indecisive encounters, but has stimulated strategic and tactical ingenuity. One approach is to focus on social institutions well-attested in the literary and legal sources, in particular slavery, and to present them as major characterising features of the economy of the Graeco-Roman world. Another tactic is to concentrate on what ancient authors seem to reveal about ancient attitudes to wealth and the various means of acquiring and using it, in an attempt to define the ancient economy in terms of its economic mentality. Or one can turn to comparative data, and use mediaeval and later statistics about peasant production, transport costs and so on to construct models for the economic functioning of the ancient world. And there is also the constantly growing body of archaeological data, in particular the results of field surveys and of studies in the production and distribution of ceramic wares, which does provide a certain, factual, even statistical basis for discussion of some key aspects of the ancient economy. These various approaches, especially in combination, have greatly extended the horizons and increased the subtlety of academic debate about the economy of the Graeco-Roman world, but they all have their own internal problems of validity, and they all tend to produce competing hypothetical explanatory models on a grand scale, very different, for example, from the elaboration of F. Braudel's *Civilization and Capitalism [: The Perspective of the World,] 15th–18th Century* from a mass of detailed studies of local documentary sources.

Ancient economic historians in contrast possess relatively few and isolated 'facts', as is reflected in the excitement generated by finds of minor archives such as the tablets from the ager Murecinus and those from Vindolanda. Whether they care to admit it or not, anyone who writes about broad topics such as slavery, economic mentality, peasant livelihood or trade builds hypothetical models, in which comparative data are used to control the classical evidence or to fill lacunae in it. But this tactic has nasty risks. As one scholar wrote, after noting the unreliability of the shipping rates laid down in Diocletian's Price Edict, 'if we can accept ancient evidence only if it accords with comparative evidence, and reject it if it diverges widely, why bother with the ancient evidence?'[1] The answer is that while comparative evidence is useful in delimiting the possible and the probable in ancient economic history, it cannot in itself provide the detailed specifics which are needed to distinguish between the economy of the classical world and those of other pre-industrial societies, or between the economies of different areas and of different periods within the classical world.

There is little excuse, therefore, for the continuing failure to exploit the uniqueness of Graeco-Roman Egypt, its legacy of an ever-growing corpus of documentary evidence which, even if it might seem relatively pitiful to historians of later periods, nonetheless provides us with a quantity and quality of economic data which are without parallel in the classical world. Admittedly this evidence is not easy to use. The few synthetic works which collect and present Egyptian economic data are now dated.[2] Few ancient historians are as students given even a rudimentary introduction to Egypt and its papyri – a failing which teachers of ancient history should perhaps make more effort to remedy. But initial unfamiliarity with the material is no real bar to a historian who thinks there is something to be gained from its study, as is demonstrated by the fact that economic studies of the Hellenistic and Byzantine periods do not ignore the Egyptian evidence in the way that is pretty standard for the Roman period. The problem here is that while Egypt has always been seen as an integral part of both the Hellenistic and the Byzantine worlds, the tradition is to view it as a unique province in the Roman empire, information from which therefore has little or no use as an indicator of what was happening in other parts of the empire.

There is little mileage in abstract debate about the value and wider relevance of the Egyptian evidence. My starting assumptions are that there was great regional diversity in the society and economy of the classical world in general, rather than a peculiar chasm between Egypt and the rest of that world, but that behind this general diversity there were also similar and at times even identical economic

---

[1] K. Hopkins, 'Models, ships and staples,' in P. Garnsey and C. R. Whittaker (eds), *Trade and Famine in Classical Antiquity* (1983), 84–109 (at 104).
[2] The standard works are: A. C. Johnson, 'Roman Egypt', in T. Frank (ed.), *An Economic Survey of the Roman World*, II (1936); S. L. Wallace, *Taxation in Egypt from Augustus to Diocletian* (1938); L. C. West and A. C. Johnson, *Currency in Roman and Byzantine Egypt* (1944); A. C. Johnson and L. C. West, *Byzantine Egypt Economic Studies* (1949). More recent is R. S. Bagnall, 'Currency and Inflation in fourth century Egypt', *BASP* Suppl. 5 (1985).

developments for which the Egyptian evidence provides a keyhole on a much wider panorama. To convert the sceptics we need concrete examples of how studies of aspects of the economy of Graeco-Roman Egypt, apart from their intrinsic value because of the importance of Egypt as a unit of the classical world, can further our understanding of economic life in other parts of that world. The three common topics which I have chosen for review here are the economic position of the rural population, the character of ancient economic behaviour, and the nature and scale of Roman taxation. I apologise in advance for two failings: a necessary brevity which may seem sometimes to border on the superficial, and a focus on the Roman period which is deliberate since it is the value of the evidence from the Roman period which most needs advocacy. I shall also, inevitably, be raising issues rather than solving problems, and discussing what might [be] rather than what has been.

In the case of the first topic, the economic position of the rural population, we need to look as much at Ptolemaic as at Roman Egypt. One way in which the economy of Graeco-Roman Egypt was apparently exceptional in the classical world was the relative paucity of chattel slaves.[3] We start with a picture of classical Greece and classical Rome as slave-based societies, and expect them to have exported this mode of production to the other areas which they came to control. It is, however, becoming increasingly orthodox to believe that the mass of agricultural producers in the ancient world as a whole were in a position between slavery and freedom – leaving aside Egypt, examples are the helots and *penestai* of classical Greece, the indigenous *oiketai* of Magna Graecia, the so-called temple slaves and the crown peasants of the Seleucid and Attalid kingdoms, the Mancian coloni of North Africa, the *ambacti* and *obaerati* of the Celts in Gaul, and eventually the colonate of the later Roman empire.[4] Hence, incidentally, the growing tendency for historians of Marxist inspiration to talk of the slave mode of production being dominant in the ancient world in a qualitative or ideological rather than a simple quantitative sense.[5] The corollary is that it was classi-

---

[3] I. Biezunska-Malowist, *L'esclavage dans l'Egypte gréco-romaine*, I (1974), II (1977); W. L. Westermann, *Upon Slavery in Ptolemaic Egypt* (1929).

[4] [Helots, *penestai*, *oiketai*, coloni, *ambacti* and *obaerati* were types of slaves and unfree labourers in different parts of the Graeco-Roman world.] See for example: M. I. Finley, 'Between slavery and freedom', *Comparative Studies in Social History*, 6 (1964), 233–49; [...] C. R. Whittaker, 'Rural labour in three Roman provinces', in P. Garnsey (ed.), *Non-Slave Labour in the Greco-Roman World* (1980), 73–99.

[5] A. Carandini, *L'anatomia della scimmia* (1979), 129, 151–2, 196–9 etc.; G. E. M. de Ste Croix, *The Class Struggle in the Ancient Greek World* (1981), especially 52–4, 133–4 – cf. the

cal Greece and Italy with their related phenomena of free citizen smallholders and chattel slavery in agriculture which were the exceptions, and even these sharply bipolar systems were the products of socio-political revolutions which had abolished more 'normal' pre-existing systems based on an unfree peasantry – notably the *hektemoroi* ['sixth-part' tenants at the time of Solon] at Athens and the *nexi* [semi-free tenants] at Rome. These revolutions, the emergence of what we might call these 'super-economies', must surely play a large part in any attempt to explain the military expansion of these states. But for present purposes the important point is that the labour situation in Egypt was in broad terms 'normal' rather than 'exceptional'.

That said, we should not forget that in Egypt in the urban and domestic contexts the Greeks did import and the Romans maintained chattel slavery on a considerable scale.[6] Indeed we dispose of a fair amount of documentary evidence for the distribution, employment and treatment of urban and domestic slaves in Graeco-Roman Egypt which at the least has comparative value for wider studies of slavery in the classical world.[7] Far richer, however, is the evidence for unfree labour. Of course it cannot be used as a simple proxy for evidence for the many different unfree statuses elsewhere. There are, however, some important areas of overlap where the Egyptian evidence can have a direct bearing on agrarian systems found elsewhere, and the Egyptian evidence can always be used indirectly, in a comparative or suggestive manner. When writing about land-tenure and land-use in the classical world, it is very tempting to draw analogies or construct models from post-classical peasant societies. One scholar, for instance, recommends Lambton's study of landlords and peasants in Iran before 1962: 'A reading of at least chapters 13–18 and 21–2 of that book might do something to lessen the overconfidence of modern scholars who do not hesitate to generalise about land tenure in Seleucid Asia Minor and Syria or the Pergamene kingdom on the

---

criticisms of B. D. Shaw, 'The economy of the vampire bat', *Economy & Society*, 13 (1984), 208–49.

[6] For the question of the extent, nature and influence of slavery – if it existed – in pre-Ptolemaic Egypt see H. Heinen, 'Ägyptische und griechische Traditionen der Sklaverei im ptolemäischen Ägypten', in H. Maehler and V. M. Strocka (eds), *Das ptolemäische Ägypten* (1978), 227–35, with discussion 235–7; A. B. Lloyd, 'Egypt, 664–323 BC', in B. Trigger et al. (eds), *Ancient Egypt: A Social History* (1983), 279–348 (at 314–15).

[7] [...] See for example K. Hopkins, 'Brother–sister marriage in Roman Egypt', *Comparative Studies in Social History*, 22 (1980), 303–54 (329–31 on the distribution of slaves); K. R. Bradley, 'The age at time of sale of female slaves', *Arethusa*, 11 (1978), 243–52 (on the breaking up of slave 'families').

basis of a handful of isolated and often fragmentary texts'.[8] This is fair enough, but I would also or instead recommend consideration of the situation in contemporary Ptolemaic Egypt, where circumstances were not dissimilar in that Egypt too was an area which had passed from Persian to Graeco-Macedonian rule and exploitation. It is always possible to locate and emphasise differences between the economy of Ptolemaic Egypt and those of other Hellenistic kingdoms, but there are also common elements which deserve more attention.[9]

In the Zenon archive, to digress for a moment, we have an extremely rich source of formation on the composition and management of a *dorea* gift-estate – that of Apollonius, the *dioiketes* [treasurer] of Ptolemy II Philadelphus – which has yet to be set and interpreted in its historical context. Taken in isolation this archive has provided the documentary basis for construction of the historical thesis of the 'royal economy', the great dirigiste economic development which allegedly took place under Ptolemy II.[10] But the novelty of the enterprise has been exaggerated: schemes of agricultural development are attested throughout the Persian empire (and in Egypt under the Saïte pharaohs, as under previous dynasties), and among the many known Achaemenid gift-estates it is particularly worth comparing the Egyptian estate of Arsames, an Achaemenid prince and governor of Egypt in the later fifth century BC, which is documented in a small archive of letters in Aramaic.[11] A re-examination of the nature and function of Ptolemaic *doreai* in the light of earlier traditions might in turn illuminate some of the problems posed by the often terse epigraphic evidence for Seleucid gift-estates. So too we could reasonably expect fruitful results from comparison of the organisation of Graeco-Macedonian military settlements in

---

[8] De Ste. Croix, op. cit. (n. 5), 150–1, referring to A. K. S. Lambton, *Landlord and Peasant in Persia* (2nd edn, 1969).

[9] See the brief comments of J. K. Davies, 'Cultural, social and economic features of the Hellenistic world', *CAH*, VIII.1 (1984), 257–320 (esp. 299–304).

[10] The basic studies are: M. I. Rostovtzeff, *A Large Estate in Egypt in the Third Century* BC (1922); C. Préaux, *L'économie royale des Lagides* (1939); M. I. Rostovtzeff, *The Social and Economic History of the Hellenistic World* (1941), Ch. 4, B; C. Préaux, *Les Grecs en Egypte d'aprés les archives de Zénon* (1949); C. Orrieux, *Les papyrus de Zénon. L'horizon d'un grec en Egypte au IIIe siècle avant J.C.* (1983); id., *Zénon de Caunos, parépidémos, et le destin grec* (1985).

[11] See in general P. Briant, *Rois, Tributs et Paysans* (1982), 310–16, 418–30, 484–8; references to pre-Ptolemaic agricultural development schemes also in K. W. Butzer, *Early Hydraulic Civilisation in Egypt* (1979), 95–6 (Delta); J. M. Cook, *The Persian Empire* (1983), 72 (Khargeh Oasis). For the Arsames archive see the references in J. C. Greenfield, 'A new corpus of Aramaic texts of the Achaemenid period from Egypt', *AOS*, 96 (1979), 131–5; for discussion of the estate see J. Harmatta, 'Das Problem der Kontinuität im frühhellenistischen Ägypten', *Acta Antiqua Hung.*, 11 (1963), 199–213.

Egypt and other Hellenistic kingdoms insofar as it stemmed from two common influences: on the one hand the Achaemenid practice of settling soldiers by unit or ethnic group on allotments which though free of rent to the crown still owed taxes, and on the other the development of Philip II's new model army with soldiers settled on allotments in the newly drained plain of Philippi.[12] Thus while the immediate stimulus for Ptolemaic expansion of the cultivable area of the Fayum may have come from this Macedonian experience, its execution and success probably owed much to previous local experience of such developments. Attempts to determine the balance between Greek innovation and native tradition will always be controversial, but in general it would seem that the economic centralisation and development which we associate with early Ptolemaic Egypt owed far more to the Achaemenids and the Saïte pharaohs than is commonly recognised by classical scholars.

Returning now to the proper topic of the economic position of the rural population, study of the evidence from Graeco-Roman Egypt provides both comparative material and specific overlapping points with the classical world in general. One feature which is striking for its regular recurrence throughout this period in Egypt is the diversity of the 'peasant' economy, the many and varied economic activities pursued contemporaneously by members of family units, whether we look, to give but two instances, at the family of Dionysius son of Cephalas at Akoris in the later second century BC or at the family of Kronion in Tebtunis in the early second century AD.[13] This should serve to warn us against treating people in categories such as *basilikos georgos* [royal farmer], military settler, lessee of sheep, fisherman or carpenter as if these occupations were all mutually exclusive. For the topic of rural monetisation too we have abundant evidence from Egypt which provides a unique documentary control for interpretation of the numismatic evidence which elsewhere has to be used by itself. Here we meet a major economic innovation by the Graeco-Macedonian conquerors: they first introduced coinage and monetised exchange to Egypt in civil life on a significant scale, although under the Ptolemies it appears that monetisation barely percolated through to the native population. By the Roman period,

---

[12] [...] N. G. L. Hammond, *A History of Macedonia*, I (1972), 149, 160, 207; II (1979), 366–71.
[13] E. Boswinkel and P. W. Pestman, *Les archives privées de Dionysios, fils de Kephalas* (*Pap. Lugd.-Bat.*, XXII, 1982), = *P. Dion.*; cf. N. Lewis, *Greeks in Ptolemaic Egypt* (1986), Ch. 8.1; D. Foraboschi, *L'archivio di Kronion* (1971), = *P. Kron.*; cf. N. Lewis, *Life in Egypt under Roman Rule* (1983), 69–73.

however, despite the strong persistence in the countryside of exchanges in kind, virtually everyone was involved in the money economy, and it was largely their success in obtaining cash which
determined individuals' level of prosperity – see, for example, the
archives of the Fayum farmers Soterichus in the first century AD and
Aurelius Isidorus in the early fourth century.[14] This picture of a
diverse and monetised peasant economy is a model which can with
profit be used in considering the rural economy of other areas of
the Roman world. So too the Egyptian evidence allows us to assess
changes in rural prosperity across time, and to examine the probable
causes. It should be possible to trace the effects on rural prosperity
of factors such as the development of rights of private ownership
of land by the first century AD, of the later growth of large private
estates, of changes in the system of taxation and so on, in part by
tabulating rents, wages and food costs. The harvest is waiting, but
the labourers are lacking.

Perhaps more valuable, however, is what we can learn from the
Egyptian evidence of all periods about the specifics of the linking of
the rural labour-force to the land, the complex matrices of rights and
obligations which put many of the rural population in a position
between freedom and slavery. Here the *basilikoi georgoi* of Ptolemaic
Egypt have come in for some recent attention. Against the traditional
view that their tenure was extremely precarious, highly unfavourable
and virtually compulsory, the idea is gaining ground that the position
of *basilikoi georgoi*, who in fact mostly had other economic interests,
was more normally one of privilege.[15] Indeed this is one facet of a
growing appreciation of the rights and liberties of tenants in the
native Egyptian tradition.[16] Within Egypt this helps to explain the
very slow and partial development of rights of private ownership of
land in the Ptolemaic period – presumably even the Greeks did not
feel this was a pressing desideratum. Outside of Egypt we might
now be stimulated to re-evaluate the position of the apparently tied

[14] J. Bingen, 'Economie grecque et société égyptienne au IIIe siècle', in Maehler and Strocka
(eds), op. cit. (n. 6), 211–18, with discussion 218–19; A. E. Samuel, 'The money economy and
the Ptolemaic peasantry', *BASP*, 21 (1984), 187–206; D. Foraboschi and A. Gara, 'L'economia
dei crediti in natura (Egitto)', *Athenaeum*, 60 (1982), 69–83; S. Omar, *Das Archiv von
Soterichos* (*Pap. Colon.*, VIII, 1979), = *P. Soterichos*; cf. R. S. Bagnall, 'Theadelphian archive',
BASP, 17 (1980), 97–104 (at 98–9); A. E. R. Boak and H. C. Youtie, *The Archive of Aurelius
Isidorus in the Egyptian Museum, Cairo, and the University of Michigan* (1960), = *P. Cair. Isid.*
[15] See the recent discussion of J. Rowlandson, 'Freedom and subordination in ancient agriculture: the case of the basilikoi georgoi of Ptolemaic Egypt', in P. Cartledge and F. D. Harvey
(eds), *Crux. Essays in Greek History Presented to G.E.M. de Ste. Croix on his 75th Birthday*
(1985), 327–47.
[16] See in particular the articles of B. Menu collected in *Recherches sur l'histoire juridique,
économique et sociale de l'ancienne Egypte* (1982), Ch. 1.

tenants, not least the crown peasants, found in other areas of the Hellenistic world.

Still in the category of unfree labour, though advancing rapidly through time, I move to the relevance of the Egyptian evidence for the emergence and nature of the late Roman colonate. There have always been difficulties with the simple view that the colonate was the empire-wide product of Diocletian's legislation. Major problems include the length of time after Diocletian before evidence for the colonate in the sense of tenants tied to the land emerges, the survival of apparently free tenants and imperial edicts which reveal that the system was not, at least originally, found in all provinces.[17] Evidence from third-century Egypt, more precisely from the Heroninos archive, shows that at least fifty years before Diocletian tax-collectivities of tenants and workers had been set up on some larger estates, through which the landowner paid all the taxes for the members of the collectivity.[18] This disposes of the need to posit specific legislation by Diocletian to create the colonate. When he re-enacted, perhaps more stringently, the old Roman rule that taxpayers should be hereditarily liable for payments in their local administrative unit of origin, he will inadvertently have made hereditary any pre-existing local arrangements such as the tax-collectivities attested in the Heroninos archive. These tax-collectivities were the reality of the original 'colonate'. They involved private tenants, not the tenants of state land; they had been formed for local administrative convenience, and were not created through a deliberate policy of the central imperial government; and in many provinces they probably affected only a minority of the rural population. Later developments in the Roman use of the word '*colonus*' are beyond my scope here, but what may well have happened – and can probably be documented from the Egyptian evidence – is that the central government made a simplistic bureaucratic attempt to define in a single category, that of '*coloni*', the many forms of unfree rural labour which were to be found in the Roman empire. It was another admission, following the distinction between *honestiores* [the better off] and *humiliores* [the economically weaker], that the classical legal distinction between slave and free had little practical relevance for the majority of the subjects of Greek

[17] The classic view is that of A. H. M. Jones, 'The Roman colonate', *Past & Present*, 13 (1958), 1–13, repr. in P. A. Brunt (ed.), *The Roman Economy* (1974), Ch. XV; cf. *The Later Roman Empire* (1972), II, 795–803; for some problems of interpretation see W. Goffart, *Caput and Colonate: Towards a History of Late Roman Taxation* (1974), Ch. V.

[18] D. W. Rathbone, 'The Heroninos archive and the estate of Aurelius Appianus', PhD, Cambridge (1986), 73–7 [now published in revised form under the title *Economic Rationalism and Rural Society in 3rd Century BC Egypt* (1991)].

and Roman rule. But whether and how legislation about *coloni* actually affected the bulk of the rural population is a question which again is open to considerable debate, as is well illustrated by the recent re-interpretation of the evidence of the Apion estate in the Oxyrhynchite nome to mount a rousing challenge to established opinions on the emergence of feudalism in early Byzantine Egypt.[19]

I move now to my second topic in ancient economic history for which evidence from Egypt can be particularly useful, the character of ancient economic behaviour. Were the wealthy élite of the ancient world just like capitalists? Or were they, as many scholars hold, quite different, with no concept of or interest in the long-term accumulation of capital by productive investment?[20] This not the place to review this extensive debate, and instead I focus on two issues, archaeological evidence for manufacture and trade, and the level of sophistication of ancient accounting. In recent years there has been an enormous output of scholarly work on the production and distribution of ceramic artefacts in the classical world – especially fine tablewares, lamps and amphorae, and especially in the western Mediterranean. This alluringly quantitative evidence is often used to paint dramatic pictures of changing patterns of production and trade, despite a constant chorus of doubters who stress the difficulties of interpretation caused by the large silences in the archaeological material: the silence, for instance, about the production and movement of perishable items, the silence about the motives – not necessarily commercial – for movements of goods even over long distances, the normal silence about the identity of producers, transporters and purchasers, and so on.[21]

Even though the common pottery of Graeco-Roman Egypt has rather lost out to the mass of more immediately exciting finds, the material is there and current work holds out the hope of an improvement in the rate and quality of publication of such finds.[22] Where

---

[19] [...] J. G. Keenan, 'On law and society in late Roman Egypt', *ZPE*, 17 (1975), 237–50.

[20] M. I. Finley, *The Ancient Economy* (1973; 2nd edn, 1985), with M. Frederiksen, 'Theory, evidence and the ancient economy', *JRS*, 65 (1975), 164–71; P. Garnsey and R. Saller, *The Roman Empire* (1987), Chs. 3 and 4.

[21] For an introduction to the extensive literature see the items in n. 20 and the widely divergent views expressed in P. Garnsey, K. Hopkins and C. R. Whittaker (eds), *Trade in the Ancient Economy* (1983); also J. Paterson, 'Salvation from the sea: amphorae and trade in the Roman West', *JRS*, 72 (1982), 146–57; K. Greene, *The Archaeology of the Roman Economy* (1986), 156–68; D. P. S. Peacock and D. F. Williams, *Amphorae and the Roman Economy* (1986); M. Fulford, 'Economic interdependence among urban communities of the Roman Mediterranean', *World Archaeology*, 19 (1987), 58–75.

[22] The finds from Karanis are an important example: see L. A. Shier, *Terracotta Lamps from Karanis, Egypt. Excavations of the University of Michigan* (1978) [...]; B. Johnson, *Pottery from Karanis* (1981) [...]; cf. also A. L. Kelly, *The Pottery of Ancient Egypt: Dynasty I to*

Egypt is different is in the existence, in addition to all the data for prices (and for customs dues and sales taxes), of all kinds of texts to do with the production, sale and use of amphorae, of numerous contracts, accounts and letters which give information about the movement of goods, including perishable goods, within Egypt and also beyond it, with the bonus that these documents often make clear the social status of the persons involved. We thus have an opportunity, unique in the classical world, to submit interpretation of the archaeological material to documentary control.

Little has yet been done in this field, but for two topics at least the potential gains are already clear. For Rome's trade with the East via Egypt we can add to the brief comments in Roman literary sources two monographs of Egyptian origin, the *Periplus Maris Erythraei* and the *Christian Topography* of Cosmas Indicopleustes, inscriptions which range from private dedications to the Domitianic tax-schedule from Coptos, archaeological traces of traded items from sites in India and from the Red Sea ports and Coptos, and archives of and individual papyri and ostraka dealing with all kinds of facets of this trade-route. Despite two recent and sizeable monographs on Roman trade with the East there is still need of a study which uses the latest evidence [...] in an attempt to reconstruct the economics of this trade-route – the scale of the profits, how and where they were made, and above all who, including the state, took what share of the profits and by what types of agreements and mechanisms.[23] The results, even if tentative, would be illuminating for ancient economic history in general. For the topic of the production and distribution of amphorae, we should be able to match the names in the papyri with extant recognised types, providing a documentary control on the chronologies and distribution ranges suggested by the archaeological evidence, while the papyri already provide us with evidence for aspects like the system, scale, control, speed and costs of production which should be applicable to amphora production elsewhere in the classical world.[24] Conversely historians of Graeco-

---

Roman Times (1976). For amphorae see G. Nachtergael, *La Collection Marcel Hombert I, Timbres amphoriques et autres documents écrits acquis en Egypte* (1978); V. Grace and J.-Y. Empereur, 'Un groupe d'amphores ptolémaïques estampillées', *Bulletin du Centenaire (BIFAO, Suppl.)* (1981), 409–26; L. Criscuolo, *Bolli d'anfora greci e romani. La collezione dell'Università Cattolica di Milano* (1982).

[23] The monographs: M. G. Raschke, 'New studies in Roman commerce with the East', *ANRW* II 9.2 (1978), 604–1378; S. E. Sidebotham, *Roman Economic Policy in the Erythra Thalassa 30 BC–AD 217* (1986).

[24] Some examples: J. Riley, 'Industrial standardisation in Cyrenaica during the second and third centuries AD: the evidence for locally manufactured pottery', *Libyan Studies* (1979–80), 73–8 (though rather dubious!); H. Cockle, 'Pottery manufacture in Roman Egypt, a new

Roman Egypt could themselves benefit from greater integration of the archaeological with the papyrological evidence, as is shown, to give one example, by the recent study of the pattern of ownership and occupation of houses in Soknopaiou Nesos and Karanis.[25] We should not forget that papyri and ostraka are archaeological finds which can only lose by divorce from their original archaeological context.

Moving to another dusty corner in the warehouse of documentary papyrology, we come across the numerous private accounts from Graeco-Roman Egypt. Their sad neglect must be attributed largely to the malign influence of earlier studies, still taken as the standard view, which were rather rude about the level of sophistication achieved in these accounts.[26] But these judgments require modification. On the general plane historians and practitioners of accountancy are changing their criteria for assessing the usefulness of accounting systems, which means that 'simple' accounts are no longer necessarily taken as second best. At a lower, more specific level study of the third-century Heroninos archive, which relates to the large private estate of the Alexandrian magnate Aurelius Appianus, has persuaded me that the accounts kept on it were by far the most sophisticated yet recognised from the ancient world, and probably enabled calculation of profitability in cash terms, while the estate as a whole was structured and run in a highly centralised, efficient, resource-sharing and cash-conscious manner.[27] Of course if the outcome is that we are readier to believe that the élite of Roman Egypt ran their estates (and perhaps other businesses too) in an economically rational manner, the sceptical may try to confine this economic behaviour to Egypt, making it another example of Egypt's supposed uniqueness. But the evidence cannot be evaded so easily. These sophisticated accounts were the result of a development in Egypt after it had come under Roman rule, and although the precise stages of this development are yet to be traced, one important influence appears to have been the system of individual salary accounts used by the Roman army.[28] There is, furthermore, evidence that the

papyrus', *JRS*, 71 (1981), 87–97; D. W. Rathbone, 'Italian wines in Egypt', *Opus*, 2 (1983), 81–98.

[25] D. Hobson, 'House and household in Roman Egypt', *YCS*, 28 (1985), 211–29; cf. the useful work of G. Husson, *OIKIA. Le vocabulaire de la maison privée en Égypte d'après les papyrus grecs* (1983).

[26] G. Mickwitz, 'Economic rationalism in Graeco-Roman agriculture', *English Historical Review*, 52 (1937), 577–89; G. E. M. de Ste Croix, 'Greek and Roman accounting', in A. C. Littleton and B. S. Yamey (eds), *Studies in the History of Accounting* (1956), 14–74.

[27] R. H. Macve, 'Some glosses on Ste Croix's *Greek and Roman accounting*', in Cartledge and Harvey (eds), op. cit. (n. 15), 233–64; Rathbone, op. cit. (n. 18), Chs 8 and 9.

[28] Rathbone, op. cit. (n. 18), 178 n. 9, with reference to R. O. Fink, *Roman Military Records on Papyrus* (1971), nos. 68–73.

senatorial and equestrian élite and the upper classes of Roman Egypt had mutual knowledge of each other's agricultural systems: Seneca, for example, had a grace-and-favour estate in Egypt from which he received progress reports, while on Egyptian estates the Latin word 'cella' came to be used for barrack-type accommodation for the labour-force.[29] If sophisticated accounting and economically rational estate management were practised in Roman Egypt, the probability must be that they were practised in Roman Italy too and at a much earlier date. The nature of the accounts kept on large private estates in Italy cannot be deduced from Columella's rhetorical and exaggerated advocacy of the profitability of viticulture, and the fact that the extant Roman agricultural treatises contain a few incidental references to the keeping of accounts but no discussion of them does not indicate either that accounts were often not kept or that they were extremely simple.[30] It is rather a matter of literary tradition and choice that while the agronomists describe the basics of farming exhaustively, they omit crucial aspects of estate management such as accounting. Didactic muses have tackled some stodgy subjects in their time, but apparently even they could not stomach accountancy.

The last topic of ancient economic history which I wish to use to illustrate the value of the Egyptian evidence is Roman taxation. Questions of perennial debate here are how oppressive the rates of taxation were, whether the overall rate of taxation rose, especially in the later empire, and whether there were significant fluctuations in the proportion of taxes collected in cash against those collected in kind, and so on. Debate is perennial because it disposes of few hard facts. Normally the evidence from Roman Egypt is ignored or treated separately. Admittedly the Egyptian evidence is dense and difficult to interpret, and recent studies have tended to focus on particular problems, often without solving them.[31] However, the possible gains to be made from further work in this field can be illustrated by a rapid survey of just some of the more obvious pieces of evidence for the overall rate of taxation in cash and in kind.

The Arab historian Baladhuri claims that under the first Arab

[29] Sen., *Ep.*, 77.3; [...].

[30] R. P. Duncan-Jones, *The Economy of the Roman Empire, Quantitative Studies* (2nd edn, 1982), pp. 39–59; A. Carandini, 'Columella's vineyard and the rationality of the Roman economy', *Opus*, 2 (1983), 177–204. Cato, *De Agr.*, 2, expects various accounts to be kept and examined by the master; Columella reports Celsus' opinion that one advantage of an illiterate vilicus is that he cannot falsify the accounts (1.8.4), and regrets disregard of the old rule that the vilicus [bailiff] should not speculate with the master's cash because it impedes checking the accounts (1.8.13; also 11.1.24).

[31] Wallace, op. cit. (n. 2) remains fundamental [...]. For other more specific studies consult section 630 of the 'Bibliografia metodica' in *Aegyptus*.

governor of Egypt – when the Byzantine fiscal system was still in use – the total annual assessment of land and capitation taxes came to 2 million units (unspecified), which are probably to be taken as solidi.[32] A rough check on this figure is provided by a sixth-century papyrus from Antaeopolis which gives for a certain year the nome's total tax dues in both cash and kind, which in cash terms work out at around 0.32 solidus per aroura.[33] At this rate a total assessment of 2 million solidi would imply a taxable base of some $6\frac{1}{4}$ million arouras, which is a plausible figure for the total cultivable area of Byzantine Egypt. Of course part of the total tax assessment to the value of 2 million solidi was actually assessed and, in theory, was payable in kind. In the Antaeopolite text 37% of the total was due in kind, which works out in terms of wheat at an average rate of 1.2 artabas per aroura of all cultivable land. And a similar average rate for sixth-century Egypt as a whole is implied by the total annual tax revenue of 8 million artabas given in *Edict* 13.8 of Justinian. The plausibility of these figures stems not only from the congruence of the literary sources but also from the support of the extremely informative Antaeopolite document.

The question now is how these Byzantine–early Arab rates of taxation and the ratio between taxes due in kind and in cash compare with fiscal practice before the sixth century. As yet we have no document like the Antaeopolite one to give us total dues in cash in previous centuries, but rates of tax-assessment in wheat very similar to those of 1.2 to 1.3 artabas per aroura can be traced back to much earlier times. An early fourth-century papyrus gives the rates of wheat tax in the Oxyrhynchite as 3 artabas per aroura on public land and 1 artaba per aroura on private land, giving an average for the whole nome of 1.6 artabas per aroura, while in the same period land in the Arsinoite nome was taxed at exactly half the rates current in the Oxyrhynchite, but plus a small supplement assessed in barley, which in effect meant an average overall rate of roughly 1 artaba of wheat per aroura.[34] The rates on private land can be traced back even further to the low fixed rates levied on the old catoecic or cleruchic land [royal land given to soldiers settling in Egypt] from the time

[32] Here and in what follows I draw heavily on the presentation and interpretation of these Arab sources by M. A. H. El Abbadi, 'Historians and the papyri on the finances of Egypt at the Arab conquest', *Proc. XVI Int. Cong. Pap.* (1981), 509–16.

[33] P. Cairo Masp. 67057, in Johnson and West, op. cit. 1949 (n. 2), 275–80, but using the corrected figures of A. H. M. Jones, *JHS*, 71 (1951), 271–2.

[34] H. C. Youtie, 'P. Mich. inv. 335 verso: a summary register of wheatland', *ZPE*, 32 (1978), 237–40; with R. S. Bagnall and K. A. Worp, 'Grainland in the Oxyrhynchite nome', *ZPE*, 37 (1980), 263–4.

of its privatisation under Augustus. Those on public land appear to represent eventual official acceptance of the long-standing tendency to apply an average rate for the tax-rents due on public land instead of calculating a separate figure each year on the basis of the level of the Nile flood.[35] It thus seems that the average rate of taxation on land in Egypt, expressed in terms of wheat, remained broadly stable from at least the late first century BC to the later seventh century AD; indeed there was, if anything, a slight reduction in the overall average rate after the mid-third century [...] What may have changed in different periods is the ratio of actual receipts in kind as against receipts in cash, and the level of irregular exactions. If there were rises in tax rates in the third and the fourth centuries, they must have been cancelled subsequently, or perhaps they merely maintained the status quo by countering the cumulative tax-exemptions and evasions of the previous two centuries. It is also possible that collection of a greater percentage of taxes in kind rather than cash caused short-term disruption and aggravation. But this is a problem which cries out for more detailed work on the evidence from third century Egypt.[36] The fundamental stability of rates of taxation in Egypt, the flexibility of the medium of payment; the non-payment or recycling within the province of about half of the taxes assessed; these are all features of Roman and Byzantine fiscality which are of general significance for the economic history of those empires. In this field too the evidence of Egypt cannot be ignored with impunity.

[35] Wallace, op. cit. (n. 2), Ch. II; Johnson, op. cit. 1936 (n. 2), Ch. IV. iii; for the averaging out of rentals see G. Chalon, *L'édit de Tiberius Julius Alexander* (1964), 222–9.

[36] See D. Van Berchem, 'L'annone militaire est-elle un mythe?' *Armées et fiscalité dans le monde antique* (1977), 351–6, with discussion 337–9.

PART IV

Trade and Transfer

9 *Agricultural Products Transported in Amphorae: Oil and Wine*[†]

CLEMENTINA PANELLA
and ANDRÉ TCHERNIA

This article develops the theme of Chapter 4, moving from the production of cash crops to their transfer to the consumers. The geographical distribution patterns of the physical remains of ceramic containers for wine and olive oil, known as *amphorae*, have enabled modern scholars to reconstruct the main networks of trade in these goods. Thanks to the durability and large number of these artifacts, *amphora* studies have become a thriving sub-discipline within the field of classical archaeology that continues to make substantial contributions to the study of ancient economies. The present piece stands out for the unusually broad perspective taken by its authors.

Here, Clementina Panella, one of the leading Italian experts on Roman containers who is able to build on her own noteworthy surveys of this material,[‡] and the French archaeologist André Tchernia, best known for his fundamental study of the Roman wine trade,[§] team up to provide a succinct synthesis of a vast body of specialised research on the transport of liquid goods to Italy, tracing changes in the relative representation of containers from different regions from the late Republican to the early Byzantine periods (first century BC to sixth century AD). Although some of the details and technical language will be unfamiliar to novices to the field, their survey

---

† Originally published as 'Produits agricoles transportés en amphores: l'huile et surtout le vin', in *L'Italie d'Auguste à Dioclétien. Actes du Colloque International organisé par l'École Française de Rome, l'École des Hautes Études en Sciences Sociales, il Dipartimento di Scienze Storiche, Archeologiche, Antropologiche dell'Antichità dell'Università di Roma La Sapienza et lo Dipartimento di Scienze dell'Antichità dell'Università di Trieste (Rome, 25–28 mars 1992)*, Rome: École Française de Rome, 1994, pp. 145–65. Translated from the French by Antonia Nevill. Reprinted with permission.

‡ 'La distribuzione e i mercati', in A. Giardina and A. Schiavone (eds), *Società romana e produzione schiavistica*, Rome and Bari: Laterza, 1981, vol. II, 55–80; 'Le merci: produzione, itinerari e destini', in A. Giardina (ed.), *Società romana e impero tardoantico*, Rome and Bari: Laterza, 1986, vol. III, 431–59.

§ *Le vin de l'Italie romaine: essai d'histoire économique d'après les amphores*, Paris: École Française de Rome, 1986.

offers an accessible introduction to the methods and concerns of this particular approach. The authors' caution in drawing historical conclusions from
their data highlights both the potential and the limits of economic interpretations of this particular type of evidence. *Amphora* studies shed light on
geographical and chronological shifts in inter-regional trade but do not
normally allow us to measure changes in the overall scale of commercial
exchange or to explain the underlying economic forces of supply and
demand. Owing to the deficiencies of the primary sources, these more
general issues are best addressed with the help of theoretical models
(Hopkins, Ch. 10 below).

The aim of this article† is to determine, at some years' distance from
works published independently by the two authors,[1] the development of Italian trade as regards the products for which amphorae
have left remains – oil and, chiefly, wine. Fresh data have been
contributed by excavations recently carried out in Rome. These will
be combined for the first time with those from Ostia in a single graph,
whose interpretation provides an opportunity to demonstrate the
numerous points of agreement which now draw the writers' stand-
points closer together.

I STARTING POINTS

1 The reign of Augustus [...] places us at the heart of changes in
trading in Italy, especially for the products that interest us. This is a
point no longer in any doubt.

  a) *Oil.* Let us begin with what has least been commented upon. In
the Benaki collection of the Museum of Alexandria there are almost
600 stamped amphora handles from Brindisi, and these represent
over half of the stamped Latin handles. These same amphorae,
together with what have been called the 'ovoid amphorae of the
Republic' (Empereur and Hesnard, 1987), have been found distributed in small or very small numbers, but fairly widely, in the western Mediterranean area, where they penetrated farther inland than
was first believed – as far as Mont Beuvray, for instance. Both types
disappear shortly before or during Augustus' reign. Subsequently,
oil exports would be confined to Istrian oil, contained in Dr. 6B
amphorae, exported to Magdalensberg and the Danube (but not to
the Mediterranean) at least until the reign of Hadrian, perhaps
complemented and superseded by funnel-necked amphorae ('collo ad

---

  † Two maps and three tables included in the original article have been omitted here. All
dates are AD unless specified otherwise.
  [1] Panella, 1986, 1992; Tchernia, 1986, 1989.

imbuto'), which might also have been produced in certain places in the Cisalpine region (Pesavento, 1992).

b) *Wine*. The considerable visible decline between exports of the Dr. 1 and of the Dr. 2/4 has been stressed too often for us to refer to it again. But let us go further: where and when, after the end of the Republic, do we find a massive presence of Italian amphorae? At Carthage, either in the wall of Byrsa, dated between about 45 BC and 15 BC (where, with 40 stamps of *L. Eumachius* and 30 of *Maes(ianus) Cels(ius)*, which is a mark of Suessa Arunca, there is the largest known concentration of Italian amphora stamps), or around the beginning of the first century AD, with many Dr. 6 amphorae. Underwater archaeology provides evidence that leads in the same direction, as the last datable shipwrecks laden completely or partly with Dr. 2/4 or 6 Italian amphorae date to the time of Augustus.[2]

Thereafter, evidence of exports is not rare, but no longer gives the impression of massive amounts.[3] We have to wait until the second century for the flat-bottomed amphorae of Emilia to provide signs of exports, probably less important but nevertheless quantitatively noteworthy, to which we shall return later. Of course, these remarks relate only to mass exports and not those of the great vintages: the literary sources that demonstrate their persistence are now complemented, in the second half of the second century and right into the third, by the evidence of some amphora stamps and some 'late Campanian' (Arthur and Williams, 1992; Tchernia, 1996).

What were the consequences of the drop in overseas trade for Italian vineyards? We will not return to the transformation in types of vine, a necessary adaptation to different demands; but it is probable that certain vineyards on the Tyrrhenian coast disappeared in that period: at Dugenta, Astura and Gravisca, amphora-producing workshops stopped operating at the end of the Republic.[4] There were doubtless other disappearances in Augustus' time and during the first century. Henceforward, the remaining vineyards would find their main outlets in their production region and, for several of them, in Rome's vast market.

---

[2] Grand-Ibaud, D., Ladispoli, Tradelière (Hesnard et al., 1988; Gianfrotta and Hesnard, 1987; Fiori and Joncheray, 1975).

[3] For Gaul, among the most recent publications, see (on the drop in the percentages of amphorae from Lyon): Desbat and Martin-Kilcher, 1989; Desbat and Dangréaux, 1992, and the references cited therein; for Africa, see Riley, 1979; Fulford, 1983; Panella, 1983; Tchernia, 1996. Note, however, that this question is less clear regarding the eastern Mediterranean because the exact dates of Dr. 6 amphorae from Athens and Alexandria are not precisely known and we lack data from shipwrecks in the Aegean.

[4] Hesnard et al., 1989; Incitti, 1986.

2 During the same period, we find at Ostia, coming from Baetica and Tarraconensis, imports of three essential products transported in amphorae: oil, wine and fish. Other areas of provenance (Gaul, Africa and Lusitania) would add to or replace these, but the size of these imports was unfailing.

3 The end of overseas exports and the start of provincial imports are far from implying the end of commercial agricultural production in Italy taken as a whole. For wine, the amphorae of exporting areas under the Republic are found again in abundance in Rome up to the middle (Dr. 6) or end of the first century (Dr. 2/4). After that date, the latter tend to disappear fairly gradually, replaced by products from other regions (see below). For oil, although amphorae from peninsular Italy are no longer known after Augustus,[5] written proof exists of the continued use, up to the end of the first century, at least of oil from Venafrum and chiefly, up to the third or fourth century, of Sabine oil.[6] In fact, an entire zone of production around Rome permanently eludes the testimony of amphorae. Of particular concern are the wine and oil of the Sabine area, the wine of Tibur, Nomentum and the Montes Albani. In the latter case, the area has been relatively well examined and numerous presses are known (Bellini and Rea, 1985) without any trace of the production of amphorae having been discovered. Rome was near enough for savings to be made in transporting liquids, which were probably held in goatskins. In all these regions, there is textual evidence of a continuity which the proximity of the capital might in any case have led one to assume.

II PRESENTATION AND INTERPRETATION OF THE GRAPHS ON THE WINE TRADE

A *Presentation of the graphs*

I ARCHAEOLOGICAL CONTEXTS

An examination was made of the amphorae from several well-dated collections found in the stratigraphic excavations recently carried out in the centre of Rome. These groups were selected on the basis of the

---

[5] At Giancola, workshops producing 'ovoid [egg-shaped] amphorae' disappeared at the end of the Augustan period: Manacorda, 1990, 1993.

[6] Venafrum: Plin. *HN* 15.8; 17.31; Mart. 12.63.1; 13.101; Sabine: Columella, *Rust.* 5.8.5; Plin. *HN* 15.13. Galen was familiar with the characteristics of Sabine oil and oil from Istria: Sabine: Galen 6.196, 220, 287; 10.287, 577, 822; 11.392, 869, 872; Istria: 10.791, 822 (ed. Kühn). Sabine oil is also cited in the *Mulomedicina* 874, 875, 899, 903.

quantitative importance of the material, their representativeness, and thus the reliability of the figures deduced from them. In one instance only, average values were calculated on the basis of two different excavations (of the Meta Sudans near the Coliseum and of the Via Nova on the Palatine), because the areas excavated are not only of the same period, but also the result of the same process of formation, the levelling following the fire of 64.

For the periods not yet well attested in the Rome material, we have used the data provided by the stratigraphies of Ostia (the House of the Porch, the store of La Longarina and the Baths of the Swimmer). Ostia was the transit point for seaborne goods destined for Rome and, so to speak, lived in symbiosis with it. Although methodologically speaking not very strict (the material culture of Ostia is certainly not identical with that of Rome), this operation was made necessary in order to begin to formulate a hypothesis on the overall development of Rome's wine supplies over a long period. Obviously, this reconstruction will have to take stock of the new data which the Roman excavations will soon supply.

Within the chronological sequence that we offer (50 BC to 600), the period in which data are most lacking is from 250 to 400. We have available, in fact, only two Roman contexts, qualitatively poor (that of the crypt of Saint Bonaventure in 250–300 and of the temple of the Magna Mater in 350–90), and the only reasonably contemporary level at Ostia (layer 1 of room XVI) is one of slow formation (250–400) which, covering a very extended chronological arc, gives a hardly representative sample. However, we are dealing with a period that is fundamental to an understanding of certain phenomena of production that need to be better known.

2 AREAS OF PRODUCTION AND TYPES OF AMPHORAE

a) Wine amphorae from Italy

Forming part of the 'wine amphorae of the Tyrrhenian coast' are the 'Graeco-italic' and the Dr. 1 for the Republican period, the Dr. 2/4 and 'late Campanian' for the imperial era.[7]

Wine amphorae of internal central Italy include the type *Ostia III*, 369–70 (known from Spello in Umbria: Panella, 1989), present up to the levels of 190–210, and the type *Ostia IV*, 279–90 (known from Empoli in Tuscany: Cambi, 1989) attested starting from the levels of 230–50.

To the Adriatic wine amphorae belong (from the first century BC

---

[7] For the latter, see Panella, 1989; Arthur and Williams, 1992.

to the first century AD) the Lamboglia 2 and the Dr. 6A, and, from the levels of 130–50, the type *Ostia IV*, 440–2 (known from Forlimpopoli: Panella, 1989).

The amphorae of Calabria are represented by the type Keay LII, produced in Bruttium and possibly Sicily from the first decades of the fourth century (Andronico, 1991; Gasperetti and Di Giovanni, 1991; Arthur and Williams, 1992).

b) Other wine amphorae

Alongside the Italian amphorae just mentioned, we included in the wine amphorae all the provincial types that are believed with enough certainty to have been used for transporting wine, and a few other types that were undoubtedly for wine but whose origin is still doubtful (as for example the type *Ostia II*, 522–3/*Ostia I*, 553–4 = *Benghazi Mid Roman 1*, considered until now to be north African, but recently attributed by Wilson, 1990, to Sicily). Among the late amphorae, the *Carthage Late Roman 1* were regarded as wine transporters and have been taken into account in the calculations of these containers.

3 PERCENTAGES AND CORRECTION FACTORS

The graphs present a complex series of percentages inferred from each of the groups examined: wine amphorae out of the total number of amphorae (Figure 9.1), and Italian wine amphorae – separated in their turn by region of origin – out of the total number of amphorae (Figures 9.2 and 9.3). As these groups are spread fairly regularly in time, it was possible to show the development by a series of continuous lines and thus to follow over a long period not only arrivals in Rome of wine amphorae in comparison with arrivals of amphorae containing other products, but also the performance of Italian wine amphorae compared with provincial wine amphorae (Hispanic, Gaulish, African, Aegean and oriental taken as a whole).

The reader must be warned, however, of the risks of error inherent in this operation. Starting from percentages within each of the groups examined, it relies on a comparison of them to reconstruct, through the increase or decrease in these percentages, the development of arrivals of a specific product (wine) at a specific site (Rome/ Ostia). The supposition is that this can be shown from the trace of the curve (on this see Panella, 1983).

In the instance that concerns us here, it would have been necessary to introduce several correction factors in order to reach a less approximate evaluation of the figures to be interpreted. First, among

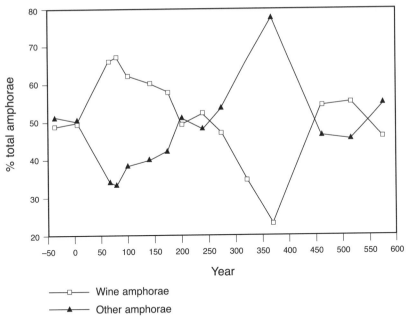

Figure 9.1 Development of the percentages of wine amphorae (Italian and provincial together) and amphorae intended for transporting products other than wine (oil, fish preserve) in the contexts of Rome and Ostia.

the most important, is the capacity of the types of amphorae, which is far from being uniform (flat-bottomed amphorae from those of Spello to those of Forlimpopoli – and almost all the late amphorae – from the Keay LII to the *Carthage Late Roman* 1, 3, 5/6 – transport a lower, and in some instances very much lower, quantity than the Italian amphorae of the end of the Republic and beginning of the Empire); second, the demographic evolution of the sites under consideration. Rome seems to have seen its population decline by half after 410 (Mazzarino, 1951; Durliat, 1990, p. 117), while the very existence of Ostia in the early fifth century is attested only by scarce and poor evidence.

The first point (the capacity of the various types of amphorae) leads one to qualify the apparent stability of the place of Italic wine amphorae between 10 and 190 – between 29% and 21%, as shown in Figure 9.2. In fact, the majority of the Italian amphorae attested in the levels of the second century contain on average one-third less liquid than those of the first century. We may thus assume that between 100 and 200 the percentage of arrivals of wine (if not of amphorae) in the sites studied should be decreased by a few points.

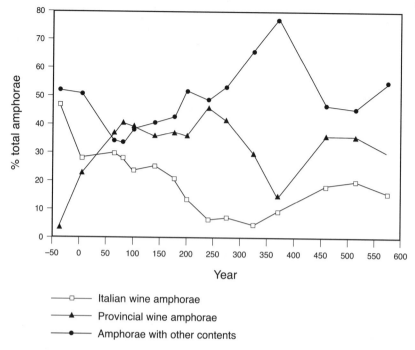

Figure 9.2 Development of the percentages of Italian wine amphorae, provincial wine amphorae and amphorae intended for transporting goods other than wine on the sites of Rome and Ostia.

Similarly, in Figure 9.1, the spectacular increase starting in 350–90 of the proportion of wine amphorae to the total number of amphorae of that period (Italian, Aegean and oriental) had a low capacity (only 3–6 litres for the *Carthage Late Roman 3*!), whereas in the same period (from 430) some African oil or garum amphorae increased their capacity.

As regards the second point (demographic evolution), if one accepts the hypothesis that Rome's population dwindled from the early fifth century and subsequently continued to decline (for some months during the Graeco-Gothic war of the sixth century the inhabitants deserted the town), one obviously has to accept a heavy drop in demand, and consequently in arrivals of amphorae.

The percentages curve cannot take this factor into account. However, it would be possible to introduce a correction element based on hypotheses of the development of demand. If this were done, it would naturally become apparent that there had been no increase, between the third to fourth centuries and the fifth to sixth centuries, in the arrivals of wine-carrying amphorae in Rome.

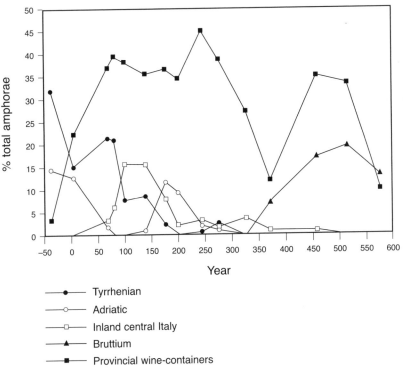

Figure 9.3 Development of the percentages of Italian wine amphorae, sorted by place of origin, and provincial wine amphorae on the sites of Rome and Ostia.

B Interpretation of the chief movements in the curve

For the Italian wine-carrying amphorae, there are clearly two fundamental interruptions.

1 The first is in the time of Augustus. From the House of the Porch around 40 BC to La Longarina several decades later, the collapse in the percentage of Italian amphorae chiefly illustrates the development of provincial imports in all products, but especially in that of wine (Figure 9.2). The proportion of Italian amphorae decreases heavily whereas those of wine amphorae over amphorae as a whole, regardless of content, tends to increase slightly (Figure 9.1).

2 The situation illustrated by Figure 9.2 between the Julio-Claudian era and the end of the Antonine era raises more interesting problems. Commencing from the first half of the first century, and up to the years 160–90, the figures for Italian wine amphorae tend to stabilise, with a slight decrease, to be seen from context to context and mainly noticeable if their capacity is taken into account. Before descending in its turn, the curve of imported wine amphorae con-

tinues at first to grow and reaches its highest points between the time of Nero and that of Trajan, peaking in the Flavian period (Figure 9.2). Since at that time the figures for Italian amphorae remain pretty constant, it would appear that the overall quantities of wine sold in Rome's market increased, and that this increase was due exclusively to provincial production.

This last aspect of the situation could be related to the destruction in the eruption of 79 of the vineyards in the region of Vesuvius, whose amphorae had previously been fairly well attested in Rome. However, it must be noted that, in the context of 64, provincial wines already had a very strong presence. The catastrophe that struck part of Campania does not therefore seem to have played a big part – unless very momentarily – in imports. On the other hand, it must have had a certain impact (and how could it be otherwise?) on the internal balance of Italian production (Tchernia, 1986).

The relative stability of Italian production as a whole, which we have emphasised, in fact masks profound internal changes (Figure 9.3). Up to the time of the Flavians, production on the Tyrrhenian coast represents over half the Italian amphorae. Starting from the end of the first century and the early second, it is inland central Italy that dispatches little flat-bottomed amphorae in large numbers, reaching levels of the same kind as the Tyrrhenian amphorae of the preceding period. With a new flat-bottomed shape, amphorae from the Adriatic coast also make their reappearance; in the Antonine era, they have percentages that are fairly close to those of the Dr. 6 in the reign of Augustus.

We must pause a moment over the two strands of production that become established and develop during the period when the villa of Settefinestre ceases producing wine and starts receiving it from Gaul, as does the surrounding region.

The amphorae of inland central Italy appear under Tiberius and are attested up to the Severan era. Until now, workshops have been found only at Spello in Umbria, but other production centres did exist, no doubt especially in north Etruria (*Ager Pisanus, Ager Volterranus*: see Menchelli, 1990–1). Their spread was fairly limited and they were primarily intended for the mass consumption of Rome. This explains the difference in the percentages for Rome and Ostia. Coming down the Tiber, they did not continue their journey to Ostia, where the proportion of amphorae from Gaul was greater.

Around the same time, Pliny the Younger (*Ep.* 5.6) depicts the *region* (we follow the interpretation of De Neeve, 1990) of *Tifernum Tiberinum* in the upper valley of the Tiber as covered in vines: *sub his (collibus) per latus omne vineae porriguntur, unamque faciem longe lateque contexunt; quarum a fine imoque quasi margine arbusta nascuntur* [Below them (i.e., the hills) the vineyards spreading down every slope weave their uniform pattern far and wide, their lower limit bordered by a plantation of trees]. His letter is intended to reassure a correspondent who believed he was going to coastal Etruria; no, he is going to inland Etruria: *Ne facerem suasisti, dum putas insalubres. Et sane gravis ac pestilens ora Tuscorum, quae per litus extenditur. Sed hi procul a mari recesserunt* [Nor shall I allow myself to be persuaded, while you think them unhealthy. The stretch of Tuscany along the coast is certainly unhealthy and rife with pestilence; but these (i.e., my lands) are far from the sea]. The excavations of the villa Settefinestre have revealed, however, not any traces of malaria in coastal Etruria in Pliny's time, but a reconversion of the villa's production and ways of life that is just as significant. One of the causes of malaria was in fact the depopulation of the countryside and the abandonment of systems of drainage and irrigation (the trenches of centuriation) which for centuries had contributed to keeping at bay from this region the hazards of malarial marshes (Carandini, 1989).

The amphorae of Emilia make a timid appearance under the Flavians, establish themselves in the Antonine era and disappear from the sites under consideration at the end of the Severan period. With them, non-sporadic archaeological traces of distant exports of Italian wine are found, since there are numbers of them in the reserves of the Agora Museum of Athens, and they are similarly attested at Knossos and Tripolitanian Berenice. Let us remember that third-century Egyptian papyri mention amphorae *Hadrianai* (Rathbone, 1983). A wrecked ship laden with these amphorae recently discovered at Sant'Alessio near the Strait of Messina must have been on its way to Rome, however.

3 The second break, as spectacular as the first, occurred at the end of the second century and the beginning of the third. During this period, evidence of provincial amphorae remains relatively stable and even, around the mid-third century, reaches a second peak (after that of the Flavian era) (Figure 9.2). At the end of the second century, the decline in the curve of wine amphorae as a whole (Figure 9.1) is solely due to the decrease of the percentage of Italian amphorae (Figure 9.2). This would seem to indicate that the decrease in commercial Italian wine in amphorae was partially compensated for by arrivals from the provinces, but without their being sufficient to maintain the whole at the level of the preceding decades. After 250,

we witness a sudden drop in provincial amphorae, and wine amphorae as a whole reach their lowest level during the fourth century (350–90) (Figures 9.1 and 9.2). As it is impossible to suppose that wine consumption in Rome had diminished so considerably, this evidence can be set beside the hypothesis of a contemporary spread of the use of casks in the wine trade.

4 Let us take stock of this problem, on the subject of which the assessments made by the authors of this article may sometimes diverge by a few degrees, but are based on the following common findings.

a) The bas-relief of Cabrières d'Aigues proves that the use of amphorae could occur in the same production area as the use of the cask.

b) The texts of the Digest confirm that the use of casks began to be widespread in Italy at the latest in the early third century. There is no proof of their use on the western side of Italy before then. Neither the bas-relief of the Capitoline Museum, close to the third Pompeian style, nor the casks on Trajan's column, which might concern the north of Italy, have as yet had any explanation that could integrate them in a coherent system. That is why we do not want to use casks to interpret the drop in the percentage of wine amphorae between the middle and the end of the second century (Figure 9.1). This explanation would be all the more difficult to adopt, since at the same time the proportion of Adriatic amphorae clearly increases (Figure 9.2), whereas this region would be the best candidate for an early development of the use of casks.

c) On the other hand, iconography and epigraphy bear witness that casks were in quite common use in Rome in the late third century and the fourth.

d) Although the existence of casks casts doubt on the discontinuities that emerge from a study of the amphorae, it does not prove continuity either, in the absence of material traces and in each of the local instances. It cannot be ruled out, in particular, that casks could have replaced goatskins, and to a greater or lesser degree been used for transporting wines from regions bordering on Rome, the containers leaving no traces, as we have just said. If one comes down to the level of each production region, one notices that the only zone for which precise argument puts it beyond doubt that casks were added to amphorae is the north Adriatic region. There we have the combined evidence of casks found by Maximinus' army among the winegrowers of the region of Aquileia in 238, according to Herodian's account (8.4.4), bas-reliefs of Aquileia and Ancona (Tchernia, 1986,

Fig. 4), and, for the continuity of production in an area which in the time of the Dr. 6 probably contained an amphora workshop, a letter from Constantius and Constans (354) to the *ordo Caesenatianum* regarding wine *'quod ad cellarii usus ministrari solet'* [which is customarily furnished for use as cellar supplies] (*Cod. Theod.* 11.1.6). Elsewhere, it can only be a question of hypotheses which are a matter of personal assessment.

III THE END OF THE CURVE

The recovery of the percentage of Italian wine amphorae from the second half of the third century is due to the presence of one type alone, which makes up almost all the total of Italian amphorae: the Keay LII. These are small, flat-bottomed, fairly crude amphorae, with a capacity of from 12 to 14 litres. They are very widespread in the late fourth century and in the fifth century in Greece (Athens, Argos), southern Gaul, Spain and Italy. In 1989 P. Arthur advanced the theory that they came from Bruttium, and that hypothesis was confirmed more recently by the discovery of workshops near Reggio di Calabria. Some also very probably came from Sicily, and there is nothing to say that other centres of production did not exist.

Nevertheless, it is interesting to note that there had previously been production of amphorae in Lucania and Bruttium, from the late Graeco-Italic in the mid-second century BC up to the first century AD (De Caro, 1985). These amphorae were marketed locally and in small quantities elsewhere. When, with the Keay LII, much more widespread production reappeared in the fourth century, a whole range of texts supports the archaeological data. The *Expositio totius mundi* (53) says that Bruttium *'emittit [...] vinum multum et optimum'* [produces a lot of excellent wine]. It is the only passage in the text that mentions exports from Italy, since it is mostly concerned with those from Cilicia, Cappadocia, Dalmatia, Spain and Africa. The Theodosian Code (14.4.4) bears witness in 367 to the arrival in Rome of fiscal wines from Lucania and Bruttium (which created problems, since in response to their complaints, the owners were authorised to replace them by other allowances). In the sixth century, Cassiodorus, in two very interesting letters (*Variae* 12.12 and 14), explains that the Reggio region is poorly endowed with grassland and wheat but rich in olive trees and vines; he describes the wines of Bruttium, which are of high quality and much esteemed at the royal table. A native of the region, he boasts of a vintage named *Palmatianum*, which has 'full body and a creamy smoothness; it is robust and ages well; it has a forceful nose, a remarkable sparkle, and its bouquet, when spat out, has justly merited its taking its name from the palm'.

Once more, texts whose real economic scope has been difficult to evaluate up to the present acquire more meaning and weight from archaeological data. But let us not be under any illusion. As we said above, fifth- to sixth-century Rome did not belong to the same world as Rome in the second to third centuries. For a heavily diminished population, with a different tax system, imports no longer played the same role. Not only their quantity, but also their structure, and especially the respective shares of luxury and mass produced goods, must have been profoundly altered. Moreover, the cask doubtless won the day at that time for the western wine-containers. In fact, there were only oriental wine amphorae or those from the Aegean to compete with the Keay LII. Among such a reduced population of amphorae, the increase in one of the factors is enough to modify the percentages radically. We must therefore be careful not to think that the occurrences represented by the extreme right of the curve are of the same kind as those revealed by its left side.

CONCLUSION

To conclude the discussion of data on Italian production, supplied mainly by the amphorae of Rome and Ostia, and the methodological reflections they inspire, we shall avoid dealing with the problems posed by the establishment of causal links and seeking the origin of changes. One point alone seems to us sufficiently evident to be worth emphasising.

Shifts of balance in agricultural production and exports between Italy and the provinces have long been the source of much argument and, speaking of Italy, one nearly always thinks of Campania, Latium and Etruria. Now it increasingly appears that the Tyrrhenian coast of central Italy did not have the monopoly on farming as an investment and overseas trading. Since the Lamb. 2 of the Republic are attributed to the northern half of the Adriatic coast (Carre and Cipriano, 1989), the vineyards of this region assume an economic importance almost equalling that of the vineyards of Etruria or Campania, and in the long term their prosperity poses fewer problems of continuity than that of the mass vineyards of the western side: except for the interruption in the second half of the first century, they do not seem to have stopped sending their wine by sea, throughout at least four centuries, chiefly in the direction of Rome and the

Aegean Sea. However, the archaeological landscape of the Adriatic coast differs considerably from that of the Tyrrhenian coast, and one does not find the impressive remains of villas which still adorn Etruria, Latium and Campania. What is implied here? Perhaps simply the glaring inequality in excavations (Fentress, 1990–1) and the less visible vestiges in a region where fine and durable building materials are harder to find.

But several other regions of Italy in their turn have demonstrated their ability to pass from an agriculture with local outlets to one directed towards distance trading, in particular to Rome. Even though we have just warned against the risk of over-interpreting them, the amphorae of Bruttium in the fourth century provide an example. The expansion of the vineyards of the Tiber basin, concomitant with the decline of those on the Tyrrhenian coasts, in the first and second centuries, give another particularly eloquent instance. The percentage curves show clearly that consideration of the changes in Italy's internal equilibrium, and their causes, would today prove a more fruitful task, and one more likely to give an account of the economic history of the heart of the Empire, than continuing to make overall comparisons between Italy and the provinces. But of course, it should not make us forget the considerable amount of food products coming from the provinces, from the time of Augustus, to Italy's urban centres, Rome in particular, and their surrounding areas.

BIBLIOGRAPHY

Andronico, E. (1991), 'Il sito archeologico di Pellaro (fraz. di Reggio Calabria', *MEFRM*, 103, 2, pp. 731–6.

Arthur, P. (1989), 'Some observations on the economy of Bruttium under the Later Empire', *JRA*, 2, pp. 133–42.

Arthur, P. and Williams, D. (1992), 'Campanian wine, Roman Britain and the third century', *JRA*, 5, pp. 250–60.

Bellini, G. R. and R. Rea (1985), 'Note sugli impianti di produzione vinicolo-olearia nel suburbio di Roma', in *Misurare la terra: centuriazione e coloni nel mondo romano. Città, agricoltura e commercio: materiali da Roma e dal suburbio*, Rome, pp. 119–31.

Cambi, F. (1989), 'L'anfora di Empoli', in *ARHE*, pp. 564–6.

Carandini, A. (1989), 'La villa romana e la piantagione schiavistica', in *Storia di Roma*, 4, Turin, pp. 101–92.

Carre, M. B. and M. T. Cipriano (1989), 'Production et typologie des amphores de la côte adriatique de l'Italie', in *ARHE*, pp. 67–104.

De Caro, S. (1985), 'Anfore per pece del Bruzio', in *Klearchos*, 105–8, pp. 21–32.

De Neeve, P. W. (1990), 'A Roman landowner and his estates: Pliny the Younger', *Athenaeum*, 68, 2, pp. 363–400.

Desbat, A. and B. Dangréaux (1992), 'La distribution des amphores dans la région lyonnaise. Étude de deux sites de consommation', in F. Laubenheimer (ed.), *Les Amphores en Gaule. Production et circulation*, Besançon, pp. 151–6.

Desbat, A. and S. Martin-Kilcher (1989), 'Les amphores sur l'axe Rhône-Rhin à l'époque d'Auguste', in *ARHE*, pp. 339–65.

Durliat, J. (1990), 'De la ville antique à la ville byzantine. Le problème des subsistances', in *CEFR*, 134, Rome.

Empereur, J.-Y. and H. Hesnard (1987), 'Les amphores hellénistiques', in *Céramiques hellénistiques et romaines*, II, Besançon-Paris, pp. 9–71.

Fentress, E. (1990–1), 'Les prospections en Italie', *Nouvelles de l'archéologie*, 42, pp. 9–14.

Fiori, P. and J.-P. Joncheray (1975), 'L'épave de la Tradelière. Premiers résultats des fouilles entreprises en 1975', *CAS*, 4, pp. 59–70.

Fulford, M. G. (1983), 'Pottery and the economy of Carthage and its Hinterland', *Opus*, 2, pp. 5–14.

Gasperetti, G. and V. Di Giovanni (1991), 'Precisazioni sui contenitori calabresi della tarda antichità (le anfore tipo Keay LII)', *MEFRM*, 103, 2, pp. 875–85.

Gianfrotta, P. and A. Hesnard (1987), 'Due relitti augustei carichi di dolia: quelli di Ladispoli e del Grand Ribaud D', in *El vi a l'Antiguitat, economia, producció i comerç al Mediterrani Occidental*, Actes du Colloque de Badalona, 28 Nov. to 1 Dec. 1985, Badalona.

Hesnard, A., M. B. Carre, M. Rival and B. Dangréaux, 'L'épave romaine Grand Ribaud D (Hyères, Var)', *Archaeonautica*, 8.

Hesnard, A., M. Ricq, P. Arthur, M. Picon and A. Tchernia, 'Aires de production des gréco-italiques et des Dr. 1', in *ARHE*, pp. 21–65.

Incitti, M. (1986), 'Recenti scoperte lungo la costa dell'alto Lazio. Una produzione di anfore nell'ager di Graviscae', *BA*, Suppl. to 37–8, *Archeologia Subacquea*, 3, Rome, pp. 198–202.

Manacorda, D. (1990), 'Le fornaci di Visellio a Brindisi. Primi risultati dello scavo', *Vetera Christianorum*, 27, pp. 375–415.

Manacorda, D. (1993), 'Produzione agricola, produzione ceramica e proprietà della Calabria romana tra Repubblica e Impero', in *Epigrafia della produzione e della distribuzione*, Rome, pp. 3–59.

Mazzarino, S. (1951), *Aspetti sociali del IV secolo*, Rome, pp. 217–47.

Menchelli, S. (1990–1), 'Una fornace di anfore Dressel 2–4 nell'ager Pisanus ed alcune considerazioni sui contenitori vinari prodotti nell'Etruria settentrionale in età romana', *Opus*, 9–10, pp. 169–82.

Panella, C. (1983), 'La anfore di Cartagine: nuovi elementi per la ricostruzione dei flussi commerciali del Mediterraneo in età imperiale romana', *Opus*, 2, pp. 53–74.

Panella, C. (1986), 'Le anfore tardoantiche: centri di produzione e mercati preferenziali', in A. Giardina (ed.), *Società romana e Impero tardoantico*, III, *Le merci, gli insediamenti*, Bari–Rome.

Panella, C. (1989), 'Le anfore italiche del II secolo', in *ARHE*, pp. 139–78.

Panella, C. (1992), 'Mercato di Roma e anfore galliche nella prima età imperiale', in F. Laubenheimer (ed.), *Les amphores en Gaule. Production, Circulation*, Bescançon, pp. 185–218.

Pesavento Mattioli, S. (1992), *Anfore romane a Padova: ritrovamenti dalla città*, Modena.

Rathbone, D. W. (1983), 'Italian wines in Roman Egypt', *Opus*, 2, pp. 81–98.

Riley, J. A. (1979), 'Coarse pottery', in J. A. Lloyd (ed.), *Excavations at Sidi Khrebish-Benghazi (Berenice)*, Suppl. to *Libya Antiqua*, 6, p. 91.

Tchernia, A. (1986), *Le vin de l'Italie romaine*, Rome.

Tchernia, A. (1989), 'Encore sur les modèles économiques et les amphores', in *ARHE*, pp. 529–36.

Tchernia, A. (1996), 'Maesianus Celsus et Caedicia Victrix sur des amphores de Campanie', in M. Cébeillac-Gervasoni (ed.), *Les élites municipales de l'Italie péninsulaire des Gracques à Néron*, Rome.

Wilson, R. J. A. (1990), *Sicily under the Roman Empire. The Archaeology of a Roman province 36 BC–AD 536*, Warminster.

10 *Rome, Taxes, Rents and Trade*[†]

KEITH HOPKINS

In 1980, Keith Hopkins presented a general model of the interdependence of movements of taxes, traded goods and money in the Roman empire.[‡] This bold attempt to construct a comprehensive explanatory framework for the expansion of market exchange in the wake of Roman conquest attracted considerable attention as well as criticism. One and a half decades later, Hopkins restated and refined his position in an article that took full account of the debate triggered by his original argument. Published in an academic journal of limited circulation, this important contribution is now being made more readily accessible. Hopkins, who held Moses Finley's chair at Cambridge, stands out among ancient historians for his professional background and research in both classics and sociology. As a social scientist, he has consistently preferred deductivist arguments and comparativist analogy over positivist and inductivist readings of ancient source material. After successfully redefining the terms of the debate in Roman population studies, Hopkins soon turned to the study of the Roman economy, devising sweeping models of urbanisation, the spread of chattel slavery, and the expansion of trade that have left their mark on the field.[§]

Here and elsewhere, he takes a mildly developmental approach, allowing for a measure of real economic growth in response to the increasingly efficient coercion of surplus from subject populations. Moving beyond the empirical analysis of ancient source material and generalisations from particular texts and artifacts, Hopkins seeks to identify the principal forces driving economic development and commercial exchange in the Roman empire, and to explore the logical implications of their interactions. Less constrained by disparate and often inadequate sources and the absence

---

[†] Originally published as 'Rome, Taxes, Rents and Trade', *Kodai: Journal of Ancient History* VI/VII (1995/6), 41–75. Reprinted with permission.

[‡] 'Taxes and Trade in the Roman Empire, 200 BC–AD 400', *Journal of Roman Studies* LXX (1980), 101–25.

[§] 'Economic Growth and Towns in Classical Antiquity', in P. Abrams and E. A. Wrigley (eds), *Towns in Societies: Essays in Economic History and Historical Sociology*, Cambridge: Cambridge University Press, 1978, pp. 35–77; *Conquerors and Slaves: Sociological Studies in Roman History, 1*, Cambridge: Cambridge University Press, 1978; 'Models, Ships and Staples', in P. Garnsey and C. R. Whittaker (eds), *Trade and Famine in Classical Antiquity*, Cambridge: Cambridge Philological Society, 1983, pp. 84–109.

of ancient statistics than more traditional modes of enquiry, this approach sheds light on underlying mechanisms that would otherwise remain obscure. This strength, however, has also been considered a weakness by scholars who have emphasised apparent discrepancies between predictions generated by the model (such as the reciprocity of tax and trade flows) and samples of empirical evidence, above all coinage. Richard Duncan-Jones in particular, in a series of studies of the movement of coins and goods, has repeatedly challenged crucial elements of Hopkins's argument.¶ In this paper, Hopkins responds to these criticisms, discusses methodological issues, and defends a revised version of his model. The only comprehensive attempt to explain the dynamics of the Roman imperial economy currently available, this restatement will remain the starting point for further research for the foreseeable future.

INTRODUCTION

The purpose of this article is to review some working-methods in Roman economic history, to make some propositions, to analyse their implications, and to understand the criticisms levelled against these methods and conclusions. In some sense, the article is unashamedly apologetic, but it is also, I hope, revisionist and self-critical. Inevitably, I made errors in my previous work, and it seems only sensible to acknowledge some of them. And yet in the end I still want to reassert the broad utility of models in ancient economic history, and the basic validity of the specific model of the Roman economy and of the main conclusions, which I put forward nearly twenty years ago.[1] In sum, I want to go over some old arguments, assess criticisms, confess some faults, and break new ground.

Some of the greatest fun I have had in Roman history has been in constructing models. A model is, roughly speaking, a simplification of a complex reality, designed to show up the logical relationships between its constituent parts. The utility of models in Roman history, as I see it, is twofold. First, models allow us to perceive the structures or repeated patterns which lie behind the superficial flow of indi-

---

¶ R. Duncan-Jones, *Structure and Scale in the Roman Economy*, Cambridge: Cambridge University Press, 1990, Ch. 2; *Money and Government in the Roman Empire*, Cambridge: Cambridge University Press, 1994.

[1] 'K. Hopkins, Taxes and Trade in the Roman Empire, *JRS* 70 (1980) 101ff. Two synoptic reviews of the current state in the field are intelligently incisive: William Harris, 'Between Archaic and Modern', in W. V. Harris ed., *The Inscribed Economy* (Ann Arbor, 1993) 11ff and E. Lo Cascio, 'Forme dell'economia imperiale', in A. Schiavone ed., *Storia di Roma* (Torino, 1991) 313ff especially 351ff. The book of Hans-Ulrich von Freyberg, *Kapitalverkehr im römischen Kaiserreich* (Freiburg im Bresgau, 1989), represents a real advance in sophistication, and is now essential reading: see the discussion by J. Andreau, *L'Italie d'Auguste à Dioclétian* (Rome, 1994) 175ff.

vidual actors and events, which fill the pages of traditional Roman narrative histories. Secondly, models allow us to construct whole pictures, into which the surviving fragments of ancient source material can be plausibly fitted. The model is a sort of master picture, as on the front of a jigsaw puzzle box; the fragments of surviving ancient sources provide only a few of the jigsaw pieces.

All this may still seem heresy to some. The dominant orthodoxy among traditional ancient historians is still induction; they move from evidence to conclusion, or at the very least that is how they prefer to present their arguments. For some Roman historians, even that is going too far; for a significant conservative minority, the primary focus is on the acquisition and display of knowledge, used often enough as a defence against arguing propositionally. For such people, speculation is a term of abuse, and they sometimes affect to sneer at models as though they are frivolous and irresponsible.[2]

Actually, there is ample room for both compromise and overlap between model-builders and inductivists; their positions are more complementary than opposed. After all, deduction like induction is partly a rhetorical pose. The model-builder, if he/she is going to have any chance of success, has to know much of what the sources tell us. The pure inductivist, if he/she is going to be understood outside a narrow range of committed specialists, has to think through what the implications are of his/her, detailed arguments. Quite a few conservative historians nowadays have a nodding, if uneasy, acquaintance with deductive arguments, model-building, and comparative evidence.[3] The gap between the various schools is not as wide as it once was. That said, I still think that the style and shape of my arguments on Roman economic history are distinctively different from the norm; and so, their assumptive frame is not always understood, and

---

[2] A recent and amusing case, *exempli causa*, is in the excitingly innovative book by Roger S. Bagnall, *Egypt in Late Antiquity* (Princeton, 1993). It is self-consciously inductivist, and presents a huge amount of well-documented detail. The care put into the detail is then used to legitimate the generalising inferences, which are often disproportionate to the evidentiary base. Per contra, Bagnall explicitly denies the utility of models (p. 310), and then proceeds to present a rather good simplifying model of the Egyptian agricultural economy.

[3] Harry Pleket, who would I think call himself a conservative historian, provides a wealth of comparative data in his long and interesting discussion of Roman economic history: 'Wirtschaft', in F. Vittinghoff ed., *Handbuch der Europäischen Wirtschafts- und Sozialgeschichte* (Stuttgart, 1990) vol. 1, 25–160. But his comparisons illustrate more often the possible than the probable. I agree with him completely that the agriculture of the Roman empire was a patchwork of varied agricultural practices and productivity, and that the area under cultivation and total product probably grew in the first two centuries AD. But his broad conclusions (pp. 78–9) on average agricultural productivity (yields of 8–10 times seed for Italy) seem much too optimistic, if only because he fails to fit them into a matrix of cognate probabilities (e.g. population and demand). See below.

their utility and its limits are not always appreciated. This is a slightly shame-faced, perhaps also two-faced apologia.

A MODEL OF THE ROMAN ECONOMY: FIVE PRINCIPLES OF CONSTRUCTION

Five interconnected principles form the frame for the model of the Roman economy constructed here. The first principle is that we are dealing here primarily with logical relationships, for example with the necessary interconnections between rents, taxes and trade, more than with their precise measurement. We are dealing with arguments, which order facts, more than with the facts themselves. But awkward facts, and arguments about disputed facts, can be very helpful, since they increase puzzlement (the search for new solutions), induce humility (the acknowledgment of failure to find them), and push us to clarify the exposition of logical relationships (some objections arose because the old model was not clearly explained). Facts and arguments together allow us to see more clearly how the Roman economy worked.

The second principle is that the larger the problem, and the larger the universe which it covers, the smaller the chances of large proportionate error. By this, I mean that it is easier and more profitable to draw up a model to cover the economy of the whole Roman empire, over a longish period, than to investigate a single town or province, at a single point in time. For example, if we investigate the population size of a single town in Roman Britain, or of a single province, we can be wildly wrong. But if we are careful in our construction of a model on a large scale, with luck and good judgement, some of our errors, and some local or temporary fluctuations, should be self-cancelling.

There is a corollary to this second principle which deserves a brief discussion, partly because it goes against the grain of much scholarly historical practice. A network of estimated probabilities deals only with probabilities. Because of our imperfect knowledge, each argument by itself may be weak, but in an elegantly constructed model, the imperfect, but complementary arguments prop each other up; the principle of construction is similar to a Red Indian wigwam. The area circumscribed by the arguments considered as a set should cover and account for much of the surviving relevant evidence. Or put another [way], constructing a model is just one out of several possible heuristic tactics. We make a simplifying assumption, to see where it leads us, without facing up initially to all the complexities of the real world. It is as though, in order to guess the weight of an elephant, you first imagine it to be a solid cube.

The third principle is that it is very much easier and more profitable to construct a model in the field of economic history than in other fields, because we are dealing here with finite variables. For example, Roman population size and money supply may be unknown quantities, but their unknownness lies within guessable limits. So as a first approximation, we might guess that the total population of the Roman empire was probably between 30 million and 120 million people; and the more probable limits are much narrower.

The fourth framing principle helps us set narrower limits to probabilities. After all, we are concerned with networks of economic factors which affect each other. For example, population size affects total product, especially in a predominantly agricultural society, and total product in turn affects the amount of tax which a government can easily raise. The more people, the more food they produce, the more possible it is for labour to be specialised, the more taxes can be raised. So the second principle runs: the choice of a value for any one factor affects the range of probable values of all other cognate variables. Or put another way, it does not make much sense trying to find out about x, unless we think of the impact of our findings about x on the interrelated variables $yzabc$. Once stated, this principle is obvious; but it is surprisingly often forgotten.[4]

The fifth principle is only an extension of the fourth principle. It restates the compatibility or coherence theory of truth: the conclusion which we reach is more likely to be accepted if it is compatible with whatever else we wish to believe. At first hearing, this may sound too reductionist and too cowardly. Surely scholars should pursue truth straightforwardly, without servile obedience to what everyone else believes? Perhaps. But I suspect that the life chances are short for a conclusion which no one believes to be true. In history, as distinct from philosophy or science, the tautology is a favourite figure of argument; to be sure it should not be a simple tautology of the type

---

[4] For example, Roger S. Bagnall and Bruce W. Frier, *The Demography of Roman Egypt* (Cambridge, 1994) 56, by extrapolating from isolated and puzzling data, propose levels of urbanisation in Roman Egypt which are three times the levels found in Europe in 1800. Richard Duncan-Jones is also, in my view, quite often guilty of this error. For example, in *Structure and Scale in the Roman Economy* (Cambridge, 1990) Chapter 12, he argues for the importance of taxes in kind, without analysing the patterns of their consumption. In Chapter 2 of the same book, and in *Money and Government in the Roman Empire* (Cambridge, 1994), Chapter 12, he argues for the restricted local circulation of both money and pots, without considering the macro-economic implications of his conclusions. No doubt each author would defend his conclusions by saying that this is what the evidence shows; but no; it is what *their interpretation* of patchily surviving testimony shows.

'good generals win battles', but a complex tautology, elegant and economical in its construction, fitting many of the known facts, and not easily controvertible.

The proof or disproof of the model cannot be accomplished by illustration. For example, if I put forward the proposition that, in general, height and weight, education and income correlate highly, and for particular reasons, it is no proof of the proposition if I produce an exemplary fat giant, or super-rich professor. Nor is it a defeat of the proposition if someone produces one thin, or even several thin, undereducated millionaire Welsh dwarfs (I call this the Welsh dwarf gambit). Finally, it is not helpful to claim that the data are too diverse to make generalisation possible.[5]

Three problems then: diversity, exceptions, and proof/disproof. Diversity is relatively easy; after all, generalisations were invented to cope with diversity. Exceptions, whether extreme cases (which are sometimes called outliers) or problematic marginal cases, pose quite different problems. At one level, they helpfully remind us that the world is not so carefully ordered that everything fits into a single, and necessarily imperfect, intellectual scheme. At another level, as we shall see, exceptions, and the objections which various scholars have raised about those exceptions, force us to revise the model, or make us clarify its workings, or recognise the limits within which it holds true.[6] All that said, I now think that a good model can be defeated properly only by other means: for example, by showing that its assumptive frame is wrongly conceived, or even better by showing that an alternative model will cover more evidence, more elegantly, with fewer moving parts, and more persuasively.

A BRIEF REVIEW OF THE MODEL

My present purpose is to figure out the interconnections between several salient features of the Roman economy. As a preliminary, let us deal with four factors:

a) the total population of the Roman empire
b) average agricultural yields
c) the Gross Product of the Roman empire
d) the state budget, i.e. the total tax income of the Roman state.

---

[5] There is another common variant of these false arguments: the citation of a single exceptional exemplar. I call this the Mt Everest gambit.

[6] See the seductive self-awareness of Albert O. Hirschman, *A Propensity to Self-Subversion* (Cambridge, Mass., 1996) Chapter 1.

Specialists in Roman economic history know all too well that the exact size of each of these factors is unknown. Our information about each is scanty, fragmentary, and often suspect. That has not prevented its repeated use. For example, the geographer Strabo (17.1.13), citing his near contemporary Cicero, reports that the state income of Egypt in the middle of the last century BC was 300 million HS.[7] Yet the tax income of the whole Roman empire in the first century AD has been estimated as being in the region of 650–900 million HS per year (see below). Is it likely that Egypt alone generated 35–45% of the revenue of an empire covering the whole of the Mediterranean basin and beyond? It seems doubtful, and in the circumstances, it seems safer to distrust Cicero's figure.

This simple procedure illustrates my main point here, which is innocent enough. Even when we are given precious information by an ancient source, we have to think whether it is reasonable, probable, compatible with what else we know about the Roman empire. That does not seem too contentious, but its corollary is quite interesting. As Collingwood observed long ago, it is our critical intelligence which is prior to the sources; history is based on critical intelligence and reconstructive imagination plus sources, not on the sources alone (in spite of the many authenticating footnotes filled with citations from sources).[8] Or put another way, it is not the *evidence*, referred to in hushed tones, which dictates our conclusions, but our *selection* and *interpretation* of the evidence.

If we agree that the plausibility of ancient sources has to be checked, how are we to do it? When I first learnt ancient history, the dominant method in England seemed to reflect the English class system; sources were examined and ranked in order. Ancient history at Oxford, I remember reading the claim in a reference for a young scholar applying for a job in Cambridge, is taught only from first-class historical sources. Nowadays we are perhaps not so sure about rank and order; even inferior sources are widely admitted to represent views which are useful for historical reconstruction. But there are other methods. One is the comparative method, recently displayed to considerable effect, for example by Wim Jongman and

---

[7] Duncan-Jones (1994: 46 and 53, albeit with some reservations) accepts this income for Egypt, even though he estimates the total revenue of the whole Roman empire one hundred years later at 670 million HS.

[8] R. G. Collingwood, *An Autobiography* (Oxford, 1939) 79ff, for a scathing criticism of ancient history's 'scissors-and-paste men' who are not really historians at all. See similarly his *The Idea of History* (Oxford, 1946) 257ff or the revised edition, edited by J. van der Dussen (New York, 1993). Alas, scissors-and-paste people still dominate the ancient history profession, and some even pride themselves for it.

Harry Pleket.[9] It is a very useful method; we can compare what we know about later economies with what we know about the Roman economy. But strictly speaking, comparative data show only what was possible in other societies, not what happened in Rome. Comparisons have to be used cautiously, suggestively, not imperialistically. And they are particularly useful to indicate how Rome was different.[10]

The method I want to illustrate now is an exercise in co-ordinate thinking. Let me begin with three simple and unproblematic propositions:

1) Tax is a proportion of Gross Domestic Product (GDP).
2) We do not know the GDP of the Roman empire, but we can think of a *minimum*, which its *actual* GDP must have exceeded.
3) This *minimum* GDP must equal Population × (Minimum Subsistence plus Seed).

Taking one year with another, the population as a whole must eat enough to survive, and overall must grow enough seed to supply food for the next year. This self-maintaining sufficiency is, of course, not predetermined, and indeed may not always have happened. But the minimalist, stable assumption is a simplifying and useful heuristic tactic. After all, it seems more sensible to assume a hungry and stable population first, before we add the more speculative finesses of assuming a rising (or falling) population. To estimate minimum subsistence needs, we can rely on fieldwork by agricultural economists specialising in the modern third world.[11] They reckon that humans can survive and reproduce if they consume a minimum of 250 kg wheat

---

[9] Pleket *op. cit.*, see above note 3, and W. Jongman, *The Economy and Society of Pompeii* (Amsterdam, 1988). Of the two, Jongman is much more analytically sophisticated in his use of comparisons.

[10] This point is meant to deal with the objection which I have often heard voiced that you have to compare like with like. I can see no justification for this limitation. Part of the utility of comparisons lies in contrast; (some) apples are sweeter than (some) oranges. The Roman imperial economy was less sophisticated than the Chinese imperial economy in the seventeenth century. For a fruitful discussion of the economy of the Chinese empire, with repeated references to Rome, see Mark Elvin, *The Pattern of the Chinese Past* (London, 1973).

[11] Colin Clark and M. Haswell, *The Economics of Subsistence Agriculture* (London, fourth edition 1970) 57ff and 135. I should stress that these are actual minima, not optimistic minima prescribed by welfare agencies (such as the FAO) in order to boost foreign aid. I purposely use a rounded figure (250 kg wheat equivalent per person/year) in order to express the necessarily rough character of such calculations. Minimum intake depends on age, weight, climate, energy expended etc. The average food intake is equal to about 2000 calories per person/day, with about 15 kg wheat equivalent per person/year for a) clothing, plus an equal amount for b) heat and housing. At this rate of consumption, many/most people would feel hungry and lethargic.

equivalent per person/year; I stress the word *minimum*; we are dealing with an underemployed population surviving on minimum
subsistence. This minimum survival ration includes some small
allowance for clothing, housing and heat. The concept 'wheat equivalent' or 'rice equivalent' reflects the predominance of cereals in the
diet of hungry third-world countries, and also allows for inter-
cultural comparisons across time. Needless to say, it does not mean
that any population, or that Romans, ate only wheat. Nor does it
imply that all, or even that most, inhabitants of the Roman empire
necessarily lived at the level of minimum subsistence. These are only
provisional, simplifying calculations, useful for establishing a base
line.

We are now in a position to move to the next stage of our argument. Let us guess, without any commitment for the moment about
the truth of our guesses (though each of them is defensible and quite
close to scholarly conventions), that:

a) the population of the Roman empire was 60 million,
b) *minimum* subsistence was 250 kg wheat equivalent per person/
    year,
c) average yields were 4 × seed, i.e. that one quarter of gross
    agricultural product had to be saved each year in order to grow a
    similar crop in the next year.[12]

Now all these guesses can be put together in a single matrix, so
that we can see the implications of each separate guess for all the
other guesses. Let me emphasise that the objective here is *not* to estimate the GDP of the Roman empire, but to use the minimum GDP
as an intermediate element in a network of calculations.

We have already asserted (see 3 above) that *minimum* GDP =
Population × (Minimum Subsistence plus seed). Using the estimates
cited above a–c), *minimum* GDP therefore equals:

> 60 million (Population) × (Minimum Subsistence = 250 kg wheat equivalent
> plus Seed = 83.3 kg) = 15 million tonnes plus 5 million tonnes seed =
> 20 million tonnes wheat equivalent.

We can now return to proposition 1), and factor in price. Let us
also guess that: d) farm-gate prices for wheat averaged 3 sesterces per

---

[12] For average wheat yields of barely four times seed in first-century Italy, see Columella
3.3.4. On sowing rates for wheat at 4 modii per iugerum see Varro (1.44), 4–5 modii per
iugerum Columella (2.9, 2.12 and 11.2.75), and 5–6 modii per iugerum (Plin. *HN* 18.198).
Actual sowing rates obviously varied. Assuming an average sowing rate of 5 modii per iugerum
= 130 kg/ha seems reasonable enough. For a discussion, see best M. S. Spurr, *Arable Cultivation
in Roman Italy* (London, 1988) 41–88, or R. P. Duncan-Jones, *The Economy of the Roman
Empire* (Cambridge, 1982) 33ff.

modius of 6.55 kg = 450 HS per tonne.[13] If so, then *minimum* GDP at 20 million tonnes was worth 9000 million HS. But tax is necessarily a proportion of this minimum gross product. If, as a final guess in this matrix of guesses, we estimate the average tax rate as 10% of *minimum* gross product, then total tax revenues = 2 million tonnes wheat, at 450 HS per tonne = 900 million HS.[14] Need I stress that all these figures are, and can be, only rough orders of magnitude? They are better treated as metaphors than as reliable statistics.

DOUBTS AND USES

The exact size of each element in this simple equation is unknown and untested. And yet, in spite of that, the conclusion is, in a curious way, both compelling and useful. Let me explain why I think so.

The only known element in the Roman state budget is the total cost of the army; perhaps 'known' is an exaggeration, but there is in broad terms a rough agreement among modern scholars that the army cost say 450–500 million HS in the middle of the first century.[15] But several Roman writers tell us or imply that army costs were the single most important item in the state budget.[16] And besides, other

[13] On wheat prices, see conveniently Duncan-Jones 1982: 145–6 and 345–6, with some minor adjustments since it is now commonly agreed that the artaba equalled 4½ not 3⅓ Roman modii, so that wheat prices in Egypt in the first century were probably often below 2 HS per modius. Wheat prices obviously varied significantly, according to season, year and place (see below note 64). 3 HS per modius as an average farm-gate price can only be a crude simplifying assumption.

[14] It is easy to see why some traditional historians object to this form of reasoning. It seems so unhistorical. Duncan-Jones dismissively calls it 'a priori not empirical' (1994: 46). But then his estimates are based on army costs plus a series of arbitrary and unsubstantiated guesses, including a complete guess that Vespasian increased total revenues 'perhaps by as much as 20%', which becomes 20% in his statistical table (1994: 33–46). Anyhow, mutual recrimination apart, our results are roughly similar: his 670 million, rising to 804 (*sic*) million HS in about AD 80; mine is 900 million HS. Willy-nilly, we are playing a similar game, with similar results. The real difference is that his reasoning is consciously inductive, mine is what I prefer to consider as matrix thinking. And all of us in economic history need some such thinking to check on the plausibility/utility of a) untrustworthy ancient sources and b) modern scholars' competing estimates.

[15] We know the notional size of the Roman legionary army and the pay of legionaries, but there is some debate about how many auxiliaries (non-citizen soldiers) there were at different periods and about how much pay auxiliaries received. M. A. Speidel, 'Roman Army Pay Scales', *JRS* 82 (1992) 87ff, argued plausibly that auxiliaries received ⅚ of legionary pay. R. Alston, 'Roman Military Pay from Caesar to Diocletian', *JRS* 84 (1994) 113ff, is radically agnostic. But there is not a huge room for manoeuvre. Duncan-Jones (1994: 36) estimates 493–554 million HS for army pay and retirement benefits in the mid-first century (the higher estimate if auxiliaries were paid retirement benefits). This can be only a rough order of magnitude. I suspect there was systematic underpayment and some considerable fluctuations in numbers. I personally therefore still prefer an estimate of 450±50 million HS.

[16] 'Our present revenues are insufficient to provide for the army and everything else' (Dio 52.6). And the early third-century jurist Ulpian explains tribute 'as being clearly called tribute because it is attributed to soldiers' (Digest 50.16.27).

scholars have come to similar conclusions about the size of the Roman state budget, though by more inductive methods. Duncan-Jones, for example, estimates it as 670–804 million HS in the mid-first century AD.[17] My provisional estimate is 900 million HS. Given the uncertainties in such estimates, I personally regard these results as roughly similar – in the same ball-park. So the arbitrarily chosen figures for population size, average yields, wheat prices and tax rates, placed in conjunction, produce a roughly plausible result, of the correct order of magnitude.

What is wrong? There is one obvious and large omission. The *actual* Gross Domestic Product of the Roman empire must have exceeded the *minimum* Gross Domestic Product [Population × (Minimum Subsistence plus Seed)] by a very considerable margin. Many Romans ate much more than mere subsistence. A considerable minority of Romans did not produce their own food, but lived in towns, ate food produced by slaves or peasants, and produced goods or provided services (legal, religious, educational) for sale; others were peasants who produced goods for sale in their spare, non-agricultural time.[18] We have to include their total (though unknown) product in the Roman empire's actual GDP. It is difficult to estimate this *actual* Gross Domestic Product of the Roman empire, though occasionally a scholar has tried.[19] At least it seems reasonable, given the high level of urbanization in the provinces around the Mediterranean Sea in the first two centuries AD, accounting for say 10–20% of the total population, to imagine that non-agricultural production also accounted for more than a fifth and less than two fifths of total produce. After all, towns concentrated higher value labour and services, so that average product there would have been higher than in the countryside. And so, for these two reasons (1) widespread consumption above minimum subsistence, and (2) sizeable non-agricultural production, the *actual* GDP was significantly higher,

---

[17] Duncan-Jones 1994: 33–46, and see note 14 above. See also note 19 below.

[18] For a quick description of the growth of the Roman economy under the impact of imperial expansion, see K. Hopkins, *Conquerors and Slaves* (Cambridge, 1978) Chapter 1. For a sophisticated summary and revision see E. Lo Cascio, 'Forme dell'economia imperiale', in A. Schiavone ed., *Storia di Roma* (Torino, 1991) vol. 2, 313ff esp. at 328ff. For a balanced survey of the economy in the first two centuries AD, see Peter Garnsey and R. Saller, *The Roman Empire* (London, 1987) 43ff.

[19] Surprisingly, serious academic estimates of the GDP of the Roman empire do exist. See R. W. Goldsmith, 'An Estimate of the Size and Structure of the National Produce of the Early Roman Empire', *The Review of Income and Wealth* 30 (1984) 263ff. His *Comparative National Balance Sheets* (Chicago, 1985) adds nothing relevant here. In detail, his method seems error prone, since his dominant tactic was to make estimates based on the average of all previous scholarly guesses. But there are some very useful hints for ancient historians, based on his knowledge of other pre-industrial economics. See note 20 below.

perhaps between a third and a half higher, than our minimum GDP.[20]

These speculative calculations suggest some positive conclusions and negative exclusions. By exclusions, I mean here that these calculations can be used to exclude as improbable some estimates advanced by reputable scholars. The first positive conclusion which leaps to the modern eye is that the Roman tax-rate was low.[21] If 10% of the *minimum* Gross Domestic Product would have produced as much or more tax (900 million HS) than the Roman government spent (Duncan-Jones estimates a budget of 670 million HS in the middle of the first century AD), then taxes must have been significantly less than 10% of the *actual* Gross Product. If we factor in our rough guess about the *actual* GDP as 50% above *minimum* GDP, then it looks as though taxes were levied at about 5–7% of *actual* GDP, to raise 700–900 million HS per year in tax in the mid-first century AD. At the very least, this model of the Roman economy raises the serious suggestion that Roman tax-rates were, objectively speaking, low.

Let us now turn to two exclusions. Some scholars have argued that the population of the Roman empire grew significantly above 60 million people, or that average yields were higher than 4 times seed, or both.[22] Let me try to show that both these conclusions seem improbable. If the total population of the Roman empire, because of general prosperity, grew to and stayed at about 100 million, and if

[20] Goldsmith 1984 (see note 19 above) reckons that total actual agricultural product (net of seed) was about 50% above minimum subsistence needs, and that non-agricultural product probably equalled at least 40% of GNP, and that average Roman living standards were significantly lower than in England in the seventeenth century. His final estimate of average product in the Roman empire in mid-first century AD at 380 HS or 125 modii per head is 3 times my estimate of minimum GDP, and to me seems too high. It implies a tax-rate of only 3%, and emphasises the weakness of the Roman government. On his side is the argument that a similar split between subsistence, above subsistence agricultural product and non-agricultural product has been found in other under-developed states.

[21] See the review by P. A. Brunt of Lutz Neesen, *Untersuchungen zu den direkten Staatsangaben der römischen Kaiserzeit* (Bonn, 1980) in *Roman Imperial Themes* (Oxford, 1990) 324ff.

[22] K. J. Beloch, 'Die Bevölkerung im Altertum', *Zeitschrift für Sozialwissenschaft* 2 (1899) 620, revised his earlier estimate of the population of the Roman empire from 54 million in 28 BC (in *Bevölkerung der griechisch-römischen Welt* 1 886: 507) to 100 million, plus or minus 20 million, in about AD 200. E. Lo Cascio, 'The Size of the Roman Population', *JRS* 84 (1994) 113ff, deals primarily with the population of Italy. He aims to reject Beloch's still standard view that Italy's population at the end of the last century BC was in the region of 5–7 million (the old view was strongly supported by P. A. Brunt, *Italian Manpower* (Oxford, 1971 and 1987) 121–30. If the Beloch–Brunt view is rejected, then I assume that Lo Cascio wants the Nissen–T. Frank estimates reinstated, and the population of Italy is estimated at 14–16 million. I cannot help wondering if apologetic national pride is partly responsible for such inflated estimates. For example, C. Jullian thought that Gaul's population in the last century BC was 20 million, and may have doubled in the first two centuries AD, thanks to the 'long famous fertility of Celtic women', *Histoire de la Gaule* (Paris, 1920) vol. 5, 25–8. In either case, the empire's population is presumably estimated at well above 60 million.

because of general prosperity GDP rose proportionately with the population, then tax-rates averaged $^{60}/_{100} = ^{3}/_{5}$ of the level argued for in the previous paragraph. Those who argue for a population of 100 million are implying an average tax-rate of 3–4% of *actual* GDP, and that with average yields of four times seed. If average yields were higher, then tax-rates were even lower. But if taxes were so low, the Roman government should have faced little difficulty in raising tax-rates, or in increasing army rates of pay.[23] But rises in army rates of pay were rapidly followed by difficulties with the coinage system, and were usually resolved by debasement (more precisely, by reducing the silver content of the coinage, or its weight, or both). If the Roman empire ran on a 3–4% tax-rate, it should have been able to increase revenues in an emergency. Any enemy attack would have induced a minor tax hike, and a massive increase in central government resources. This did not happen. It is therefore easy to conclude that the empire did not have at its disposal a population of 100 million people.

Other scholars have argued either that Roman wheat yields were significantly higher than four times seed, or that they were higher in important areas of Roman agriculture, in addition to the well-known exception of Egypt, irrigated by the Nile.[24] Once again, I am concerned here as much with the intellectual shape of the argument as with the (im)plausibility of the results. Let us proceed by supposing the high yield advocates are right. What are the implications of their assumptions? We can examine the argument, both macro-economically at the level of the whole economy, and micro-economically at the level of the single farm.

First, macro-economically. Let us take the example of Italy. Roughly speaking, experts argue that Romans in Italy cultivated perhaps 10 million hectares, about 40% of the surface.[25] If yields

[23] One way round this difficulty would be to argue that government revenues were so low, and could not be raised, because of the obstructive power of the aristocracy who depended on rents. I too think that rents and taxes were competitors for a limited surplus, but see the emperors in the first two centuries AD as having an edge over the aristocracy. But such perceptions are matters of judgement and of competing probabilities.

[24] For example, Pleket 1990: 78–9 (cf. note 3 above). On agricultural yields in Egypt, see, for example, A. K. Bowman, *Egypt after the Pharaohs* (London, 1986) 17–18. With several qualifications, specialists in ancient Egypt often argue for average yields there on irrigated land of about 10 times seed.

[25] See the slightly different, consumption-led calculations of Italy's total produce by Brunt, *Italian Manpower* 1971 and 1987: 126, following Beloch. He also assumes an average yield of four times seed, and an average consumption of wheat of about 250 kg wheat per person/year, and assumes that the city of Rome was fed from imports; he also thinks that Roman farmers even at those yields left half their fields fallow. I think that this calculation underestimates consumption by draught animals and horses, and also perhaps consumption

averaged six times seed (650 kg wheat/ha net of seed), then Italy alone produced enough food to feed 26 million people, or roughly speaking almost half of the population of the whole empire.[26] But we know very well from a myriad of sources that Italy and Rome in particular were importers of food. Again even with half the cultivable land fallow, the assumption of widespread high yields looks mistaken.

We reach the same critical conclusion if we think micro-economically. Let us speculate about single farms.[27] If, for the sake of example, a peasant had a farm of 5 hectares (20 iugera), and if yields averaged six times seed, then crops equalled 650 kg net of seed (sowing at 130 kg/ha = 5 modii per iugerum; see note 12 above). The farm then yielded 3250 kg wheat per year. Roughly speaking, since a family of four persons at minimum subsistence requires 1000 kg wheat equivalent per year, this assumption implies that one third of the Roman population could have fed two thirds living in non-agricultural occupations. But it is generally agreed that the non-agricultural sector of the Roman population amounted to barely 10–20% of the whole. And even if the high yield farmer restricted his output by keeping half his land fallow, he could still support one third of the population in non-agricultural occupations. No. It looks as though the conclusion of widespread high yields in Roman farming (outside irrigated areas such as Egypt or small favoured locations) is mistaken. Above all, the intellectual moral is that tentative isolated results should be scrutinised in terms of their broader implications.

---

by Italians over and above minimum subsistence. But the differences between us are a salutary reminder of the tentative nature of such calculations and of their roughness. They can provide rough orders of magnitude only.

[26] Italy's actual population was probably in the order of 5–7 million in the beginning of the first century AD. It may have risen during the first two centuries, then declined in the third century and risen again in the fourth century. We know from post-mediaeval demographic histories that there were broad long-term waves of population growth and decline, but our data from antiquity are rarely good enough to be able to quantify such changes. For short- and long-term population swings, see E. A. Wrigley, *Population and History* (London, 1969) 62ff. The best introduction to ancient demography is T. Parkin, *Demography and Roman Society* (Baltimore, 1992).

[27] Calculations about the size, yield, agricultural practices, and consumption needs of the single farm/farming family are obviously complex and require a parametric model of their own. *Exempli gratia*, a 5 hectare = 20 iugera farm, if half was left fallow each year, and if the yield was four times seed (520–130 seed = 390 kg wheat/ha), would produce 975 kg wheat per year on average. That is less than minimum subsistence for a family, with no allowance for plough oxen, rent or taxes. A 5 hectare farm, wholly cultivated, with a yield of four times seed, would produce 1950 kg wheat net of seed, enough food for a family of four at subsistence, and an ox, and still be able to produce a sizeable surplus, which could be extracted as rent or tax, or consumed by the farmer. Less or more land, yield and fallowing would dictate both the farmer's living standards and his need to work for a landlord.

LOW TAXES AND ARISTOCRATIC
SELF-ENRICHMENT

Why were Roman taxes so low? By low, I mean here less than 10% of *minimum* Gross Domestic Product, and only about 6% of probable *actual* GDP. Of course, I should stress right away that there is a fundamental distinction between taxes levied and taxes transmitted. The central Roman government was primarily interested in taxes transmitted, i.e. in the amount of taxes which eventually reached its own coffers.[28] The *actual* amounts of tax levied by tax-collectors on the ground were likely to have been significantly higher, and they were probably unfairly distributed; the powerless paid a disproportionately high share of the taxes, while the powerful, who supervised the collection of taxes or the distribution of the tax burden, understandably let themselves off lightly. So complaints about the heaviness of Roman taxation, or the cruelty of Roman tax-collectors, are quite compatible with an overall low level of transmitted taxes.[29]

All that said, an average tax burden in the rough region of 5–7% of *actual* Gross Domestic Product seems low. Why were taxes so low? Two answers come readily to mind. The first is genetic, the second structural. The genetic explanation is that the Roman empire came into being as an empire of conquest; its first taxes were devised to replace booty as a more effective method of covering the costs of war. The state's needs started at a low level; the rapid expansion of the empire in the last two centuries BC meant that the Roman state repeatedly had more revenues flowing in than ever before.[30] The

[28] The Roman tax-system seems to have involved assessing towns at a particular sum, and then leaving local leaders to allocate the tax among their own land-owners. See *IG* v (1) 1432–3 for example, dating perhaps from the first century AD. It shows that the southern Greek town of Messene was assessed at 100,000 denarii (400,000 sesterces), divided among land-owners in strict proportion to their declared capital value (self-assessment itself as a system favours the socially powerful rich – who is to challenge their assessments?). Even so, it was outsiders, including Romans, who were particularly negligent in paying their dues.

[29] For a highly rhetorical report of cruelty by tax-collectors in first-century Egypt, see Philo, *de specialibus legibus* 3, 159, who describes a tax-collector torturing the wives and children of fugitive tax-payers; cf. Lactantius, *de mortibus persecutorum* 23. More generally, still see best A. H. M. Jones, 'Taxation in Antiquity', in A. H. M. Jones, *The Roman Economy*, ed., P. A. Brunt (Oxford, 1974) 151ff, and see similarly the hostile and anti-Roman comments by rabbis on Roman tax-collectors' greed, analysed by N. de Lange, 'Jewish Attitudes to the Roman Empire', in P. Garnsey et al. eds., *Imperialism in the Ancient World* (Cambridge, 1978) 255ff, now partly superseded by M. Hadas-Lebel, 'La fiscalité romaine dans la littérature rabbinique ...', *Revue des études juives* 143 (1984) 5ff.

[30] The classic overview of Roman state income and expenditure from 268 BC onwards is to be found in T. Frank, *Economic Survey of Ancient Rome* (Baltimore, 1933) vol. 1. Although Roman leaders knew and published statements about the total income of the Roman state, only fragments have survived. According to Plut. *Life of Pompey* 45, the income of the Roman state in 62 BC was 340 million sesterces, compared with an average estimated income in the first half

conquerors provided only a sketchy service to the conquered: rudimentary corrective justice, supervision (of tax-collection), external defence, with occasional support for internal infrastructure (ports, roads, temples) and internal order. But the main provision was in external defence, divertable if needs be towards the ruthless suppression of rebellion.

The structural reason for low taxes is that the Roman conquerors had always operated a binary system of profiting from empire. By a binary system, I mean that the Roman state shared the profits of empire with its own citizens. As is well known, in the period of imperial expansion from about 200 BC–AD 14, conquering generals and provincial governors took a far greater (and increasingly larger) share than common soldiers. Equestrian tax-collectors and the relatively rich private investors in tax-collecting companies (who bid at auctions for the right to collect taxes in a district or province) profited more than private Roman citizens who stayed at home. But even ordinary citizens in Italy got some profit from empire. After 167 BC, citizen land-holders paid no tax on Italian land (except in emergencies); and citizens living in the city of Rome received a monthly dole of wheat at subsidised prices from 122 BC, and absolutely free from 58 BC. Finally, tens of thousands of Italian citizens emigrated from Italy to the provinces, especially in the second half of the last century BC, in order to get larger farms than they had had in Italy.[31] In short, Romans got richer by profiting from empire.

Two final elements in this complex process of self-enrichment need to be mentioned. First, especially after the Augustan settlement, upperclass Romans moved swiftly to occupy important tracts of provincial land. In Nero's reign, for example, six men of senatorial rank were alleged to own half the province of Africa. And, for example, rich Romans owned substantial estates in Egyptian villages.[32] How else could Romans maintain their ostentatious

of the second century BC of 55 million sesterces (Frank 1933: 145). In sum, Roman state income had increased sixfold, and was to more than double again in the next century.

[31] On the increase in booty from empire and the progressive relative enrichment of the Roman elite, and the consequent migration of Italian peasants to Rome, other Italian towns and the provinces, see Hopkins 1978: Chapter 1.

[32] The allegation that six Roman land-owners owned half the province of Africa when the emperor Nero killed them is made by the encyclopaedist Pliny (*HN* 18, 35). A mid-second-century papyrus from the Fayum in Egypt (P. Bouriant 42), for example, lists estates which had once belonged to the senator Seneca, to the equestrian praetorian prefect Macro, to various freed imperial slaves and to members of successive royal families. In the late empire, the noble Christian lady Melania owned estates in six provinces (*Life* (Greek) 11–12, 19–21, 37), see Elizabeth A. Clark, *The Life of Melania the Younger* (New York, 1984); another aristocratic lady, Olympias, owned estates in four provinces (*Life* 5); see E. A. Clark, *Jerome, Chrysostom and Friends* (New York, 1979) 107ff.

luxury, except by profiting from the whole empire?[33] Secondly, especially under the rule of the emperors, the political economy of the Mediterranean basin became increasingly integrated.[34] Not only did rich Romans own land in all the provinces, but increasingly rich provincials became Romans. By the end of the second century AD, about half of all senators were of provincial origin; and two second-century emperors passed regulations that senators should have $\frac{1}{3}$, reduced by the second emperor to $\frac{1}{4}$, of their total wealth in Italian land.[35] The mere existence of the regulation illustrates the extent to which senatorial investment in land had become provincial. Finally, in 212, most inhabitants of the empire became Roman citizens. The old dividing line between conquerors and conquered had been replaced by an empire-wide system of stratification between the more powerful (*honestiores*) and the unprivileged (*humiliores*).

The increased wealth of the Roman rich under the shelter of em-perors' rule is generally veiled by a prevailing aristocratic ideology, which reports cruelty and persecution by emperors of individual aristocratic families, and laments the decline of aristocratic political power compared with its glorious republican past.[36] But the few surviving statistics on aristocratic wealth suggest significant increases in aristocratic wealth. Cicero in the middle of the last century BC wrote that a rich Roman needed an annual income of 100–600,000 HS per year, an income clearly implying a total fortune well in excess of the minimum capital required to become a senator (1 million HS). Pliny the Younger, himself a senator of middling wealth at the end of the first century AD, may have had an annual income of at least

[33] The Roman imperial state unlike post-mediaeval European kingdoms offered aristocrats no reliable offices of profit at court. Aristocrats therefore had to meet the expenses of being courtiers basically out of their incomes from estates (including urban rents), from their mercan-tile activities (administered by their freed slaves), as well but less predictably from gifts from the emperor and profits from occasional but discontinuous office in the provinces.

[34] By political economy, I refer here to the extent to which the Roman state, by its policies, but probably unintentionally, affected the ownership of wealth. What I have in mind is that the peace and security of the state acted as a carapace protecting the interests primarily of the Roman ruling classes. For a similar broad phenomenon in past feudal European monarchies, see Perry Anderson, *Lineages of the Absolutist State* (London, 1974).

[35] On the regulations governing senatorial ownership of land, see Plin. *Ep.* 6.9 and SHA, *Marcus Aurelius* 11. On the process of integration in the Roman elite and their lowish rates of inheriting status, see K. Hopkins, *Death and Renewal* (Cambridge, 1983) Chapter 3 (by Hopkins and G. P. Burton). For some good, but mostly ill-founded, criticisms of our statisti-cal reasoning, see Johannes Hahn and P. M. M. Leunissen, 'Statistical Method', *Phoenix* 49 (1990) 60ff, and now a convincing rebuttal by G. P. Burton, 'The Inheritance of the Consul-ship', *Phoenix* 49 (1995) 218ff.

[36] The conflict between successive emperors and aristocrats is the leitmotif of surviving Roman historians of the early empire. For example, the emperor Claudius is reported to have had 35 senators and more than 300 knights put to death (Suetonius, *Claudius*, 29, cf. *Tiberius* 54, Dio 67.9).

1.1 million HS; and the historian Olympiodorus reports that middling aristocrats in the west in the late fourth century AD had incomes of 1333–2000 Roman pounds of gold, roughly equivalent to 6–9 million HS per year.[37]

If these figures are roughly indicative, aristocratic fortunes had risen two- or threefold from the late Republic to the end of the first century AD, and had risen again five- to eightfold between AD 100 and AD 400. Such skimpy data can only be suggestive. But aristocratic enrichment is what we might have expected from general trends in the politicoeconomic integration of the empire. After all, Cicero and his contemporary senators had practically all their wealth invested in Italy, whereas the fourth-century elite controlled investments from all over the Mediterranean basin. Imperial government, for all its alleged cruelty to aristocrats, provided an effective shelter for their progressive enrichment.[38]

This marked increase in average individual aristocratic wealth should also be considered as an increase in aggregate aristocratic wealth. But in an economy with a limited surplus, rents and taxes were in competition. The aggregate wealth of the political aristocracy limited the state's capacity to act.[39] Let us consider again the figures

---

[37] See Cicero, *Paradoxa Stoicorum* 45–9; for Pliny, see the detailed estimates by Duncan-Jones 1982: Chapter 1; for Olympiodorus, see R. C. Blockley, *The Fragmentary Classicising Historians of the Later Roman Empire* (Liverpool, 1983) vol. 2, frag. 41.2; Olympiodorus claimed that middling senators had an annual income of 1000–1500 Roman pounds of gold; but if they, like the richest senators, had an additional income in 'grain, wine and produce ... equal to one third of the income in gold' (ibid.), then their total incomes averaged 1333 to 2000 Roman pounds of gold. I translate that (rather crudely) into sesterces by equating each pound of gold with 45 aurei each worth 100 HS; that was the minting rate in the second half of the first century AD. Duncan-Jones also lists the size of 29 fortunes in the Principate (1982: Appendix 7). For a careful warning against trusting many figures reported in ancient sources, see Walter Scheidel, 'Finances, Figures and Fiction', *Classical Quarterly* 46 (1996) 222ff.

[38] The two arguments being advanced here clearly need to be kept separate. The first argument is that average and aggregate aristocratic wealth increased; the second argument is that this increase may have accelerated in the chaotic conditions of the third century, when local aristocrats wrested control over greater resources, probably to the disadvantage of smaller independent land-owners. Eventually, in the western empire, the local power of aristocrats prevented the central government from effectively raising its revenues sufficiently to repel barbarian attacks. Admittedly, this argument faces considerable problems of definition and fact, if only because the boundaries of the fourth-century elite are much wider than the senatorial and equestrian strata of the early empire. Even so, it seems worth bearing in mind the changing economic base of political groupings.

[39] I use political aristocracy as a vague term on purpose. What I have in mind is say the top few thousand families in the Roman empire: six hundred or so senators, a few hundred leading equestrian administrators, and the landed, mostly equestrian families from whom senatorial families had or would come. Romans had a fairly rapidly changing aristocracy of office, with only between one fifth and a third of second-ranking (*suffect*) consuls in the first or second centuries having a consular son, grandson or great-grandson. The Roman political elite was much more volatile than any post-mediaeval European nobility. See Hopkins, 1983: 142.

already cited. If Pliny the Younger, a senator of middling wealth, had an annual income of at least 1.1 million HS, then all 600 senators, plus knights plus high palace officials, must surely have had a collective aggregate income of at least say 600 million HS. This aggregate elite income was significantly more than the Roman state's income, net of army costs.[40] I cite these figures only as very rough orders of magnitude for illustrative purposes.

My overall argument here is twofold. First, taxes and aristocratic rents were rivals for a limited surplus. Secondly, disposable aristocratic incomes, which like taxes were generated mostly from landownership, were of the same rough order of magnitude as taxes, especially if we consider taxes as largely precommitted to supporting the standing army, whereas aristocratic incomes were slightly more fluid, more redirectable to alternative ends. *Cognoscenti* will already have thought of an obvious objection: imperial estates. Precisely. Emperors confiscated rich people's estates, because these estates constituted such important elements in graspable national wealth. But by the same token, emperors were caught in the delegatory bind; they could not administer these large and scattered estates themselves; and they had their own favourites to reward and keep loyal. The recipients of imperial largesse or the administrators of imperial estates were in effect replacement aristocrats (irrespective of their formal status, sometimes they were knights) for those who had had their estates confiscated.[41]

SOME IMPLICATIONS OF AND OBJECTIONS TO THE MODEL

In order to analyse the competition between taxes and rents further, I want to return once more to a central proposition of my old article, 'Taxes and Trade'.[42] I return to this proposition, partly because the sharpness of some criticisms has forced me to reconsider, and I hope improve, some of my arguments.

My basic argument then was that taxes or rents raised in place P (provinces) and spent in place R (Rome and the frontier armies) were

---

[40] Duncan-Jones (1994: 45) reckons second-century non-army government expenditure at 189–279 million HS. I suspect this guess/calculation is rather low, for example in its estimate of the emperors' household costs, and too precise. I would think in terms of 400–500 million HS. This difference illustrates our divergent intellectual styles.

[41] Duncan-Jones 1994: 5–6 and 42–3 gives examples of emperors' confiscations and gifts, and then states (p. 43): 'Clearly there was no real barrier to what the emperor could spend.' Clearly and really?

[42] See note 1 above.

necessarily, in the medium term, balanced by an equal flow of trade, through which tax-payers or rent-payers in P earned money with which to pay their taxes. The process which I had in mind was that tax- or rent-payers, in so far as they were forced to pay their taxes or rents in money, had to earn the money with which to pay their rents or taxes whether by the sale of produce or services, or both. And if the tax-users or rent-receiving landlords were at some distance, for example in the city of Rome, then goods of an equal value (roughly speaking) to the taxes and rents raised had to be exported via merchants in Rome, so that tax-/rent-payers could get their money back, with which to pay taxes and rents in a subsequent year.

Of course, I never had in mind a simple four-axis flow: from a) tax-payer or b) rent-payer on the one hand to c) tax-spenders and d) landlords on the other hand. Instead, I imagined a whole differentiated network of converters, whose mode of operation and function would differ, depending on whether they were dealing with taxes or rents, in money or in kind. For example, peasants might pay rent in kind to a local landlord or his agent; the landlord then sold the peasants' surplus to wholesale merchants, who in turn either exported it unconverted, or sold it to local artisans, located either in local villages or towns, who ate the peasants' surplus wheat and meanwhile made pots, shoes or other artefacts, whether for local sale or export.[43] But if rents or taxes were exacted in money, the peasant was forced to sell his surplus wheat to a local merchant in order to earn cash, or to work for a local landowner, or even did both. If money taxes or rents were spent at some distance from where they were collected, then a network of trade and manufacture had to be established, so that surplus produce could be sold, perhaps via a variety of towns, and original tax-payers could earn their money back. In this view then, the exaction of rents and taxes, whether in money or kind, was an, and perhaps the most important, element in the complex process of increasing the specialisation of labour (more shoemakers, barbers and lawyers), and the consequent growth of towns throughout the Mediterranean basin. Towns were undoubtedly a political and cultural phenomenon, but they needed economic underpinning, and themselves created economic repercussions.

---

[43] For taxes in kind, see below. For a fruitful discussion of local networks of trade between peasants and specialist local traders, see now L. De Ligt, *Fairs and Markets in the Roman Empire* (Amsterdam, 1993), especially Chapters 4 and 6. I still cannot help thinking that De Ligt underestimates the aggregate demand of peasants for urban produced goods, while acknowledging with him that they also consumed rural produced goods and that much of the exchange might have taken place at rural markets, outside towns. His discussion is (unlike so much ancient economic history) well informed, theoretically and comparatively.

The impact of rents and taxes probably differed. Landlords were more dispersed than the spenders of taxes. Absentee landlords lived in local and regional capitals as well as in the city of Rome. So rents had much more impact on local economies. Taxes, by contrast, were, I imagine, spent only to a limited extent in the provinces where they were raised. Mostly taxes were spent on the armies stationed in frontier provinces, and in the city of Rome, on the emperor's palace, on his self-indulgences and on administration, as well as on the palace guard and other troops in the city of Rome. Even so, the expenditure of metropolitan elite rents and taxes (net of army costs) together, totalling (say 600 million HS rents + 400–500 million HS taxes, as very rough orders of magnitude) something like 8% of *actual* GDP, concentrated in the city of Rome.[44] In so far as they were raised in money at a distance from the place where they were spent, they inevitably stimulated a network of complementary trade. Tax-payers and rent-payers had to earn back the money transmitted to Rome, as to the frontier armies. The network of exchange created by the reciprocal flows of taxes, rents and trade contributed to the integration of the Roman economy.

That is the theory. How it all worked out in practice may well be a different matter. Models do not mirror reality exactly. And for the moment I want to stress the logical, abstract, model-like nature of the proposition on the complementarity of taxes, rents and trade. It is in my view a logical equivalence, rather like Fisher's famous price equation:

$$P = \frac{M \times V}{Q}.$$

The logical connections cannot be proved or disproved by examples, or by counter-examples. The only proper disproof, I claim, is by counter-argument, i.e. by proving that there is no necessary recipro-cal flow between taxes and rents paid in money on the one hand, and trade on the other hand, or by putting forward a better (more economical, elegant or comprehensive) model.

The model has provoked some discussion, and some criticism, and thanks to that criticism I think I now see more clearly than I did in 1980 some strengths and weakness in my arguments. Howgego in two very clear and scholarly articles has been particularly helpful and

---

[44] By *actual* GDP, I mean here my very rough estimate of actual GDP at *minimum* GDP plus 50%, to allow for non-agricultural and higher value urban production. It is significantly less than Goldsmith's estimate of actual GDP; see note 20 above.

persuasive.[45] Only one of his objections seems weak. He argues that there were exceptions to the complementary flow of taxes and trade: provincials could have [paid] and probably did pay taxes out of stored treasure, they created new money out of mines, they fell into debt, their labourers migrated, and perhaps most important, they transferred their capital assets, principally land, to Roman owner-ship, perhaps to meet their accumulated debts.[46] I agree. These were all temporary expedients designed to soften the impact of the impo-sition of money taxes (mines were not temporary, but localised), and some were important transitional stages in the unification of the Roman economy, and in the transfer of capital and ownership from provincials to Romans. But they are qualifications, rather than refutations. The logical relationship between rents/taxes and trade still stands, if only after all these temporary processes had been exhausted. Methodologically, these processes constitute a marginal case, and do not defeat the basic proposition.

That said, reading Howgego made me rethink a whole series of problems. I shall deal here with three issues, which are best kept separate: first, proof and disproof of general propositions; secondly, methodology and the utility of illustrations; and third, specific points of fact, some critical, some seemingly trivial, some leading to useful revisions or clarifications of the model. Some problems have arisen, I think, because some critics, true to the positivistic traditions of history, have simply taken for granted that showing errors of fact would be sufficient disproof of my propositions.[47] I do not think that disproof is so simple. Let me illustrate and explain.

In my original article, I used four illustrative diagrams. Three have caused trouble. The first was a bar-chart showing the relative frequency of shipwrecks, by two-century periods. Basically, it showed that there were more shipwrecks (and from those I deduced more ship sailings) in the period 200 BC–AD 200 than in any period before or since, up to the early modern period. Subsequent research and refinements have, if anything, reinforced the 1980 picture.[48] Actually,

---

[45] Christopher Howgego, 'The Supply and Use of Money in the Roman World 200 BC to AD 300', *Journal of Roman Studies* 82 (1992) 1–31, and 'Coin Circulation and the Integration of the Roman Economy', *Journal of Roman Archaeology* 7 (1994) 5–21.

[46] Howgego 1994: 18.

[47] One exception is E. Lo Cascio 1991: 351ff (see note 1 above). He saw, correctly as I too now think, that my illustrations were flawed, but that the model with suitable modifications still has merits. I have incorporated most of his modifications with gratitude.

[48] It was based on the work of A. J. Parker. Parker has now refined his data. See now *Ancient Shipwrecks of the Mediterranean and the Roman Provinces* (London, 1992) 10ff. Parker's latest data cover almost 800 dated wrecks from the third century BC through the end of the fourth century AD. They show marked growth and decline. The numbers of datable wrecks

I always thought this chart merely confirmed what many scholars 'knew', namely that there was more trade in the western Mediterranean in this period, partly as a function of the Roman imperial expansion, subsequent peace and increased general prosperity, than in prehistory or after the Vandal invasions. The relative frequency of shipwrecks/ship-sailings also suggested, and that may have been anathema to some, that shipwrecks/ship-sailings diminished progressively in the third and fourth centuries AD. So some of my colleagues objected on the grounds that the evidence was biased, if only because western underwater archaeologists were much more active in southern France than in north Africa or the eastern Mediterranean. This was true and stated in my original article. But to be a powerful objection, the objector has to claim not only that some data are missing (they nearly always are in ancient history), but also that he/she thinks that the overall pattern would be different if the missing data (here shipwrecks from the eastern Mediterranean) were included.

A roughly similar objection has been made, and powerfully expressed, to the second illustration, showing the significant increase in the volume of coinage in the last century of the Republic. Again it is an objection about accurate measurement. Buttrey doubts that money growth in this period can ever be measured accurately.[49] He argues from a position of impeccable agnosticism, that the average number of coins struck per die is and must be unknown, because it varied significantly, and that the attrition rate, i.e. the rate at which coins were lost from circulation, also varied and cannot be known. My defence is simple. But first a word of caution. I did, as Buttrey generously confirms, repeatedly stress in my 1980 article the tentative and hypothetical nature of the estimates made; and not only as a rhetorical device, a *captatio benevolentiae*. That said, there are limits to reasonable caution.

We are dealing with a very large number of dies (hundreds each year) used to produce millions of silver coins in the last century of the Republic. There must be *some* average rate of production per die, and there is little reason to think that this *average* fluctuated madly. Even if Romans got better at coin production, as the volume of their

discovered peaked in the last century BC (N = 183) and first century AD (181), were almost as high in the second century BC (154) and the second century AD (158), diminished in the third century AD (86) to less than half the first-century peak, and diminished again in the fourth century AD (54) to less than one third of the peak; (cf. 64 wrecks in the third century BC). Such data can only be suggestive.

[49] T. V. Buttrey, 'Calculating Ancient Coin Production: Facts and Fantasies', *Numismatic Chronicle* 153 (1993) 335ff, and 'Calculating Ancient Coin Production II: Why It Cannot Be Done', ibid. 154 (1994) 341ff.

production increased, so that more coins on average were minted per die, then my argument, that the volume of coinage increased, holds *a fortiori*. So also for attrition rates; we do not know what the average rate of attrition was, but there must have been some attrition; 2% average loss rate per year is merely a simplifying assumption. The attrition rate could have been 3% per year, or even $x\%$ per year. In fact, any reasonable constant loss rate and any reasonable constant average number of coins minted per die make very little difference to the *shape* of the curve. My general point holds, and Buttrey does not dispute it: the volume of coins in circulation in the last century of the Republic rose considerably; I say tenfold, but that is only a rough order of magnitude, perhaps better treated, like so many numbers in ancient sources, more as a metaphor than as a statistic.[50]

Logically, the more powerful objection to both bar-charts would have been that they were only marginally relevant to the basic proposition on the reciprocity of rents/taxes and trade. From a purist point of view, the charts were only rhetorical adornments, side illustrations, which lent my general argument an air of empirical plausibility. But the basic argument itself, as I have already said, cannot be defeated by establishing the correctness or falsity of its illustrations. This point will be even clearer when we turn to the fourth illustration (Hopkins 1980: 113), in which I sought to show that coins in the Roman empire circulated, and that any increase in the volume of coinage in one province in one period was matched by a similar rise of coinage in other provinces. I hypothesised that the complementary flows of taxes and trade were the most likely vectors which brought about this effective distribution of Roman coins throughout the empire, both in provinces where the army was stationed and in other internal and non-army occupied provinces.

Both Howgego and Duncan-Jones have spent some considerable effort in examining these arguments and the evidence on which they could be based. It was Howgego's judicious article which showed me

---

[50] I would be happy enough to sacrifice my hypothetical total (based on an average of 30,000 coins per obverse die) of Roman silver coins in circulation, at about 400–500 million denarii in the middle of the last century BC (Hopkins 1980: 109). But Ian Carradice, *Coinage and Finances in the Region of Domitian* (Oxford, 1983) 83–6, estimates annual average silver coin production towards the end of the first century AD at 15 million denarii per year, and Duncan-Jones, 1994: 165–8 suggests a similar volume of production of about 17 million denarii per year for the first half of the second century AD (though apparently on the basis of 8000 coins per die on average). At 2% per year loss rate, these figures suggest a total money supply of silver coins of 750–850 million denarii, though Duncan-Jones' estimate is much higher (1994: 168, and see my note 90 below). If you reduce late Republican money supply too much, then you have a huge boom in money supply to account for in the first century AD even allowing for the fact that then Roman coinage covered the whole of the Mediterranean basin (except Egypt) and beyond.

the error of my ways. He examined the evidence of coin circulation with much more expertise than I have ever had, and came to the general conclusion (against Duncan-Jones) that in the longish run coins did circulate between provinces, except that in one particular case, i.e. Spain, just after its conquest by Rome, even though it was taxed, there is no evidence of Roman coinage.[51] In his view, conquest by itself did not induce coin circulation, but silver coins in the first two centuries AD did circulate between provinces, albeit gradually.

In other words, in Howgego's view, Hopkins' proposition may be right in fact, but it is not universally right, and it is not at all clear from this coin evidence that taxes or complementary trade were the main vectors integrating the Roman economy. On reading Howgego, I had a flash of revelation. The whole argument of coin circulation was not vital to my thesis on the complementarity of taxes and trade. Or put another way, I had been looking for a confirmatory illustration in the wrong way.

Egypt is the critical case. Egypt under Roman rule had an enclosed coinage system. Broadly speaking, no Egyptian coins are found outside Egypt, and almost no Roman coins are found in Egypt. In other words, there was no circulation of coinage between Egypt and other regions of the Roman empire. Nevertheless, I would still argue that Egyptians paid taxes in money (as well as in kind), which were largely spent outside Egypt, and that this export of taxes obliged Egyptians to export goods with which to earn money, which then had to be paid in tax in successive years. Here at least the issue of coin circulation is clearly a red herring, and so, in strict logic, coin circulation must also be not critical to the interrelation between other provinces.[52] There must have been some other form of balancing trade-, rent- and tax-flows between provinces, other than by exporting silver coin (see below). In my view, the proposition on the complementarity of rents, taxes and trade is right, because I cannot see or imagine any other way in which the broad mass of tax-payers in the long run could have got money with which to pay their taxes, except via trade. In short, it is not a question here of fact, it is a matter of argument. But more of this in a moment.

Duncan-Jones in several chapters of two books ('Trade, Taxes and Money'; 'Separation and Cohesion in Mediterranean Trade';

---

[51] Howgego 1994: particularly 17ff.; cf. Duncan-Jones 1990: Chapters 2, 3 and 12, and 1994: Chapter 12.

[52] Unless one were to argue that the economic links between Egypt and the rest of the empire were quite unlike the links between the other provinces. That is possible, but it seems unlikely that they were so different as to require a different conceptualisation.

'Taxation in Money and Taxation in Kind'; see note 51) has touched on issues which were central to my original article, 'Taxes and Trade'. His work is interesting for me on three counts: perspective, method and conclusion. I shall deal here with four of Duncan-Jones' arguments. As I understand it, he has concluded that taxes were levied to a significant extent in kind, not in money (with the implication that the reciprocity of money taxes and trade was relatively unimportant); secondly, that the circulation of goods was pocketed, i.e. that few goods were interregionally traded; thirdly, that coins also stayed within the region of their first location (with the implication that the economy of the Roman empire was not integrated); and finally, if long-distance trade did increase during the first two centuries AD (which he doubts), then it was unlikely that this was caused by levying taxes in money (Duncan-Jones 1990: 45). Each of these conclusions is important to our general understanding of the Roman economy; but in each case, my views and those of Duncan-Jones are distinctly different, in both substance and method. But once again, the conflict of views has helped clarify and, I think, improve my own arguments.

First then, let us deal with the problem as to whether taxes were levied mostly in money or in kind, beginning with technical details of source interpretation and going on to general argument.[53] Duncan-Jones begins his discussion by citing the second-century land-surveyor Hyginus: 'In some provinces, they pay part of the crop, some (provinces) paying one fifth, others one seventh, while other (provinces instead) pay in money, ... (205L)' (so Duncan-Jones 1990: 187). Duncan-Jones understandably concludes that some provinces paid land-tax in kind (at 14–20%), others in money, and he stresses the importance of the order in Hyginus' list; Hyginus gave 'first place to payment in kind' – this is section 1.1.1 of Duncan-Jones' chapter. But for this text, he cites Lachmann's 1848 edition of Hyginus. Yet the Teubner edition, edited by C. Thulin in 1913, is superior; the text reads: 'in quibusdam [provinciis] fructus partem praestant certam, alii quintas alii septimas, alii pecuniam'.[54] Thulin's *apparatus criticus* shows that a major ancient manuscript, P, has a variant reading: instead of '*other (provinces pay) money*', it reads '*now many (provinces pay) money*' nunc multi pecuniam. This variant reading is clearly either a comment added in antiquity, which indicates that at some stage taxes in money widely replaced taxes in kind, or more

---

[53] Duncan-Jones 1990: Chapter 12, called 'Taxation in Money and Taxation in Kind'.
[54] C. Thulin ed., *Corpus Agrimensorum Romanorum* (Leipzig, 1913) 168. I am grateful to Michael Reeve for advice on this point.

probably this reading was the original version of Hyginus; a scribe mistakenly added a third *alii* (others) instead of the original 'now many (pay) money.' So the strongest element in Duncan-Jones' argument from sources disintegrates.

But now for a more general, and I think more interesting, argument.[55] Overall, there must have been a serious imbalance between a) what the government raised as tax in kind and b) its needs. Once again the case of Egypt is illuminating. The Roman state needed wheat with which to supply the citizens receiving a wheat dole in Rome, and basic food for its soldiers, dispersed along its frontiers. Distributions of free wheat to the citizen population in Rome accounted for only about 100,000 tonnes per year (250,000 recipients × 5 modii of 6.6 kg per month). The army of say 300,000 soldiers needed slightly more. There was, as far as we know, no other regular demand for the government to supply taxes in wheat to state dependants. But by Duncan-Jones' own calculations, the Roman government raised 17.5 million artabae = over 500,000 tonnes annually in tax from Egypt alone (plus money equalling about 40% of the whole).[56] The amount of wheat raised in tax in Egypt was, by these calculations, more than twice as much as the government needed in the whole empire. We have to conclude, therefore, that taxes which were raised in kind, in Egypt and in other provinces, had to be transformed into money, in order for the government to be able to spend the revenue elsewhere.

These simple calculations transform the problem of taxes in money and taxes in kind. Let us first think of the problem on a large scale, interprovincially, and then consider the micro-economic problems of individual tax-payers. Macro-economically, it is now not so much a question about the relative scale of taxes in money and taxes in kind, since, as we have shown, the bulk of taxes in kind must have been sold in the market in the region where the tax was raised. Most of the money (i.e. net of local administrative costs) raised from the sale of tax-wheat was then sent out of the province where it was

---

[55] This argument is raised very briefly by Duncan-Jones 1990: 193–4, but not pursued.

[56] Duncan-Jones' estimate of average revenue in wheat in Egypt (1994: 53) is far more precise than it deserves to be. He assumes a stable ratio between private (low tax-paying) and public (high tax-paying) land, whereas his own figures suggest that over time there was a significant transfer of land from public to private status, itself a reflection of tax-payers' power against the state. I cite his estimate of wheat revenue from Egypt, therefore, *exempli causa*, rather than because I think it correct. On land tenure, now see Jane Rowlandson, *Landowners and Tenants in Roman Egypt* (Oxford, 1996) especially 63ff; she stresses diversity, underplays chronological change, but still thinks that there was an increase in private (lower-taxed) land, which was held disproportionately by richer land-owners.

raised to be spent either on the armies stretched along the frontiers, or where the emperor was, in Rome. So Duncan-Jones' argument has had the unexpected result of convincing me that taxes in kind were, macro-economically speaking, even less important than I assumed in 1980.

Micro-economically, it was quite a different matter, and here Duncan-Jones' objections allow us now to envisage in a more nuanced way how the Roman tax-economy worked, especially in under-monetised districts of the empire. Levying taxes in kind allowed the central government to get revenues even in under-monetised districts and regions, with relatively little trouble. The primitive natural economies met the monetised economy only at the point where the tax in kind was sold on the market, e.g. perhaps at a local port or district capital. There the wheat was consumed and turned by the workers it fed into marketable and exportable goods, which were sold in order to recoup the money taxes, which had been sent off to Rome or the frontier armies.

Let us now deal with Duncan-Jones' remaining and closely related arguments, that trade in both goods and money was regionally pocketed, that the economy of the Roman empire was therefore, relatively speaking, unintegrated, and that if there was any growth in long-distance trade, it was not stimulated by taxation in money.[57] Once again, we have here detailed problems of evidence, but above all we face differences in the forms of argument and in general perspective. In intellectual style, Duncan-Jones is an inductivist; he likes piling evidence up, so that his conclusions seem to flow from the pile. But he also has an informing perspective, which follows from the grand Cambridge tradition of M. I. Finley and C. R. Whittaker.[58] They are all what I call static minimalists. They stress the static nature of the ancient economy over one thousand years, and its cellular self-sufficiency; they think that the distribution of the surplus was predominantly local, or where it was not, demand was dictated by the specific needs of government and aristocracy for food, services and conspicuous consumption. In their view, the Roman economy was more a command economy than a market economy.

And so, Duncan-Jones' tactic is first to stress the continuity between the pre-Roman and Roman empires, in order to diminish the plausibility of there having been any significant economic growth

---

[57] Duncan-Jones 1990: Chapters 2 and 3; 1994, Chapter 12.
[58] See M. I. Finley, *The Ancient Economy* (London, 1973), and C. R. Whittaker, *Land, City and Trade in the Roman Empire* (Aldershot, 1993) especially Chapter 12.

in the first two centuries AD.[59] And secondly, since he thinks that conclusions follow unproblematically from the evidence, his tactic is to show that the evidentiary basis for the Hopkins 1980 model is flawed, or that there is contrary evidence which points in a different direction. Two examples will suffice. He argues from the distribution of signed terracotta lamps that trade was regionalised, i.e. there were regional limits to the pattern of trade in terracotta lamps, and different lampmakers had their lamps traded in different regions.[60] Secondly, he argues that coins of a particular type are found to a different extent in different provinces, from which he concludes that 'circulation was mainly local' and that there is little basis in coin finds for arguing that the 'coin of the Principate circulated about the empire through trade-flows'.[61]

My response could proceed on four separable levels: perspectival (what are the merits and deficiencies of our competing models?), empirical (is he right?), deductive (what are the broad implications either way?), and conciliatory (how can these objections be incorporated to help improve the original model?). But rather than pursue each of these arguments *à outrance* [to the end], it seems sensible to remodel the old model, incorporating the genuine advances which Duncan-Jones' latest research suggests, while noting differences of opinion as we proceed.

---

[59] Almost at random, as illustrations of Duncan-Jones' static minimalism, I quote, 'the world that he (Strabo) describes had not yet been changed by centuries of Roman rule' (1990: 33). For me, Roman rule had indeed radically changed the economy of Italy, and was in the process of gradually evolving the economy of much of the Mediterranean basin. Or, 'Sea-borne trade was already an active feature of the Mediterranean economy in archaic times, as the growing number of wreck-finds clearly shows' (1990: 35). But again the 'evidence' (Strabo, shipwrecks) is used to buttress an argument which does not quite follow; yes, there was sea-borne trade in archaic times. But in later times, there were much bigger ships, and progressively more wrecks have been found from later periods, at least until AD 100/200 (see note 48). As I see it, the scale of sea-borne trade developed.

[60] This is my short version of Duncan-Jones' distinctively obscure arguments. For his version see 1900: Chapter 3. For a crisply dismissive summary of this chapter, see W. V. Harris, *The Inscribed Economy* (Ann Arbor, 1993) 14, who doubts both the truth and the significance of Duncan-Jones' findings.

[61] Duncan-Jones 1994: 178, cf. 1990: 38ff. I do not agree that the evidence which he cites disproves my point. The fact that you find different proportions of different coin types in different provinces seems unproblematic. For example, few coins struck for the empress Matidia have been found in Syria (1.3% of one hoard), but more of the same type have been found in Britain (3.3% and 4% of two hoards – see 1990: 41). To me, this seems of little consequence. Such variations in small samples are completely expectable. My argument was on a different scale. I suggested that in longish periods in largish regions, the volume of coinage was of roughly the same relative order; i.e. when the volume of coinage grew in one region, it grew in others (1980: 113). I did not suppose that each region got exactly the same types of coins.

I then surmised that the *balancing* between regions may have been promoted by the reciprocal flows of taxes and trade. Now that is difficult, both to prove and to disprove (see below), but I did not mean or imply that the payment of money taxes mixed the total money supply thoroughly, like a cook tossing a salad.

THE MODEL REMODELLED

My broad perspective on the Roman economy is mildly developmental.[62] The prime cause of economic growth was the political integration of the Mediterranean basin under Roman rule. Under the impact of Roman conquest, and because of the prolonged peace which Roman rule eventually brought, the Roman empire could achieve modest, though significant, economic growth.

This economic growth came about partly through the diffusion of technical innovations (principally along the axis from the more advanced south-east towards the less developed north-west); I am thinking here of factors such as improved agricultural techniques (different crops and improved animal breeding), but also for example of the increase in the size of ships and improvements in their handling.[63] It is also likely that Roman government and prolonged peace cut transaction costs; for example, the suppression of piracy made peaceful transport across the Mediterranean Sea possible, and so reduced the risks and costs of transport, while the enforcement of law secured relatively predictable and peaceful outcomes to contracts.[64] The mere existence of a single unified state must have enhanced the possibilities and reduced the costs of medium- and long-distance trade. Finally, and you would now expect me to say this, the exaction of taxes and rents, and their expenditure at some distance from where they were raised, elongated the lines of trade, and stimulated an increased division of labour (to produce goods of lower volume and higher value for that trade), and urbanisation.[65] Towns served both as economical locations of production, and as entrepôts for medium- and long-distance trade.

The city of Rome was the prime locus of court and elite expenditure.[66] Emperors, palace officials, aristocrats and hangers on, even

[62] I set out some of these views in the Introduction to Peter Garnsey, K. Hopkins and C. R. Whittaker (eds), *Trade in the Ancient Economy* (London, 1983), and 'Models, Ships and Staples' in P. Garnsey and C. R. Whittaker eds, *Trade and Famine in Classical Antiquity* (Cambridge, 1983) 84ff.

[63] For improvements in shipping, see for example J. Rougé, *Recherches sur l'organisaion du commerce maritime sous l'empire romain* (Paris, 1966) 44ff.

[64] On the importance of reducing transaction costs in economic development, in addition to changes in production and consumption, see Douglas C. North, *Structure and Change in Economic History* (New York, 1981). On trade, see, for example, A. Giardina and A. Schiavone (eds), *Merci, mercati e scambi nel Mediterraneo* (Rome, 1981) especially pp. 55ff.

[65] The impact of conquest by Rome was probably different in the eastern and western Mediterranean basins. In the western basin, the imposition of money taxes forced peasants or local communities into the monetary economy, and helped create new towns. In the eastern Mediterranean, Roman conquest elongated the lines of trade, probably promoted further urban growth and probably enlarged the size of the monetary economy.

[66] I stress the importance of the city of Rome in the development of the Roman empire's

the plebs, spent money in Rome. The money which the emperors and elite spent derived principally from taxes and rents; their expenditure then percolated down to the rest of the population. Everyone benefited from the huge expenditure, whether on the construction of public baths, palaces and temples, or even on the simple redistribution of food, by porters, wholesalers, traders, bakers, cooks and garbage collectors, to and from Rome's teeming population. Rome had a population of about one million people; it was as large as London in 1800, when London was the largest city in the world.[67] Food, clothing, housing, heat, entertainment and occasional luxuries for such a large population, plus the elite's demand for goods and services, made the city of Rome into by far the single largest market in the Roman empire.

The city of Rome acted like an accelerator, increasing the speed of the whole Mediterranean economy. Because of the concentration of spending power and people, prices in Rome were much higher than anywhere else in the empire. Wheat, for example, cost roughly speaking four times as much at Rome as it did in Egypt, three times as much as in inland Asia Minor, and twice as much as it did in the Italian countryside.[68] Rome was at the peak of a pyramid of rising prices. Or put another way, goods were sold in Rome, macroeconomically to help debtor provinces pay rents and taxes, but micro-economically because individual traders hoped to make huge profits by selling goods in the highest-priced metropolitan market.

economy much more now than I did in 1980. The growth of the population of the city of Rome occurred mostly in the last century BC. But it seems reasonable to suppose that its elite consumption grew (cf. the growth in aristocratic wealth, note 37 above), even if the city's population remained roughly stable in the first two centuries AD. Since Alexandria, Antioch and Carthage maintained or perhaps even grew in prosperity in the first two centuries AD, even though they were no longer capitals of independent kingdoms, it follows probably that total Gross Product was higher too. And the idea that each of these regions, all bordering the Mediterranean, had pocketed, self-sufficient, cellular mini-economies (Duncan-Jones 1990: 44) seems implausible.

[67] For a wonderful study of London in the English economy from 1650 to 1750, see E. A. Wrigley, 'A Simple Model of London's Importance', in P. Abrams and E. A. Wrigley, eds, *Towns in Societies* (Cambridge, 1978) 215ff. His analysis is extremely suggestive for possible economic developments in Rome, Roman Italy and the Mediterranean basin from 200 BC onwards, especially when allied with Jan de Vries' concept of network. See Jan de Vries, *European Urbanization 1500–1800* (Cambridge, Mass., 1984).

[68] The data on wheat prices to support these broad generalisations are lamentably thin (cf. note 13 above). First-century Egyptian wheat prices were probably below 2 HS per modius. And I myself side rather with Jasny (*Wheat Studies* 20 (1944) 160ff), who estimated wheat prices in the city of Rome, from Pliny's flour price of 12 HS per modius (*HN* 18.90), at 8 HS per modius. Duncan-Jones preferred 6 HS per modius, but properly compromised on a notional normal price for wheat of 6–8 HS per modius at Rome, compared with 2.25 HS in Pisidian Antioch and 4 HS in Italy (single and not greatly reliable prices for each). That is practically all we have. The jurist Gaius noted that prices of wheat, wine and oil differed in various cities, without specifying which (Dig. 13.4.3).

When Rome burnt in AD 64, according to the Revelation of St John, the ship-merchants who grew rich from her, by bringing and selling luxuries and staples, wept to see their source of profit vanish in smoke – while the moralist crowed at the destruction of the scarlet harlot of Roman imperial power.[69]

The pyramid of prices, reaching their peak at Rome, must have encouraged the development of a *network* of 'feeder' towns around Rome. Because of cheaper sea-transport, relative to land transport, this network of towns, linked to Rome, could as easily be in southern Spain, or north Africa, as in northern Italy.[70] I use the concept *network* to underline the complexities of inter-urban relationships.[71] The term 'feeder' towns perhaps overstresses the interrelationship between the towns surrounding Rome and Rome itself. These towns presumably served the needs of their own and their surrounding populations, and each other, as well as the metropolis. What I am keen on here is to avoid understanding the high level of urbanisation in the Roman empire, particularly along the Mediterranean littoral, as an exclusively cultural and political development. Towns in the ancient economy must also have had an economic underpinning. Urbanisation, as I see it, may well have begun from the local expenditure of locally collected rents (rentier towns), but in the first two centuries AD, towns developed and benefited from their involvement in production for, and trade with, Rome.[72]

The exemplary cases here are the cities of Alexandria, Antioch and Carthage, each once the capital of a local empire, supported just as Rome later was by the expenditure of taxes and elite rents. But under Roman rule, tax expenditure in provincial centres was restricted. And as we have seen, large amounts of provincial land fell into the hands of the central Roman elite. Taxes and large amounts of rent were no longer spent locally; they were now transmitted to Rome. Nonetheless these old and very large cities (with populations in the

---

[69] *The Revelation of St John* 18. 11ff lists some of the goods which sea-merchants had sent to Babylon (= Rome) at the time of the great fire of AD 64: 'And the merchants of the earth weep and mourn over her, for no man buys their merchandise any more; merchandise of gold, silver, jewels, pearls and fine linen, purple, silk and scarlet, all kinds of scented wood, ivory, articles of costly wood, bronze, iron and marble, cinnamon, spice, incense, myrrh and frankincense, wine, oil, fine flour and wheat, cattle and sheep, horses and chariots, and slaves.'

[70] On relative transport prices, see Hopkins 1983: 102ff (note 62 above). Roughly speaking, land transport cost 55 times more than sea transport, and ten times as much as river transport. Needless to say, variations were very considerable.

[71] On the importance of urban networks, see Jan de Vries 1984: 10ff (see note 67 above).

[72] On rentier (consumer) cities, see the classic article by M. I. Finley, 'The Ancient City: From Fustel de Coulanges to Max Weber and Beyond', reprinted in his *Economy and Society in Ancient Greece* (London, 1981) 3ff.

range of 150,000–500,000) continued to flourish. As I see it, these large cities must have been significantly dependent for some of their undoubted wealth and prosperity on the goods which they managed to produce or send on to the largest market, i.e. Rome. The expenditure of taxes and elite rents, above all in the city of Rome, helped encourage a network of feeder towns engaged in the supply of goods, which had to be exported and sold in order to earn back the money with which to pay rents and taxes in subsequent years.

Of course, we do not *know* the total value of the metropolitan market in the first century AD, though I have guessed it as accounting for 800–900 million HS per year, roughly 8% of the whole empire's *actual* GDP. Such figures need to be considered sceptically; they are very rough orders of magnitude, more metaphor than fact, but useful enough to give a sense of scale.[73] That said, our evidence from the Roman world is too sparse to allow any confirmation either of the total, or of any shift say from 6% to 8% of *actual* GDP. But there are straws in the wind.

Three illustrations may help. First, from comparative data, I have estimated the capital value of the ships involved in bringing food and supplies to Rome at 100 million HS. Such a huge total investment, and the sizeable value of each large ship laden with wheat and wine (on arrival at Rome, equal in worth to the minimum fortune of a senator), indicate either that some merchants grew very rich from trade, or that the Roman rich were themselves involved, probably through agents, in financing trade with Rome.[74] Second, a single document, recently published, illustrates the huge scale of the trade in luxuries. We know in general terms from Pliny (*HN* 12.84, cf. 6.10) that Roman trade with the Middle and Far East (Arabia, India, China) was worth 100 million HS per year. This document now makes Pliny's valuation seem an underestimate. On one side it records a contract drawn up in southern India; on the other side it notes the value of six items of a cargo liable to customs duty at Alexandria, including nard from the Ganges, used as a medicinal ointment, ivory and wool; the total value of the cargo was just under seven million

---

[73] The guesstimate that metropolitan trade with Rome may have amounted to about 8% of the empire's *actual* GDP seems consonant with the estimate by D. H. Perkins for fourteenth century China, that 7–8% of agricultural produce was interregionally traded; see his *Agricultural Development in China 1368–1968* (Chicago, 1969) 115ff. The Mediterranean Sea gave the Roman empire a huge geo-political advantage, and enabled a much greater volume of interregional trade. And of course, a great proportion of the total trade was in higher value non-agricultural goods.

[74] For this estimate of the capital value of ships engaged in supplying Rome, see Hopkins 1983: 102 (see note 62 above). For senatorial interest in profits from commerce, see John H. D'Arms, *Commerce and Social Standing in Ancient Rome* (Cambridge, Mass., 1981).

HS, the minimum qualifying fortune of seven senators.[75] The luxury trade clearly required heavy investment combined with high risk. Finally, a single visit to the city of Rome and its museums should be enough even now to convince anyone of the scale and luxury which it formerly achieved. And most of that luxury was bought with money.[76]

If the concentrated purchasing of Rome was the accelerator of the Roman economy, then the city's magnetic attraction to immigrants and their high mortality served as a brake. The presence of foreigners at Rome was a literary commonplace. Rome beckoned travellers, merchants, preachers, poets, artisans and plain workers from all over the Mediterranean world. Seneca, for example, tells us that people of all sorts migrated to Rome, either to work, or for pleasure, or for education, because Rome offered unparalleled opportunities for pleasure and enrichment. We know from the population history of post-mediaeval European towns that mortality in larger cities is greater than in small towns and the countryside.[77] It seems likely that Rome's experience was similar.[78] The historian Herodian confirms this; during an epidemic, he noted, mortality was highest in Rome, 'because of its very large population, and because it took in immigrants from all over' (1.12). Rome was a huge death-trap, which consumed both goods and people.

This urban immigration and differential mortality brought significant economic benefits to different sub-populations scattered throughout the empire. At least that is what may have happened, if we can apply the experience of London and England in the seventeenth century to Rome.[79] A brief survey of a complex process will

[75] P. Vindob. G. 40822 was published by H. Harrauer and P. J. Sijpestien, 'Ein neues Dokument zu Roms Indienhandel', *Anzeiger der österreichischen Akademie der Wissenschaften, phil.-hist. Klasse* 122 (1985) 124ff. The editors take the the valuation on the reverse to be the total due in customs-charges, but that seems improbable, since then the total value of the cargo would be 35 million HS, including customs payment, which seems too large.

[76] The list of estates given to the Christian church at Rome in the fourth century shows that nearly all rents of the estates, which had previously belonged to aristocrats, were paid in money. It seems unlikely that money rents were a fourth-century innovation. See L. Duchesne ed., *Liber Pontificalis* (Paris, 1886) CL and 34; it is now translated by R. Davis, *The Book of the Pontiffs* (Liverpool, 1989).

[77] Wrigley 1978: 220 (see note 67 above).

[78] Seneca, *Consolation to Helvia* 6: 'Look at the crowds for whom there is scarcely sufficient housing in this huge city; most of the masses come from other places. They have flooded in from their towns and colonies; in fact, from all over the world.' In image, Rome was to the author of *Revelation* a scarlet harlot, bedecked with gold and jewels, drinking the golden cup full of abominations, 'Babylon, the mother of harlots' (17.4ff). For a Jewish author, Rome represented a city of wealth and unsurpassed prosperity: 'The great city of Rome has 365 streets, and in each street there are 365 palaces. Each palace has 365 stories, and each storey contains enough food to feed the whole world' (B. Talmud, *Pesahim* 118b).

[79] Wrigley 1978: 215ff (see note 67 above).

suffice. Emigration to the bigger cities helped drain off surplus population from rural areas. The rural workers who remained had to feed
a larger urban population, so their average productivity grew, and in
some areas, particularly close to Rome, agriculture became specialised.[80] Supplying Rome created increased employment in the surrounding satellite/feeder towns, both in the production of goods and
in trade. And finally, those who migrated only temporarily to Rome,
and [who] survived, learnt and took back home some of the cultured
tastes which they had learnt in the metropolis. Metropolitan fashions
affected taste well beyond the traditional elite, and some quite modest
households consumed manufactured goods. Aggregate demand rose,
not hugely but visibly. All sectors of the economy, from large cities
like Alexandria, to the smaller satellite towns from Ostia to Cadiz,
and even villagers and distant farmers, were marginally affected by
the demands and expenditures of the central government and elite in
Rome.[81]

None or little of all this can be proved or disproved. It is a reconstructive vision of what may have happened. Of course, it can be
supportively illustrated, while sceptics can adduce counter-examples.
But basically, to choose between static minimalism and local and
economically self-contained pockets on the one hand, and on the
other hand mild development plus a thin veneer of economic and
monetary integration, as basic characteristics of the Roman economy, is not so much a problem of fact and evidence, but rather a
problem of preference, of a general sense of how the Roman world
worked, and of the balance of probabilities and plausibilities. I
myself think that the political integration of the Roman empire
brought in its train a gradual integration of the economy, in the sense
that all regions of the empire were forced to pay taxes, and induced
to pay rents, to a government and to an elite whose expenditure was
relatively concentrated. The Mediterranean Sea made transport of a
traded surplus between coastal provinces relatively cheap and easy.
In my view, therefore, the balance of probability is that the economy
was integrated, in the limited sense that a smallish surplus, say about
10% of the actual Gross Product, was traded via a network of towns,
centring on, but not exclusively concerned with, the huge metropolis

---

[80] Francesco de Martino, *Storia economica di Roma antica* (Firenze, 1979) 229ff, follows
Columella (*Rust.* 1, pr. 20) in regretting Italy's lack of self-sufficiency in wheat, and looks for
internal causes of agricultural decline. But Ricardo's theory of rents clearly implies that land
near Rome would be much too expensive to use for growing wheat.

[81] Dio Chrysostom, *Oration* 11, fantasises about an ideal and secluded peasant, living a life
of simplicity and beauty. But even he has his peace shattered by the intrusions of the city, and
he has anyhow escaped to the country in order to dodge persecution.

of Rome, where prices were highest. The main stimuli to that trade were taxes and rents, which were both complements and rivals.

It is no significant objection to this revised model to show that either goods or silver coins circulated locally. Of course, they did. Or rather some did, and some did not. On the whole it must be true that in Roman conditions, local self-sufficiency predominated. Farmers ate much of their own produce; small towns were fed mostly from their immediate hinterland. Per contra, the distribution of wine and oil amphorae illustrates the wide diffusion of trade. As to coins, Howgego has shown, to my mind convincingly, that silver coins did move between provinces in the first two centuries AD, but only gradually. How then was the balance between creditor and debtor (tax-receiving and tax-paying) regions achieved?[82]

The answer is provided, I think, by conceptualising the Roman economy as operating on five intersecting planes: the natural economy, bronze coinage, silver coinage, gold coinage and credit.

1) The natural economy was large, mostly self-sufficient (in the sense that farmers ate a large proportion of their own produce) or consumed locally (after having been paid as rent in kind, or bartered). This broad generalisation holds true, even when we take account of taxes and rents in kind, delivered without any market transaction, sometimes over considerable distances.[83] This command economy became of increasing importance in the late third and early fourth centuries.

The natural economy intersected with the money economy, for example, when peasants brought food to sell in local markets, or when taxes, raised in kind, were sold by the tax-collectors on the open market, because the government needed money much more than it needed wheat. Upper-class large land-owners also needed money more than they needed themselves to consume the produce of their land; the myth of self-sufficiency ('all we eat here comes from my own farms') was a myth.[84]

2) There was a bronze coinage, which for the most part circulated locally. It intersected with the natural economy below, and with the silver economy above, when peasants sold their surplus in exchange for occasional needs, or when peasants, artisans and small shop-keepers bought goods or exchanged a handful of bronze coins for

[82] Howgego 1994: 15 and 20 (see note 45 above).
[83] For an illustrative selection of requisitions by government agents, see for example T. Frank, *Economic Survey of Ancient Rome* (Baltimore, 1936) vol. 2 620ff; for an amusing example of long-distance requisition of transport, see Augustine, *City of God* 18.18.
[84] I do not mean that myths of self-sufficiency are completely untrue, only that they do not tell the whole truth. For an instance of this myth, see Petronius, *Satyricon* 38.

silver, in order to pay their rents or taxes. Local money-changers or tax-collectors charged dearly for this exchange service (see for example *OGIS* 484). Duncan-Jones estimates the size of this bronze economy at 5–10% of the total coin stock by value, with more than 5000 million coins of low denomination in circulation in the mid-second century.[85]

3) There was a huge silver coinage. Under the Republic, silver coins had dominated the Roman monetary system. But Duncan-Jones has recently concluded, I think convincingly, that under the emperors, gold became the dominant coin, in aggregate value (see below). Even so, silver coin was still very important. Most taxes were paid in silver coin; and everyday purchases were made in silver or bronze. After all, a denarius, the most commonly minted silver coin, worth 4 HS, was more than enough, even in the city of Rome, to feed a family for a day.[86]

Duncan-Jones himself estimates the total silver coin stock in the mid-second century at some 7000 million HS. This is based on an average of only 8000 coins struck per die, and a low loss-rate of about 1% per year.[87] It is roughly four times my estimate of the stock of Roman silver coinage in circulation in the middle of the last century BC, though then Roman coinage did not cover the whole of the Mediterranean basin. Even so, we apparently both agree that the volume of the Roman silver coinage expanded.[88] The surplus had become more monetised.

4) Gold. Duncan-Jones has argued that under the emperors gold became the most important component by value in the Roman monetary system. This conclusion is based primarily on the relative value of gold and silver in coin hoards. In coin hoards in Pompeii and in the rest of the empire, gold coins account for between 70% and 75% of total value. To be sure, savings may not exactly mirror the mix of all coins available; hoarders may have selected gold coins preferentially for hideability and portability. But Duncan-Jones corroborates his conclusion by arguing from the number of coin dies found (or

---

[85] Duncan-Jones 1994: 169–70.

[86] Pliny, *HN* 18.90, gives the price of flour at Rome, and *CIL* 4.5380 from Pompeii gives the price of a substantial loaf of bread at ½ HS (enough for a slave every two days). Even if we double the Pompeian bread price, to allow for higher prices at Rome, we can still feed a family of four for a day on less than a denarius.

[87] Duncan-Jones' actual estimate for the total silver coin stock in the second century AD is 6864 million HS (1994: 170).

[88] This compares with my estimate of 400–500 million denarii in circulation in the middle of the last century BC (1980: 109). But that was based on an average of 30,000 coins struck per die and an annual loss rate of 2%.

estimable) for silver and gold coins.[89] Although I have difficulty with, and doubts about, his detailed figures, the general drift of Duncan-Jones' arguments seems convincing.

Two general points should be quickly made. First, the priority in value of gold coin, plus an expansion in the volume of silver coin, taken together, seem to confirm my mildly developmental perspective, that under the emperors the Roman economy expanded and became increasingly monetised.[90] To be sure, the volume of money in circulation is only one measure of economic activity; ideally, we also need to know the velocity of circulation. And about velocity, unfortunately we know virtually nothing. But we can assume that gold coins circulated much more slowly than silver coins. The normal gold coin of the High Empire, the aureus, was worth 25 denarii (100 HS), and would have fed a poor family at Rome for a month. Gold was a prestige currency, used for example for occasional imperial gifts to soldiers and the plebs at Rome, and reciprocally as a tax to celebrate a new emperor's accession.

Secondly, of course, the existence of a mass of gold coins in the currency system helps account for the stolidity in the local circulation of silver coins. Even if we cautiously downscale Duncan-Jones' extrapolation from the hoards, from 70–5% for the value of gold in the total coin stock to say 60% of total value, and if we allocate say 35% of total value to silver coins, and set bronze at say 5%, then we get

[89] Duncan-Jones reaches his conclusions by an ingenious series of circular arguments. Coin hoards show a high ratio of gold (71–4%) by value. There are fewer gold dies known than silver dies (about 1 or 2:40). Therefore to estimate the total in circulation, while keeping the ratio of gold to silver, we need to have a higher production of coins per gold die than per silver die, say 22–43,000 coins per gold die and 8000 per silver reverse die (1994: 164). The ratio of gold and silver coin production is then corroborated by 1) taking the relative proportion of coins from each reign a) in hoards and b) in stray finds, 2) correcting the stray find relative proportions according to the number of years they were in circulation and so available to be lost (the procedure is worked out in 1994: 113ff). Since these statistical procedures transform the original data, the consequent global estimates should be treated as only very rough orders of magnitude. I am convinced by Duncan-Jones' arguments that gold coins in circulation during the first and second centuries were of considerable value relative to silver. For the moment, his guesstimate of 70% gold, 30% silver, is the only one available. For the sake of caution, given the bias towards high value coin in hoards which might not be reflected in all coins circulating, I think a ratio of 60 gold:40 silver more sensible.

[90] Duncan-Jones 1994: 168–70 boldly calculates the total money stock of the Roman empire in the mid-second century AD at 7000 million HS in silver coins plus 12,000 million HS in gold, plus 2000 million HS in bronze (I have rounded his unnecessarily precise figures). So he values the total money stock at 20,000 million HS. This seems implausibly high, both relatively and absolutely. It is 12 times my estimate of Roman money stock in the middle of the last century BC (1980: 109), and so incompatible with Duncan-Jones' static minimalism. It is also absolutely too high. It works out at 330 HS per head of the population – equal to three times the level of minimum subsistence. Given his view, which I share, that significant sectors of the rural economy were non-monetised or under-monetised, this staggering total represents a very high level of liquidity in the monetised sectors of the economy.

a much clearer view of how the Roman monetary system may have worked. Rich Romans, or merchants, or the government, when they wanted to move money from one region to another, as part of the balancing of supply and need, would have found it far more sensible to move small amounts of gold coin than large amounts of silver coin. In the light of Duncan-Jones' radical discovery, the lumpishness or slowness to silver coin circulation really does not matter. For long-distance, high volume/high value trade (such as the trade in luxuries for sale at Rome), gold mattered much more than silver.

5) Finally, credit. When Cicero in the middle of the last century BC wanted to send money to his son at school in Athens, or draw money himself at Ephesus in Asia Minor and at Brindisium in southern Italy, he used the services of his friend and banker Atticus, to arrange for the transfer of credit to a local bank.[91] When minor tax-collectors and even tenant peasants in Roman Egypt had to pay their taxes or rents, they quite often paid their money into a local bank, whether private or public.[92] Finally, Rathbone, in his careful study of a large estate in middle Egypt in the third century, came to the considered conclusion that the rural economy in the Fayum was essentially monetised, but that 'monetisation was not limited by the quantity of coin in circulation, but was extended by the operation of credit arrangements by private banks and the estate itself'.[93] To be sure, we cannot take for granted that Egyptian practices were widespread in the rest of the empire; the economic development of the provinces differed. Nor should we assume that Romans could not do for themselves what Egyptians did regularly. We do not know the scale of credit balancing, but even this skimpy evidence indicates that the volume of coins in circulation was increased by the operation of credit, and that transfers between provinces could be made by balancing credits between bank accounts, as well as by the physical cartage of coins.

SUMMARY

The Roman economy was integrated, as a by-product of the central tax-raising power of the Roman government and the purchasing capacity of the elite, who were concentrated during the first two

---

[91] Cicero, *Letters to Atticus* 5.13; 12, 24 and 27.
[92] Among numerous examples of payments into local banks for transfer elsewhere: *P. Tebt.* 121 R. 4.12 (AD 42), *P. Tebt.* 235 (AD 41); *P. Oxy.* 309 2 (AD 217).
[93] Dominic Rathbone, *Economic Rationalism in Rural Society in Third Century Egypt* (Cambridge, 1991) 329–30.

centuries AD in the city of Rome. A high proportion of imperial and aristocratic income was spent in Rome. So the city of Rome served as the main motor of economic integration. Looked at another way, conquering Romans turned their political power into economic advantage. Even small peasants in remote villages in the provinces had their lives disrupted by the demands of a distant government for taxes, and by the demands of distant elite landlords for rents. These taxes and rents contributed to the luxury and glitter of the metropolis. The political cost of sharing the profits of empire between government and elite was that the power of the aristocracy to exact rents limited the capacity of the central government to raise taxes.

The very high prices prevailing at Rome enabled merchants to transport and sell there goods which had been produced in the provinces, at lower costs, in and via a network of satellite towns, which themselves in turn prospered, partly because of their involvement in the trade with Rome. These taxes and rents were raised predominantly in money, or if they were raised in kind, they were converted into money by government agents, in the provinces. The reason for the relative unimportance of taxes in kind, or their swift sale in the market, is simple: the government and the elite had limited demand for food; both had a much greater need for money. After all, money provides a generalised capacity to buy unspecified goods at a distance in time and place from where the rents or taxes were originally exacted.

The Roman government in the first two centuries AD produced a much greater volume of coins, by value, than it had produced in the last two centuries BC. This increased coin production was partly in silver, but above all in gold. This increase in the volume of coinage reflected the unification of the coinage system; all coins in use in the Roman world were now minted by the Roman government. But the growth in the volume of coinage was on such a scale, without any corresponding rise in prices, that it seems sensible to think that trade had also grown. The surplus had become more commercialised.

The prime stimulus to this limited economic growth was the exaction of taxes and rents. I can think of no other stimulus with the same force and coverage. The long-term balance between tax-paying and tax-receiving regions was probably achieved not so much by the transfer of silver coins, but rather by the transfer of higher value gold coins and by credit-transfers. All that said, the greatest part of the Roman economy remained local and circumscribed, in that producers, both farmers and artisans, either consumed their own produce or sold the bulk of it locally. The relatively sophisticated, relatively integrated, monetary economy sat on top of this basic natural economy. But it was the relatively sophisticated and integrated sector of the Roman economy which helped the empire maintain its political unity.

PART V

The Nature of the Ancient Economy

11 *Modernism, Economics and the Ancient Economy*[†]

SCOTT MEIKLE

Although 'modernists' and 'primitivists' differ in their judgements of the importance and complexity of trade and market exchange in the Graeco-Roman world, even the most ardent 'modernist' would agree that most goods were exchanged and traded for the sake of consumption rather than further exchange. For Scott Meikle, known for his work on ancient economic thought,[‡] this is an indication that the ancient economy was a system dominated by 'use value' rather than 'exchange value'. This distinction derives from classical economic theory and concerns the different kinds of value associated with goods in different types of exchange. Exchange value emerges where competitive buyers and sellers purchase goods for resale. Use value denotes a more individual relationship between goods and their consumers and depends on the goods' specific utility for their consumer. For example, the valuation of a donkey applied by a donkey driver is likely to differ from the price of the same donkey when purchased by a donkey dealer. In the majority of cases, Meikle holds, ancient prices were established on the basis of the use value of goods. Most importantly, money itself had above all use value rather than exchange value. This is not hard to understand if we view credit as an exchange of money for a price (i.e., the interest rate). Although much lending and borrowing took place in the ancient world, there was no competitive market for money (i.e., credit) destined to be used for further exchange (i.e., investment). Since money used for investment is known as capital, Meikle's line of reasoning implies that the ancient world lacked capital markets.

Meikle's propositions differ from arguments that concentrate on micro-economic factors for the development of modern economies such as rationality of estate management and profit orientation of production. They also improve on Finley's claims, which played down the scale of markets and monetisation in ancient economies. It remains doubtful, however, whether

---

[†] Originally published as 'Modernism, Economics, and the Ancient Economy', in *Proceedings of the Cambridge Philological Society*, 41 (1995), 174–91 (© The Cambridge Philological Society).

[‡] *Aristotle's Economic Thought*, Oxford: Clarendon Press, 1995.

the absence of a labour market – believed by Meikle to be the prime explanation for limited capital investment – was the only factor inhibiting
economic growth in the ancient world. As most productive enterprises
were agrarian in nature, and the environmental conditions of agrarian production were difficult to control, it was also hard to evaluate the risk
and productivity of investment.§ Moreover, the pressures created by a
high-mortality/high-fertility demographic regime and the shortcomings of
ancient legal institutions were also likely to curb economic development. In
the end, it is significant economic development, and not its absence, that
requires explanation.¶

I

Modernism, as a phenomenon in the study of the ancient world, has
shown miraculous powers of recuperation from repeated and apparently fatal blows, and the appearance in 1992 of Edward Cohen's
book *Athenian economy and society: a banking perspective* is a
reminder of the fact.[1] Modernism's apparent capacity to postpone
terminal decline obviously has something to do with the subject of
economics, but the connections are unclear.

It might be imagined that modernism began with the first appearance of economics as an independent science in the eighteenth century. But in fact the classical political economists did not seek to
universalize political economy backwards in time to cover the whole
of human history in the way that today's modernists try to universalize economics. Adam Smith distinguished four stages in the development of mankind from the 'rude' to the 'civilized' state. He was
perfectly aware that what he called 'the stage of commerce' was
historically recent, that earlier forms of society had been quite different in character, and that the new science of political economy
described only the operations of the last stage, that of commerce.
Grote wrote about ancient banking in ways that might raise a primitivist eyebrow today, but he did not believe anything of the kind that
the modernists of the past hundred years have believed.[2] Modernism
began in the last quarter of the nineteenth century, and this happens
to be more or less when marginalist or neo-classical economics began.

---

§ See D. Kehoe, *Management and Investment on Estates in Roman Egypt During the Early Empire*, Bonn: Habelt, 1992; T. Gallant, *Risk and Survival in Ancient Greece*, Stanford, 1991.
¶ See Saller (Ch. 12 below).
[1] Edward E. Cohen, *Athenian economy and society: a banking perspective* (Princeton, 1992).
[2] G. Grote, *A history of Greece* (London, 1869), Part II, Chapter XI. Grote speaks in nineteenth-century tones of 'the march of industry and commerce', and exaggerates the scale and nature of the lending of money at interest.

It is worth considering some of the ways in which the two might be connected, and particularly whether the view of the world that accompanies neo-classical economics might be a source of nurture and sustenance for modernism in ancient history.

Scholars have shown empirically, over and over again, that antiquity did not have the institutions, ideas, and practices which modernist claims wittingly or unwittingly attribute to it. Weber, Hasebroek, and Polanyi argued powerfully against the applicability to the ancient world of a market-centred analysis. Finley exposed the futility of the modernist case with even greater cogency and rigour. He drew attention to the persistent reliance on unrepresentative evidence; the misguided application to ancient society of modern theories of investment, banking, and credit; the absence from ancient society of 'vast conglomerations of interdependent markets'; the absence from ancient affairs of state of anything resembling 'economic policy'; and the absence from Greek literature of economics. This empirical refutation ought to be enough, but it never is. Ever since it first appeared, modernism has shown itself to be insensitive to criticism based on contrary evidence. This suggests an underlying problem which empirical evidence on its own fails to resolve.

A position which empirical evidence cannot defeat is not an empirical position, and modernism is indeed in part an *a priori* position, so that dealing with it must be partly a conceptual matter. But Finley and others have also provided much of the necessary conceptual correction. Finley argued that there is a systematic mistake involved in applying modern economic concepts to the ancient world, because that world was predominantly a world of use value, and not a system of exchange value or market economy. He argued also that economics was essentially a modern subject whose concepts were specifically devised to describe and explain modern societies based on market economy, so that it should scarcely be surprising that ancient Greek and Latin lacked words for 'labour, production, capital, investment, income, circulation, demand, entrepreneur, utility', at least in the abstract senses required for economics.[3] Unfortunately modernist authors have proved pretty thick-skinned to conceptual criticism too, and have generally shrugged it off without effectively replying to it.

Critics of modernism have sometimes drawn the conclusion, unsurprisingly, that rational ways of dealing with it seem powerless. Paul Millett expresses a commonly felt impatience in suggesting that

[3] M. I. Finley, *The ancient economy*[2] (London, 1985), p. 21.

it 'ought to have died a natural death long ago, but it still refuses to lie down'.[4] In the face of such a degree of perversity, impatience is a natural enough response. None the less, there must be a reason for the persistence of such perversity, if that is what it is.

The issues underlying the primitivist–modernist dispute are difficult to get at, and it will help to begin by sketching the very different positions from which modernists and primitivists approach ancient 'economic' behaviour. Finley's position is that market economy is a recent historical arrival, at most 400 years old, and that the subject of economics is not, and cannot be, any older, if by 'economics' we mean the study of the behaviour of things and economic agents in market economy. In Finley's sort of view, the study of economics and the existence of market economy are necessarily and not accidentally connected, and that is why they both arose together. He concludes that we should not be surprised, therefore, to find that the ancient world produced nothing that can be regarded as economics.

The modernist position, in so far as it is inspired by economics, is based on the view that economics is the study of laws which hold between humans and economic goods. In Lionel Robbins' much cited definition, 'Economics is the science which studies human behaviour as a relationship between ends and scarce means which have alternative uses.'[5] These are laws of such general character that they must apply in all periods of history and to all forms of society, so that we should expect to find some sort of economic writing in antiquity. If what we find is limited and peculiar, this is because ancient economic activity was still too undeveloped to manifest more than a few rather basic economic laws. Since the Greeks had little economic reality to reflect on, they had relatively little to say about it, and what they did say we should expect to be mixed up with other things, like ethics and administration. None the less, if the economic reality of antiquity was too undeveloped to prompt the Greeks themselves to make many discriminations, to form economic concepts, and to find the right relation between ethics and economics (i.e. none, according to Robbins), their activity was nevertheless of such a kind that it is properly described in terms of economic concepts, even though these concepts were formed later, when greater insight and discrimination had become possible. The Greeks, after all, did of necessity engage in 'economic activity' as all societies must (the scare quotes will be

---

[4] P. Millett, *Lending and borrowing in ancient Athens* (Cambridge, 1991), pp. 9 and 15.
[5] L. Robbins, *The nature and significance of economic science* (London, 1932), p. 15. See also p. 69: 'we regard [the economic system] as a series of interdependent but conceptually discrete relationships between men and economic goods'.

explained later), and economics merely makes explicit what has always been implicit in economic activity.

There is something in this modernist view. The Greeks did develop exchange value, money, and commerce, and even the most resolute primitivist cannot deny it. Aristotle, and to a lesser extent Plato, also developed systematic thought about matters which today would be called 'economic'. No primitivist can deny this either, even though they may want to insist on the point, which might be thought a quibble, that this work does not constitute 'economic analysis'.

2

The core of the controversy is the role that exchange value had in the ancient world, and the terms in which that role is to be described. There has been much exaggeration about this on both sides. In spite of primitivist exaggeration seeking to minimize the role of exchange value, it cannot be seriously contested that money and commodity exchange were vitally important to the polis. It is fruitless to argue about the relative scale of production for direct consumption and production for exchange; we do not know how much money circulated at any time, nor how many 'bankers' there were, nor what proportion of products were made to be sold. But whatever the scale of private exchange may have been, we know at any rate that it was sufficiently developed to sustain a considerable private division of labour, to have prompted Aristotle to investigate the conceptual problems that arise in trying to understand exchange value as he does in *NE* V 5, and to have prompted him to the belief that *philia* [friendship] in buying and selling was the most important form of justice in the polis, 'the salvation of states' (*NE* V 1132b33; *Pol.* II 1261a30–1).[6]

There are difficulties in attributing even this fairly indefinite degree of importance to the market relationships that existed in fourth-century Athens. Market relationships are impersonal and atomized, and the social relationships of ancient Greece generally were not. On the contrary, they embodied the sensibility of *koinōnia* [community] to a degree which is quite unfamiliar to denizens of market societies, and Millett has shown the depth and significance of the difference.[7]

[6] This is argued in my 'Aristotle and exchange value', in D. Keyt and Fred D. Miller (eds), *A companion to Aristotle's Politics* (Blackwell, Oxford, 1991), pp. 156–81.

[7] See Paul Millett, 'Sale, credit and exchange in Athenian law and society', in [P. Cartledge, P. Millett and S. Todd (eds),] *Nomos: essays in Athenian law, politics and society* (Cambridge, 1990).

But this is a line of thought which has induced other critics of modernism into underestimating the scale and importance of Athenian commerce, and into portraying the market relationships and institutions of the fourth century as less developed than they were. The work of Karl Polanyi provides ample illustration of the consequences of disregarding the danger, and so to a lesser extent does that of Finley.

Finley interpreted Aristotle in an extreme non-'economic' way, arguing that *NE* V 5 was purely ethical, and to achieve this he was prepared to ignore entirely the substance of the chapter, which is an attempt to explain the strange property of exchange value which things come to acquire as exchange develops through the four forms or circuits Aristotle distinguishes in book I of the *Politics*. It helps to make Aristotle's distinctions clearer if one introduces the notation C to represent a commodity, and M to represent money. His four circuits are (1) barter, or C–C, which is the direct exchange of goods unmediated by money; (2) selling in order to buy something needed, or C–M–C; (3) buying in order to sell and make money, or M–C–M; and (4) usury, or M–M (1256b27–58b8). Polanyi went to even greater extremes, and saw Aristotle as a defender of archaic institutions, 'the philosopher of *Gemeinschaft* [community]'.[8] He compared Aristotle's thoughts about *koinōnia, philia*, and *autarkeia* [autarky] with the reciprocity institutions of the Trobriand Islanders and the Arapesh people of Papua-New Guinea, and he attributed their importance to the fact that 'the regulation of mutual services is good since it is required for the continuance of the group'.[9] These are lamentable exaggerations. Aristotle's concern with holding together the bonds of the polis does not, in the end, take the form of a defence of archaic reciprocity in gift-giving. It takes the form of an attempt to specify reciprocity (*to antipeponthos*) as a relation of equality between proportions of products being exchanged. This means that the problem of holding the polis together in Aristotle's period was no longer a matter of preserving mutual gift-giving on the basis of status. It had become a matter of regulating, or finding some form of *philia* for, buying and selling.

Exaggerations of this kind in anti-modernist writing have naturally been seized upon by modernists to make their own cause look more plausible. Thompson, in an article pointedly entitled 'The Athenian entrepreneur', concedes that 'the "primitivist" view of the

---

[8] Polanyi, 'Aristotle discovers the economy', in G. Dalton (ed.), *Primitive, archaic, and modern economies* (New York, 1968), p. 107.

[9] Polanyi (n. 8), pp. 109 and 96.

Athenian economy originated as a healthy reaction to the naive presumption of some nineteenth-century historians that Athenian business was conducted along the lines of contemporary industry'. But the concession is granted in order to conclude that 'like most reactions it has gone to extremes, both in minimizing the importance of economic activity at Athens and in its denial of enterprise and risk-taking on the part of Athenian citizens'.[10] There is something in the claim about the extremity of the reaction, though it is another matter whether this is enough to justify all the baggage of business-speak, 'enterprise', 'economic activity', 'risk-taking', and the rest, that Thompson would like it to bear.

Primitivists have sometimes minimized the importance of 'economic activity' in Athens. But the term 'economic activity' is ambiguous, as are many economic terms, between a use-value meaning and an exchange-value meaning. If the term is used to mean the making and distributing of useful things, then the primitivist would presumably not wish to deny its importance in Athens. But if it means productive and distributive activity systematically regulated by money, as in a market economy, any primitivist worth his or her salt would deny its importance. Economic writers use the term 'economic activity' exclusively in the latter sense; *Financial Times* reports on the market reforms undertaken in Poland in the 1980s and 1990s typically say that 'economic activity' is much better than it used to be; the fact that production is down by 40 per cent on what it used to be does not affect this judgement. It is entirely understandable that primitivists should deny claims about the importance of 'economic activity' in antiquity. Such claims invariably equivocate with the term 'economic activity' between a use-value sense and an exchange-value sense.

3

Rostovtzeff had confidently assumed that 'modern capitalistic development differs from the ancient only in quantity and not in quality'.[11] He went on uninhibitedly to describe the ancient world in terms such as 'bourgeoisie', 'proletariat', 'capitalism', 'mass production', and 'factories'. Some sort of lesson was learned from these excesses, and terms of this kind are avoided today in the description of antiquity. But the measure of convergence between the primitivist and

---

[10] W. E. Thompson, 'The Athenian entrepreneur', *L'Antiquité Classique* 51 (1982), p. 53.
[11] Rostovtzeff, cited by J. H. D'Arms, *Commerce and social standing in ancient Rome* (Cambridge, Mass., 1981), p. 12.

modernist positions represented by this non-use of certain terms is superficial, and cannot always be taken as a sign of any deeper agreement, either about the nature of ancient society, or about the nature of the difference between ancient and modern society and how it is to be characterized. There is no lack of choice in the terms available for characterizing the difference: 'embedded' and 'disembedded' economies; 'pre-industrial' and 'industrial' societies; 'unspecialized' and 'specialized' societies; 'pre-capitalist' and 'capitalist' societies. The array of terms betrays the political sensitivity of the issue.

Some of the difficulties to be faced in trying to deal with it are illustrated in the account offered by D'Arms, who agrees that Rostovtzeff's descriptions 'depended too closely on assumptions which are appropriate only to an industrial, highly specialized age', and that Rostovtzeff did not sufficiently emphasize 'the fact that throughout most of antiquity ... the foundation of economic life for all persons was not commerce and industry but agriculture'. These statements are unexceptionable, and they serve to establish a distance between D'Arms and Rostovtzeff. But they do not help to explain the nature of the difference between ancient and modern society, rather they enumerate aspects of it. D'Arms expands on the differences:

> Commercial shipping and manufacturing ventures were at best ancillary, owing in large part to the smallness of the units of production, the tendency for production and distribution to remain nonspecialized and in the same hands, the difficulties, costs, and risks of distant transport, the geographically restricted nature of most markets, and the negligible progress of technological innovation and improvements.[12]

It is difficult to say what this catalogue of differences amounts to. Do they add up to a difference of quality between antiquity and modernity, or only to the difference of quantity which Rostovtzeff had assumed? Smallness of scale, lack of specialization and innovation, transport problems, limited markets, and even the predominance of agriculture over commerce and industry are elements making up the difference between antiquity and modernity which has to be understood and explained; they do not add up to an explanation of the nature of the difference. Even if there is agreement about these elements as a starting-point, as there often is, people still want to move on from them in different directions. Those favouring the sort of view advanced by Finley tend to want to move towards widening the gap between antiquity and modernity, and others towards narrowing it, as D'Arms himself does. The issue is not how

---

[12] D'Arms, op. cit. (n. 11).

'sophisticated' or 'simple' the Greeks were. People are no more subtle now in going about their affairs than they were in the ancient world. The issue is what they did and what institutions they had for getting it done.

It is difficult to see, in the tangle of interweaving threads, which thread to pull in order to unravel the tangle. The decisive question, I believe, is about the functions of money. Did money function in ancient society in the most important of the ways in which it functions in modern market economies?

Hoarding was a highly characteristic use of money in Greek society. Large amounts of gold and silver were buried in the earth over a long period, and archaeologists are still regularly discovering coin hoards. It needs to be explained why the Greeks preferred to bury their exchange value, rather than to invest it profitably as an 'economically rational' person would do today. The development of productive credit is a long process, and it presupposes the prior formation of many other institutions and conditions. One necessary condition is the development of money as a means for the settlement of credit transactions, and the Greeks had nothing like it. There were no credit instruments of any kind, and each individual transaction was settled almost always by physical transfers in person, either by the principal himself or by an accredited agent, even if this involved travelling. There was no double-entry book-keeping; notions of debit and credit were unknown; there was no accounting of debits and credits through strings of transactions to be settled at the end of a period, and there were no settlement days, quarterly or otherwise.[13]

The ancient monetary system provided a medium of circulation, not a means for the settlement of credit transactions. So the Greeks were a very long way from developing productive credit, and the hoarding of exchange value as coin, gold, or silver was simply the most useful and sensible thing to do with it. This is precisely how Aristotle identifies the usefulness of money: 'it serves as a guarantee of exchange for the future: supposing we need nothing at the moment, it ensures that exchange shall be possible when a need arises, for it meets the requirement of something we can produce in payment so as to obtain the thing we need' (*NE* V 1133b10 ff.).

Modernist explanations for the lack of productive credit, such as the high risk of lending, and the supposedly high interest rates on

[13] See G. E. M. de Ste Croix, 'Greek and Roman accounting', in A. C. Littleton and B. S. Yamey (eds), *Studies in the history of accounting* (London, 1956), pp. 28, 30; see also Millett (n. 4), pp. 8, 191.

borrowing, cut little ice, as Millett observes.[14] There simply were no 'investment opportunities', no productive function for money that was a serious alternative to hoarding. There was no market in capital, for the simple reason that there was no market in labour that was anything more than seasonal and casual.[15] Without a significant pool of unattached labour, that is, people needing to work for money-wages as their only way of acquiring use values for living, there cannot be a significant market in capital for establishing productive enterprises. These were precisely the conditions that prevailed throughout the entire history of the ancient world, and for centuries after it. Money could generally be advanced in order to grow only through circulation, or buying and selling, and it was not possible to use production in general as a means to this end, because money did not have the command over labour that is required to achieve it; in other words, money did not function as industrial capital. Once such a credit system arrives, with markets in labour and capital, hoarding simply disappears.

The bulk of production in the Greek world of the classical period was done by free peasant proprietors producing at or near subsistence. The rest was done by a relatively small number of craftsmen producing in workshops of very restricted scale, and by chattel-slaves mainly on the estates of the propertied class. Contracts of wage labour, which become typical with the arrival of market economy, were extremely limited. They were entered into for occasional municipal building programmes like that of Pericles, when local craftsmen were too few to do the job and others had to be attracted from abroad. They were also sometimes used on agricultural estates at harvest time when it was necessary to supplement the normal slave workforce by the addition of casual labour. But wage-labour was never more than incidental, and there was no large and permanent section of the population which had to rely exclusively on it in order to sustain themselves. That is the fundamental reason why, as Millett has convincingly shown, there was no productive credit in the ancient world, that is to say, no lending or borrowing for establishing or expanding productive enterprises, and it is also why no Greek could have made a living by lending for that purpose. The Greeks were hoarders because there was no possibility of the productive investment of money in production, and consequently there was virtually no lending for that purpose. Millett puts the numbers of

[14] Millett (n. 4), p. 72.
[15] G. E. M. de Ste Croix, *The class struggle in the ancient Greek world* (London, 1981 [corr. impr. 1983]), pp. 179–204.

instances of lending for such a purpose, for which there is evidence, and on the most liberal definition of that purpose, at eight.[16]

Markets existed in societies of many kinds for millennia without those societies being or becoming market economies. It is possible for a society to become entirely regulated by exchange value only when there is a full market in capital, and that is possible only when there is a serious market in labour, that is, when labour is generally supplied in the form of an exchange value (the capacity for labour or 'labour power') which capital can buy. These are the defining conditions of a market economy, and neither condition obtained sufficiently in the ancient world. A large part of all lending was *eranos* lending, and as Millett notes 'a survey of the known motives behind *eranos* or "friendly" loans reveals no instance of a productive use'. The purpose of commercial lending, which in any case was very restricted in scale, was consumption, not productive investment. The main reasons for loans of all kinds 'were almost invariably associated with the unpleasant necessities of life – ransoms, fines, burials, food-shortages, tax-payments and public service'.[17] Wage-labour, where it existed, was entirely seasonal or casual; free men would do almost anything to avoid it, because they regarded it as a more demeaning condition even than slavery, and usually they could avoid it. Hired labourers (*misthōtoi* or *thetes*) were not very numerous or mobile, and many were slaves hired out by their masters.

The propertied class, those who extracted surplus (in the sense defined by Ste Croix),[18] did so through rent, and through the use of unfree labour in agriculture, first debt-bondage, then chattel-slavery, and, in the Later Roman Empire, serfdom. They did not extract surplus through the employment of wage-labour. D'Arms has suggested that Finley underestimates Roman Senatorial involvement in trade in maintaining his view of Roman society as primarily a 'spectrum of statuses'.[19] But whether or not Finley exaggerates, D'Arms himself seems to agree that his own belief that there may well have been Jean Samuel Duponts (rich *arrivistes* who concealed the fact that the origin of their wealth lay in trade) in Rome, even if justified, cannot have an impact profound enough to shift the broad outlines of Finley's position. At any rate, however the evidence is interrogated, it cannot yield the conclusion that there were significant Greek and Roman markets in capital and wage-labour, because we know

[16] Millett (n. 4), p. 59.
[17] Millett (n. 4), p. 72.
[18] Ste Croix (n. 15), pp. 35–7, 43–4, 51, 52–3.
[19] D'Arms (n. 11), ch. 1.

there were not. Without them it is vain to harp on about the evidence for Athenian 'entrepreneurship', 'risk-taking', and so forth, because, even granting that there were things which can reasonably be described in these terms, they cannot have been anything more than marginal. Unless there are significant markets in capital and wage-labour, market relationships cannot be the way in which the surplus of society is extracted and appropriated, as they are in market society. In that case, such relationships can have been no more than important marginal aspects of the essential life processes of ancient society. To describe the typical productive and distributive activities of antiquity as 'economic activity', in the familiar sense remarked on at the end of the previous section, is wholly unjustified [...]

4

Primitivist work sometimes equivocates over what an 'economy' is, and it does so in a way that affects its main thesis. Finley holds that Greek society had no masses of market phenomena embodying economic laws, and that the Greeks accordingly had no occasion to engage in economic policy. The source of reasons for public decision-making was *politikē* [the art of the political], not the balance of trade or theories about competition or money. Finley cites Schumpeter as his authority for the view that economics is the science of the masses of such phenomena, and he concludes that their absence from the Greek world explains why the Greeks did no economics. But if they had neither the phenomena, nor the study of the phenomena, nor the need to contend with the phenomena by means of policy, it would seem that, in the sense that matters most, the Greeks did not have what we normally mean by an 'economy' at all. In this sense Austin and Vidal-Naquet seem justified in saying that 'the very concept of "the economy" in the modern sense is untranslatable in Greek, because it simply did not exist'.[20]

On the other hand, Finley is prepared to speak of 'the ancient economy'. He concedes that the Greeks and other 'non-capitalist or pre-capitalist societies have economies, with rules and regularities ... whether they can conceptualise them or not', and that these can be studied. But the study of these 'economies', he seems to be suggesting, can be a matter only for us in the present, not for the contem-

---

[20] M. M. Austin and P. Vidal-Naquet, *Economic and social history of ancient Greece* (London, 1977), p. 8.

poraries of those 'economies' who were incapable of conceptualizing them.[21]

Did Greek society have a lawlike economy, or didn't it? And if it did, why should it have been impossible for the Greeks to make some sort of attempt to study those laws, rules, and regularities? The position looks contradictory, and Finley makes no attempt at reconciliation, for instance, by arguing that these are regularities or laws of different kinds. It remains a puzzle why, if the Greeks had an 'economy' with regularities which made a difference to their lives, we should be able to think about them but the Greeks could not. There is a related contradiction over whether or not the Greeks wrote anything that could count as economics. Finley holds that they did not, and that it is a mistake to think that even Aristotle did economics rather than ethics. But he also holds that they did write economics, though it was of 'crashing banality'.[22] There is evidently a confusion somewhere.

The confusion was already present earlier in the work of Polanyi. He had concluded that the source of the persistent anachronism in modern attempts to interpret ancient economic life lay in a failure to appreciate the nature of the difference between modern capitalist market economy and all pre-capitalist 'economies'. He sought to register the difference by distinguishing between the 'embedded economy', one which is integral to the whole social fabric and does not stand above it, and the 'disembedded economy', one which is torn out of the social fabric to become an independent entity that dominates social decision-making.[23] Pre-capitalist societies had embedded economies, and only capitalist society has a disembedded one.

The difference was real enough, but the terms of the distinction Polanyi drew in order to mark it were ambiguous between two quite different conceptions of how to resolve the problem he faced. The ambiguity is in the term 'economy'. The 'economy' could be conceived as a single species of thing, with 'embedded' and 'disembedded' variants. As members of a single species, these variants, though they would differ from each other in accidental features, would share their essential features and have a common nature. Alternatively, the 'disembedded' economy might be a thing of quite a different kind from the 'embedded' economy, rather than both

---

[21] Finley (n. 3), p. 23.
[22] See Finley (n. 22), *passim*, and id. (n. 3), p. 22, for the first view. For the second view see (n. 3), pp. 19–20.
[23] Polanyi (n. 8), p. 81.

being variants of a single kind. In this case, they would not share a common nature, though they might share a common appearance in features that are accidental rather than essential. To call them both by the same name of 'economy', in this case, would invite puns on the word. The puns would be serious, because they would tend to defeat the very purpose for which the distinction between 'embedded' and 'disembedded' was introduced in the first place, which was to correct the source of the persistent anachronism.

In non-market societies, decisions operate directly over the realm of natural kinds, things or use values that are needed, and the main constraints are natural necessities and social mores. Under market economy, decisions operate primarily over exchange values, and the most imperative constraints, overriding even custom and ethics, are laws and cycles arising largely from the social system of exchange value itself rather than from natural causes. A market economy, or 'disembedded economy', has a nature of its own, which expresses itself in laws that we have to discover by scientific inquiry, in something like the way in which we have to discover the laws of physical nature, and which are inflexible constraints on our decision-making in much the way that laws of nature are. A market society is predominantly a system of exchange value, and exchange value is the regulator of its production and distribution. Economics is the study of the developed forms of exchange value, of the regularities in its movement, and of its interaction with use value.[24] The science of economics came into being historically only with the appearance of market economy, that is, with the appearance of markets in labour and capital. Antiquity was predominantly a system of use value, not of exchange value, and if it had regularities in its nature, these were not the laws and cycles which characterize a system of exchange value, which economics studies, and which economic policy tries to contend with.

These are the differences that Polanyi and Finley had in mind in emphasizing the world of difference between the ancient 'economy' and the modern one. Finley did not follow Polanyi in using the terms 'embedded' and 'disembedded' to mark the difference, and prudently avoided committing himself firmly to any particular pair of terms. In order to capture those differences, the obvious distinction to use is that between use value and exchange value. Pre-market or pre-capitalist societies are systems in which use value is predominant,

---

[24] See my 'Aristotle on money', *Phronesis* 39 (1994), pp. 26–44. The issue is looked at in greater detail in my *Aristotle's economic thought* (Oxford, 1995).

and market or capitalist society is a system in which exchange value is predominant. Perhaps it was Finley's prudence which prevented him using these terms, but whatever the reason, the distinction between use-value and exchange-value economies is one which constantly comes to mind throughout his book *The ancient economy*.

The fact that both sorts of system are, by established usage, called 'economies' need not in itself be a cause of confusion. But it is usual to think that the object of the study of economics is the 'economy', and since ancient society is said to have had an economy, it is tempting to suppose that ancient society is a suitable object for study in terms of economics. But this would be to suppose that a use-value economy can be described and explained in the terms in which an exchange-value economy is described and explained, and this has effectively been shown to be false.

Within ancient society there were early forms of exchange value. There was money, for instance, and ancient money was subject to some of the things money is subject to, debasement and inflation, for example. These things did not always escape ancient writers, and Aristotle notes that money is not always worth the same though it tends to be more stable (*NE* V 1133b13–4). In studying these aspects of antiquity, we may at times need to use economics, because economics is the science of that kind of thing. But in doing this we are studying relations and institutions that were far from being central and defining features of ancient society. The institutions and relations of exchange value were peripheral to ancient society, not central and dominating as they have become in modernity. The nub of the objection to modernism is that it fails to take sufficient account of this. In insisting on trying to describe and explain ancient social behaviour in modern economic terms, modernism implicitly and constantly insinuates a view of the nature of ancient society which is known to be false. Ancient society had money, but it was not regulated by it as capitalist society is. Cohen goes badly adrift in suggesting that fourth-century Athens underwent a 'transition to an economy governed (in Aristotle's words) by "monetary acquisition" rather than by traditional social motivations'.[25] I don't think Aristotle ever uses an expression corresponding exactly to those words, and he certainly never said that Athens had an 'economy', or that it was 'governed' by money.

---

[25] Cohen (n. 1), p. 3.

Modernists might want to reply that they accept that this view of antiquity is false, and that the modernist position of Meyer, Rostovtzeff, and their descendants, who wrote of ancient society as if it had been a market economy, was an extreme modernism which they do not endorse. With such a moderate modernism it might seem reasonable to continue to describe at least some ancient behaviour in modern economic terms, provided it were made clear with suitable qualifications that only marginal aspects of the society were being so described, and that the wider historical implication that antiquity had been an exchange-value economy, with its associated institutions, behaviour, values, and attitudes, was not intended. But there are problems with this more moderate line too.

Even the attempt to use economic terms judiciously, confining them strictly to the description of ancient practices to which they genuinely apply, carries risks, because of the ambiguity that many economic terms have between a use-value meaning and an exchange-value meaning. A term like 'productivity', for example, may be used in evaluations of exchange-value phenomena, but it has a purely use-value application as well. If we consider the method that was used in the ancient world to produce some good, we may try to work out the number of people who would have been needed to produce a unit of it, and how long they would have taken on average using that method. This is a use-value calculation, and there is no reason in principle why we should not speak of 'productivity' in this sense in relation to the ancient world. But in practice, the use of the term carries a heavy burden of exchange-value connotations which it can be difficult to set aside. Its use would be misleading, for instance, if it induced the supposition that productivity was a systematic concern in the ancient world as it is today. In fact, there is little or no evidence that the Greeks bothered much about yields per acre, 'throughput', and so forth, and throughout antiquity there was relatively little innovation in methods of production. A term like 'investment' is even more difficult to detach from its modern associations with capital. As a result of the pretensions of economics to be a universal science of use value as well as exchange value, the temptation has proved too great for some writers to describe even the ploughing of manure into the soil as 'investment', so that the manure itself becomes 'capital'.[26] The use of economic terms, even in their use-value senses when they have them, constantly invites the assimilation of ancient behaviour

---

[26] On the uses of economic terms to describe pre-capitalist societies see C. Meillassoux, 'From reproduction to production', *Economy and society* 1 (1972), pp. 93–105.

and mentality to modern market behaviour and mentality. This mentality is, for good or ill, second nature to us, and it is all too easy for us to transfer it to the Greeks, and for that reason great caution is needed if ancient behaviour is to be described in such market terms as 'risk-taking', 'enterprise', 'entrepreneur', and the rest, even when those terms might in some ways seem to fit.

If the modernist accepts neo-classical economics, as experience suggests is likely to be the case, adopting the more moderate modernist line is not as straightforward as it might appear. According to the neo-classical economic view, there is no categorical distinction to be drawn between use value and exchange value, and it is not easy to see that a subscriber to neo-classical economics could, or should want to, allow a distinction between a use-value economy and an exchange-value economy. It would be a fairly natural extension of the present economic view of the world to hold that 'economies' constitute a single species with a common nature, and that may be why many modern historians of economic thought, and some ancient economic historians, have in practice taken that view. According to neo-classical principles, there should be no objection in principle to describing the ancient economy in general in terms of modern economic theory, and not merely marginal aspects of it.

5

The main difference between non-market societies and market ones lies in the fact that in the former the primary end is exchange value, and in the latter use value. Smith, Marx, and Keynes each recognized a categorical distinction between use value and exchange value, and a problem about how the pursuit of one could be reconciled with the pursuit of the other. Since they are distinct ends their pursuit calls for different courses of action respectively, and there is a problem in reconciling these. All three held that a capitalist economy pursues exchange value as the primary goal rather than use value. Smith thought business to be essentially M–C–M in character, rather than C–M–C, and he thought it needed public regulation for that reason if use value was to be safeguarded. He also held that, given suitable regulation, the totality of these operations produced a result for the society that is C–M–C in character, and he resolved the tensions between use value and the pursuit of exchange value in that way. In Marx's theory, market economy is a lawlike system of exchange value which can be interfered with to make it serve human ends better only to a limited degree. Use value is not the end but a means, and exchange value or money is not a means but the end. The two may intersect to a limited degree, but not enough for human good. Keynes wanted to increase the extent of the intersection. He also took the view that the end pursued in a capitalist economy is exchange value or money: 'He [Marx] pointed out that the nature of production in the actual world is not, as economists seem to suppose, a case of C–M–C′, i.e. of exchanging commodity (or effort) for money in order to obtain another commodity (or effort). That may be the standpoint of the private consumer. But it is not the attitude of business, which is a case of M–C–M′, i.e. of parting with money for commodity (or effort) in order to obtain more money.'[27] Keynes's reconciliation consisted in both accepting that money is 'tremendously useful' as an engine of accumulation and that we need to stick with it until we have enough, but also in recognizing that once we do have enough we will then need to dispense with it as something damaging, which has brought us accumulation at a huge moral cost.[28]

This confrontation between use value and exchange value has always lain at the heart of the economic debate. But the problem of deciding whether they can be reconciled, or whether they are irreconcilable alternatives between which we must choose, is evaded in neo-classical economics. Since use value and exchange value are fused in the neo-classical version of the notion of 'utility' the problem cannot even be posed, and the distinction between C–M–C and M–C–M cannot be drawn. Modernism is a consequence of this course taken by economics. It is easy to see why economists, and the historians influenced by them, should be so strongly inclined to extend market economy backwards over history. If the categorical distinction between use value and exchange value is elided, then the basis of the distinction between capitalist and pre-capitalist societies is elided too. [...]

---

[27] *The collected writings of J. M. Keynes* (London, 1973), vol. 29, p. 81.
[28] J. M. Keynes, *Essays in persuasion* (London, 1931), p. 369.

12 *Framing the Debate over Growth in the Ancient Economy*†

RICHARD SALLER

Taking stock of some of the recurrent themes of the previous three chapters, this piece explores ways of advancing beyond established controversies. Richard Saller is one of the foremost authorities on Roman social history, above all on patronage and the history of the Roman family.‡ As one of the editors of the forthcoming *Cambridge Economic History of the Graeco-Roman World*, Saller has most recently begun to address economic questions from the perspective of neo-institutional and development economics, and to link his work on families and households to the study of the Roman economy. Contrary to Finley (and Cartledge, Ch. 1), Saller defends the application of the concepts and concerns of modern economics to the study of the ancient world. In this paper, he challenges the common perception of a clear-cut dichotomy of 'modernist' and 'primitivist' positions in twentieth-century scholarship on the nature of the ancient economy as represented by the works of Mikhail Rostovtzeff and Moses Finley. Urging conceptual clarification of the terms of the debate, he then focuses on the pivotal question of how to define 'significant growth' in the Roman economy.

Ancient economic history has been the arena for what must be the most voluminous debate in ancient history over the past 30 years. Much valuable research has been published, and yet, in my view, the debate is in something of a conceptual rut, and as a result the debate has not been as productive as it might have been. Moses Finley's *The Ancient Economy* has been at the center of the controversy. Since its publication in 1973, a series of scholars have attacked it and pronounced the central thesis 'demolished'. And yet 27 years later, it has

---

† Forthcoming as 'Framing the Debate over Growth in the Ancient Economy', in J. Manning and I. Morris (eds), *The Ancient Economy: Evidence and Models*, Stanford: Stanford University Press, in press. Reprinted by permission.

‡ See for example *Personal Patronage under the Early Empire*, Cambridge: Cambridge University Press, 1982; *The Roman Empire: Economy, Society and Culture*, London: Duckworth, 1987, esp. Chs 6–8 (with P. Garnsey); *Patriarchy, Property and Death in the Roman Family*, Cambridge: Cambridge University Press, 1994.

recently been republished in a third edition, edited by Ian Morris, and continues to be the target of attack for new work.

Indeed, Finley's name has become a kind of glib shorthand used to summarize one side of the debate, in opposition to Rostovtzeff and his *Social and Economic History of the Roman Empire* – the so-called "primitivist" versus "modernist" debate (despite Andreau 1995 [Ch. 2 above]). This discourse has taken on a life of its own, sometimes far removed from anything Rostovtzeff or Finley wrote. This becomes obvious when one reads characterizations of Finley's position, with no page reference to *The Ancient Economy* but, rather, a reference to one of the hostile critiques. As a first step toward getting out of the rut, I want to go back to original texts to clarify what Rostovtzeff and Finley really wrote and point out the considerable common ground. Next, I offer a bit of speculation about why the debate has become distorted by exaggerated or false polarities. Then, I want to suggest some possibilities for ways in which recent economic theory of development and modern economic history can frame the ancient debate for the purposes of intellectual progress.

The contrast between Finley and Rostovtzeff is commonly summed up in the following polarities: primitivist versus modernist, no-trade versus long-distance trade, autarky versus integrated markets, technological stagnation versus technological progress; no-economic-growth versus growth, non-rational traditionalist versus rational individualists. These polarities are grossly misleading for two related reasons: 1) they seriously misrepresent the views of both Rostovzeff and Finley, and 2) the polarities are very far from representing the full spectrum of possibilities, as both Rostovtzeff and Finley knew. By the latter, I mean that it is as if historians have framed the possible views as Black and White, and then proceeded with ferocious arguments against either White or Black, all the while tacitly conceding that the most probable truth is somewhere in between, in the gray. The futility of such posturing need hardly be stressed. This is not to say that there are not substantive disagreements; rather, that those disagreements are narrower than sometimes thought, and may in many cases be beyond decisive resolution, as both sides agree on closer reading.

Before going to the text of *The Ancient Economy*, let me sketch what I take to be the current characterization of Finley's position, starting with brief phrases drawn from two very distinguished Roman historians. One describes Finley's view as that of "a primitive Roman economy" (Harris 1993: 15). The other describes Finley as a "static minimalist," who stressed the "cellular self-sufficiency" of local town-country units (Hopkins 1995/6: 56 [see p. 217 above]). Notice two aspects of these characterizations: "primitive," meaning household self-sufficiency at subsistence, and "static," meaning no growth. Most recently, Horden and Purcell (2000: 106–7) have repeated the association of Finley with the descriptors "primitivist," "minimalist," and a "stagnant" economy.

To begin with the characterization of Finley as a "primitivist" in his interpretation of the ancient economy, it is true that he asserted that modern concepts of economic analysis designed for capitalist industrial economies are inappropriate for antiquity, which is only to say that there is an incomparability in economic organization between economies before the eighteenth century and those modern European industrializing economies of the late-eighteenth, nine-teenth, and twentieth centuries analyzed by Adam Smith, Ricardo, Marx, and the neo-classical economists. It is not to say that Finley believed that the classical ancient economy was so primitive as to have consisted of autarkic households producing only for themselves without relation to markets. Indeed, the irony here is that in the early 1950s Finley broke with Polanyi who denied the significance of com-mercial markets in antiquity precisely because, in Finley's view, the ancient economy was *not* primitive. Contrary to Polanyi's thesis, Finley wrote in 1972, "the intrusion of genuine market (commercial) trade, on a *very considerable scale and over very great distances*, into the Graeco-Roman world had a feedback effect on peasant markets and the rest to such degree as *to render the primitive models* [of Polanyi] *all but useless*" (1975: 117, my emphases).

Finley's very definition of peasant – in his view the predominant type of laborer in the Empire – included linkage to wider markets and taxation systems. This characteristic distinguishes "the peasant on the one hand from the primitive agriculturist or pastoralist, who is not involved in a "wider economic system," and also differentiates the peasant from the modern family farm, in which the family is an "entrepreneurial unit, rather than a productive unit'" (1973: 105). Finley placed the labor system of antiquity in an intermediate pos-ition between primitive and modern, and cited for comparisons a number of studies of peasants in early modern European and modern colonial economies.[1] To burden Finley with the label "primitivist" is

---

[1] Finley's choice of comparisons is revealing of where he placed the Roman economy in the spectrum of development. Many of his comparisons were drawn from Shanin's classic collec-tion on peasants (1971) and cover a range including twentieth-century Russia and colonial Africa (Finley 1973: ch. 4, nn. 29–30), Europe of the 1930s (ch. 4, n. 33), post-colonial Brazil (ch. 4, n. 49) – none of which is a "primitive society."

to ignore what he wrote or to use the word "primitive" so broadly as to be meaningless.

Clearly, Finley acknowledged the existence of markets in antiquity, and, further, noted that peasants specialized in cash crops for markets if they lived close enough to urban areas or sites of religious festivals (1973: 106). What he denied was the *integration* of markets empire-wide to a point that they can be analyzed as a single unit of supply and demand. There were markets, even linked markets, but not integrated markets. Had the markets been fully integrated, there should not have been desperate grain shortages in individual cities, at the same time that other cities were well supplied (1973: 33f.). In such cases, hungry urban dwellers did not depend solely on higher market prices to draw larger supplies from elsewhere in the Empire, but resort was made to imperial intervention.[2]

Related to markets is trade. By now, the number of scholarly papers demonstrating that Finley was wrong because of the large-scale material remains of trade is legion. Yet, Finley himself noted the amphorae "manufactured in the millions" (1973: 190), "the important foreign trade in famed regional wines" (133), and the significant group of commercial "cities which by their location were clearing houses and transfer points, deriving *substantial* income from tolls, harbor-dues and dock charges" (130, my emphasis). The major limiting factor in the expansion of trade was the cost of land transport. Yet noting the great grain mill at Arles, Finley wrote that for the towns on the rivers and sea "water transport ... created radical new possibilities ... In the first place, imports of food and other bulk commodities permitted a substantial increase in the size of the population, ... and improvement in the quality of life, through a greater variety of goods, a greater abundance of slave labor for domestic as well as productive work." This in turn opened possibilities for "specialized production" in the countryside. But "the tempo of development [was] slow and sometimes abortive" (128).

Why was the tempo slow? Because technological progress was slow – not non-existent, but slow. Finley underlined the fact of "some technological progress precisely where slavery showed its most brutal and oppressive face, in the Spanish mines and on the Roman latifundia" (1973: 83). Overall, however, comparative

---

[2] Similarly, Rostovtzeff (1957: 145) noted that one of the main duties of the emperor in Rome and town magistrates elsewhere was to secure the basic food supply. "The conditions under which a plentiful supply of food had to be secured were not very favourable." In an integrated market, this sort of supervision would have been superfluous because pricing would have drawn grain to areas in need.

evidence suggests that rentier systems of peasant agriculture are not conducive to innovation (109).

Finley added that we should not expect the kind of fast-paced innovation which in the history of mankind is peculiar to the nineteenth and twentieth centuries with their capitalist economic rationality (1973: 144). It is essential to stress here that Finley was not denying the rationality of the ancients, but was asserting that their rationality was framed by a different set of values and did not include some of the basic modern concepts such as amortization and double-column bookkeeping. Finley acknowledged that Romans kept accounts, even detailed accounts, but these were aimed at tracking production, sales, and expenditures – the sort of monitoring function so crucial to, and typical of, the absentee landlord. Monitoring is of course a rational strategy for the absentee landlord, but it is not the same as an analysis to identify profit rates in various parts of the business operation with the aim of directing investments to the points of highest profitability. Overall, Finley did not deny growth or assert that the ancient economy was "static." In fact, "the level of consumption increased in the course of ancient history, at times to fabulous proportions" (139). More particularly, "the expanded commercial activity of the first two centuries of the Empire was not [solely] a Roman phenomenon. It was shared by many peoples within the Empire" (158). As a result, Rome enjoyed some growth, but not "significant growth in *productivity*," to be distinguished from aggregate production (175, my emphasis, also p. 140) – a point to which I will return.

Curiously, some of Finley's prominent critics have heroized Rostovtzeff as the anti-Finley. And yet on certain fundamental points, the two agree. Above all, Rostovtzeff believed that the peasants constituted "an enormous majority of the population of the Roman Empire" who "lived in *very primitive* conditions" (1957: 346, my emphasis) – a stronger assertion of primitivism than I can discover in Finley. Furthermore, Rostovtzeff was far from arguing for integrated markets, allowing for the fact that "every inland city tried to become self-sufficient and to produce on the spot the goods needed by the population" (177). The reason was the expense of overland transport (146). And even sea transport was costly enough to prompt decentralization of manufacture to the provinces in order to save those costs. In addition, Rostovtzeff believed that the *annona* was the largest consumer of imperial trade (158f.), stressing the command aspect of the economy – the very stress for which Finley has been taken to task.

Where Rostovtzeff and Finley did part company was in Rostovtzeff's statements about the emergence of "big men, capitalists on a large scale" (1957: 153). Even here, however, Rostovtzeff clearly limited his assertion. He wrote that the numbers and associations of such merchants "may seem to indicate that the commerce of the first and second centuries began ... to assume the form of modern capitalistic commerce, based on large and wealthy trade-companies. The facts, however, do not support this view. Business life throughout the history of the Greco-Roman world remained wholly individualistic" (170).

Though Rostovtzeff and Finley did disagree over the characterization of villa production as "scientific," they agreed on the ultimate domination of the wealthy rentier class of absentee landlords who looked for "safe investment" – Rostovtzeff's phrase (1957: 197, 203) – in land and loans, rather than trying to maximize profits.

For Rostovtzeff, the reason that industry did not develop in the empire was a fundamental lack of demand for goods in a population whose great majority were impoverished peasants. The cities enjoyed greater wealth, but "we must not exaggerate the wealth of the cities," many of whose residents were also poor: the cities' "external aspect is misleading" (191).

Overall, I confess that I was surprised at the fundamental points of agreement between Rostovtzeff and Finley, after years of reading about the "dichotomy" between their interpretations, to quote a recent important publication (Harris 1993: 15). I have quoted in some detail, because after years of tendentious representations it is important to understand what these two great historians wrote in order to stop the fruitless jousting at straw men. Why the persistent misrepresentation of Rostovtzeff's modernism versus Finley's primitivism? A number of explanations come to mind, ranging from the individual to the late-twentieth-century cultural. First, soon after the publication of *The Ancient Economy*, a polemical tone encouraged the polarization of issues along the lines of growth/no-growth, trade/no-trade, and so on, in a way that quickly lost sight of the texts. Finley himself contributed to the polemic, for instance in the 1985 Postscript to the second edition. Second, on some issues of real disagreement, there may simply be insufficient evidence to bring the debate to a conclusion. In *The Ancient Economy*, Finley actually points to areas where further research needs to be done, but these points get lost in the polemic. Third, the polemic has been transformed into a controversy over the value of new archaeological finds. Finley was skeptical about some of the claims of archaeologists and demanded that they address more precise issues than the question, "Was there trade?" – which he clearly acknowledged. In retrospect, I wish that he had addressed his challenge to archaeologists in a more constructive and precise way. Fourth, the debate over the ancient economy has taken on a strident, political edge as it has been caught up in the larger politics of the later twentieth century. In the first years after publication, *The Ancient Economy* was tossed around in the Marxist/anti-Marxist controversies, attacked by both sides. A recent internet publication by a Danish scholar, Peter Fibiger Bang (1998), argues that in the late twentieth century the primitivist–modernist debate about classical antiquity goes well beyond the economy to religion and other areas, and should be situated in the politics of the post-colonial era. That is, classicists are covertly arguing about whether their own European heritage is like or unlike the colonial Third World. Bang's idea is suggestive.

I am certainly not the only historian to feel that the Finley/anti-Finley debate has become increasingly sterile, but it is less easy to figure out how to break out of it. A first step would be to dispense with the misleading polarities. The next step, to my mind, is to try to specify the areas of contention more precisely, both through models and through more conceptual sophistication.[3] To argue endlessly over whether there was "significant" growth or not is futile, unless we specify what we mean by "significant." It is quite possible that the answer is both "yes" and "no," depending on the implicit frame of reference. By making explicit the frame of reference, by insisting on certain critical conceptual distinctions, and by drawing on recent economic theory of development, some progress may be possible.

Let me begin with a few brief assertions about development economics. Given the vast research in the field, they will necessarily be simple and crude. Yet, for all that economists disagree among themselves, certain basic points have gained broad adherence and have stood up to repeated empirical tests. In thinking about economic growth, it is absolutely essential to distinguish conceptually between per capita growth in production and aggregate growth. Hopkins (1980) has made this point, but it has been ignored in the debates. Total economic production can grow either because the productivity of each worker grows or because the number of workers grows or both. The two extremes would be, on the one hand, the recent experience in the US when productivity per worker

---

[3] Finley (1985: 182) made a similar programmatic statement, but did not develop it in a constructive fashion.

Table 12.1 Fastest growing economies (Ray 1998: 48)

Country	Period	%/year
Netherlands	1580–1820	+0.2
United Kingdom	1820–1890	+1.2
United States	1890–1970	+2.2
Total growth OECD countries	1870–1978:	570%

has jumped and, then, on the other hand, some densely populated Third World countries today where total population and production are multiples of what they were a century ago, but much of the population hovers around subsistence income, not noticeably more productive or better off than ancient rural populations. Even Finley at times conflated those two types of growth (e.g., 1973: 146f.), and that has muddled the argument. It seems beyond doubt to me that some regions of the Roman Empire increased aggregate production as the population increased (as Finley and Rostovtzeff recognized), but it does not follow that the per capita productivity noticeably increased. It is in the latter type of growth that development economists are interested, because it is the only type of growth that raises living standards in the long run. But if the issue in question is the tax base of the Empire, then aggregate production is the relevant measure. In the end, to assert only an increase in aggregate production based on an increase in population is a fairly weak claim in as much as it is to assert no more than that the Roman Empire fits into a very much longer progression of humans more densely populating the earth over the millennia.

A second fundamental point is that scale is critical, and in particular, scale over time. To have much meaning, the phrase "significant growth" should be pegged to some notion of rate of growth. To say, for instance, that productivity and standard of living increased by 50% sounds "significant," but takes on a different meaning if one adds "over a thousand years." It may well be that time span is the element in the estimation of growth rate that can be guessed at most confidently. Some comparative figures for economic growth can offer a sense of perspective. The fastest growing economies in per capita GDP through the modern era have been the Netherlands during the seventeenth and eighteenth centuries, followed in the nineteenth century by the United Kingdom, and in the twentieth century by the United States (Table 12.1).

Clearly, the great threshold here is between the Netherlands and Britain, and comes around 1800. Before 1800, growth in per capita

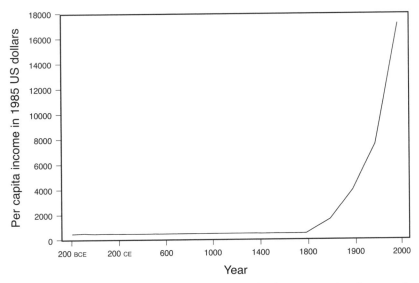

Figure 12.1 GDP per capita 200 BCE–2000 CE in leading economies. Source: after Lucas 1998: Figure 3

production was almost imperceptible, and the classical economists writing around 1800 simply did not dream of the possibility of dramatic increases (Lucas 1998;[4] Johnson 2000). At the early modern growth rate of the Netherlands, productivity would have improved only 6% over a generation of 30 years. By contrast, in nineteenth-century Britain from one generation to the next productivity improved by 50%; and in the twentieth century US productivity and living standards doubled with each generation.

Perspective is essential to ground the claims about growth. To the economist Robert Lucas, the very long-term graph of economic growth looks something like Figure 12.1 (from Lucas 1998: Figure 3). Looked at from a closer perspective, the section of the graph for the Roman Empire could – without contradicting Lucas – look like Figure 12.2. This graph postulates economic growth in the first centuries of Roman rule of the Mediterranean. Let me stress that it is a heuristic device to clarify the debate, designed to illustrate that it is possible to specify a growth curve consistent with both sides. In particular, it is consistent with the arguments of Keith Hopkins, who has put forward a sophisticated case for some economic growth stimulated by imperial taxes (Hopkins 1980, 1995/6 [Ch. 10 above], and personal correspondence). In total, the growth amounts to per-

---

[4] I am especially grateful to the author for permission to cite this work prior to publication.

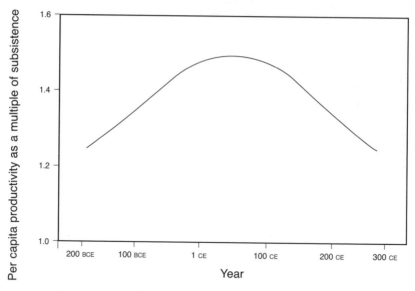

Figure 12.2 GDP per capita productivity 200 BCE–300 CE. Source: from lower lefthand corner of Figure 12.1, after Hopkins 1995/6 [Chapter 10 in this volume]

haps as much as 25%. The peak of production allows room for urbanization and for 4 billion HS per year in non-agricultural production, and hence for plenty of trade to generate those millions of amphorae and hundreds of shipwrecks that Finley, Hopkins, and the many critics of Finley point to. And yet, in comparison with the nineteenth century – the comparison of interest to Finley and Lucas – it is still correct to stress the limits of the growth. After all, total growth of 25% over three centuries would amount to less than 0.1% per year, and even that rate was not sustained.

Was there "significant" growth? From the perspective of a near-subsistence economy in parts of the western empire in 100 BCE, the answer could be "yes." But from the perspective of Robert Lucas at the end of the twentieth century, the answer is "no" (1998). I see no point whatever in arguing about which perspective is the right one: that would be tantamount to arguing about whether the glass is half-empty or half-full. The critics of Finley might well say: "of course, Rome did not have a modern, industrial economy; that is so obvious, why make the claim?" To which the ghost of Finley, or at least his student, might respond: "Earlier in the twentieth century some prominent historians argued that there was no serious gap between imperial Rome and modern Europe; and even today, it is useful to place Rome in that top graph in order to be reminded of some basic limitations of Rome's predominantly agrarian economy."[5] On the other side, this is not to minimize the value of the perspective of 100 BCE and Hopkins' suggestion of "modest, though significant, economic growth" (1995/6: 57 [p. 219 above]).

Some basic theory of economic development can, I believe, help us to understand why the growth was no more than modest and why, ultimately, it was limited. One might start with four or five basic causes for growth in per capita production identified by economists (Mokyr 1990). The first was emphasized by Adam Smith: trade, which in turn allows for specialization. The most obvious aspect of specialization was the fundamental split between rural and urban production. A second cause of growth is intensification of capital investment. That is, the more that a society saves in order to invest in tools of production, the more productive each worker can be. But over 40 years ago, Robert Solow (1956) made the fundamental observation that additional capital investment will have diminishing returns, unless the technology of the capital also improves. The logic is clear: give a farmer an ox and iron plough in place of hand tools, and his productivity will increase; but a second or third plough for the same farmer won't double or triple the production. Hence, the emphasis of Joseph Schumpeter (1934) on improved technology as the engine of sustained growth: this is a third basic cause of growth and the one of central concern in much contemporary research. Over the past 15 years, Chicago economists and others have refocused their theories on a more fundamental cause than technology, and that is the human capital that invents and uses the technology (Becker, Murphy, and Tamura 1990; Lucas 2000; Johnson 2000). That is to say, sustained technological improvements should not be treated as random strokes of good luck, but as an outcome of the education and training of people. It is a striking fact that in the late twentieth century the total value of human capital in the US economy – the investment in education and training – was larger than the value of physical capital. These economists make the theoretical argument that human capital investment is the only basis for indefinite *sustained* economic growth in productivity per worker (Ehrlich 1990), and that increased education of ordinary workers explains a large part of the economic growth of the twentieth century (Lucas 1998).

There is an important corollary of the human capital argument, and that is its tie to the demographic transition [more people work-

---

[5] This broad understanding, from the point of view of an agricultural economist, is the point of Johnson 2000.

ing in service sector than in production] (though cause and effect are unclear). Increased investment in education makes sense against a background of longer life expectancy and fewer children per family, each of whom receives more attention and education, which is then employed through a longer working life (Becker, Murphy, and Tamura 1990). One other dimension of economic growth has been emphasized by Douglass North (1973, 1990): the institutional framework for economic activities. In particular, North argues that some societies have frameworks that do more to encourage productive innovation and to reduce the difficulties and costs of economic activity than others.

Let me offer a few reflections about how we might think about each of these factors in regard to the Roman Empire. First, consider trade. Clearly, as both Rostovtzeff and Finley wrote, the Empire benefited from trade in volume, and that long-distance trade probably increased under Roman rule. Hopkins (1980, 1995/6) has further argued that the increase was stimulated by taxation that required the provincials to earn back at least some of their denarii taken as taxes – in other words, to reach a balance of payments. Even with all of the caveats of the critics (e.g., Duncan-Jones 1994), Hopkins' argument is likely to be right, in my view. But we should understand the limits of his claim about the importance of long-distance trade in the economy by comparison with agriculture (and, in fact, Hopkins himself is careful to circumscribe it). For instance, Hopkins (1995/6: 59, pp. 222–3 above]) calculates the amount of grain consumed by Rome as the huge consumption center of the Empire, and then estimates the number of ships needed to supply the grain, and suggests that the capital investment in these ships must have been of the order of 100 million HS – a large number that underlines the significance of this trade. But how far does this modify the stress on land as the overwhelming investment of Rome's wealthy? 100 million HS is less than some individual fortunes of a few senators and imperial freedmen, and less than 1% of the total capital assets of senators (if we take Pliny's fortune as the rough average for senators).

Now, it is reasonable to suppose, with Hopkins, that Roman taxation demanded more surplus from rural labor, forcing peasants to intensify their labor, and that the surplus supported larger urban populations who manufactured goods for trade. Hopkins' evidence, though indirect, does point to an increment in trade in the last two centuries BCE (1980; revised numbers in 1995/6: n. 48 [p. 211 above]). It is also true that Hopkins' graph of dated shipwrecks, used as a proxy for trade and growth, does *not* show a rise in the first two centuries CE. If we accept the logic of his argument, we should ask for an economic model that explains not only the growth in wrecks through the first century BCE, *but also the absence of growth thereafter, before the decline of the third century.* It would be wrong to read this graph to show that the Roman economy displayed a consistent capacity for sustained growth through the Principate before the political shocks of the third century.

My second cause of growth is the intensification of capital investment. Here the fundamental starting point, agreed by all sides, is that production was predominantly agricultural – probably of the order of at least 75 or 80%. In some regions of the Empire, there was agricultural investment in the sense of extending cultivation, including specialized crops for market. This would have increased aggregate production, and to a lesser extent per capita production. But limits were reached in the absence of major improvements. The willingness of Roman landowners to invest more intensively was limited. As Dennis Kehoe (1992, 1997) has argued, the best description of the dominant attitude toward investment was "satisficing" – that is, the strategy of a safe return for a minimum investment in land. It is plausible to think that there were narrow limits to increases in productivity to be had by pressing peasants and slaves to work more intensively with more or less the same capital (the Hopkins scenario). And such pressure in the longer run may have turned out to be counterproductive in some areas, as capital was sucked out of the countryside, depriving peasants of, e.g., their plough animals and even their capacity to raise children (the scenario in Plin., *Ep.* 3.19). Kehoe's research on rural investment, especially in Roman Egypt (1992), suggests that economic decline in some areas in the Principate is consistent with the evidence and with comparative studies in development economics.[6]

Of course, there were exceptions to the rentier mentality – emphasized by Finley's critics, but on a closer look some of them actually support Finley's view of land acquisition as a matter of windfall rather than efficient markets and calculated capitalist investment. The elder Pliny (*HN* 14.49–51) reports the exceptional example of Remmius Palaemon, who in the mid-first century CE bought a rundown vineyard outside Rome, invested in it heavily with traditional technology, and increased annual production so much that he sold

---

[6] Comparative studies show that the more skewed the wealth between rich landowners and tenants, the lower the productivity (Rosenzweig and Binswanger 1993).

one year's crop for two-thirds the original cost of the land just a few years after purchase. One could stop at that point and take the story as an instance of a capitalist investment, but the end of the story also bears emphasis. Pliny does not say that Palaemon's example inspired similar capital investment by other Romans, but rather that Seneca moved in to buy the vineyard at four times its original price because he was captivated by a desire (*amore*) to possess this model estate, not to make his own profit by similar investments elsewhere.

Another example recently held up to exemplify capitalist investment is Claudius' draining of Lake Fucinus, studied by Philippe Leveau (1993) as an illustration of entrepreneurship. The elder Pliny (*HN* 36.124), Tacitus (*Annals* 12.56f.), and Suetonius (*Claudius* 20) all noted this massive project, and Suetonius claimed that Claudius did it as much for profit as for glory. According to the biographer, the project required the labor of 30,000 men over 11 years. Archaeologists estimate that 5,000 hectares were recovered. The land was distributed to those private individuals who offered to help finance the project. If we take Suetonius and his numbers at face-value, we can do a simple calculation: at a cost of 36 million HS (30,000 men × 11 years × 110 HS in bare subsistence/man-year), Claudius recovered 20,000 *iugera* of land, worth something less than 20 million HS[7] – that is, the project cost nearly twice the value of the land. Leveau, who did not do the arithmetic as far as I can see, concluded that "this is a rare example for Antiquity of agricultural investment, i.e., of an expense made in the hope of a profit in return" (1993: 12). Ironically, given the cost and benefits, its rarity may attest more to Roman rationality than the project itself. What's more, the drainage was allowed to fall into disrepair soon after, suggesting that it cannot have been profitable to maintain and that some of the colossal investment must have been at least partially wasted.

To crystallize my point about capital investment, let me briefly comment on Columella's famous illustration of a model investment in a vineyard – a comment unrelated to the ongoing debate about Columella's accounting. My point is more basic: Columella exhorts his readers to invest in a productive vineyard: 7,000 HS for the land, about as much again for a slave vinedresser, and 14,000 HS for stakes and slips (3.3.8). This kind of investment no doubt had the capacity to increase productivity above subsistence production, but it had

[7] Duncan-Jones (1982) argues convincingly from the indirect evidence of returns to investment that Columella's 1000 HS per *iugerum* is likely to be on the high side for land prices in Italy.

no capacity to generate sustained growth, only one-time growth. The fact that Columella was writing about essentially the same mode of intensification to increase productivity as Cato more than *two centuries earlier* says something obvious about economic growth.

Sustained growth per capita requires sustained technological improvement. There were certainly some technological innovations through the Principate – to assert this as if it were an attack on Finley seems pointless, since he acknowledged as much. The important questions are how much did productive technology improve over what timeframe, and for what proportion of the work force. Scale is essential, as one example may illustrate. Orjan Wikander has written about the invention and diffusion of animal- and water-powered mills. On Wikander's account (1984), the mills could save labor and improve production of basic food processing by as much as 10%; the use of these mills required three to five centuries to spread around the Empire. On the assumption that this improvement was exploited to the very fullest (clearly it was not), it would have contributed to growth at a rate of less than 0.025% per year. I say this not to trivialize the water mill, but to suggest that it would have required a whole series of such inventions that increased the productivity of the mass of rural workers to reach growth levels comparable to the early modern Netherlands. Perhaps the argument can be made, but Rostovtzeff and White (1970: 450), like Finley, saw little evidence for dramatic innovation in peasant agriculture.

In the urban sector, technical progress – much of it in the public domain in the form of building techniques, aqueducts, and other amenities – certainly did improve living standards, and that fact should be taken into account in assessing economic growth. At the same time, the limitations of improved technology should also be acknowledged, as Rostovtzeff and Hopkins have been careful to do. It is generally agreed that the urban population constituted no more than 20% of the population. It follows that if the productivity and living standard of the urban minority increased as much as 50% over several centuries (say, 100 BCE to CE 200), that would constitute growth of only 10% for the Empire as a whole, spread over three centuries – that is, much less than 0.1% per year. And there are reasons to think that such a rate is too generous, because, as Rostovtzeff noted, much of the urban population remained underemployed and at bare subsistence (as in Third World economies today).

Perhaps most fundamentally, those urban amenities did not have the effect of changing the basic demographic regime of the popu-

lation in a way to change the decisions about human capital investments, as happened in the nineteenth century. That is to say, recent
research has reaffirmed the sense that, despite the aqueducts and
sewers, mortality in Rome and other cities of the Empire remained
appallingly high and life expectancies very low (Shaw 1996; Scheidel
1996: Ch. 4 and 1999). In that environment, there was no shift
toward smaller family size, more investment in the education of each
child, and a longer average work life to utilize that human capital.
Education and training outside the household were the privilege of
the elite few for the most part, and the standard elite education in
literature and rhetoric would have had little benefit in increased
productivity. To state this is only to state the obvious about differences in cultural values, recognized by Finley and his critics (e.g.,
Wikander 1984: 40).

The question of the institutional framework for economic growth
– the last on my list of causes of growth – is quite interesting and
complex – too complex for a satisfactory discussion here. Suffice it
to say that the Roman Empire may be used as a test case for Douglass
North's claim about the importance of institutions. In many respects,
Roman imperial institutions should have encouraged growth on
North's theory: the large potential market of the Empire, the long
periods of peace across much of the empire, the relatively low average taxes, the legal system protecting property rights. And yet, the
area of the Empire in which these characteristics were most strongly
felt, tribute-exempt Italy, did not lead the Empire in sustained
growth. Historians argue about whether and when the Italian economy declined, but no one to my knowledge argues that Italy led the
empire with consistent growth through the Principate, as would be
predicted by North's neo-institutionalism.

To conclude, the framing of the debate over growth in the Roman
imperial economy in the polar terms of primitive vs. modern seems
pointless to me: it misrepresents the positions of the supposed pro-
tagonists, and it obscures areas of both agreement and disagreement.
I have suggested that, rather than arguing about whether or not there
was "significant" growth, without defining the adjective, we might
imagine a gentle growth curve for the Roman Empire that is consonant with the observations of Finley and Rostovtzeff, and with the
propositions of Hopkins and Lucas. It can accommodate a rise in the
level of urbanization in the western Empire to a point commensurate
with the eastern provinces, and also an accompanying increase in
trade. From the perspective of the period of Roman annexation of
the eastern Mediterranean, the aggregate growth could be defined as

"significant;" from the perspective of the industrial age, the growth as represented in Figure 12.1 is imperceptible and unsustained. Most recent work in the economic theory of development would lead us to expect nothing else.

My hope is that this broad framing will lead either to some consensus about the parameters of the debate or to more clarity in the challenges to Finley (and Rostovtzeff). Are the critics prepared to argue that the growth was so "significant" as to exceed substantially that depicted in Figure 12.2 (say, to exceed "twice subsistence")? That would be a claim of major importance, of interest not only to ancient historians but also to economists. If that claim is advanced, what evidence would be required in corroboration? "Millions of amphorae" and monumental urban architecture will have to be taken into account but will not be enough, because Figure 12.2, despite the very modest growth postulated (modest not only by late modern standards, but also by early modern standards), can accommodate one trillion HS in urban production over the two and a half centuries of the Principate.

REFERENCES

Andreau, J. (1995) "Vingt ans après *L'économie antique* de Moses I. Finley," *Annales ESC* 50: 947–60 [repr. as Ch. 2 in this volume].

Bang, P. F. (1998) "Antiquity between "Primitivism" and "Modernism." Electronic publication: URL: www.hum.aau.dk/dk/ckulturf/DOCS/PUB/pfb/antiquity.htm

Becker, G., Murphy, K., and Tamura, R. (1990). "Human Capital, Fertility, and Economic Growth," *Journal of Political Economy* 98 Supplement: S12–S37.

Duncan-Jones, R. P. (1982) *The Economy of the Roman Empire: Quantitative Studies*. Second edition. Cambridge.

Duncan-Jones, R. P. (1994) *Money and Government in the Roman Empire*. Cambridge.

Ehrlich, I. (1990) "The Problem of Development: Introduction," *Journal of Political Economy* 98 Supplement: S1–S11.

Finley, M. I. (1973) *The Ancient Economy*. Berkeley and Los Angeles.

Finley, M. I. (1975) *The Use and Abuse of History*. New York.

Finley, M. I. (1985) *The Ancient Economy*. Second edition. Berkeley and Los Angeles.

Finley, M. I. (1999) *The Ancient Economy*. Expanded edition with Preface by I. Morris. Berkeley and Los Angeles.

Harris, W. V., ed. (1993) *The Inscribed Economy: Production and Distribution in the Roman Empire in the Light of* instrumentum domesticum. Ann Arbor.

Hopkins, K. (1980) "Taxes and Trade in the Roman Empire," *JRS* 70: 101–25.

Hopkins, K. (1995/6) "Rome, Taxes, Rents and Trade," *Kodai: Journal of Ancient History* 6/7: 41–74 [repr. as Ch. 10 in this volume].

Horden, P. and Purcell, N. (2000) *The Corrupting Sea: A Study of Mediterranean History*. Oxford.

Johnson, D. G. (2000) "Population, Food, and Knowledge," *American Economic Review* 90: 1–14.

Kehoe, D. (1992) *Management and Investment on Estates in Roman Egypt during the Early Empire*. Bonn.

Kehoe, D. (1997) *Investment, Profit, and Tenancy: The Jurists and the Roman Agrarian Economy*. Ann Arbor.

Leveau, P. (1993) "Mentalité économique et grands travaux: la frainage du Lac Fucin," *Annales ESC* 48: 3–16.

Lucas, Robert E., Jr. (1998) "The Industrial Revolution: Past and Future," University of Chicago working paper. Originally presented as the 1996 Kuznets Lectures, Yale University.

Lucas, Robert E., Jr. (2000) "Some Macroeconomics for the 21st Century," *Journal of Economic Perspectives* 14: 159–68.

Mokyr, J. (1990) *The Lever of Riches: Technological Creativity and Economic Progress*. New York.

North, D. and Thomas, R. (1973) *The Rise of the Western World: A New Economic History*. Cambridge.

North, D. (1990) *Institutions, Institutional Change and Economic Performance*. Cambridge.

Ray, D. (1998) *Development Economics*. Princeton.

Rosenzweig, M. R. and Binswanger, H. P. (1993) "Wealth, Weather Risk, and the Composition and Profitability of Agricultural Investments," *Economic Journal* 103: 56–78.

Rostovtzeff, M. I. (1957) *The Social and Economic History of the Roman Empire*. Second edition, revised by P. M. Fraser. Oxford.

Scheidel, W. (1996) *Measuring Sex, Age and Death in the Roman Empire: Explorations in Ancient Demography*. JRA Supplement 21. Ann Arbor.

Scheidel, W. (1999) "Emperors, Aristocrats, and the Grim Reaper: Towards a Demographic Profile of the Roman Elite," *Classical Quarterly* 49: 254–81.

Schumpeter, J. (1934) *The Theory of Economic Development: An Inquiry into Profits, Capital, Credit, Interest, and the Business Cycle*. Cambridge MA.

Shanin, T., ed. (1971) *Peasants and Peasant Societies: Selected Readings*. Harmondsworth.

Shaw, B. D. (1996) "Seasons of Death: Aspects of Mortality in Imperial Rome," *JRS* 86: 100–38.

Solow, R. (1956) "A Contribution to the Theory of Economic Growth," *Quarterly Journal of Economics* 70: 65–94.

White, K. D. (1970) *Roman Farming*. London.

Wikander, O. (1984) *Exploitation of Water-Power or Technological Stagnation? A Reappraisal of the Productive Forces in the Roman Empire*. Lund.

Intellectual Chronology

For reasons of space, this overview has been limited to particularly influential or otherwise noteworthy works of pertinent scholarship published after 1800. All dates refer to first editions (or, in two cases, the year(s) of composition).

1817	A. Böckh, *Die Staatshaushaltung der Athener*
1840	A. J. C. A. Dureau de la Malle, *Economie politique des Romains*
1847	H. Wallon, *Histoire de l'esclavage dans l'antiquité*
1857/58	K. Marx, *Grundrisse der Kritik der politischen Ökonomie* (first published 1939/41)
1867–94	K. Marx, *Das Kapital*
1869	B. Büchsenschütz, *Besitz und Erwerb im griechischen Alterthume*
1885	N. D. Fustel de Coulanges, 'Le colonat romain'
1891	M. Weber, *Die römische Agrargeschichte in ihrer Bedeutung für das Staats- und Privatrecht*
1893	K. Bücher, *Die Entstehung der Volkswirtschaft*
1893–1904	K. J. Beloch, *Griechische Geschichte*
1895	E. Meyer, 'Die wirtschaftliche Entwicklung des Altertums'
1899	H. Dressel, *Corpus Inscriptionum Latinarum* XV 1
1902	W. Sombart, *Der moderne Kapitalismus*
1906	G. Salvioli, *Le capitalisme dans le monde antique*
1909	M. Weber, 'Agrarverhältnisse im Altertum'
c.1918	K. J. Beloch, 'Wirtschaftsgeschichte Athens' (unpublished)
1921/22	M. Weber, *Wirtschaft und Gesellschaft*
1926	M. I. Rostovtzeff, *The Social and Economic History of the Roman Empire*
1928	J. Hasebroek, *Staat und Handel im alten Griechenland*
1931	J. Hasebroek, *Griechische Wirtschafts- und Gesellschaftsgeschichte bis zur Perserzeit*
1933–40	T. Frank (ed.), *An Economic Survey of Ancient Rome*
1938	F. M. Heichelheim, *Wirtschaftsgeschichte des Altertums vom*

	Paläolithikum bis zur Völkerwanderung der Germanen, Slaven und Araber
1941	M. I. Rostovtzeff, *The Social and Economic History of the Hellenistic World*
1949	F. Braudel, *La Méditerranée et le monde méditerranéen à l'époque de Philippe II*
1957	K. Polanyi et al. (eds), *Trade and Market in the Early Empires*
1957	E. C. Welskopf, *Die Produktionsverhältnisse im Alten Orient und in der griechisch-römischen Antike*
1964	A. H. M. Jones, *The Later Roman Empire*
1965	*Proceedings of the Second International Conference of Economic History, Aix-en-Provence, 1962, I: Trade and Politics in the Ancient World*
1972	M. M. Austin and P. Vidal-Naquet, *Economies et sociétés en Grèce ancienne*
1973	M. I. Finley, *The Ancient Economy*
1974	R. Duncan-Jones, *The Economy of the Roman Empire: Quantitative Studies*
1974	A. H. M. Jones, *The Roman Economy*
1978	K. Hopkins, *Conquerors and Slaves*
1979	F. De Martino, *Storia economica di Roma antica*
1980	M. I. Finley, *Ancient Slavery and Modern Ideology*
1980	K. Hopkins, 'Taxes and Trade in the Roman Empire'
1981	G. E. M. de Ste. Croix, *The Class Struggle in the Ancient Greek World from the Archaic Age to the Arab Conquests*
1981	M. I. Finley, *Economy and Society in Ancient Greece*
1981	A. Giardina and A. Schiavone (eds), *Società romana e produzione schiavistica*
1988	W. Jongman, *The Economy and Society of Pompeii*
1990	F. Vittinghoff (ed.), *Europäische Wirtschafts- und Sozialgeschichte in der römischen Kaiserzeit*
1991	P. Millett, *Lending and Borrowing in Ancient Athens*
1991	D. Rathbone, *Economic Rationalism and Rural Society in Third-Century AD Egypt*
1996	R. Duncan-Jones, *Money and Government in the Roman Empire*
1999	L. Kurke, *Coins, Bodies, Games, and Gold*
2000	P. Horden and N. Purcell, *The Corrupting Sea*
(c.2005)	*The Cambridge Economic History of the Graeco-Roman World*

Guide to Further Reading

With an eye to the intended audience of this series, we have limited our bibliographical essay to noteworthy books and more occasionally articles published in English. In addition to the first two chapters in this volume, another pair of complementary articles provides critical overviews of recent research: I. Morris, 'The Ancient Economy Twenty Years after *The Ancient Economy*', *Classical Philology* LXXXIX (1994), 351–66, and W. V. Harris, 'Between Archaic and Modern: Some Current Problems in the History of the Roman Economy', in W. V. Harris (ed.), *The Inscribed Economy: Production and Distribution in the Roman Empire in the Light of Instrumentum Domesticum*, Ann Arbor: *Journal of Roman Archaeology*, 1993, pp. 11–29. Important new collections of articles on the ancient economy are D. Mattingly and J. Salmon (eds), *Economies beyond Agriculture in the Classical World*, London: Routledge, 2001, and P. Cartledge, E. E. Cohen and L. Foxhall (eds), *Money, Land and Labour. Approaches to the Economies of Ancient Greece*, London: Routledge, 2000.

The single most influential study of the ancient economy is M. I. Finley, *The Ancient Economy*, first published in 1973, followed by a second edition in 1985, and now reissued as an expanded edition with a foreword by I. Morris (Berkeley and Los Angeles: University of California Press, 1999). Finley's seminal articles are readily accessible in his *Economy and Society in Ancient Greece* (eds B. D. Shaw and R. P. Saller), London: Harmondsworth, 1981. On methodological issues in general, see also M. I. Finley, *Ancient History: Evidence and Models*, New York: Viking Penguin, 1986.

The most significant contributions to the first major debate about the nature of the ancient economy around 1900 have been gathered by M. I. Finley (ed.), *The Bücher–Meyer Controversy*, New York: Arno, 1979. For a modernising perspective of ancient (post-classical) economic history and rich source references, see M. I. Rostovtzeff, *The Social and Economic History of the Hellenistic World*, 3 vols, Oxford: Oxford University Press, 1941, corr. repr. 1953, and *The Social and Economic History of the Roman Empire*, 2 vols, Oxford: Oxford University Press, rev. edn 1957 (first edn

1926). More recent accounts of economic conditions in particular periods and regions of the ancient world can be found in the second edition of the *Cambridge Ancient History*, vols 3.1– (Cambridge: Cambridge University Press, 1982–).

M. M. Austin and P. Vidal-Naquet, *Economic and Social History of Ancient Greece: An Introduction*, Berkeley: University of California Press, 1977, offers a coherent vision of the ancient Greek economy accompanied by a broad selection of annotated primary sources in translation. More recently, P. Millett's *Lending and Borrowing in Ancient Athens*, Cambridge: Cambridge University Press, 1991, has been the most influential contribution to the discussion on the ancient Greek economy, although it covers only one aspect of it. For a different interpretation, contrast E. E. Cohen, *Athenian Economy and Society: A Banking Perspective*, Princeton: Princeton Unviersity Press, 1992. R. Osborne, *Classical Landscape with Figures: The Ancient Greek City and its Countryside*, London: George Philip, 1987, demonstrates the importance of rural production and exchange within a broader political and ritual context. D. W. Tandy, *Warriors into Traders: The Power of the Market in Early Greece*, Berkeley: University of California Press, 1997, albeit controversial as a historical analysis, includes stimulating considerations of theoretical issues. For a sophisticated Marxist account of the Greek economy and society (liberally construed to encompass the entire Mediterranean world down to late antiquity), see G. E. M. de Ste Croix, *The Class Struggle in the Ancient Greek World from the Archaic Age to the Arab Conquests*, London: Duckworth, 1981 (corr. repr. 1983). Z. H. Archibald, J. Davies, G. Oliver and V. Gabrielsen (eds), *Hellenistic Economies*, London and New York: Routledge, 2001, showcases a wide range of approaches to the study of Hellenistic economies after Rostovtzeff.

For a recent account of the Roman imperial economy, see P. Garnsey and R. Saller, *The Roman Empire: Economy, Society, Culture*, London: Duckworth, 1987, Chs 3–5. T. Frank (ed.), *An Economic Survey of Ancient Rome*, 6 vols, Baltimore: Johns Hopkins University Press, 1933–40 (repr. 1959), offers positivistic readings of a huge amount of pertinent evidence. A. H. M. Jones, *The Roman Economy: Studies in Ancient Economic and Administrative History* (ed. P. A. Brunt), Oxford: Oxford University Press, 1974, an updated collection of articles, portrays the Roman imperial economy in 'primitivist' terms. Operating within the primitivist/substantivist framework established by Jones and Finley, R. P. Duncan-Jones seeks to quantify economic structures and processes in *The Economy of the Roman Empire: Quantitative Studies*, second edn, Cambridge: Cambridge University Press, 1982, and *Structure and Scale in the Roman Economy*, Cambridge: Cambridge University Press, 1990. On late antiquity, see A. H. M. Jones, *The Later Roman Empire, 284–602: A Social, Economic and Administrative Survey*, 3 vols, Oxford: Oxford University Press, 1964. K. Greene, *The Archaeology of the Roman Economy*, London: Batsford, 1986, demonstrates the importance of archaeological evidence.

Recent work on the economy of individual provinces of the Roman empire includes R. S. Bagnall, *Egypt in Late Antiquity*, Princeton: Princeton University Press, 1993, and Z. Safrai, *The Economy of Roman Palestine*, London and New York: Routledge, 1994. In addition to Finley's *Economy and Society* (cited above), relevant articles by leading scholars have been reprinted in volumes such as C. R. Whittaker, *Land, City and Trade in the Roman Empire*, Aldershot and Brookfield: Variorum, 1993, and P. Garnsey, *Cities, Peasants and Food in Classical Antiquity: Essays in Social and Economic History* (ed. with addenda by W. Scheidel), Cambridge: Cambridge University Press, 1998. J. Manning and I. Morris (eds), *The Ancient Economy: Evidence and Models*, Stanford: Stanford University Press, in press, contains the results of a recent conference.

Chapters 6–9 of P. Horden and N. Purcell, *The Corrupting Sea: A Study of Mediterranean History*, Oxford: Blackwell, 2000, a sweeping survey in the tradition of Fernand Braudel ranging across classical antiquity and the Middle Ages, deal with economic conditions. Their detailed bibliographical essays for each chapter are particularly helpful. A new synthesis of ancient economic history ranging from 1000 BC to late antiquity is currently in preparation: I. Morris, R. Saller and W. Scheidel (eds), *The Cambridge Economic History of the Graeco-Roman World*, Cambridge: Cambridge University Press.

Farming, as the principal sector of ancient economies, has recently attracted a fair amount of attention. For the Greek world, see S. Isager and J. E. Skydsgaard, *Ancient Greek Agriculture: An Introduction*, London and New York: Routledge, 1992; A. Burford, *Land and Labor in the Greek World*, Baltimore and London: Johns Hopkins University Press, 1993; and the articles in B. Wells (ed.), *Agriculture in Ancient Greece*, Stockholm: Swedish Institute in Athens, 1992. R. Sallares, *The Ecology of the Ancient Greek World*, London: Duckworth, 1991, 294–389, addresses this topic from an interdisciplinary ecological perspective. Ethnoarchaeological and comparative approaches have enriched our understanding of Greek land use: e.g., H. Forbes, 'The Ethnoarchaeological Approach to Ancient Greek Agriculture', in Wells (ed.), *Agriculture* (cited above), 87–101. M. H. Jameson, C. N. Runnels and T. H. van Andel, *A Greek Countryside: The Southern Argolid from Prehistory to the Present Day*, Stanford: Stanford University Press, 1994, is a particularly ambitious case study. For further references, see Horden and Purcell, *Corrupting Sea* (cited above), 572–4.

For Roman estate management and its contribution to economic growth, see D. P. Kehoe, *The Economics of Agriculture on Roman Imperial Estates in North Africa*, Göttingen: Vandenhoeck & Ruprecht, 1988, *Management and Investment on Estates in Roman Egypt during the Early Empire*, Bonn: Habelt, 1992, and *Investment, Profit, and Tenancy: The Jurists and the Roman Agrarian Economy*, Ann Arbor: University of Michigan Press, 1997, which deal with issues of agricultural management and investment. On farm-tenancy in Italy, see P. W. de Neeve, *Colonus: Private Farm-*

Tenancy in Roman Italy during the Republic and the Early Principate, Amsterdam: Gieben, 1984. D. Rathbone, *Economic Rationalism and Rural Society in Third-Century AD Egypt: The Heroninus Archive and the Appianus Estate*, Cambridge: Cambridge University Press, 1991, offers a sophisticated analysis of papyrological records from Roman Egypt. The potential of survey archaeology is well brought out by G. Barker and J. Lloyd (eds), *Roman Landscapes: Archaeological Survey in the Mediterranean Region*, London: British School at Rome, 1991, and G. Barker, R. Hodges and G. Clark, *A Mediterranean Valley: Landscape Archaeology and 'Annales' History in the Biferno Valley*, London and New York: Leicester University Press, 1995. For Roman farming techniques, see K. D. White, *Roman Farming*, Ithaca: Cornell University Press, 1970, and M. S. Spurr, *Arable Cultivation in Roman Italy, ca. 200 BC–ca. AD 200*, London: Society for the Promotion of Roman Studies, 1986.

The articles in C. R. Whittaker (ed.), *Pastoral Economies in Classical Antiquity*, Cambridge: Cambridge Philological Society, 1988, discuss various aspects of animal husbandry. On fishing, see T. Gallant, *A Fisherman's Tale*, Ghent: Belgian Archaeological Mission in Greece, 1985. There is no recent synthesis in English on the economy of ancient mining; for references, see Horden and Purcell, *Corrupting Sea* (cited above), 607–9. J. F. Healy, *Mining and Metallurgy in the Greek and Roman World*, London: Thames and Hudson, 1978, deals with technological issues.

The study of slavery has often been given pride of place in modern research on ancient labour. Essential reading includes M. I. Finley, *Ancient Slavery and Modern Ideology*, expanded edn, ed. B. D. Shaw, Princeton: Wiener, 1998; Chs 6–10 in Finley's *Economy and Society* (cited above); and de Ste Croix's *Class Struggle* (cited above). On Greek slavery, see Y. Garlan, *Slavery in Ancient Greece*, Ithaca and London: Cornell University Press, 1988, and N. R. E. Fisher, *Slavery in Classical Greece*, London: Bristol Classical Press, 1993; for Rome, see K. Bradley, *Slavery and Society at Rome*, Cambridge: Cambridge University Press, 1994, and (for the social and economic consequences of the creation of a slave society in Roman Italy) K. Hopkins, *Conquerors and Slaves: Sociological Studies in Roman History, 1*, Cambridge: Cambridge University Press, 1978, Chs 1–2. For more detailed bibliography, readers are referred to K. Bradley's volume in this series.

P. Garnsey (ed.), *Non-Slave Labour in the Graeco-Roman World*, Cambridge: Cambridge Philological Society, 1980, deals with aspects of free labour. On labour and gender, see, e.g., R. Brock, 'The Labour of Women in Classical Athens', *Classical Quarterly* XLIV (1994), 336–46; S. Treggiari, 'Jobs for Women', *American Journal of Ancient History* I (1976), 76–104; J. K. Evans, *War, Women and Children in Ancient Rome*, London and New York: Routledge, 1991; W. Scheidel, 'The Most Silent Women of Greece and Rome: Rural Labour and Women's Life in the Ancient World', *Greece and Rome* XLII (1995), 202–17, and XLIII (1996), 1–10.

Research on mechanisms of economic exchange has revolved around questions of the nature and scale of trade in ancient societies. P. Garnsey, K. Hopkins and C. R. Whittaker (eds), *Trade in the Ancient Economy*, Berkeley and Los Angeles: University of California Press, 1983, is a suitable starting point. For a more recent collection, see H. Parkin and C. Smith (eds), *Trade, Traders, and the Ancient City*, London and New York: Routledge, 1998. F. Meijer and O. van Nijf, *Trade, Transport and Society in the Ancient World: A Sourcebook*, London and New York: Routledge, 1992, translates pertinent source material. S. von Reden, *Exchange in Ancient Greece*, London: Duckworth, 1995, gives an anthropological account. R. Osborne, 'Pots, Trade and the Archaic Greek Economy', *Antiquity* LXX (1996), 31–44, seeks to reassess the scope of early Greek trade with the help of archaeological evidence.

J. H. D'Arms, *Commerce and Social Standing in Ancient Rome*, Cambridge MA and London: Harvard University Press, 1981, explores discrepancies between attitudes and conduct regarding mercantile activities among the Roman elite. K. Hopkins, 'Models, Ships and Staples', in P. Garnsey (ed.), *Trade and Famine in Classical Antiquity*, Cambridge: Cambridge Philological Society, 1983, pp. 84–109, estimates the probable scale and capital requirements of Roman trade. For a model of trade stimulated by coercive surplus extraction, see K. Hopkins, 'Taxes and Trade in the Roman Empire, 200 BC–AD 400', *Journal of Roman Studies* LXX (1980), 101–25, and his reprise, 'Rome, Taxes, Rents and Trade', *Kodai* VI/VII (1995/6), 41–75 (= Ch. 10 above). D. P. S. Peacock and D. F. Williams, *Amphorae and the Roman Economy: An Introductory Guide*, London and New York: Longman, 1986, give an introduction to the economic interpretation of ceramic containers (compare Ch. 9 above). The study of the distribution of amphorae is complemented by research on the distribution patterns of shipwrecks: A. J. Parker, *Ancient Shipwrecks of the Mediterranean and the Roman Provinces*, Oxford: BAR, 1992. L. de Ligt, *Fairs and Markets in the Roman Empire*, Amsterdam: Gieben, 1993, is now the most sophisticated study of ancient markets.

Recent work on ancient money has been reviewed by S. von Reden, 'Money in Classical Antiquity: A Survey of Recent Literature', *Klio* LXXXIV (2002), 141–74. The best introduction to ancient money and coinage in the Graeco-Roman economy is C. Howgego, *Ancient History from Coins*, London: Routledge, 1995. Still valuable are the introductory chapters by C. Kraay, *Archaic and Classical Greek Coins*, London: Methuen, 1976. The origins and functions of Greek coinage have been reconsidered by S. von Reden, 'Money, Law and Exchange: Coinage in the Greek Polis', *Journal of Hellenic Studies* CXVII (1997), 154–76, and L. Kurke, *Coins, Bodies, Games, and Gold: The Politics of Meaning in Archaic Greece*, Princeton: Princeton University Press, 1999. On the development and circulation of Roman money, see in particular the complex discussion by C. Howgego, 'The Supply and Use of Money in the Roman World 200 BC to AD 300',

Journal of Roman Studies 82 (1992), 1–31, the statistical analyses in R. Duncan-Jones, *Money and Government in the Roman Empire*, Cambridge: Cambridge University Press, 1996, and the general, though not always reliable, survey by K. M. Harl, *Coinage in the Roman Economy, 300 BC–AD 700*, Baltimore and London: Johns Hopkins University Press, 1996.

The most sophisticated studies of ancient prices are G. Reger, *Regionalism and Change in the Economy of Independent Delos 314–167 BC*, Berkeley and Los Angeles: University of California Press, 1994, and Duncan-Jones, *Economy* (cited above). On banking and finance, see the debate between Millett, *Lending and Borrowing* (cited above), and E. E. Cohen, *Athenian Economy and Society: A Banking Perspective*, Princeton: Princeton University Press, 1992, as well as the new survey by J. Andreau, *Banking and Business in the Roman World*, Cambridge: Cambridge University Press, 1999.

P. Garnsey, *Food and Society in Classical Antiquity*, Cambridge: Cambridge University Press, 1999, gives an overview of diet and nutrition in Greece and Rome. T. W. Gallant, *Risk and Survival in Ancient Greece: Reconstructing the Rural Domestic Economy*, Cambridge: Polity, 1991, discusses production and consumption in Greek subsistence farming. Disruptions of the food supply and risk-buffering strategies are the central themes of P. Garnsey, *Famine and Food Supply in the Graeco-Roman World: Responses to Risk and Crisis*, Cambridge: Cambridge University Press, 1988.

The economic impact of urbanisation has been considered by K. Hopkins, 'Economic Growth and Towns in Classical Antiquity', in P. Abrams and E. A. Wrigley (eds), *Towns in Societies: Essays in Economic History and Historical Sociology*, Cambridge: Cambridge University Press, 1978, pp. 35–77; N. Morley, *Metropolis and Hinterland: The City of Rome and the Italian Economy 200 BC–AD 200*, Cambridge: Cambridge University Press, 1996; H. Parkins (ed.), *Roman Urbanism: Beyond the Consumer City*, London and New York: Routledge, 1997; and H. Parkins and C. Smith (eds), *Trade, Traders and the Ancient City*, London and New York: Routledge, 1998. W. Jongman, *The Economy and Society of Pompeii*, Amsterdam: Gieben, 1988, is the most sophisticated case study in the Finley tradition.

For the relationship between technological and economic development, see the classic statement by M. I. Finley, 'Technical Innovation and Economic Progress in the Ancient World', *Economic History Review* XVIII (1965), 29–45, reprinted as Chapter 11 of Finley, *Economy and Society* (cited above), with the recent critique by K. Greene, 'Technological Innovation and Economic Progress in the Ancient World: M. I. Finley Reconsidered', *Economic History Review* LIII (2000), 29–59. On technology in general, see K. D. White, *Greek and Roman Technology*, London: Thames and Hudson, 1984. Labour-saving devices are discussed by J. P.

Oleson, *Greek and Roman Water-Lifting Devices: The History of a Technology*, Toronto and Buffalo: University of Toronto Press, 1984, and O. Wikander, *Exploitation of Water-Power or Technological Stagnation? A Reappraisal of the Productive Forces in the Roman Empire*, Lund: Gleerup, 1984. J. W. Humphrey, J. P. Oleson and A. N. Sherwood (eds), *Greek and Roman Technology: A Sourcebook*, London and New York: Routledge, 1998, gathers ancient references. The limits of ancient economic thought are further explored by S. Meikle, *Aristotle's Economic Thought*, Oxford: Clarendon Press, 1995 (cf. Ch. 11 above).

Index